Lectionary for Worship
YEAR A

Revised Common Lectionary

Study Edition

Augsburg Fortress
Minneapolis

LECTIONARY FOR WORSHIP
YEAR A
Revised Common Lectionary

Study Edition
with Pronunciation Helps and Reader Notes

December 2, 2007 — November 23, 2008   November 30, 2025 — November 22, 2026
November 28, 2010 — November 20, 2011   December 3, 2028 — November 25, 2029
December 1, 2013 — November 23, 2014   November 30, 2031 — November 21, 2032
November 27, 2016 — November 26, 2017   December 3, 2034 — November 25, 2035
December 1, 2019 — November 22, 2020   November 29, 2037 — November 21, 2038
November 27, 2022 — November 26, 2023   December 2, 2040 — November 24, 2041

Cover and interior art: Nicholas T. Markell, Markell Studios, Inc.
Reader notes: Christopher G. Hoyer

Manufactured in Canada

ISBN 978-0-8066-5614-4

16 15 14 13 12 11 10 09 08 07   1 2 3 4 5 6 7 8 9 10

CONTENTS

Introduction

THE WORD OF GOD

The Christian church believes and confesses that Jesus Christ is the eternal Word of God incarnate in a human being. The word through which God created all things, liberated and sustained the chosen Hebrew people, and continues to give life, became truly human for our salvation. Therefore, when we speak of God's word, we refer above all to this Word who "became flesh and lived among us" (John 1:14), "God the only Son, who is close to the Father's heart, who has made [God] known" (1:18).

However, the canonical scriptures of the Old and New Testaments are also regarded by most Christians as the word of God in written form. This word communicates the mighty acts of God in the Torah or Pentateuch, the first five books of the Bible. This written word also relates how God inspired the judges and psalmists and spoke to the prophets. This testimony was collected by the children of Israel, passed from generation to generation, written down, and proclaimed when they gathered daily and weekly.

The Christian church grew out of this tradition. Jesus of Nazareth was raised attending services centered on the proclamation of the holy scriptures. The apostolic witnesses to his life, death, and resurrection knew those same scriptures and worship patterns. As the new church grew and spread, apostles and evangelists taught communities of believers through gospels that told of the life of Jesus Christ as well as letters that expanded upon the understandings of this new covenant with God.

The proclaimed word of God continues to be essential to Christian worship. Despite ongoing changes in the ways people communicate, public reading of scripture remains foundational to proclamation within the assembly. Using patterns of worship inherited from the generations that have preceded us, we gather weekly as communities of faith. Here the triune God speaks to each person, to the gathered community of faith, and to the whole creation. Within the context of the whole liturgy, we hear readings from Old and New Testaments, attend as the word is further proclaimed and interpreted in the sermon, and respond in song, prayer, and praise. Both word and sacrament connect us not only to God, but also to the whole body of believers of all times and places.

SELECTION OF SCRIPTURES

Among all the books of the Bible, the gospels have particular prominence for Christians because they proclaim "the good news of Jesus Christ, the Son of God" (Mark 1:1), telling the story of his life, his teachings, and most important, his saving death and resurrection. In worship, the reading of the gospel for the day is similarly lifted up: we stand for that reading, and surround it with acclamations.

From the earliest years of the Christian church, it has also been customary to read from letters of the apostles, valuable both for their theological insights and for their encouragement in the life of faith. In the liturgy, this reading precedes the gospel, much as all other witnesses testify to the centrality of Jesus Christ.

The Old Testament or Hebrew scriptures, too, are acknowledged as God's authentic word for us today. Since the middle of the twentieth century, Christian churches increasingly have been including a reading from the Old Testament in corporate worship, usually as the first reading. Additionally, as a response to the first reading, a psalm is frequently sung by the assembly. (These psalm texts, though part of the Revised Common Lectionary, are not included here, both because there are many choices of versions available, and because the psalms are traditionally sung by the assembly or the choir.)

Though Protestant churches usually do not regard the books of the Apocrypha as part of the core, canonical Bible, they have generally esteemed them as worthy teachings for Christians. In this light, readings from these books are sometimes suggested as alternate choices for a given day.

This procedure opens up the entire Bible as potential source of scripture reading in the assembly. That is both gift and challenge. Certainly, the Bible is an inexhaustible storehouse, overflowing with the riches of God's word. No part of it is unworthy of our attention. On the contrary, "All scripture is inspired by God and is useful for teaching, for reproof, for correction, and for training in righteousness" (2 Tim. 3:16). But with such a treasury available to us, how do we choose what to read on a given Sunday? If we are not to rely on individual preference, a system is needed. For centuries, the church has employed a lectionary method to address this issue. Over most of that time, a one-year lectionary repeated the same lessons on a given Sunday each year. In the last third of the twentieth century, in an attempt to make a wider selection of scripture available for reading in the assembly, many Christian denominations adopted a three-year lectionary. And most of those worked together to prepare the Revised Common Lectionary, toward the goal that the readings would be largely the same across the denominations on a given day. The present volume, based on the outcome of that ecumenical effort, uses the Revised Common Lectionary as it appears in *Evangelical Lutheran Worship* (2006). This version includes additional readings for a number of festivals and occasions, as well as the church year calendar and terminology from *Evangelical Lutheran Worship.*

In the Revised Common Lectionary, the gospels remain the core. In year A, most of the gospel readings are from the gospel of Matthew; in year B, from the gospel of Mark; and in year C, from the gospel of Luke. Readings from the gospel of John appear in all three years and are most numerous in year B. In Advent through Holy Trinity, the gospels relate to the season or festival. In the rest of the year, the gospel readings are excerpts from the life and teachings of Jesus, generally following the order of the gospel books.

The first readings are chosen for their relationship to the gospels, especially in the Advent through Holy Trinity time and, in the complementary series, throughout the year. An alternative series for the time after Pentecost within the Revised Common Lectionary, the semicontinuous series, provides Old Testament readings and psalms that, while not as explicitly connected to the gospels, explore many of the books and stories not covered by the complementary series. Both series are provided in this volume in separate sections for clarity and ease of use.

The second readings more often stay within a book for a number of Sundays, providing a more prolonged exposure to a given writer's thought. Although these readings are usually not intentionally tied to the gospel, a community that uses the lectionary will often find that it opens up the scriptures in unexpected ways, allowing the Bible to converse with itself as well as its hearers.

READING FROM THE LECTIONARY

Proclaiming God's word in the assembly is an important and blessed task. Any who are chosen to read the scriptures in public, though, will need to prepare. Training, rehearsal, and prayerful preparation assist those who read the scriptures to proclaim the word of God so that it can be clearly heard and its meaning conveyed.

Repeated reading—silently and aloud—of the assigned texts in advance will allow the reader to communicate the meaning behind the words, as well as to prepare for any difficulties in pronunciation or syntax. Practice in the worship space with the sound system, as necessary. Then, when actually proclaiming the texts in the assembly, remember that all need to hear and understand them. Speak loudly enough—through the end of each phrase— that the person farthest away can hear clearly. Speak slowly—there is no hurry. Pay attention to consonants, which aid greatly in understanding, and to phrasing. The readings in this book are laid out in "sense lines" to assist in logical breaks for breath and for meaning.

This volume provides introductions and conclusions for each reading. Although these are widely accepted formulas, if your assembly uses other wording, that may be substituted.

Brackets around verses indicate that those sections are optional within the reading. Because the spirit of the lectionary is to bring more of scripture to the assembly, providing the fuller readings deserves consideration. Half brackets ⌐ ⌐ denote where explanatory words have been added or substituted to make the context of the reading clear.

The translation provided here is the New Revised Standard Version, highly regarded for its accuracy and its clear and readable translation.

A NOTE ABOUT THE READER HELPS

At the bottom of the pages of the study edition, each reading is provided with pronunciation helps as needed, and with notes to assist the reader. The notes were written by Christopher G. Hoyer, whose background and gifts enable him to provide helps that are useful to skilled and novice readers alike. At the same time, these paragraphs are not canonical; readers are invited to make use of them as they see fit.

The pronunciation helps, also, bear no official stamp. They are an attempt to render difficult words (mostly from Hebrew or Greek origin) into American-inflected English (thus *eye-ZAY-uh* rather than the British *eye-ZY-uh*). Most sounds are presented in a consistent manner—a long "a" is pronounced *ay*; a long "o" is *oh*, and so forth. The long "i" sound is most often shown with a *y*, but where it stands alone, it is represented by *eye*, and as a way of differentiating the noun prophecy from the verb prophesy, the long "i" at the end of the latter is designated *PROF-eh-sigh*. Note that an "h" at the end of a syllable relates only to the vowel preceding it, and should not be voiced. Thus, in *sheh-OHL*, the second "h" is intended only to show a short "e" sound. Some of the pronunciations may seem obvious; the intent is to be relatively comprehensive. Pronunciations may, of course, be altered from these suggestions if another usage is preferred.

The holy scriptures, the written and proclaimed word of God, never fail to reward those who encounter them. Those who worship in community owe their gratitude to those who give breath to that word. May this lectionary assist in that holy ministry.

COMPARISON OF NAMES
Sundays in the Time after Epiphany and the Time after Pentecost

TIME AFTER EPIPHANY

Evangelical Lutheran Worship	Other naming conventions
BAPTISM OF OUR LORD	
First Sunday after Epiphany	Baptism of the Lord
Sunday, January 7–13, Lectionary 1	
SECOND SUNDAY AFTER EPIPHANY	
Sunday, January 14–20	Second Sunday in Ordinary Time
Lectionary 2	
THIRD SUNDAY AFTER EPIPHANY	
Sunday, January 21–27	Third Sunday in Ordinary Time
Lectionary 3	
FOURTH SUNDAY AFTER EPIPHANY	
Sunday, Jan. 28–Feb. 3 *(if before Transfiguration)*	Fourth Sunday in Ordinary Time
Lectionary 4	
FIFTH SUNDAY AFTER EPIPHANY	
Sunday, February 4–10 *(if before Transfiguration)*	Fifth Sunday in Ordinary Time
Lectionary 5	
SIXTH SUNDAY AFTER EPIPHANY	
Sunday, February 11–17 *(if before Transfiguration)*	Sixth Sunday in Ordinary Time
Lectionary 6	Proper 1
SEVENTH SUNDAY AFTER EPIPHANY	
Sunday, February 18–24 *(if before Transfiguration)*	Seventh Sunday in Ordinary Time
Lectionary 7	Proper 2
EIGHTH SUNDAY AFTER EPIPHANY	
Sunday, Feb. 25–March 1 *(if before Transfiguration)*	Eighth Sunday in Ordinary Time
Lectionary 8	Proper 3

Time after Pentecost

Evangelical Lutheran Worship	Other naming conventions
SUNDAY, MAY 24–28 *(if after Holy Trinity)*	
Lectionary 8	Proper 3 8th Sunday in Ordinary Time
SUNDAY, MAY 29–JUNE 4 *(if after Holy Trinity)*	
Lectionary 9	Proper 4 9th Sunday in Ordinary Time
SUNDAY, JUNE 5–11 *(if after Holy Trinity)*	
Lectionary 10	Proper 5 10th Sunday in Ordinary Time
SUNDAY, JUNE 12–18 *(if after Holy Trinity)*	
Lectionary 11	Proper 6 11th Sunday in Ordinary Time
SUNDAY, JUNE 19–25 *(if after Holy Trinity)*	
Lectionary 12	Proper 7 12th Sunday in Ordinary Time
SUNDAY, JUNE 26–JULY 2	
Lectionary 13	Proper 8 13th Sunday in Ordinary Time
SUNDAY, JULY 3–9	
Lectionary 14	Proper 9 14th Sunday in Ordinary Time
SUNDAY, JULY 10–16	
Lectionary 15	Proper 10 15th Sunday in Ordinary Time
SUNDAY, JULY 17–23	
Lectionary 16	Proper 11 16th Sunday in Ordinary Time
SUNDAY, JULY 24–30	
Lectionary 17	Proper 12 17th Sunday in Ordinary Time
SUNDAY, JULY 31–AUGUST 6	
Lectionary 18	Proper 13 18th Sunday in Ordinary Time
SUNDAY, AUGUST 7–13	
Lectionary 19	Proper 14 19th Sunday in Ordinary Time
SUNDAY, AUGUST 14–20	
Lectionary 20	Proper 15 20th Sunday in Ordinary Time

Evangelical Lutheran Worship	Other naming conventions
SUNDAY, AUGUST 21–27	
Lectionary 21	Proper 16 21st Sunday in Ordinary Time
SUNDAY, AUGUST 28–SEPTEMBER 3	
Lectionary 22	Proper 17 22nd Sunday in Ordinary Time
SUNDAY, SEPTEMBER 4–10	
Lectionary 23	Proper 18 23rd Sunday in Ordinary Time
SUNDAY, SEPTEMBER 11–17	
Lectionary 24	Proper 19 24th Sunday in Ordinary Time
SUNDAY, SEPTEMBER 18–24	
Lectionary 25	Proper 20 25th Sunday in Ordinary Time
SUNDAY, SEPTEMBER 25–OCTOBER 1	
Lectionary 26	Proper 21 26th Sunday in Ordinary Time
SUNDAY, OCTOBER 2–8	
Lectionary 27	Proper 22 27th Sunday in Ordinary Time
SUNDAY, OCTOBER 9–15	
Lectionary 28	Proper 23 28th Sunday in Ordinary Time
SUNDAY, OCTOBER 16–22	
Lectionary 29	Proper 24 29th Sunday in Ordinary Time
SUNDAY, OCTOBER 23–29	
Lectionary 30	Proper 25 30th Sunday in Ordinary Time
SUNDAY, OCTOBER 30–NOVEMBER 5	
Lectionary 31	Proper 26 31st Sunday in Ordinary Time
SUNDAY, NOVEMBER 6–12	
Lectionary 32	Proper 27 32nd Sunday in Ordinary Time
SUNDAY, NOVEMBER 13–19	
Lectionary 33	Proper 28 33rd Sunday in Ordinary Time
SUNDAY, NOVEMBER 20–26	
Christ the King Last Sunday after Pentecost, Lectionary 34	Proper 29 Reign of Christ, Last Sunday of the Church Year

Dates for Easter and Related Days

LECTIONARY	YEAR	ASH WEDNESDAY	EASTER	PENTECOST
A	2008	February 6	March 23	May 11
B	2009	February 25	April 12	May 31
C	2010	February 17	April 4	May 23
A	2011	March 9	April 24	June 12
B	2012	February 22	April 8	May 27
C	2013	February 13	March 31	May 19
A	2014	March 5	April 20	June 8
B	2015	February 18	April 5	May 24
C	2016	February 10	March 27	May 15
A	2017	March 1	April 16	June 4
B	2018	February 14	April 1	May 20
C	2019	March 6	April 21	June 9
A	2020	February 26	April 12	May 31
B	2021	February 17	April 4	May 23
C	2022	March 2	April 17	June 5
A	2023	February 22	April 9	May 28
B	2024	February 14	March 31	May 19
C	2025	March 5	April 20	June 8
A	2026	February 18	April 5	May 24
B	2027	February 10	March 28	May 16
C	2028	March 1	April 16	June 4
A	2029	February 14	April 1	May 20
B	2030	March 6	April 21	June 9
C	2031	February 26	April 13	June 1
A	2032	February 11	March 28	May 16
B	2033	March 2	April 17	June 5
C	2034	February 22	April 9	May 28
A	2035	February 7	March 25	May 13
B	2036	February 27	April 13	June 1
C	2037	February 18	April 5	May 24
A	2038	March 10	April 25	June 13
B	2039	February 23	April 10	May 29
C	2040	February 15	April 1	May 20

Advent

✠ First Sunday of Advent

FIRST READING: Isaiah 2:1-5

A reading from Isaiah.

[1]The word that Isaiah son of Amoz saw concerning Judah and Jerusalem.

[2]In days to come
   the mountain of the LORD's house
shall be established as the highest of the mountains,
   and shall be raised above the hills;
all the nations shall stream to it.

   [3]Many peoples shall come and say,
"Come, let us go up to the mountain of the LORD,
   to the house of the God of Jacob;
that he may teach us his ways
   and that we may walk in his paths."

For out of Zion shall go forth instruction,
   and the word of the LORD from Jerusalem.
[4]He shall judge between the nations,
   and shall arbitrate for many peoples;
they shall beat their swords into plowshares,
   and their spears into pruning hooks;
nation shall not lift up sword against nation,
   neither shall they learn war any more.

[5]O house of Jacob,
   come, let us walk in the light of the LORD!

The word of the Lord.　　　*or*　　　Word of God, word of life.

PSALMODY: Psalm 122

FIRST READING　　*Isaiah = eye-ZAY-uh　Amoz = AY-moz*
Verse 1 is a headline. A significant pause before the beginning of verse 2 will help to make that clear. The mountain image is a vision of grandeur. See the majesty of the mountain in your mind, and help the hearer to see it in the sound of your description. Another substantial pause following verse 4 will set up the invitation to journey in the light of the Lord offered in verse 5.

SECOND READING: Romans 13:11-14

A reading from Romans.

^{11}Besides this,
you know what time it is,
how it is now the moment for you to wake from sleep.
For salvation is nearer to us now than when we became believers;
^{12}the night is far gone, the day is near.

Let us then lay aside the works of darkness
and put on the armor of light;
^{13}let us live honorably as in the day,
not in reveling and drunkenness,
not in debauchery and licentiousness,
not in quarreling and jealousy.

^{14}Instead, put on the Lord Jesus Christ,
and make no provision for the flesh,
to gratify its desires.

The word of the Lord.   *or*   Word of God, word of life.

SECOND READING   *licentiousness = ly-SEN-chus-ness*
Think "immediacy" and provide the reader with a feel for the reading. Now is the moment. The day is near.
Help the hearer feel the urgency of the author's appeal. Additionally, note that the image of living or walking
in the light makes an apparent connection to the first reading. Make certain that the hearer can sense that
connection.

GOSPEL: Matthew 24:36-44

The holy gospel according to Matthew.

⌈Jesus said to the disciples,⌉
36"About that day and hour no one knows,
neither the angels of heaven, nor the Son,
but only the Father.

37"For as the days of Noah were,
so will be the coming of the Son of Man.
38For as in those days before the flood they were eating and drinking,
marrying and giving in marriage,
until the day Noah entered the ark,
39and they knew nothing until the flood came and swept them all away,
so too will be the coming of the Son of Man.

40"Then two will be in the field;
one will be taken and one will be left.
41Two women will be grinding meal together;
one will be taken and one will be left.
42Keep awake therefore,
for you do not know on what day your Lord is coming.

43"But understand this:
if the owner of the house had known
in what part of the night the thief was coming,
he would have stayed awake
and would not have let his house be broken into.

44"Therefore you also must be ready,
for the Son of Man is coming at an unexpected hour."

The gospel of the Lord.

GOSPEL
"Be ready" is the clear thrust of the text, but the images are mixed and will take the assembly a little effort to absorb. Also, verses 38–39 are one long sentence. The hearer will be helped by a reading that is deliberately paced and provides plenty of breathing room between paragraphs.

SECOND SUNDAY OF ADVENT

FIRST READING: Isaiah 11:1-10

A reading from Isaiah.

¹A shoot shall come out from the stump of Jesse,
    and a branch shall grow out of his roots.
²The spirit of the LORD shall rest on him,
    the spirit of wisdom and understanding,
    the spirit of counsel and might,
    the spirit of knowledge and the fear of the LORD.
³His delight shall be in the fear of the LORD.

He shall not judge by what his eyes see,
    or decide by what his ears hear;
⁴but with righteousness he shall judge the poor,
    and decide with equity for the meek of the earth;
he shall strike the earth with the rod of his mouth,
    and with the breath of his lips he shall kill the wicked.
⁵Righteousness shall be the belt around his waist,
    and faithfulness the belt around his loins.

⁶The wolf shall live with the lamb,
    the leopard shall lie down with the kid,
the calf and the lion and the fatling together,
    and a little child shall lead them.
⁷The cow and the bear shall graze,
    their young shall lie down together;
    and the lion shall eat straw like the ox.
⁸The nursing child shall play over the hole of the asp,
    and the weaned child shall put its hand on the adder's den.
⁹They will not hurt or destroy on all my holy mountain;
for the earth will be full of the knowledge of the LORD
    as the waters cover the sea.

¹⁰On that day the root of Jesse shall stand as a signal to the peoples;
the nations shall inquire of him,
and his dwelling shall be glorious.

The word of the Lord.   *or*   Word of God, word of life.

FIRST READING   *Isaiah = eye-ZAY-uh*
The text is in two parts. Verses 1–5 are a startling word picture of the "Promised One." Paint the picture with your reading. Help us to see him. Do not miss the fearsome nature of the prophecy that "he shall strike the earth with the rod of his mouth, and with the breath of his lips he shall kill the wicked." Verses 6–9 describe the glorious dwelling of the Promised One. It is the inspiration for the famous painting *The Peaceable Kingdom*. The reader will be helped by viewing a copy of that painting in preparation for this reading. Help us to see the painting in Isaiah's writing.

PSALMODY: Psalm 72:1–7, 18–19

SECOND READING: Romans 15:4-13

A reading from Romans.

[4]Whatever was written in former days
was written for our instruction,
so that by steadfastness and by the encouragement of the scriptures
we might have hope.

[5]May the God of steadfastness and encouragement
grant you to live in harmony with one another,
in accordance with Christ Jesus,
[6]so that together you may with one voice
glorify the God and Father of our Lord Jesus Christ.

[7]Welcome one another, therefore,
just as Christ has welcomed you,
for the glory of God.
[8]For I tell you that Christ has become a servant of the circumcised
on behalf of the truth of God
in order that he might confirm the promises given to the patriarchs,
[9]and in order that the Gentiles might glorify God for his mercy.
As it is written,
     "Therefore I will confess you among the Gentiles,
         and sing praises to your name";
[10]and again he says,
     "Rejoice, O Gentiles, with his people";
[11]and again,
     "Praise the Lord, all you Gentiles,
         and let all the peoples praise him";
[12]and again Isaiah says,
     "The root of Jesse shall come,
         the one who rises to rule the Gentiles;
     in him the Gentiles shall hope."

[13]May the God of hope
fill you with all joy and peace in believing,
so that you may abound in hope by the power of the Holy Spirit.

The word of the Lord.   *or*   Word of God, word of life.

SECOND READING   *Isaiah = eye-ZAY-uh*
Hope is the theme of the reading. The Promised One from the first reading (also described as "the root of Jesse") is identified as our Lord Jesus Christ by the author of Romans. The "circumcised" are the Jews, and the author wants to make it clear that both Jew and Gentile have cause for rejoicing, because their common hope is in Christ (the root of Jesse). The quotations in verses 9–12 are what was referred to in verse 4 as "whatever was written in former days" and in verse 8 as "the promises given to the patriarchs." Help the hearer sense each set of quotation marks. Verse 13 is a little prayer of blessing. Pause—really pause—between verses 12 and 13, and then pray the blessing for the hearer.

GOSPEL: Matthew 3:1-12

The holy gospel according to Matthew.

¹In those days John the Baptist appeared in the wilderness of Judea,
proclaiming,
²"Repent, for the kingdom of heaven has come near."
³This is the one of whom the prophet Isaiah spoke when he said,
"The voice of one crying out in the wilderness:
'Prepare the way of the Lord,
make his paths straight.'"

⁴Now John wore clothing of camel's hair
with a leather belt around his waist,
and his food was locusts and wild honey.
⁵Then the people of Jerusalem and all Judea were going out to him,
and all the region along the Jordan,
⁶and they were baptized by him in the river Jordan,
confessing their sins.

⁷But when he saw many Pharisees and Sadducees coming for baptism,
he said to them,
"You brood of vipers!
Who warned you to flee from the wrath to come?
⁸Bear fruit worthy of repentance.
⁹Do not presume to say to yourselves,
'We have Abraham as our ancestor';
for I tell you,
God is able from these stones to raise up children to Abraham.
¹⁰Even now the ax is lying at the root of the trees;
every tree therefore that does not bear good fruit
is cut down and thrown into the fire.

¹¹"I baptize you with water for repentance,
but one who is more powerful than I is coming after me;
I am not worthy to carry his sandals.
He will baptize you with the Holy Spirit and fire.
¹²His winnowing fork is in his hand,
and he will clear his threshing floor
and will gather his wheat into the granary;
but the chaff he will burn with unquenchable fire."

The gospel of the Lord.

GOSPEL   *Isaiah = eye-ZAY-uh   Sadducees = SAD-yuh-seez*
Do not allow the assembly to miss the threatening sound of this text. There is genuine excitement
surrounding the advent of the Baptizer (verses 4–6)—dire warnings and not a little sarcasm in his preaching.
Bring some passion to the reading. Bring it to life.

THIRD SUNDAY OF ADVENT

FIRST READING: Isaiah 35:1-10

A reading from Isaiah.

¹The wilderness and the dry land shall be glad,
　　the desert shall rejoice and blossom;
like the crocus ²it shall blossom abundantly,
　　and rejoice with joy and singing.
The glory of Lebanon shall be given to it,
　　the majesty of Carmel and Sharon.
They shall see the glory of the LORD,
　　the majesty of our God.

³Strengthen the weak hands,
　　and make firm the feeble knees.
⁴Say to those who are of a fearful heart,
　　"Be strong, do not fear!
Here is your God.
　　He will come with vengeance,
with terrible recompense.
　　He will come and save you."

⁵Then the eyes of the blind shall be opened,
　　and the ears of the deaf unstopped;
⁶then the lame shall leap like a deer,
　　and the tongue of the speechless sing for joy.
For waters shall break forth in the wilderness,
　　and streams in the desert;
⁷the burning sand shall become a pool,
　　and the thirsty ground springs of water;
the haunt of jackals shall become a swamp,
　　the grass shall become reeds and rushes.

⁸A highway shall be there,
　　and it shall be called the Holy Way;
the unclean shall not travel on it,
　　but it shall be for God's people;
　　no traveler, not even fools, shall go astray. ▸

FIRST READING　　*Isaiah = eye-ZAY-uh　Carmel = CAR-mul　Sharon = SHAR-un*
The tone of the reading is upbeat. The wilderness and the dry land "shall be glad." The reader will do well
to bring a confident and optimistic voice to the reading. (A happy face underscores an optimistic voice!)
Note carefully the promise in verses 5 and 6 that "the eyes of the blind shall be opened, and the ears of the
deaf unstopped." Jesus will make reference to this text in the gospel, and you will want to make certain the
hearers in the congregation still have these words of promise from the prophet ringing in their memory.

⁹No lion shall be there,
    nor shall any ravenous beast come up on it;
they shall not be found there,
    but the redeemed shall walk there.
¹⁰And the ransomed of the LORD shall return,
    and come to Zion with singing;
everlasting joy shall be upon their heads;
    they shall obtain joy and gladness,
    and sorrow and sighing shall flee away.

The word of the Lord.   *or*   Word of God, word of life.

PSALMODY: Psalm 146:5-10 or Luke 1:46b-55

SECOND READING: James 5:7-10

A reading from James.

⁷Be patient, therefore, beloved,
until the coming of the Lord.
The farmer waits for the precious crop from the earth,
being patient with it until it receives the early and the late rains.
⁸You also must be patient.
Strengthen your hearts,
for the coming of the Lord is near.

⁹Beloved, do not grumble against one another,
so that you may not be judged.
See, the Judge is standing at the doors!
¹⁰As an example of suffering and patience, beloved,
take the prophets who spoke in the name of the Lord.

The word of the Lord.   *or*   Word of God, word of life.

SECOND READING
The reading is an appeal for patience. With the exception of verse 9 (which changes the mood by painting a picture of the imminent arrival of the Judge, who is standing at the door!) these verses will profit from a carefully paced, patient tone. Take your time.

GOSPEL: Matthew 11:2-11

The holy gospel according to Matthew.

[2]When John heard in prison what the Messiah was doing,
he sent word by his disciples [3]and said to him,
"Are you the one who is to come,
or are we to wait for another?"
[4]Jesus answered them,
"Go and tell John what you hear and see:
[5]the blind receive their sight, the lame walk,
the lepers are cleansed, the deaf hear,
the dead are raised, and the poor have good news brought to them.
[6]And blessed is anyone who takes no offense at me."

[7]As they went away,
Jesus began to speak to the crowds about John:
"What did you go out into the wilderness to look at?
A reed shaken by the wind?
[8]What then did you go out to see?
Someone dressed in soft robes?
Look, those who wear soft robes are in royal palaces.
[9]What then did you go out to see?
A prophet?
Yes, I tell you, and more than a prophet.
[10]This is the one about whom it is written,
    'See, I am sending my messenger ahead of you,
        who will prepare your way before you.'
[11]Truly I tell you, among those born of women
no one has arisen greater than John the Baptist;
yet the least in the kingdom of heaven is greater than he."

The gospel of the Lord.

GOSPEL
In two distinct episodes, the gospel presents a marvelous portrait of John. Help the assembly sense John's uncertainty as well as our Lord's blessed assurance. Separate the episodes with a healthy pause. Allow a moment for each of Jesus' rhetorical questions in verses 7–9 to hang in the air a moment before proceeding. This is too rich a text to rush.

FIRST READING: Isaiah 7:10-16

A reading from Isaiah.

^{10}The LORD spoke to Ahaz, saying,
^{11}Ask a sign of the LORD your God;
let it be deep as Sheol or high as heaven.
^{12}But Ahaz said,
I will not ask, and I will not put the LORD to the test.

^{13}Then Isaiah said:
"Hear then, O house of David!
Is it too little for you to weary mortals,
that you weary my God also?
^{14}Therefore the LORD himself will give you a sign.
Look, the young woman is with child and shall bear a son,
and shall name him Immanuel.
^{15}He shall eat curds and honey
by the time he knows how to refuse the evil and choose the good.
^{16}For before the child knows how to refuse the evil and choose the good,
the land before whose two kings you are in dread
will be deserted."

The word of the Lord.   *or*   Word of God, word of life.

PSALMODY: Psalm 80:1-7, 17-19

FIRST READING   *Isaiah = eye-ZAY-uh   Ahaz = AY-haz   Sheol = sheh-OHL*
Tread carefully here; this is a complicated little lesson. The reader will need to know where it is going if the hearer is to be helped. There are three characters in this scene: Ahaz, the king; Isaiah, the prophet; and Almighty God. God invites the king to seek a sign of God's care for him. The king says, "No thanks," suggesting that he does not wish to force God to prove himself ("I will not put the Lord to the test.") In fact, the king's unwillingness to ask for a sign is a reflection of the king's indifference toward God. It is to that indifference that Isaiah responds in verse 13, saying, in effect: "Exhausting the patience of the people you deal with isn't enough for you?! You have to try the patience of God as well?" The prophet's words are dripping with sarcasm. Then Isaiah announces that God will provide a sign in spite of the king's indifference. Although Isaiah is likely making reference to a child born in his own day, the hearer today will hear in this

SECOND READING: Romans 1:1-7

A reading from Romans.

¹Paul, a servant of Jesus Christ,
called to be an apostle,
set apart for the gospel of God,
²which he promised beforehand
through his prophets in the holy scriptures,
³the gospel concerning his Son,
who was descended from David according to the flesh
⁴and was declared to be Son of God
with power according to the spirit of holiness
by resurrection from the dead,
Jesus Christ our Lord,
⁵through whom we have received grace and apostleship
to bring about the obedience of faith among all the Gentiles
for the sake of his name,
⁶including yourselves who are called to belong to Jesus Christ,

⁷To all God's beloved in Rome,
who are called to be saints:
Grace to you and peace
from God our Father and the Lord Jesus Christ.

The word of the Lord.   *or*   Word of God, word of life.

---

promise a reference to the birth of Jesus. That's what the reader will want to help the assembly to hear, because today's gospel in Matthew will make reference to this word of Isaiah.

SECOND READING
The whole reading is one sentence! It is the salutation of a letter. First, Paul establishes his credentials by describing his relationship to Jesus. Then he tells the reader who Jesus is. Finally, he summarizes the reason for his writing ("to bring about the obedience of faith among all the Gentiles, . . . including yourselves"). All this leads up to that most familiar greeting: "Grace to you and peace from God our Father. . . ." A substantial pause just before those words may help the assembly to hear them more clearly.

GOSPEL: Matthew 1:18-25

The holy gospel according to Matthew.

¹⁸Now the birth of Jesus the Messiah took place in this way.
When his mother Mary had been engaged to Joseph,
but before they lived together,
she was found to be with child from the Holy Spirit.

¹⁹Her husband Joseph, being a righteous man
and unwilling to expose her to public disgrace,
planned to dismiss her quietly.
²⁰But just when he had resolved to do this,
an angel of the Lord appeared to him in a dream and said,
"Joseph, son of David,
do not be afraid to take Mary as your wife,
for the child conceived in her is from the Holy Spirit.
²¹She will bear a son,
and you are to name him Jesus,
for he will save his people from their sins."
²²All this took place to fulfill
what had been spoken by the Lord through the prophet:
    ²³"Look, the virgin shall conceive and bear a son,
    and they shall name him Emmanuel,"
which means, "God is with us."

²⁴When Joseph awoke from sleep,
he did as the angel of the Lord commanded him;
he took her as his wife,
²⁵but had no marital relations with her until she had borne a son;
and he named him Jesus.

The gospel of the Lord.

GOSPEL
The gospel celebrates the name of Jesus. Consider allowing the first sentence to serve as a kind of title for the reading. A sense of quiet wonder will advance the reading and allow the assembly to focus on the names "Jesus" (verses 18, 21, and 25), and "Emmanuel" (verse 23).

Christmas

Nativity of Our Lord

Set I — *particularly appropriate for Christmas Eve*

FIRST READING: Isaiah 9:2-7

A reading from Isaiah.

²The people who walked in darkness
    have seen a great light;
those who lived in a land of deep darkness—
    on them light has shined.
³You have multiplied the nation,
    you have increased its joy;
they rejoice before you
    as with joy at the harvest,
    as people exult when dividing plunder.
⁴For the yoke of their burden,
    and the bar across their shoulders,
    the rod of their oppressor,
    you have broken as on the day of Midian.
⁵For all the boots of the tramping warriors
    and all the garments rolled in blood
    shall be burned as fuel for the fire.

⁶For a child has been born for us,
    a son given to us;
authority rests upon his shoulders;
    and he is named
Wonderful Counselor, Mighty God,
    Everlasting Father, Prince of Peace.
⁷His authority shall grow continually,
    and there shall be endless peace
for the throne of David and his kingdom.
    He will establish and uphold it
with justice and with righteousness
    from this time onward and forevermore.

The zeal of the Lord of hosts will do this.

The word of the Lord.   *or*   Word of God, word of life.

FIRST READING   *Isaiah = eye-ZAY-uh   Midian = MID-ee-un*
"Joy to the world!" is the strong sense of this text from the prophet. The first four verses build toward the birth announcement in verse 6. A pause of some duration between verses 5 and 6 will help us hear that the birth of the child is the cause for rejoicing. Readers of texts as familiar as this too often rush through what everybody knows. But do not hurry. Take time to savor each name: "Wonderful Counselor. Mighty God. Everlasting Father. Prince of Peace." Take time to help the reader feel the strength of every sentence. Finally, provide another pause before the dramatic ending pronouncement, "The zeal of the Lord of hosts will do this."

PSALMODY: Psalm 96

SECOND READING: Titus 2:11-14

A reading from Titus.

[11]The grace of God has appeared,
bringing salvation to all,
[12]training us to renounce impiety and worldly passions,
and in the present age
to live lives that are self-controlled, upright, and godly,
[13]while we wait for the blessed hope
and the manifestation of the glory
of our great God and Savior, Jesus Christ.

[14]He it is who gave himself for us
that he might redeem us from all iniquity
and purify for himself a people of his own
who are zealous for good deeds.

The word of the Lord.   *or*   Word of God, word of life.

GOSPEL: Luke 2:1-14 [15-20]

The holy gospel according to Luke.

[1]In those days a decree went out from Emperor Augustus
that all the world should be registered.
[2]This was the first registration
and was taken while Quirinius was governor of Syria.
[3]All went to their own towns to be registered.
[4]Joseph also went from the town of Nazareth in Galilee to Judea,
to the city of David called Bethlehem,
because he was descended from the house and family of David.
[5]He went to be registered with Mary,
to whom he was engaged and who was expecting a child.
[6]While they were there, the time came for her to deliver her child.
[7]And she gave birth to her firstborn son
and wrapped him in bands of cloth,

SECOND READING   *Titus = TY-tus*
The author accents the implications of Christmas for all who believe. Now that the "grace of God has appeared" in the birth of the child, Jesus, we will want to live disciplined lives as we await Jesus' coming again in glory. Help the assembly hear the urgency in the author's encouragement to be "zealous for good deeds."

GOSPEL   *Augustus = aw-GUS-tus   Quirinius = kwih-RIN-ee-us*
The trick with the gospels we know by heart is to bring some "newness of life" to the reading. Spending some devotional time with the text before the arrival of the feast day can be very helpful. Take the gospel to heart; then—bring it to life!

and laid him in a manger,
because there was no place for them in the inn.

[8]In that region there were shepherds living in the fields,
keeping watch over their flock by night.
[9]Then an angel of the Lord stood before them,
and the glory of the Lord shone around them,
and they were terrified.
[10]But the angel said to them,
"Do not be afraid;
for see—
I am bringing you good news of great joy for all the people:
[11]to you is born this day in the city of David
a Savior, who is the Messiah, the Lord.
[12]This will be a sign for you:
you will find a child wrapped in bands of cloth
and lying in a manger."
[13]And suddenly there was with the angel
a multitude of the heavenly host, praising God and saying,
    [14]"Glory to God in the highest heaven,
        and on earth peace among those whom he favors!"

[[15]When the angels had left them and gone into heaven,
the shepherds said to one another,
"Let us go now to Bethlehem
and see this thing that has taken place,
which the Lord has made known to us."
[16]So they went with haste
and found Mary and Joseph, and the child lying in the manger.
[17]When they saw this,
they made known what had been told them about this child;
[18]and all who heard it were amazed at what the shepherds told them.
[19]But Mary treasured all these words and pondered them in her heart.

[20]The shepherds returned,
glorifying and praising God for all they had heard and seen,
as it had been told them.]

The gospel of the Lord.

NATIVITY OF OUR LORD

SET II — *particularly appropriate for Christmas Day*

FIRST READING: Isaiah 62:6-12

A reading from Isaiah.

⁶Upon your walls, O Jerusalem,
    I have posted sentinels;
all day and all night
    they shall never be silent.
You who remind the LORD,
    take no rest,
⁷and give him no rest
    until he establishes Jerusalem
    and makes it renowned throughout the earth.

⁸The LORD has sworn by his right hand
    and by his mighty arm:
I will not again give your grain
    to be food for your enemies,
and foreigners shall not drink the wine
    for which you have labored;
⁹but those who garner it shall eat it
    and praise the LORD,
and those who gather it shall drink it
    in my holy courts.

¹⁰Go through, go through the gates,
    prepare the way for the people;
build up, build up the highway,
    clear it of stones,
    lift up an ensign over the peoples.
¹¹The LORD has proclaimed
    to the end of the earth:
Say to daughter Zion,
    "See, your salvation comes;
his reward is with him,
    and his recompense before him."

FIRST READING   *Isaiah = eye-ZAY-uh*

Find a prophetic voice for this celebrative but complex reading. It is a word to prophets to press the Lord to make good on the Lord's promises. It is a word to the prophets to proclaim and to participate in the Lord's plan of salvation. Let this announcement ring out.

¹²They shall be called, "The Holy People,
    The Redeemed of the L<small>ORD</small>";
and you shall be called, "Sought Out,
    A City Not Forsaken."

The word of the Lord.   *or*   Word of God, word of life.

PSALMODY: Psalm 97

SECOND READING: Titus 3:4-7

A reading from Titus.

⁴When the goodness and loving kindness of God our Savior appeared,
⁵he saved us,
not because of any works of righteousness that we had done,
but according to his mercy,
through the water of rebirth
and renewal by the Holy Spirit.
⁶This Spirit he poured out on us richly
through Jesus Christ our Savior,
⁷so that, having been justified by his grace,
we might become heirs
according to the hope of eternal life.

The word of the Lord.   *or*   Word of God, word of life.

GOSPEL: Luke 2:[1-7] 8-20

The holy gospel according to Luke.

[¹In those days a decree went out from Emperor Augustus
that all the world should be registered.
²This was the first registration
and was taken while Quirinius was governor of Syria.
³All went to their own towns to be registered.
⁴Joseph also went from the town of Nazareth in Galilee to Judea,
to the city of David called Bethlehem,
because he was descended from the house and family of David. ▸

SECOND READING   *Titus = TY-tus*
This is a lovely and gentle summary of Christmas and baptismal truth. It might profitably be delivered rather softly—certainly gently—and slowly. (Softly is a relative term. People in the last row still need to hear.)

GOSPEL   *Augustus = aw-GUS-tus   Quirinius = kwih-RIN-ee-us*
The story, the whole story, bears repeating. Read all twenty verses on the Eve and on the Day. Avoid the tendency to rush the familiar. Read slowly. Visualize each scene. Take time for the beauty, the wonder, the mystery of it all.

[5]He went to be registered with Mary,
to whom he was engaged and who was expecting a child.
[6]While they were there, the time came for her to deliver her child.
[7]And she gave birth to her firstborn son
and wrapped him in bands of cloth,
and laid him in a manger,
because there was no place for them in the inn.]

[8]In that region there were shepherds living in the fields,
keeping watch over their flock by night.
[9]Then an angel of the Lord stood before them,
and the glory of the Lord shone around them,
and they were terrified.
[10]But the angel said to them,
"Do not be afraid;
for see—
I am bringing you good news of great joy for all the people:
[11]to you is born this day in the city of David
a Savior, who is the Messiah, the Lord.
[12]This will be a sign for you:
you will find a child wrapped in bands of cloth
and lying in a manger."
[13]And suddenly there was with the angel
a multitude of the heavenly host, praising God and saying,
[14]"Glory to God in the highest heaven,
        and on earth peace among those whom he favors!"

[15]When the angels had left them and gone into heaven,
the shepherds said to one another,
"Let us go now to Bethlehem
and see this thing that has taken place,
which the Lord has made known to us."
[16]So they went with haste
and found Mary and Joseph, and the child lying in the manger.
[17]When they saw this,
they made known what had been told them about this child;
[18]and all who heard it were amazed at what the shepherds told them.
[19]But Mary treasured all these words and pondered them in her heart.

[20]The shepherds returned,
glorifying and praising God for all they had heard and seen,
as it had been told them.

The gospel of the Lord.

NATIVITY OF OUR LORD

SET III — *particularly appropriate for Christmas Day*

FIRST READING: Isaiah 52:7-10

A reading from Isaiah.

⁷How beautiful upon the mountains
 are the feet of the messenger who announces peace,
who brings good news,
 who announces salvation,
 who says to Zion, "Your God reigns."

⁸Listen! Your sentinels lift up their voices,
 together they sing for joy;
for in plain sight they see
 the return of the LORD to Zion.

⁹Break forth together into singing,
 you ruins of Jerusalem;
for the LORD has comforted his people,
 he has redeemed Jerusalem.
¹⁰The LORD has bared his holy arm
 before the eyes of all the nations;
and all the ends of the earth shall see
 the salvation of our God.

The word of the Lord.   *or*   Word of God, word of life.

PSALMODY: Psalm 98

SECOND READING: Hebrews 1:1-4 [5-12]

A reading from Hebrews.

¹Long ago God spoke to our ancestors
in many and various ways by the prophets,
²but in these last days
he has spoken to us by a Son, ▸

FIRST READING   *Isaiah = eye-ZAY-uh*
This text provides a kind of afterglow to all the excitement of the night before. While historically it speaks to
a nation that has been exiled, we see "the salvation of our God" in the Babe in the manger. This is our God in
"plain sight." Help the hearer experience the joy and wonder of the miracle of Christmas. Bring that joy and
wonder to the sound of the reading.

whom he appointed heir of all things,
through whom he also created the worlds.
³He is the reflection of God's glory
and the exact imprint of God's very being,
and he sustains all things by his powerful word.
When he had made purification for sins,
he sat down at the right hand of the Majesty on high,
⁴having become as much superior to angels
as the name he has inherited is more excellent than theirs.

[⁵For to which of the angels did God ever say,
    "You are my Son;
        today I have begotten you"?
Or again,
    "I will be his Father,
        and he will be my Son"?
⁶And again, when he brings the firstborn into the world, he says,
    "Let all God's angels worship him."
⁷Of the angels he says,
    "He makes his angels winds,
        and his servants flames of fire."

⁸But of the Son he says,
    "Your throne, O God, is forever and ever,
        and the righteous scepter is the scepter of your kingdom.
    ⁹You have loved righteousness and hated wickedness;
    therefore God, your God, has anointed you
        with the oil of gladness beyond your companions."
¹⁰And,
    "In the beginning, Lord, you founded the earth,
        and the heavens are the work of your hands;
    ¹¹they will perish, but you remain;
        they will all wear out like clothing;
    ¹²like a cloak you will roll them up,
        and like clothing they will be changed.
    But you are the same,
        and your years will never end."]

The word of the Lord.   *or*   Word of God, word of life.

SECOND READING

The text is a marvelous comparison of the Son (Jesus! Born this day!) and the angels. Verses 5–12 are challenging to read because of the frequent use of quotations. This makes the pause points marked by commas of critical importance. Help the hearer to see the quotation marks around the quotes by making good use of the pauses. The tone of the reading is one of great joy at the unsurpassed marvel that this Jesus (born this day!) is the very Son of God.

GOSPEL: John 1:1-14

The holy gospel according to John.

¹In the beginning was the Word,
and the Word was with God,
and the Word was God.
²He was in the beginning with God.
³All things came into being through him,
and without him not one thing came into being.
What has come into being ⁴in him was life,
and the life was the light of all people.
⁵The light shines in the darkness,
and the darkness did not overcome it.

⁶There was a man sent from God, whose name was John.
⁷He came as a witness to testify to the light,
so that all might believe through him.
⁸He himself was not the light,
but he came to testify to the light.
⁹The true light, which enlightens everyone,
was coming into the world.

¹⁰He was in the world,
and the world came into being through him;
yet the world did not know him.
¹¹He came to what was his own,
and his own people did not accept him.
¹²But to all who received him,
who believed in his name,
he gave power to become children of God,
¹³who were born,
not of blood or of the will of the flesh or of the will of man,
but of God.

¹⁴And the Word became flesh and lived among us,
and we have seen his glory,
the glory as of a father's only son,
full of grace and truth.

The gospel of the Lord.

GOSPEL
A slow start is essential. Allow each of the three assertions to stand on its own. Verse 1 sets the stage for the "incarnation in a nutshell" in verse 14. Verses 6–9 are parenthetical and require less emphasis than the other three paragraphs. The gospel provides a dramatic contrast between the pre-existent Christ at the center of the creation of the universe and the baby in the manger on Christmas Eve. Make it a strong reading.

FIRST SUNDAY OF CHRISTMAS

FIRST READING: Isaiah 63:7-9

A reading from Isaiah.

⁷I will recount the gracious deeds of the LORD,
    the praiseworthy acts of the LORD,
because of all that the LORD has done for us,
    and the great favor to the house of Israel
that he has shown them according to his mercy,
    according to the abundance of his steadfast love.

⁸For he said,
"Surely they are my people,
    children who will not deal falsely";
and he became their savior ⁹in all their distress.

It was no messenger or angel
    but his presence that saved them;
in his love and in his pity he redeemed them;
he lifted them up and carried them all the days of old.

The word of the Lord.   *or*   Word of God, word of life.

PSALMODY: Psalm 148

SECOND READING: Hebrews 2:10-18

A reading from Hebrews.

¹⁰It was fitting that God,
for whom and through whom all things exist,
in bringing many children to glory,
should make the pioneer of their salvation
perfect through sufferings.

FIRST READING   *Isaiah = eye-ZAY-uh*

On this side of Bethlehem we hear the words of the prophet as a concise summary of the mystery of Christmas—the mystery of the incarnation. "It was no messenger or angel" (in the manger!) but the very "presence" of God that "saved them." It is a very brief text. The reader can afford to take extra time. Share the sense of wonder in the text.

SECOND READING

It is a bit startling to contemplate the suffering and death of Jesus this close to Christmas. Yet this is what the reading does. That startling contrast can help to drive the reading. It is complicated writing. Invest some time in understanding the author's point so that you may help the hearer to do the same. The "direct quotes" of

¹¹For the one who sanctifies
and those who are sanctified
all have one Father.
For this reason
Jesus is not ashamed to call them brothers and sisters, ¹²saying,
    "I will proclaim your name to my brothers and sisters,
        in the midst of the congregation I will praise you."
¹³And again,
    "I will put my trust in him."
And again,
    "Here am I and the children whom God has given me."

¹⁴Since, therefore, the children share flesh and blood,
he himself likewise shared the same things,
so that through death
he might destroy the one who has the power of death,
that is, the devil,
¹⁵and free those who all their lives
were held in slavery by the fear of death.
¹⁶For it is clear that he did not come to help angels,
but the descendants of Abraham.
¹⁷Therefore he had to become like his brothers and sisters
in every respect,
so that he might be a merciful and faithful high priest in the service of God,
to make a sacrifice of atonement for the sins of the people.
¹⁸Because he himself was tested by what he suffered,
he is able to help those who are being tested.

The word of the Lord.   *or*   Word of God, word of life.

GOSPEL: Matthew 2:13–23

The holy gospel according to Matthew.

¹³Now after the wise men had left,
an angel of the Lord appeared to Joseph in a dream and said,
"Get up, take the child and his mother, and flee to Egypt,
and remain there until I tell you;
for Herod is about to search for the child, to destroy him." ▸

---

our Lord in verses 12 and 13 provide a challenge to the reader. Take your time. A pause of some substance after the preceding commas will help us "hear the quotation marks" without the reader actually saying, "quote" and "unquote."

GOSPEL   *Jeremiah = jehr-eh-MY-uh   Ramah = RAY-muh   Archelaus = ar-kuh-LAY-us   Nazorean = naz-uh-REE-un*
The story contains considerable drama; allow it to surface naturally to good effect. Note that verses 15b as well as 17 and 18 have a parenthetical sound to them, yet both footnotes demand a degree of passion. The words Archelaus and Nazorean serve as helpful reminders that, although we have read these texts many times before, careful preparation well serves even the most seasoned lector.

¹⁴Then Joseph got up,
took the child and his mother by night, and went to Egypt,
¹⁵and remained there until the death of Herod.
This was to fulfill
what had been spoken by the Lord through the prophet,
"Out of Egypt I have called my son."

¹⁶When Herod saw that he had been tricked by the wise men,
he was infuriated,
and he sent and killed all the children in and around Bethlehem
who were two years old or under,
according to the time that he had learned from the wise men.
¹⁷Then was fulfilled what had been spoken through the prophet Jeremiah:
    ¹⁸"A voice was heard in Ramah,
        wailing and loud lamentation,
    Rachel weeping for her children;
        she refused to be consoled, because they are no more."

¹⁹When Herod died,
an angel of the Lord suddenly appeared in a dream to Joseph in Egypt
and said,
²⁰"Get up, take the child and his mother,
and go to the land of Israel,
for those who were seeking the child's life are dead."
²¹Then Joseph got up, took the child and his mother,
and went to the land of Israel.
²²But when he heard that Archelaus was ruling over Judea
in place of his father Herod,
he was afraid to go there.
And after being warned in a dream,
he went away to the district of Galilee.
²³There he made his home in a town called Nazareth,
so that what had been spoken through the prophets might be fulfilled,
"He will be called a Nazorean."

The gospel of the Lord.

SECOND SUNDAY OF CHRISTMAS

FIRST READING: Jeremiah 31:7-14   *Alternate Reading: Sirach 24:1-12 (p. 499)*

A reading from Jeremiah.

⁷Thus says the LORD:
Sing aloud with gladness for Jacob,
    and raise shouts for the chief of the nations;
proclaim, give praise, and say,
    "Save, O LORD, your people,
    the remnant of Israel."

⁸See, I am going to bring them from the land of the north,
    and gather them from the farthest parts of the earth,
among them the blind and the lame,
    those with child and those in labor, together;
    a great company, they shall return here.
⁹With weeping they shall come,
    and with consolations I will lead them back,
I will let them walk by brooks of water,
    in a straight path in which they shall not stumble;
for I have become a father to Israel,
    and Ephraim is my firstborn.

¹⁰Hear the word of the LORD, O nations,
    and declare it in the coastlands far away;
say, "He who scattered Israel will gather him,
    and will keep him as a shepherd a flock."
¹¹For the LORD has ransomed Jacob,
    and has redeemed him from hands too strong for him.

¹²They shall come and sing aloud on the height of Zion,
    and they shall be radiant over the goodness of the LORD,
over the grain, the wine, and the oil,
    and over the young of the flock and the herd;
their life shall become like a watered garden,
    and they shall never languish again.
¹³Then shall the young women rejoice in the dance,
    and the young men and the old shall be merry. ▸

FIRST READING   *Jeremiah = jehr-eh-MY-uh   Ephraim = EEF-rih-um*
"Sing aloud with gladness" is the best advice for the reader! The whole text should sing of joy and great
gladness. The people who have been exiled in Babylon are returned by God's hand to their homeland, which
is overflowing with the "goodness of the Lord." Verse 7 serves as an introduction. From verse 8 onwards
we hear the voice of God declaring God's intention. Help the people hear the voice of authority that is God's
voice in yours, declaring the Lord's intention to give the people "gladness for sorrow."

I will turn their mourning into joy,
   I will comfort them, and give them gladness for sorrow.
[14]I will give the priests their fill of fatness,
   and my people shall be satisfied with my bounty, says the LORD.

The word of the Lord.   *or*   Word of God, word of life.

PSALMODY: Psalm 147:12-20 or Wisdom 10:15-21

SECOND READING: Ephesians 1:3-14

A reading from Ephesians.

[3]Blessed be the God and Father of our Lord Jesus Christ,
who has blessed us in Christ
with every spiritual blessing in the heavenly places,
[4]just as he chose us in Christ before the foundation of the world
to be holy and blameless before him in love.
[5]He destined us for adoption as his children through Jesus Christ,
according to the good pleasure of his will,
[6]to the praise of his glorious grace
that he freely bestowed on us in the Beloved.

[7]In him we have redemption through his blood,
the forgiveness of our trespasses,
according to the riches of his grace [8]that he lavished on us.

With all wisdom and insight
[9]he has made known to us the mystery of his will,
according to his good pleasure that he set forth in Christ,
[10]as a plan for the fullness of time,
to gather up all things in him,
things in heaven and things on earth.

[11]In Christ we have also obtained an inheritance,
having been destined according to the purpose of him
who accomplishes all things according to his counsel and will,
[12]so that we, who were the first to set our hope on Christ,
might live for the praise of his glory.

SECOND READING   *Ephesians = eh-FEE-zhunz*
In a rather complex but wonderful way, the second reading echoes the first. Here the author explicitly describes how God has gathered us to God's self in Christ Jesus. (God brings us back from our exile in sin.) The thought patterns are circuitous, however, and will require the reader to spend some time getting into the text, becoming familiar with the twists and turns of the sentence structure. It is a Christmas message in a very real sense, and it will help listeners if we hear in the voice of the reader the gladness that is in the heart of every adopted child of God.

¹³In him you also, when you had heard the word of truth,
the gospel of your salvation, and had believed in him,
were marked with the seal of the promised Holy Spirit;
¹⁴this is the pledge of our inheritance
toward redemption as God's own people,
to the praise of his glory.

The word of the Lord.   *or*   Word of God, word of life.

GOSPEL: John 1:[1-9] 10-18

The holy gospel according to John.

[¹In the beginning was the Word,
and the Word was with God,
and the Word was God.
²He was in the beginning with God.
³All things came into being through him,
and without him not one thing came into being.
What has come into being ⁴in him was life,
and the life was the light of all people.
⁵The light shines in the darkness,
and the darkness did not overcome it.

⁶There was a man sent from God, whose name was John.
⁷He came as a witness to testify to the light,
so that all might believe through him.
⁸He himself was not the light,
but he came to testify to the light.
⁹The true light, which enlightens everyone,
was coming into the world.]

¹⁰He was in the world,
and the world came into being through him;
yet the world did not know him.
¹¹He came to what was his own,
and his own people did not accept him.
¹²But to all who received him,
who believed in his name,
he gave power to become children of God, ▸

GOSPEL
If the congregation opts for the abbreviated reading, verse 10 will require an especially sharp attack. In that case, it may be helpful to replace "He" in verse 10 with "The Word who was God," to help readers get on the moving train of thought. Allow each of that verse's three phrases its own significant space. Provide a significant pause at each paragraph break to help the hearer to "keep up."

¹³who were born, not of blood or of the will of the flesh
or of the will of man,
but of God.

¹⁴And the Word became flesh and lived among us,
and we have seen his glory,
the glory as of a father's only son,
full of grace and truth.

¹⁵(John testified to him and cried out,
"This was he of whom I said,
'He who comes after me ranks ahead of me because he was before me.'")
¹⁶From his fullness we have all received,
grace upon grace.
¹⁷The law indeed was given through Moses;
grace and truth came through Jesus Christ.

¹⁸No one has ever seen God.
It is God the only Son,
who is close to the Father's heart,
who has made him known.

The gospel of the Lord.

EPIPHANY OF OUR LORD

FIRST READING: Isaiah 60:1-6

A reading from Isaiah.

¹Arise, shine; for your light has come,
    and the glory of the LORD has risen upon you.
²For darkness shall cover the earth,
    and thick darkness the peoples;
but the LORD will arise upon you,
    and his glory will appear over you.
³Nations shall come to your light,
    and kings to the brightness of your dawn.

⁴Lift up your eyes and look around;
    they all gather together, they come to you;
your sons shall come from far away,
    and your daughters shall be carried on their nurses' arms.

⁵Then you shall see and be radiant;
    your heart shall thrill and rejoice,
because the abundance of the sea shall be brought to you,
    the wealth of the nations shall come to you.
⁶A multitude of camels shall cover you,
    the young camels of Midian and Ephah;
    all those from Sheba shall come.
They shall bring gold and frankincense,
    and shall proclaim the praise of the LORD.

The word of the Lord.   *or*   Word of God, word of life.

PSALMODY: Psalm 72:1-7, 10-14

FIRST READING   *Isaiah = eye-ZAY-uh   Midian = MID-ee-un   Ephah = EE-fah   Sheba = SHE-buh*
From this side of the crèche and this side of the cross we see the kings in Isaiah's wonderful words and can
practically hear the camel bells! This reading begs for the sound of unadulterated joy!

SECOND READING: Ephesians 3:1-12

A reading from Ephesians.

[1]This is the reason that I Paul am a prisoner for Christ Jesus
for the sake of you Gentiles—
[2]for surely you have already heard of the commission of God's grace
that was given me for you,
[3]and how the mystery was made known to me by revelation,
as I wrote above in a few words,
[4]a reading of which will enable you
to perceive my understanding of the mystery of Christ.

[5]In former generations this mystery was not made known to humankind,
as it has now been revealed to his holy apostles and prophets by the Spirit:
[6]that is, the Gentiles have become fellow heirs,
members of the same body,
and sharers in the promise in Christ Jesus through the gospel.

[7]Of this gospel I have become a servant
according to the gift of God's grace
that was given me by the working of his power.
[8]Although I am the very least of all the saints,
this grace was given to me
to bring to the Gentiles the news of the boundless riches of Christ,
[9]and to make everyone see
what is the plan of the mystery hidden for ages
in God who created all things;
[10]so that through the church
the wisdom of God in its rich variety might now be made known
to the rulers and authorities in the heavenly places.
[11]This was in accordance with the eternal purpose
that he has carried out in Christ Jesus our Lord,
[12]in whom we have access to God
in boldness and confidence through faith in him.

The word of the Lord.   *or*   Word of God, word of life.

SECOND READING   *Ephesians = eh-FEE-zhunz*
We hear the apostle Paul celebrating the privilege of bearing the good news of God in Christ to the Gentiles.
The reader has that same privilege, and should celebrate it in the care and spirit given to the reading.

GOSPEL: Matthew 2:1-12

The holy gospel according to Matthew.

[1]In the time of King Herod,
after Jesus was born in Bethlehem of Judea,
wise men from the East came to Jerusalem, [2]asking,
"Where is the child who has been born king of the Jews?
For we observed his star at its rising, and have come to pay him homage."

[3]When King Herod heard this, he was frightened, and all Jerusalem with him;
[4]and calling together all the chief priests and scribes of the people,
he inquired of them where the Messiah was to be born.
[5]They told him,
"In Bethlehem of Judea; for so it has been written by the prophet:
　[6]'And you, Bethlehem, in the land of Judah,
　　are by no means least among the rulers of Judah;
　for from you shall come a ruler
　　who is to shepherd my people Israel.'"

[7]Then Herod secretly called for the wise men
and learned from them the exact time when the star had appeared.
[8]Then he sent them to Bethlehem, saying,
"Go and search diligently for the child;
and when you have found him,
bring me word so that I may also go and pay him homage."

[9]When they had heard the king, they set out;
and there, ahead of them, went the star that they had seen at its rising,
until it stopped over the place where the child was.
[10]When they saw that the star had stopped,
they were overwhelmed with joy.

[11]On entering the house, they saw the child with Mary his mother;
and they knelt down and paid him homage.
Then, opening their treasure chests,
they offered him gifts of gold, frankincense, and myrrh.

[12]And having been warned in a dream not to return to Herod,
they left for their own country by another road.

The gospel of the Lord.

GOSPEL

Wise men come inquiring. King Herod is frightened. He calls the magi secretly. He lies outright. By the end of the text, the wise men are "overwhelmed with joy." Inquiry, fright, secrecy, lies, and joy each have unique sounds. Explore them. Employ them.

Time after Epiphany

Baptism of Our Lord

First Sunday after Epiphany

Sunday, January 7–13

Lectionary 1

FIRST READING: Isaiah 42:1-9

A reading from Isaiah.

¹Here is my servant, whom I uphold,
   my chosen, in whom my soul delights;
I have put my spirit upon him;
   he will bring forth justice to the nations.
²He will not cry or lift up his voice,
   or make it heard in the street;
³a bruised reed he will not break,
   and a dimly burning wick he will not quench;
   he will faithfully bring forth justice.
⁴He will not grow faint or be crushed
   until he has established justice in the earth;
   and the coastlands wait for his teaching.

⁵Thus says God, the LORD,
   who created the heavens and stretched them out,
   who spread out the earth and what comes from it,
who gives breath to the people upon it
   and spirit to those who walk in it:
⁶I am the LORD,
I have called you in righteousness,
   I have taken you by the hand and kept you;
I have given you as a covenant to the people,
   a light to the nations,
      ⁷to open the eyes that are blind,
to bring out the prisoners from the dungeon,
   from the prison those who sit in darkness.

⁸I am the LORD, that is my name;
   my glory I give to no other,
   nor my praise to idols.
⁹See, the former things have come to pass, ▸

FIRST READING   *Isaiah = eye-ZAY-uh*
This is a song by the prophet celebrating the servant of the Lord. From our vantage point we can see the face of Jesus as the face of that servant. Celebrate the Lord's chosen one, the bringer of justice and the light to the nations. The reading requires a celebrative sound. Smile, even!

and new things I now declare;
before they spring forth, I tell you of them.

The word of the Lord.   *or*   **Word of God, word of life.**

PSALMODY: Psalm 29

SECOND READING: Acts 10:34-43

A reading from Acts.

³⁴Peter began to speak to ⌈Cornelius and his household⌉:
"I truly understand that God shows no partiality,
³⁵but in every nation
anyone who fears him and does what is right
is acceptable to him.

³⁶"You know the message he sent to the people of Israel,
preaching peace by Jesus Christ—
he is Lord of all.
³⁷That message spread throughout Judea,
beginning in Galilee after the baptism that John announced:
³⁸how God anointed Jesus of Nazareth with the Holy Spirit and with power;
how he went about doing good
and healing all who were oppressed by the devil,
for God was with him.
³⁹We are witnesses to all that he did both in Judea and in Jerusalem.
They put him to death by hanging him on a tree;
⁴⁰but God raised him on the third day
and allowed him to appear,
⁴¹not to all the people
but to us who were chosen by God as witnesses,
and who ate and drank with him after he rose from the dead.

⁴²"He commanded us to preach to the people
and to testify that he is the one ordained by God
as judge of the living and the dead.
⁴³All the prophets testify about him
that everyone who believes in him
receives forgiveness of sins through his name."

The word of the Lord.   *or*   **Word of God, word of life.**

SECOND READING   *Cornelius = cor-NEE-lee-us*
Peter celebrates Jesus as God's anointed one in this little sermon to Cornelius and his family. This reading, too, yearns for a joyful sound as Peter summarizes the love of God in Christ Jesus as the one "ordained by God as judge of the living and the dead" and the one of whom the prophets testified.

GOSPEL: Matthew 3:13-17

The holy gospel according to Matthew.

[13]Jesus came from Galilee to John at the Jordan,
to be baptized by him.
[14]John would have prevented him, saying,
"I need to be baptized by you, and do you come to me?"
[15]But Jesus answered him,
"Let it be so now;
for it is proper for us in this way to fulfill all righteousness."
Then he consented.

[16]And when Jesus had been baptized,
just as he came up from the water,
suddenly the heavens were opened to him
and he saw the Spirit of God descending like a dove
and alighting on him.
[17]And a voice from heaven said,
"This is my Son, the Beloved,
with whom I am well pleased."

The gospel of the Lord.

GOSPEL
The strength of the first half of the gospel lies in its terse phrases. An understated reading of these might provide a meaningful contrast to the awe and wonder that the vision of verses 16 and 17 should inspire. Separate the two paragraphs with a solid "passage of time" pause.

✠ Second Sunday after Epiphany

Sunday, January 14–20

Lectionary 2

FIRST READING: Isaiah 49:1-7

A reading from Isaiah.

¹Listen to me, O coastlands,
     pay attention, you peoples from far away!
The LORD called me before I was born,
     while I was in my mother's womb he named me.
²He made my mouth like a sharp sword,
     in the shadow of his hand he hid me;
he made me a polished arrow,
     in his quiver he hid me away.

³And he said to me, "You are my servant,
     Israel, in whom I will be glorified."
⁴But I said, "I have labored in vain,
     I have spent my strength for nothing and vanity;
yet surely my cause is with the LORD,
     and my reward with my God."

⁵And now the LORD says,
     who formed me in the womb to be his servant,
to bring Jacob back to him,
     and that Israel might be gathered to him,
for I am honored in the sight of the LORD,
     and my God has become my strength—
⁶he says,
"It is too light a thing that you should be my servant
     to raise up the tribes of Jacob
     and to restore the survivors of Israel;
I will give you as a light to the nations,
     that my salvation may reach to the end of the earth."

⁷Thus says the LORD,
     the Redeemer of Israel and his Holy One,
to one deeply despised, abhorred by the nations,

FIRST READING   *Isaiah = eye-ZAY-uh*
The first two lines of the reading set the tone. This announcement by God's servant demands the attention of all people. Make the hearer take notice. Help the people in the pew hear the text as a detailing of the credentials of Jesus of Nazareth. It is an epiphany ("showing forth") reading selected for this day to make it clear that Jesus has been chosen as the one in whom God would be revealed most fully to the world. Do not be timid in your reading!

the slave of rulers,
"Kings shall see and stand up,
    princes, and they shall prostrate themselves,
because of the LORD, who is faithful,
    the Holy One of Israel, who has chosen you."

The word of the Lord.   *or*   Word of God, word of life.

PSALMODY: Psalm 40:1-11

SECOND READING: 1 Corinthians 1:1-9

A reading from First Corinthians.

[1]Paul, called to be an apostle of Christ Jesus by the will of God,
and our brother Sosthenes,
[2]To the church of God that is in Corinth,
to those who are sanctified in Christ Jesus,
called to be saints,
together with all those who in every place
call on the name of our Lord Jesus Christ,
both their Lord and ours:
[3]Grace to you and peace
from God our Father and the Lord Jesus Christ.

[4]I give thanks to my God always for you
because of the grace of God that has been given you in Christ Jesus,
[5]for in every way you have been enriched in him,
in speech and knowledge of every kind—
[6]just as the testimony of Christ has been strengthened among you—
[7]so that you are not lacking in any spiritual gift
as you wait for the revealing of our Lord Jesus Christ.

[8]He will also strengthen you to the end,
so that you may be blameless on the day of our Lord Jesus Christ.
[9]God is faithful;
by him you were called into the fellowship of his Son,
Jesus Christ our Lord.

The word of the Lord.   *or*   Word of God, word of life.

SECOND READING   *Sosthenes = SOS-then-eez*
These are the warm, loving, introductory words of Paul and Sosthenes to the congregation at Corinth. Be encouraging in your reading. Help us hear the love!

GOSPEL: John 1:29-42

The holy gospel according to John.

29 ⌜John the Baptist⌝ saw Jesus coming toward him and declared,
"Here is the Lamb of God who takes away the sin of the world!
30This is he of whom I said,
'After me comes a man who ranks ahead of me
because he was before me.'
31I myself did not know him;
but I came baptizing with water for this reason,
that he might be revealed to Israel."

32And John testified,
"I saw the Spirit descending from heaven like a dove,
and it remained on him.
33I myself did not know him,
but the one who sent me to baptize with water said to me,
'He on whom you see the Spirit descend and remain
is the one who baptizes with the Holy Spirit.'
34And I myself have seen and have testified
that this is the Son of God."

35The next day John again was standing with two of his disciples,
36and as he watched Jesus walk by, he exclaimed,
"Look, here is the Lamb of God!"
37The two disciples heard him say this, and they followed Jesus.
38When Jesus turned and saw them following, he said to them,
"What are you looking for?"
They said to him,
"Rabbi" (which translated means Teacher),
"where are you staying?"
39He said to them,
"Come and see."
They came and saw where he was staying,
and they remained with him that day.
It was about four o'clock in the afternoon.

40One of the two who heard John speak and followed him
was Andrew, Simon Peter's brother.

GOSPEL   *Cephas = SEE-fus*
There is a simple, cinematic quality to this gospel. Each of its four paragraphs contains an independent scene. There is an enigmatic quality about each, as if there is much more to come. An excellent reading will help the assembly to hear that.

[41]He first found his brother Simon and said to him,
"We have found the Messiah" (which is translated Anointed).
[42]He brought Simon to Jesus, who looked at him and said,
"You are Simon son of John.
You are to be called Cephas" (which is translated Peter).

The gospel of the Lord.

THIRD SUNDAY AFTER EPIPHANY

FIRST READING: Isaiah 9:1-4

A reading from Isaiah.

¹There will be no gloom for those who were in anguish.
In the former time ⌐the LORD⌐ brought into contempt
the land of Zebulun and the land of Naphtali,
but in the latter time he will make glorious the way of the sea,
the land beyond the Jordan, Galilee of the nations.

²The people who walked in darkness
    have seen a great light;
those who lived in a land of deep darkness—
    on them light has shined.
³You have multiplied the nation,
    you have increased its joy;
they rejoice before you
    as with joy at the harvest,
    as people exult when dividing plunder.
⁴For the yoke of their burden,
    and the bar across their shoulders,
    the rod of their oppressor,
    you have broken as on the day of Midian.

The word of the Lord.   *or*   **Word of God, word of life.**

PSALMODY: Psalm 27:1, 4–9

FIRST READING   *Isaiah = eye-ZAY-uh   Zebulun = ZEB-yuh-lun   Naphtali = NAF-tuh-lye   Midian = MID-ee-un*
The sound of the reading is bold and assertive (and laced with joy in verses 2–4!). In the gospel appointed for the day (Matt. 4:12-23), Matthew will point to Jesus as the fulfillment of this prophecy. An important part of the lector's assignment today is to help the people recognize the prophecy when they hear it quoted in the gospel.

SECOND READING: 1 Corinthians 1:10-18

A reading from First Corinthians.

[10]Now I appeal to you, brothers and sisters,
by the name of our Lord Jesus Christ,
that all of you be in agreement
and that there be no divisions among you,
but that you be united in the same mind and the same purpose.
[11]For it has been reported to me by Chloe's people
that there are quarrels among you, my brothers and sisters.
[12]What I mean is that each of you says,
"I belong to Paul," or "I belong to Apollos,"
or "I belong to Cephas," or "I belong to Christ."
[13]Has Christ been divided?
Was Paul crucified for you?
Or were you baptized in the name of Paul?

[14]I thank God that I baptized none of you except Crispus and Gaius,
[15]so that no one can say that you were baptized in my name.
[16](I did baptize also the household of Stephanas;
beyond that, I do not know whether I baptized anyone else.)
[17]For Christ did not send me to baptize
but to proclaim the gospel,
and not with eloquent wisdom,
so that the cross of Christ might not be emptied of its power.

[18]For the message about the cross
is foolishness to those who are perishing,
but to us who are being saved
it is the power of God.

The word of the Lord.   *or*   Word of God, word of life.

SECOND READING   *Apollos = uh-POL-us   Cephas = SEE-fus   Gaius = GAY-us*
All of the apostle's instruction leads to the conclusion in verse 18. Build toward it in the reading of the text.
The sound of the reading is that of a parent or a pastor making an important appeal to maturing children or
parishioners.

GOSPEL: Matthew 4:12-23

The holy gospel according to Matthew.

¹²Now when Jesus heard that John had been arrested,
he withdrew to Galilee.
¹³He left Nazareth and made his home in Capernaum by the sea,
in the territory of Zebulun and Naphtali,
¹⁴so that what had been spoken through the prophet Isaiah
might be fulfilled:

> ¹⁵"Land of Zebulun, land of Naphtali,
> on the road by the sea, across the Jordan, Galilee of the Gentiles—
> ¹⁶the people who sat in darkness
> have seen a great light,
> and for those who sat in the region and shadow of death
> light has dawned."

¹⁷From that time Jesus began to proclaim,
"Repent, for the kingdom of heaven has come near."

¹⁸As he walked by the Sea of Galilee, he saw two brothers,
Simon, who is called Peter, and Andrew his brother,
casting a net into the sea—for they were fishermen.
¹⁹And he said to them,
"Follow me, and I will make you fish for people."
²⁰Immediately they left their nets and followed him.

²¹As he went from there, he saw two other brothers,
James son of Zebedee and his brother John,
in the boat with their father Zebedee, mending their nets,
and he called them.
²²Immediately they left the boat and their father, and followed him.

²³Jesus went throughout Galilee, teaching in their synagogues
and proclaiming the good news of the kingdom
and curing every disease and every sickness among the people.

The gospel of the Lord.

GOSPEL   *Capernaum = kuh-PER-nih-um   Zebulun = ZEB-yuh-lun   Naphtali = NAF-tuh-lye   Isaiah =
eye-ZAY-uh   Zebedee = ZEB-uh-dee*
Map the reading out—literally. Use an atlas. Verses 12–16 will be the richer for it. Separating the remaining
four paragraphs with substantial pauses will help mark the passage of time and give the reading the
breadth it demands.

Fourth Sunday after Epiphany

Sunday, January 28–February 3   *(if before Transfiguration)*
Lectionary 4

FIRST READING: Micah 6:1-8

A reading from Micah.

¹Hear what the LORD says:
    Rise, plead your case before the mountains,
    and let the hills hear your voice.
²Hear, you mountains, the controversy of the LORD,
    and you enduring foundations of the earth;
for the LORD has a controversy with his people,
    and he will contend with Israel.

³"O my people, what have I done to you?
    In what have I wearied you?
    Answer me!
⁴For I brought you up from the land of Egypt,
    and redeemed you from the house of slavery;
and I sent before you Moses, Aaron, and Miriam.
⁵O my people, remember now what King Balak of Moab devised,
    what Balaam son of Beor answered him,
and what happened from Shittim to Gilgal,
    that you may know the saving acts of the LORD."

⁶"With what shall I come before the LORD,
    and bow myself before God on high?
Shall I come before him with burnt offerings,
    with calves a year old?
⁷Will the LORD be pleased with thousands of rams,
    with ten thousands of rivers of oil?
Shall I give my firstborn for my transgression,
    the fruit of my body for the sin of my soul?"

⁸He has told you, O mortal, what is good;
    and what does the LORD require of you
but to do justice, and to love kindness,
    and to walk humbly with your God?

The word of the Lord.   *or*   Word of God, word of life.

FIRST READING   *Micah = MY-kuh   Balak = BAY-lak   Moab = MOH-ab   Balaam = BAY-lum   Beor =
BEE-or   Shittim = SHIH-teem   Gilgal = GIL-gal*
This reading sounds much like the bailiff of the court announcing the list of charges God is bringing against
God's people. Notice, however, that this bailiff is addressing the "mountains" and the "enduring foundations
of the earth." This requires a big voice. The charges need to ring out! At verse 6 the voice changes to that
of the people. It is the voice of self-examination and should sound less like an announcement and more like
introspection.

PSALMODY: Psalm 15

SECOND READING: 1 Corinthians 1:18-31

A reading from First Corinthians.

¹⁸The message about the cross
is foolishness to those who are perishing,
but to us who are being saved
it is the power of God.

¹⁹For it is written,
    "I will destroy the wisdom of the wise,
    and the discernment of the discerning I will thwart."
²⁰Where is the one who is wise?
Where is the scribe?
Where is the debater of this age?
Has not God made foolish the wisdom of the world?

²¹For since, in the wisdom of God,
the world did not know God through wisdom,
God decided, through the foolishness of our proclamation,
to save those who believe.
²²For Jews demand signs and Greeks desire wisdom,
²³but we proclaim Christ crucified,
a stumbling block to Jews and foolishness to Gentiles,
²⁴but to those who are the called, both Jews and Greeks,
Christ the power of God and the wisdom of God.
²⁵For God's foolishness is wiser than human wisdom,
and God's weakness is stronger than human strength.

²⁶Consider your own call, brothers and sisters:
not many of you were wise by human standards,
not many were powerful,
not many were of noble birth.
²⁷But God chose what is foolish in the world to shame the wise;
God chose what is weak in the world to shame the strong;
²⁸God chose what is low and despised in the world,
things that are not,
to reduce to nothing things that are,
²⁹so that no one might boast in the presence of God.

SECOND READING
This is the central argument of the Christian faith. It is the reader's job to make it a persuasive argument. Bring all the energy and conviction you can muster to this reading. Take plenty of time. The assembly will need time to follow the argument.

³⁰He is the source of your life in Christ Jesus,
who became for us wisdom from God,
and righteousness and sanctification and redemption,
³¹in order that, as it is written,
"Let the one who boasts, boast in the Lord."

The word of the Lord.   *or*   Word of God, word of life.

GOSPEL: Matthew 5:1-12

The holy gospel according to Matthew.

¹When Jesus saw the crowds, he went up the mountain;
and after he sat down, his disciples came to him.
²Then he began to speak, and taught them, saying:

³"Blessed are the poor in spirit, for theirs is the kingdom of heaven.
⁴Blessed are those who mourn, for they will be comforted.
⁵Blessed are the meek, for they will inherit the earth.
⁶Blessed are those who hunger and thirst for righteousness,
for they will be filled.
⁷Blessed are the merciful, for they will receive mercy.
⁸Blessed are the pure in heart, for they will see God.
⁹Blessed are the peacemakers, for they will be called children of God.

¹⁰"Blessed are those who are persecuted for righteousness' sake,
for theirs is the kingdom of heaven.
¹¹Blessed are you when people revile you and persecute you
and utter all kinds of evil against you falsely on my account.
¹²Rejoice and be glad, for your reward is great in heaven,
for in the same way they persecuted the prophets who were before you."

The gospel of the Lord.

GOSPEL
It may be possible to bring the assembly to the mountain of Matthew 5 by allowing each "Blessed are"
to hang in the air a bit once it has been voiced. Give the hearer a sense of our Lord's "thinking up" the
Beatitudes rather than "reading" them. A reading textured with thoughtful pauses may help the people in
the pew to hear them as for the first time.

FIFTH SUNDAY AFTER EPIPHANY

SUNDAY, FEBRUARY 4–10   *(if before Transfiguration)*
LECTIONARY 5

FIRST READING: Isaiah 58:1-9a [9b-12]

A reading from Isaiah.

¹Shout out, do not hold back!
    Lift up your voice like a trumpet!
Announce to my people their rebellion,
    to the house of Jacob their sins.
²Yet day after day they seek me
    and delight to know my ways,
as if they were a nation that practiced righteousness
    and did not forsake the ordinance of their God;
they ask of me righteous judgments,
    they delight to draw near to God.

³"Why do we fast, but you do not see?
    Why humble ourselves, but you do not notice?"
Look, you serve your own interest on your fast day,
    and oppress all your workers.
⁴Look, you fast only to quarrel and to fight
    and to strike with a wicked fist.
Such fasting as you do today
    will not make your voice heard on high.

⁵Is such the fast that I choose,
    a day to humble oneself?
Is it to bow down the head like a bulrush,
    and to lie in sackcloth and ashes?
Will you call this a fast,
    a day acceptable to the LORD?

⁶Is not this the fast that I choose:
    to loose the bonds of injustice,
    to undo the thongs of the yoke,
to let the oppressed go free,
    and to break every yoke?
⁷Is it not to share your bread with the hungry,
    and bring the homeless poor into your house;

FIRST READING   *Isaiah = eye-ZAY-uh*
The reader will find the best advice in the first line of verse 1: "do not hold back!" This is the voice of an angry God, dripping with sarcasm. Help the assembly feel the wrath. Do not hold back. The voice changes to the voice of the prophet at verse 9b. Establish the change with a significant pause and a more tempered sound.

when you see the naked, to cover them,
    and not to hide yourself from your own kin?

[8]Then your light shall break forth like the dawn,
    and your healing shall spring up quickly;
your vindicator shall go before you,
    the glory of the LORD shall be your rear guard.
[9a]Then you shall call, and the LORD will answer;
    you shall cry for help, and he will say, Here I am.

[[9b]If you remove the yoke from among you,
    the pointing of the finger, the speaking of evil,
[10]if you offer your food to the hungry
    and satisfy the needs of the afflicted,
then your light shall rise in the darkness
    and your gloom be like the noonday.
[11]The LORD will guide you continually,
    and satisfy your needs in parched places,
    and make your bones strong;
and you shall be like a watered garden,
    like a spring of water, whose waters never fail.
[12]Your ancient ruins shall be rebuilt;
    you shall raise up the foundations of many generations;
you shall be called the repairer of the breach,
    the restorer of streets to live in.]

The word of the Lord.   *or*   Word of God, word of life.

PSALMODY: Psalm 112:1-9 [10]

SECOND READING: 1 Corinthians 2:1-12 [13-16]

A reading from First Corinthians.

[1]When I came to you, brothers and sisters,
I did not come proclaiming the mystery of God to you
in lofty words or wisdom.
[2]For I decided to know nothing among you except Jesus Christ,
and him crucified.
[3]And I came to you in weakness and in fear and in much trembling. ▸

SECOND READING
This is one of those readings that merits a warning siren. If it is to be effectively read, the reader will need to invest some significant time pondering, in advance of practicing out loud. The words themselves are instructive and demand a careful and patient reading if the assembly is to follow the line of reasoning and be edified.

[4]My speech and my proclamation were not with plausible words of wisdom,
but with a demonstration of the Spirit and of power,
[5]so that your faith might rest not on human wisdom
but on the power of God.

[6]Yet among the mature we do speak wisdom,
though it is not a wisdom of this age
or of the rulers of this age, who are doomed to perish.
[7]But we speak God's wisdom, secret and hidden,
which God decreed before the ages for our glory.
[8]None of the rulers of this age understood this;
for if they had, they would not have crucified the Lord of glory.

[9]But, as it is written,
    "What no eye has seen, nor ear heard,
        nor the human heart conceived,
    what God has prepared for those who love him"—
[10]these things God has revealed to us through the Spirit;
for the Spirit searches everything,
even the depths of God.
[11]For what human being knows what is truly human
except the human spirit that is within?
So also no one comprehends what is truly God's
except the Spirit of God.

[12]Now we have received not the spirit of the world,
but the Spirit that is from God,
so that we may understand the gifts bestowed on us by God.

[[13]And we speak of these things in words not taught by human wisdom
but taught by the Spirit,
interpreting spiritual things to those who are spiritual.
[14]Those who are unspiritual do not receive the gifts of God's Spirit,
for they are foolishness to them,
and they are unable to understand them
because they are spiritually discerned.
[15]Those who are spiritual discern all things,
and they are themselves subject to no one else's scrutiny.

    [16]"For who has known the mind of the Lord
        so as to instruct him?"
But we have the mind of Christ.]

The word of the Lord.   *or*   Word of God, word of life.

GOSPEL: Matthew 5:13-20

The holy gospel according to Matthew.

⌈Jesus said:⌉
¹³"You are the salt of the earth;
but if salt has lost its taste, how can its saltiness be restored?
It is no longer good for anything,
but is thrown out and trampled under foot.

¹⁴"You are the light of the world.
A city built on a hill cannot be hid.
¹⁵No one after lighting a lamp puts it under the bushel basket,
but on the lampstand,
and it gives light to all in the house.
¹⁶In the same way, let your light shine before others,
so that they may see your good works
and give glory to your Father in heaven.

¹⁷"Do not think that I have come to abolish the law or the prophets;
I have come not to abolish but to fulfill.
¹⁸For truly I tell you,
until heaven and earth pass away,
not one letter, not one stroke of a letter,
will pass from the law until all is accomplished.
¹⁹Therefore, whoever breaks one of the least of these commandments,
and teaches others to do the same,
will be called least in the kingdom of heaven;
but whoever does them and teaches them
will be called great in the kingdom of heaven.

²⁰"For I tell you,
unless your righteousness exceeds that of the scribes and Pharisees,
you will never enter the kingdom of heaven."

The gospel of the Lord.

GOSPEL
Lay readers will be helped to slow their reading pace by pastors who read more slowly—especially when approaching familiar texts such as this one. Give each image, each line of reasoning in these four paragraphs adequate breathing space. The pastoral ministry is one of word and sacrament. Give the word its due.

SIXTH SUNDAY AFTER EPIPHANY

FIRST READING: Deuteronomy 30:15-20   *Alternate Reading: Sirach 15:15-20 (p. 500)*

A reading from Deuteronomy.

⌐Moses said to the people:⌐
¹⁵See, I have set before you today
life and prosperity,
death and adversity.

¹⁶If you obey the commandments of the LORD your God
that I am commanding you today,
by loving the LORD your God,
walking in his ways,
and observing his commandments, decrees, and ordinances,
then you shall live and become numerous,
and the LORD your God will bless you
in the land that you are entering to possess.

¹⁷But if your heart turns away and you do not hear,
but are led astray to bow down to other gods and serve them,
¹⁸I declare to you today that you shall perish;
you shall not live long in the land
that you are crossing the Jordan to enter and possess.

¹⁹I call heaven and earth to witness against you today
that I have set before you life and death,
blessings and curses.
Choose life so that you and your descendants may live,
²⁰loving the LORD your God,
obeying him, and holding fast to him;
for that means life to you and length of days,
so that you may live in the land
that the LORD swore to give to your ancestors,
to Abraham, to Isaac, and to Jacob.

The word of the Lord.   *or*   Word of God, word of life.

FIRST READING   *Deuteronomy = dew-ter-ON-uh-mee*
Moses calls on "heaven and earth" to bear witness to his proclamation. Such a summons demands an expansive voice. The issue is a life-and-death matter and must sound that way. The command "Choose life" in verse 19 will profit from a significant pause before it and after it.

PSALMODY: Psalm 119:1-8

SECOND READING: 1 Corinthians 3:1-9

A reading from First Corinthians.

¹Brothers and sisters,
I could not speak to you as spiritual people,
but rather as people of the flesh, as infants in Christ.
²I fed you with milk, not solid food,
for you were not ready for solid food.
Even now you are still not ready,
³for you are still of the flesh.

For as long as there is jealousy and quarreling among you,
are you not of the flesh,
and behaving according to human inclinations?
⁴For when one says, "I belong to Paul,"
and another, "I belong to Apollos,"
are you not merely human?
⁵What then is Apollos?
What is Paul?
Servants through whom you came to believe,
as the Lord assigned to each.
⁶I planted, Apollos watered,
but God gave the growth.

⁷So neither the one who plants
nor the one who waters is anything,
but only God who gives the growth.
⁸The one who plants and the one who waters have a common purpose,
and each will receive wages according to the labor of each.
⁹For we are God's servants, working together;
you are God's field, God's building.

The word of the Lord.   *or*   Word of God, word of life.

SECOND READING   *Apollos = uh-POL-us*
This impassioned appeal to put an end to "jealousy and quarreling" and to factions loyal to one evangelist or another is akin to "tough love." It will most effectively sound earnest, not angry.

GOSPEL: Matthew 5:21-37

The holy gospel according to Matthew.

⌐Jesus said to the disciples:⌐
²¹"You have heard that it was said to those of ancient times,
'You shall not murder';
and 'whoever murders shall be liable to judgment.'
²²But I say to you that if you are angry with a brother or sister,
you will be liable to judgment;
and if you insult a brother or sister,
you will be liable to the council;
and if you say, 'You fool,'
you will be liable to the hell of fire.
²³"So when you are offering your gift at the altar,
if you remember that your brother or sister has something against you,
²⁴leave your gift there before the altar and go;
first be reconciled to your brother or sister,
and then come and offer your gift.
²⁵Come to terms quickly with your accuser
while you are on the way to court with him,
or your accuser may hand you over to the judge,
and the judge to the guard,
and you will be thrown into prison.
²⁶Truly I tell you,
you will never get out until you have paid the last penny.

²⁷"You have heard that it was said,
'You shall not commit adultery.'
²⁸But I say to you that everyone who looks at a woman with lust
has already committed adultery with her in his heart.
²⁹If your right eye causes you to sin,
tear it out and throw it away;
it is better for you to lose one of your members
than for your whole body to be thrown into hell.
³⁰And if your right hand causes you to sin,
cut it off and throw it away;
it is better for you to lose one of your members
than for your whole body to go into hell.

GOSPEL
Long readings bring out some readers' tendency to hurry. There is no need. Apparently our Lord has discovered a teachable moment with his disciples and takes full advantage. Allow plenty of time for these colorful illustrations of the amplified law to sink into the soul of the hearer.

³¹"It was also said,
'Whoever divorces his wife,
let him give her a certificate of divorce.'
³²But I say to you that anyone who divorces his wife,
except on the ground of unchastity,
causes her to commit adultery;
and whoever marries a divorced woman commits adultery.

³³"Again, you have heard that it was said to those of ancient times,
'You shall not swear falsely,
but carry out the vows you have made to the Lord.'
³⁴But I say to you,
Do not swear at all,
either by heaven, for it is the throne of God,
³⁵or by the earth, for it is his footstool,
or by Jerusalem, for it is the city of the great King.
³⁶And do not swear by your head,
for you cannot make one hair white or black.
³⁷Let your word be 'Yes, Yes' or 'No, No';
anything more than this comes from the evil one."

The gospel of the Lord.

Seventh Sunday after Epiphany

Sunday, February 18–24   (*if before Transfiguration*)

Lectionary 7

FIRST READING: Leviticus 19:1-2, 9-18

A reading from Leviticus.

¹The LORD spoke to Moses, saying:
²Speak to all the congregation of the people of Israel and say to them:
You shall be holy,
for I the LORD your God am holy.

⁹When you reap the harvest of your land,
you shall not reap to the very edges of your field,
or gather the gleanings of your harvest.
¹⁰You shall not strip your vineyard bare,
or gather the fallen grapes of your vineyard;
you shall leave them for the poor and the alien:
I am the LORD your God.

¹¹You shall not steal;
you shall not deal falsely;
and you shall not lie to one another.
¹²And you shall not swear falsely by my name,
profaning the name of your God: I am the LORD.

¹³You shall not defraud your neighbor;
you shall not steal;
and you shall not keep for yourself the wages of a laborer until morning.
¹⁴You shall not revile the deaf
or put a stumbling block before the blind;
you shall fear your God: I am the LORD.

¹⁵You shall not render an unjust judgment;
you shall not be partial to the poor or defer to the great:
with justice you shall judge your neighbor.
¹⁶You shall not go around as a slanderer among your people,
and you shall not profit by the blood of your neighbor:
I am the LORD.

FIRST READING   *Leviticus = leh-VIT-ih-cuss*
Recall the Lord's claim on the name "I Am" in Exodus 3:14. Then consider "signing off" on each of these fascinating commandments with a dramatic and authoritative flair by pausing before the ending phrase and punching the "I Am."

[17]You shall not hate in your heart anyone of your kin;
you shall reprove your neighbor,
or you will incur guilt yourself.
[18]You shall not take vengeance or bear a grudge against any of your people,
but you shall love your neighbor as yourself:
I am the LORD.

The word of the Lord.   *or*   Word of God, word of life.

PSALMODY: Psalm 119:33-40

SECOND READING: 1 Corinthians 3:10-11, 16-23

A reading from First Corinthians.

[10]According to the grace of God given to me,
like a skilled master builder I laid a foundation,
and someone else is building on it.
Each builder must choose with care how to build on it.
[11]For no one can lay any foundation other than the one that has been laid;
that foundation is Jesus Christ.

[16]Do you not know that you are God's temple
and that God's Spirit dwells in you?
[17]If anyone destroys God's temple,
God will destroy that person.
For God's temple is holy,
and you are that temple.

[18]Do not deceive yourselves.
If you think that you are wise in this age,
you should become fools so that you may become wise.
[19]For the wisdom of this world is foolishness with God.
For it is written,
    "He catches the wise in their craftiness,"
[20]and again,
    "The Lord knows the thoughts of the wise,
        that they are futile."
[21]So let no one boast about human leaders.
For all things are yours,
[22]whether Paul or Apollos or Cephas
or the world or life or death
or the present or the future—
all belong to you,
[23]and you belong to Christ,
and Christ belongs to God.

The word of the Lord.   *or*   Word of God, word of life.

SECOND READING   *Apollos = uh-POL-us   Cephas = SEE-fus*
Each of these three words of instruction—Christ as foundation, Christians as the temple of God's Spirit, and what's really wise or foolish—can stand alone. Separate them with pauses of substance. Bring to each the same impassioned tone you recall in the voice of the best teacher you ever had.

GOSPEL: Matthew 5:38-48

The holy gospel according to Matthew.

⌈Jesus said to the disciples:⌉
³⁸"You have heard that it was said,
'An eye for an eye and a tooth for a tooth.'
³⁹But I say to you,
Do not resist an evildoer.
But if anyone strikes you on the right cheek,
turn the other also;
⁴⁰and if anyone wants to sue you and take your coat,
give your cloak as well;
⁴¹and if anyone forces you to go one mile,
go also the second mile.
⁴²Give to everyone who begs from you,
and do not refuse anyone who wants to borrow from you.

⁴³"You have heard that it was said,
'You shall love your neighbor and hate your enemy.'
⁴⁴But I say to you,
Love your enemies and pray for those who persecute you,
⁴⁵so that you may be children of your Father in heaven;
for he makes his sun rise on the evil and on the good,
and sends rain on the righteous and on the unrighteous.
⁴⁶For if you love those who love you,
what reward do you have?
Do not even the tax collectors do the same?
⁴⁷And if you greet only your brothers and sisters,
what more are you doing than others?
Do not even the Gentiles do the same?
⁴⁸Be perfect, therefore,
as your heavenly Father is perfect."

The gospel of the Lord.

GOSPEL
These amplifications of the law parallel those of the gospel for Epiphany 6. At first hearing they must surely have sounded outrageous! The reader might take advantage of that anticipated reaction with an understated (though clearly enunciated) delivery.

Eighth Sunday after Epiphany

Sunday, February 25–March 1   (*if before Transfiguration*)

Lectionary 8

FIRST READING: Isaiah 49:8-16a

A reading from Isaiah.

⁸Thus says the LORD:
In a time of favor I have answered you,
    on a day of salvation I have helped you;
I have kept you and given you
    as a covenant to the people,
to establish the land,
    to apportion the desolate heritages;
⁹saying to the prisoners,
"Come out,"
    to those who are in darkness,
    "Show yourselves."

They shall feed along the ways,
    on all the bare heights shall be their pasture;
¹⁰they shall not hunger or thirst,
    neither scorching wind nor sun shall strike them down,
for he who has pity on them will lead them,
    and by springs of water will guide them.
¹¹And I will turn all my mountains into a road,
    and my highways shall be raised up.
¹²Lo, these shall come from far away,
    and lo, these from the north and from the west,
    and these from the land of Syene.

¹³Sing for joy, O heavens, and exult, O earth;
    break forth, O mountains, into singing!
For the LORD has comforted his people,
    and will have compassion on his suffering ones.

¹⁴But Zion said, "The LORD has forsaken me,
    my Lord has forgotten me."

FIRST READING   *Isaiah = eye-ZAY-uh   Syene = sy-EE-nih*
This dramatic celebration of the Lord's salvation is accompanied by singing heavens and an exultant earth. Bring plenty of joy and intensity to the reading. Do not miss the breathtaking beauty of verse 16a.

¹⁵Can a woman forget her nursing child,
   or show no compassion for the child of her womb?
Even these may forget,
   yet I will not forget you.
¹⁶See, I have inscribed you on the palms of my hands.

The word of the Lord.   *or*   Word of God, word of life.

PSALMODY: Psalm 131

SECOND READING: 1 Corinthians 4:1-5

A reading from First Corinthians.

¹Think of us in this way,
as servants of Christ and stewards of God's mysteries.
²Moreover, it is required of stewards that they be found trustworthy.
³But with me it is a very small thing
that I should be judged by you or by any human court.
I do not even judge myself.
⁴I am not aware of anything against myself,
but I am not thereby acquitted.
It is the Lord who judges me.

⁵Therefore do not pronounce judgment before the time,
before the Lord comes,
who will bring to light the things now hidden in darkness
and will disclose the purposes of the heart.
Then each one will receive commendation from God.

The word of the Lord.   *or*   Word of God, word of life.

SECOND READING
There is a slightly bemused, even flippant, tone attendant to the author's warning. Bring a sense of confidence to the reading.

GOSPEL: Matthew 6:24-34

The holy gospel according to Matthew.

⌐Jesus said to the disciples:¬
²⁴"No one can serve two masters;
for a slave will either hate the one and love the other,
or be devoted to the one and despise the other.
You cannot serve God and wealth.

²⁵"Therefore I tell you,
do not worry about your life,
what you will eat or what you will drink,
or about your body, what you will wear.
Is not life more than food, and the body more than clothing?
²⁶Look at the birds of the air;
they neither sow nor reap nor gather into barns,
and yet your heavenly Father feeds them.
Are you not of more value than they?
²⁷And can any of you by worrying
add a single hour to your span of life?
²⁸And why do you worry about clothing?
Consider the lilies of the field, how they grow;
they neither toil nor spin,
²⁹yet I tell you, even Solomon in all his glory
was not clothed like one of these.
³⁰But if God so clothes the grass of the field,
which is alive today and tomorrow is thrown into the oven,
will he not much more clothe you—you of little faith?

³¹"Therefore do not worry, saying,
'What will we eat?' or 'What will we drink?' or 'What will we wear?'
³²For it is the Gentiles who strive for all these things;
and indeed your heavenly Father knows that you need all these things.
³³But strive first for the kingdom of God and his righteousness,
and all these things will be given to you as well.

³⁴"So do not worry about tomorrow,
for tomorrow will bring worries of its own.
Today's trouble is enough for today."

The gospel of the Lord.

GOSPEL
Appropriately spaced pauses will allow the assembly to hear our Lord "think up" one phrase, one illustration after another in his attempt to teach his followers something about contentment. Do not merely read the text. Bring it to life.

Transfiguration of Our Lord

FIRST READING: Exodus 24:12-18

A reading from Exodus.

¹²The LORD said to Moses,
"Come up to me on the mountain, and wait there;
and I will give you the tablets of stone,
with the law and the commandment,
which I have written for their instruction."
¹³So Moses set out with his assistant Joshua,
and Moses went up into the mountain of God.
¹⁴To the elders he had said,
"Wait here for us, until we come to you again;
for Aaron and Hur are with you;
whoever has a dispute may go to them."

¹⁵Then Moses went up on the mountain,
and the cloud covered the mountain.
¹⁶The glory of the LORD settled on Mount Sinai,
and the cloud covered it for six days;
on the seventh day he called to Moses out of the cloud.
¹⁷Now the appearance of the glory of the LORD
was like a devouring fire on the top of the mountain
in the sight of the people of Israel.
¹⁸Moses entered the cloud, and went up on the mountain.
Moses was on the mountain for forty days and forty nights.

The word of the Lord.   *or*   Word of God, word of life.

PSALMODY: Psalm 2 or Psalm 99

FIRST READING   *Sinai = SY-ny*
"Now the appearance . . . was like a devouring fire." Let the reading sound like a devouring fire. Let it be full of majesty and awe as well as a little fearsome heat!

SECOND READING: 2 Peter 1:16-21

A reading from Second Peter.

[16]We did not follow cleverly devised myths when we made known to you
the power and coming of our Lord Jesus Christ,
but we had been eyewitnesses of his majesty.
[17]For he received honor and glory from God the Father
when that voice was conveyed to him by the Majestic Glory, saying,
"This is my Son, my Beloved,
with whom I am well pleased."
[18]We ourselves heard this voice come from heaven,
while we were with him on the holy mountain.

[19]So we have the prophetic message more fully confirmed.
You will do well to be attentive to this
as to a lamp shining in a dark place,
until the day dawns and the morning star rises in your hearts.
[20]First of all you must understand this,
that no prophecy of scripture is a matter of one's own interpretation,
[21]because no prophecy ever came by human will,
but men and women moved by the Holy Spirit spoke from God.

The word of the Lord.   *or*   Word of God, word of life.

SECOND READING   *prophecy = PROF-uh-see*
The eyewitness account of the transfiguration of our Lord anticipates today's gospel in which that story is told, and at the same time echoes the experience of Moses in the first reading in being an eyewitness to the majesty of God. This text also requires a sense of majesty and awe coupled with the sound of apostolic instruction and authority.

GOSPEL: Matthew 17:1-9

The holy gospel according to Matthew.

[1]Jesus took with him Peter and James and his brother John
and led them up a high mountain, by themselves.
[2]And he was transfigured before them,
and his face shone like the sun, and his clothes became dazzling white.

[3]Suddenly there appeared to them Moses and Elijah, talking with him.
[4]Then Peter said to Jesus,
"Lord, it is good for us to be here;
if you wish, I will make three dwellings here,
one for you, one for Moses, and one for Elijah."

[5]While he was still speaking, suddenly a bright cloud overshadowed them,
and from the cloud a voice said,
"This is my Son, the Beloved; with him I am well pleased;
listen to him!"
[6]When the disciples heard this,
they fell to the ground and were overcome by fear.
[7]But Jesus came and touched them, saying,
"Get up and do not be afraid."
[8]And when they looked up, they saw no one except Jesus himself alone.

[9]As they were coming down the mountain, Jesus ordered them,
"Tell no one about the vision
until after the Son of Man has been raised from the dead."

The gospel of the Lord.

GOSPEL
Help the hearer sense a vision that was breathtaking. Verse 2 ought to sound "awe-full." See the vision; don't settle for describing it.

Lent

Ash Wednesday

FIRST READING: Joel 2:1-2, 12-17
OR Isaiah 58:1-12, following

A reading from Joel.

¹Blow the trumpet in Zion;
　　sound the alarm on my holy mountain!
Let all the inhabitants of the land tremble,
　　for the day of the LORD is coming, it is near—
²a day of darkness and gloom,
　　a day of clouds and thick darkness!
Like blackness spread upon the mountains
　　a great and powerful army comes;
their like has never been from of old,
　　nor will be again after them
　　in ages to come.

¹²Yet even now, says the LORD,
　　return to me with all your heart,
with fasting, with weeping, and with mourning;
　　¹³rend your hearts and not your clothing.
Return to the LORD, your God,
　　for he is gracious and merciful,
slow to anger, and abounding in steadfast love,
　　and relents from punishing.
¹⁴Who knows whether he will not turn and relent,
　　and leave a blessing behind him,
a grain offering and a drink offering
　　for the LORD, your God?

¹⁵Blow the trumpet in Zion;
　　sanctify a fast;
call a solemn assembly;
　　¹⁶gather the people.
Sanctify the congregation;
　　assemble the aged;
gather the children,
　　even infants at the breast. ▸

FIRST READING (Joel)

The darkness and invasion images are a reference to "the day of the locust"—a plague of locusts. This threat is immediate and extraordinary, and the tone of the reading is ominous. Bring a sense of urgency to the reading. It is a complex text. Pay particular attention to the paragraph divisions (and pause when you come to them), because they often mark a change to a new voice—that of the prophet or that of the Lord—or the introduction of a new idea. For that reason, include a break between lines one and two in verse 13 as well.

Let the bridegroom leave his room,
  and the bride her canopy.

[17]Between the vestibule and the altar
  let the priests, the ministers of the LORD, weep.
Let them say, "Spare your people, O LORD,
  and do not make your heritage a mockery,
  a byword among the nations.
Why should it be said among the peoples,
  'Where is their God?'"

The word of the Lord.   *or*   Word of God, word of life.

OR: Isaiah 58:1-12

A reading from Isaiah.

[1]Shout out, do not hold back!
  Lift up your voice like a trumpet!
Announce to my people their rebellion,
  to the house of Jacob their sins.
[2]Yet day after day they seek me
  and delight to know my ways,
as if they were a nation that practiced righteousness
  and did not forsake the ordinance of their God;
they ask of me righteous judgments,
  they delight to draw near to God.

[3]"Why do we fast, but you do not see?
  Why humble ourselves, but you do not notice?"
Look, you serve your own interest on your fast day,
  and oppress all your workers.
[4]Look, you fast only to quarrel and to fight
  and to strike with a wicked fist.
Such fasting as you do today
  will not make your voice heard on high.

[5]Is such the fast that I choose,
  a day to humble oneself?
Is it to bow down the head like a bulrush,
  and to lie in sackcloth and ashes?

FIRST READING (Isaiah) *Isaiah = eye-ZAY-uh*
The voice in verses 1–5 is that of an angry God—even a bitingly sarcastic God. That tone abruptly shifts at verse 6 to one of impassioned instruction. The text's images are rich and varied. Help the assembly hear each and every one by reading slowly and enunciating.

Will you call this a fast,
    a day acceptable to the LORD?

⁶Is not this the fast that I choose:
    to loose the bonds of injustice,
    to undo the thongs of the yoke,
to let the oppressed go free,
    and to break every yoke?
⁷Is it not to share your bread with the hungry,
    and bring the homeless poor into your house;
when you see the naked, to cover them,
    and not to hide yourself from your own kin?
⁸Then your light shall break forth like the dawn,
    and your healing shall spring up quickly;
your vindicator shall go before you,
    the glory of the LORD shall be your rear guard.
⁹Then you shall call, and the LORD will answer;
    you shall cry for help, and he will say, Here I am.

If you remove the yoke from among you,
    the pointing of the finger, the speaking of evil,
¹⁰if you offer your food to the hungry
    and satisfy the needs of the afflicted,
then your light shall rise in the darkness
    and your gloom be like the noonday.
¹¹The LORD will guide you continually,
    and satisfy your needs in parched places,
    and make your bones strong;
and you shall be like a watered garden,
    like a spring of water,
    whose waters never fail.
¹²Your ancient ruins shall be rebuilt;
    you shall raise up the foundations of many generations;
you shall be called the repairer of the breach,
    the restorer of streets to live in.

The word of the Lord.   *or*   Word of God, word of life.

PSALMODY: Psalm 51:1-17

SECOND READING: 2 Corinthians 5:20b—6:10

A reading from Second Corinthians.

20bWe entreat you on behalf of Christ,
be reconciled to God.
21For our sake he made him to be sin who knew no sin,
so that in him we might become the righteousness of God.

6:1As we work together with him,
we urge you also not to accept the grace of God in vain.
2For he says,
   "At an acceptable time I have listened to you,
       and on a day of salvation I have helped you."
See, now is the acceptable time;
see, now is the day of salvation!

3We are putting no obstacle in anyone's way,
so that no fault may be found with our ministry,
4but as servants of God we have commended ourselves in every way:
through great endurance,
in afflictions, hardships, calamities,
5beatings, imprisonments, riots,
labors, sleepless nights, hunger;
6by purity, knowledge, patience,
kindness, holiness of spirit, genuine love,
7truthful speech, and the power of God;
with the weapons of righteousness for the right hand and for the left;
8in honor and dishonor,
in ill repute and good repute.
We are treated as impostors, and yet are true;
9as unknown, and yet are well known;
as dying, and see—we are alive;
as punished, and yet not killed;
10as sorrowful, yet always rejoicing;
as poor, yet making many rich;
as having nothing, and yet possessing everything.

The word of the Lord.   *or*   Word of God, word of life.

SECOND READING
The author urges the reader (and the reader will urge the hearer) to be imitators of the apostles as servants of God who have lived commendably. Urges means the issue is urgent. "Now is the acceptable time" for this kind of living. It is for this kind of life that we have accepted the grace of God.

GOSPEL: Matthew 6:1-6, 16-21

The holy gospel according to Matthew.

⌐Jesus said to the disciples:¬
[1]"Beware of practicing your piety before others
in order to be seen by them;
for then you have no reward from your Father in heaven.
[2]So whenever you give alms, do not sound a trumpet before you,
as the hypocrites do in the synagogues and in the streets,
so that they may be praised by others.
Truly I tell you,
they have received their reward.
[3]But when you give alms,
do not let your left hand know what your right hand is doing,
[4]so that your alms may be done in secret;
and your Father who sees in secret will reward you.

[5]"And whenever you pray, do not be like the hypocrites;
for they love to stand and pray in the synagogues and at the street corners,
so that they may be seen by others.
Truly I tell you,
they have received their reward.
[6]But whenever you pray,
go into your room and shut the door
and pray to your Father who is in secret;
and your Father who sees in secret will reward you.

[16]"And whenever you fast, do not look dismal, like the hypocrites,
for they disfigure their faces so as to show others that they are fasting.
Truly I tell you,
they have received their reward.
[17]But when you fast,
put oil on your head and wash your face,
[18]so that your fasting may be seen not by others
but by your Father who is in secret;
and your Father who sees in secret will reward you.

[19]"Do not store up for yourselves treasures on earth,
where moth and rust consume
and where thieves break in and steal; ▸

GOSPEL   *hypocrites = HIP-uh-crits   synagogues = SIN-uh-gogz*
Explore the natural rhythm of the text generated by the three repeated phrases: "whenever," "truly I tell you,"
and "but when." From the outset the reading is about "where your heart is." Allow all four illustrations—
almsgiving, prayer, fasting, and worldly goods—to lead the hearer to the powerful conclusion of verse 21.
A pause before that crucial verse might be just the thing to help the assembly hear it clearly.

[20]but store up for yourselves treasures in heaven,
where neither moth nor rust consumes
and where thieves do not break in and steal.
[21]For where your treasure is,
there your heart will be also."

The gospel of the Lord.

First Sunday in Lent

FIRST READING: Genesis 2:15-17; 3:1-7

A reading from Genesis.

[15]The LORD God took the man
and put him in the garden of Eden to till it and keep it.
[16]And the LORD God commanded the man,
"You may freely eat of every tree of the garden;
[17]but of the tree of the knowledge of good and evil you shall not eat,
for in the day that you eat of it you shall die."

[3:1]Now the serpent was more crafty
than any other wild animal that the LORD God had made.
He said to the woman,
"Did God say, 'You shall not eat from any tree in the garden'?"
[2]The woman said to the serpent,
"We may eat of the fruit of the trees in the garden;
[3]but God said,
'You shall not eat of the fruit of the tree
that is in the middle of the garden,
nor shall you touch it, or you shall die.'"
[4]But the serpent said to the woman,
"You will not die;
[5]for God knows that when you eat of it your eyes will be opened,
and you will be like God, knowing good and evil."

[6]So when the woman saw that the tree was good for food,
and that it was a delight to the eyes,
and that the tree was to be desired to make one wise,
she took of its fruit and ate;
and she also gave some to her husband, who was with her,
and he ate.

[7]Then the eyes of both were opened, and they knew that they were naked;
and they sewed fig leaves together and made loincloths for themselves.

The word of the Lord.   *or*   Word of God, word of life.

FIRST READING

The story is well known; that should serve as a warning to the reader. The story is high drama; for the reader that's a singular opportunity. There is nothing ho-hum about the narrative surrounding the original sin. Tell the story as to a group hearing it for the first time. Bring to the reading an understanding that appreciates the naïveté of Eve and Adam, respects the treachery of the serpent, and mourns the tragedy of the fall.

PSALMODY: Psalm 32

SECOND READING: Romans 5:12-19

A reading from Romans.

¹²Just as sin came into the world through one man,
and death came through sin,
and so death spread to all because all have sinned—
¹³sin was indeed in the world before the law,
but sin is not reckoned when there is no law.
¹⁴Yet death exercised dominion from Adam to Moses,
even over those whose sins were not like the transgression of Adam,
who is a type of the one who was to come.

¹⁵But the free gift is not like the trespass.
For if the many died through the one man's trespass,
much more surely have the grace of God
and the free gift in the grace of the one man, Jesus Christ,
abounded for the many.
¹⁶And the free gift is not like the effect of the one man's sin.
For the judgment following one trespass brought condemnation,
but the free gift following many trespasses brings justification.
¹⁷If, because of the one man's trespass,
death exercised dominion through that one,
much more surely will those who receive the abundance of grace
and the free gift of righteousness
exercise dominion in life through the one man, Jesus Christ.

¹⁸Therefore just as one man's trespass led to condemnation for all,
so one man's act of righteousness leads to justification and life for all.
¹⁹For just as by the one man's disobedience the many were made sinners,
so by the one man's obedience the many will be made righteous.

The word of the Lord.   *or*   Word of God, word of life.

SECOND READING
This is not a simple reading. It is a logical argument leading to the conclusion of verses 18 and 19. It is essential that the reader be absolutely clear as to the progression of the argument before presenting it to the assembly. It is a reading that demands practice. The pace must be slower than usual so that the hearer has time to capture and follow the argument.

GOSPEL: Matthew 4:1-11

The holy gospel according to Matthew.

¹Jesus was led up by the Spirit into the wilderness
to be tempted by the devil.
²He fasted forty days and forty nights,
and afterwards he was famished.
³The tempter came and said to him,
"If you are the Son of God,
command these stones to become loaves of bread."
⁴But he answered,
"It is written,
   'One does not live by bread alone,
     but by every word that comes from the mouth of God.'"

⁵Then the devil took him to the holy city
and placed him on the pinnacle of the temple, ⁶saying to him,
"If you are the Son of God, throw yourself down;
for it is written,
   'He will command his angels concerning you,'
     and 'On their hands they will bear you up,
   so that you will not dash your foot against a stone.'"
⁷Jesus said to him,
"Again it is written,
'Do not put the Lord your God to the test.'"

⁸Again, the devil took him to a very high mountain
and showed him all the kingdoms of the world and their splendor;
⁹and he said to him,
"All these I will give you,
if you will fall down and worship me."
¹⁰Jesus said to him,
"Away with you, Satan! for it is written,
   'Worship the Lord your God,
     and serve only him.'"

¹¹Then the devil left him,
and suddenly angels came and waited on him.

The gospel of the Lord.

GOSPEL
Perhaps the relief and wonder of being "waited on" by angels (a delightful scene to imagine) will be
heightened if the words of our Lord sound as though they were spoken by one at the end of an arduous
wilderness fast.

✝ SECOND SUNDAY IN LENT

FIRST READING: Genesis 12:1-4a

A reading from Genesis.

¹The LORD said to Abram,
"Go from your country and your kindred and your father's house
to the land that I will show you.
²I will make of you a great nation,
and I will bless you, and make your name great,
so that you will be a blessing.
³I will bless those who bless you,
and the one who curses you I will curse;
and in you all the families of the earth shall be blessed."

⁴So Abram went, as the LORD had told him; and Lot went with him.

The word of the Lord.   *or*   Word of God, word of life.

PSALMODY: Psalm 121

SECOND READING: Romans 4:1-5, 13-17

A reading from Romans.

¹What are we to say was gained by Abraham,
our ancestor according to the flesh?
²For if Abraham was justified by works,
he has something to boast about, but not before God.
³For what does the scripture say?
"Abraham believed God,
and it was reckoned to him as righteousness."
⁴Now to one who works,
wages are not reckoned as a gift but as something due.
⁵But to one who without works trusts him who justifies the ungodly,
such faith is reckoned as righteousness.

FIRST READING   *Abram = AY-brum*
This is simple, straightforward reading. God directs Abram (later to be called Abraham) with a simple command coupled with a grand promise. The punch line is in verse 4a: "So Abram went." A good, solid pause preceding those words might helpfully prepare the person in the pew to better hear them.

SECOND READING
This reading is a bit more difficult than the first. It doesn't entirely hang together. Steer the assembly through it carefully. The point is that faith is reckoned to the believer as righteousness. Verse 15 feels much like an awkward insert. Treat it as though it were in parentheses. Verses 16 and 17 are one, long, complicated sentence. Move the hearers through it slowly and confidently.

¹³For the promise that he would inherit the world
did not come to Abraham or to his descendants through the law
but through the righteousness of faith.
¹⁴If it is the adherents of the law who are to be the heirs,
faith is null and the promise is void.
¹⁵For the law brings wrath;
but where there is no law,
neither is there violation.

¹⁶For this reason it depends on faith,
in order that the promise may rest on grace
and be guaranteed to all his descendants,
not only to the adherents of the law
but also to those who share the faith of Abraham
(for he is the father of all of us, ¹⁷as it is written,
"I have made you the father of many nations")—
in the presence of the God in whom he believed,
who gives life to the dead
and calls into existence the things that do not exist.

The word of the Lord.   *or*   Word of God, word of life.

GOSPEL: John 3:1-17

The holy gospel according to John.

¹Now there was a Pharisee named Nicodemus, a leader of the Jews.
²He came to Jesus by night and said to him,
"Rabbi, we know that you are a teacher who has come from God;
for no one can do these signs that you do apart from the presence of God."
³Jesus answered him,
"Very truly, I tell you,
no one can see the kingdom of God without being born from above."

⁴Nicodemus said to him,
"How can anyone be born after having grown old?
Can one enter a second time into the mother's womb and be born?"
⁵Jesus answered,
"Very truly, I tell you,
no one can enter the kingdom of God
without being born of water and Spirit. ▸

GOSPEL   *Pharisee = FAIR-uh-see   Nicodemus = nick-uh-DEEM-us*
If the words of Nicodemus sound like those of one who is struggling hard to understand, Jesus' words ought to sound like those of one who is struggling hard to help the inquiring disciple to see that the Son of God is within arm's length.

[6]What is born of the flesh is flesh,
and what is born of the Spirit is spirit.
[7]Do not be astonished that I said to you,
'You must be born from above.'
[8]The wind blows where it chooses, and you hear the sound of it,
but you do not know where it comes from or where it goes.
So it is with everyone who is born of the Spirit."

[9]Nicodemus said to him,
"How can these things be?"
[10]Jesus answered him,
"Are you a teacher of Israel,
and yet you do not understand these things?
[11]Very truly, I tell you,
we speak of what we know and testify to what we have seen;
yet you do not receive our testimony.
[12]If I have told you about earthly things and you do not believe,
how can you believe if I tell you about heavenly things?

[13]"No one has ascended into heaven
except the one who descended from heaven, the Son of Man.
[14]And just as Moses lifted up the serpent in the wilderness,
so must the Son of Man be lifted up,
[15]that whoever believes in him may have eternal life.

[16]"For God so loved the world that he gave his only Son,
so that everyone who believes in him may not perish
but may have eternal life.
[17]Indeed, God did not send the Son into the world to condemn the world,
but in order that the world might be saved through him."

The gospel of the Lord.

✠ Third Sunday in Lent

FIRST READING: Exodus 17:1-7

A reading from Exodus.

¹From the wilderness of Sin the whole congregation of the Israelites
journeyed by stages, as the LORD commanded.
They camped at Rephidim, but there was no water for the people to drink.
²The people quarreled with Moses, and said,
"Give us water to drink."
Moses said to them,
"Why do you quarrel with me?
Why do you test the LORD?"
³But the people thirsted there for water;
and the people complained against Moses and said,
"Why did you bring us out of Egypt,
to kill us and our children and livestock with thirst?"

⁴So Moses cried out to the LORD,
"What shall I do with this people?
They are almost ready to stone me."
⁵The LORD said to Moses,
"Go on ahead of the people,
and take some of the elders of Israel with you;
take in your hand the staff with which you struck the Nile, and go.
⁶I will be standing there in front of you on the rock at Horeb.
Strike the rock, and water will come out of it, so that the people may drink."

Moses did so, in the sight of the elders of Israel.
⁷He called the place Massah and Meribah,
because the Israelites quarreled and tested the LORD, saying,
"Is the LORD among us or not?"

The word of the Lord.   *or*   Word of God, word of life.

PSALMODY: Psalm 95

FIRST READING   *Rephidim = REF-uh-dim   Horeb = HOR-eb   Massah = MAS-uh   Meribah = MAIR-uh-buh*
There is a great deal of dialogue and a great deal of drama in this reading. Do not rush. When the
people make demands, help the assembly hear them at their querulous worst. Help us hear the fear and
helplessness in Moses' plea to God. Be careful not to throw away verse 7—it underscores the whole point
of the story. Read every sentence loudly and clearly to its end.

SECOND READING: Romans 5:1-11

A reading from Romans.

[1]Since we are justified by faith,
we have peace with God through our Lord Jesus Christ,
[2]through whom we have obtained access to this grace in which we stand;
and we boast in our hope of sharing the glory of God.
[3]And not only that,
but we also boast in our sufferings,
knowing that suffering produces endurance,
[4]and endurance produces character,
and character produces hope,
[5]and hope does not disappoint us,
because God's love has been poured into our hearts
through the Holy Spirit that has been given to us.

[6]For while we were still weak,
at the right time Christ died for the ungodly.
[7]Indeed, rarely will anyone die for a righteous person—
though perhaps for a good person someone might actually dare to die.
[8]But God proves his love for us
in that while we still were sinners Christ died for us.

[9]Much more surely then, now that we have been justified by his blood,
will we be saved through him from the wrath of God.
[10]For if while we were enemies,
we were reconciled to God through the death of his Son,
much more surely, having been reconciled, will we be saved by his life.
[11]But more than that, we even boast in God through our Lord Jesus Christ,
through whom we have now received reconciliation.

The word of the Lord.   *or*   Word of God, word of life.

SECOND READING

This is a classic declaration of the efficacy of faith. It requires a voice of confidence. Note especially the energetic crescendo beginning at verse 3 and culminating in verse 5, and the logical progression of verses 9, 10, and 11. Take a little extra time to develop a confidence in your understanding of the points being made, so that you are able to deliver them with a good understanding.

GOSPEL: John 4:5-42

The holy gospel according to John.

⁵ ⌜Jesus⌝ came to a Samaritan city called Sychar,
near the plot of ground that Jacob had given to his son Joseph.
⁶Jacob's well was there,
and Jesus, tired out by his journey, was sitting by the well.
It was about noon.

⁷A Samaritan woman came to draw water,
and Jesus said to her,
"Give me a drink."
⁸(His disciples had gone to the city to buy food.)
⁹The Samaritan woman said to him,
"How is it that you, a Jew, ask a drink of me, a woman of Samaria?"
(Jews do not share things in common with Samaritans.)
¹⁰Jesus answered her,
"If you knew the gift of God,
and who it is that is saying to you, 'Give me a drink,'
you would have asked him, and he would have given you living water."
¹¹The woman said to him,
"Sir, you have no bucket, and the well is deep.
Where do you get that living water?
¹²Are you greater than our ancestor Jacob, who gave us the well,
and with his sons and his flocks drank from it?"

¹³Jesus said to her,
"Everyone who drinks of this water will be thirsty again,
¹⁴but those who drink of the water that I will give them will never be thirsty.
The water that I will give will become in them a spring of water
gushing up to eternal life."
¹⁵The woman said to him,
"Sir, give me this water, so that I may never be thirsty
or have to keep coming here to draw water."

¹⁶Jesus said to her,
"Go, call your husband, and come back."
¹⁷The woman answered him,
"I have no husband."
Jesus said to her, ▸

GOSPEL   *Samaritan = suh-MAIR-it-un   Sychar = SY-car*
The mid-Lenten gospels of year A are long. They serve as helpful reminders to even the most seasoned reader that preparation is vital to the faithful reading of scripture in the assembly. Taking adequate time to hear the text by reading it aloud in rehearsal will uncover nuances and help the reader to map the text's progression.

"You are right in saying, 'I have no husband';
[18]for you have had five husbands,
and the one you have now is not your husband.
What you have said is true!"
[19]The woman said to him,
"Sir, I see that you are a prophet.
[20]Our ancestors worshiped on this mountain,
but you say that the place where people must worship is in Jerusalem."

[21]Jesus said to her,
"Woman, believe me, the hour is coming
when you will worship the Father
neither on this mountain nor in Jerusalem.
[22]You worship what you do not know; we worship what we know,
for salvation is from the Jews.
[23]But the hour is coming, and is now here,
when the true worshipers will worship the Father in spirit and truth,
for the Father seeks such as these to worship him.
[24]God is spirit,
and those who worship him must worship in spirit and truth."
[25]The woman said to him,
"I know that Messiah is coming" (who is called Christ).
"When he comes, he will proclaim all things to us."
[26]Jesus said to her,
"I am he, the one who is speaking to you."

[27]Just then his disciples came.
They were astonished that he was speaking with a woman,
but no one said, "What do you want?"
or, "Why are you speaking with her?"

[28]Then the woman left her water jar and went back to the city.
She said to the people,
[29]"Come and see a man who told me everything I have ever done!
He cannot be the Messiah, can he?"
[30]They left the city and were on their way to him.

[31]Meanwhile the disciples were urging him,
"Rabbi, eat something."
[32]But he said to them,
"I have food to eat that you do not know about."

[33]So the disciples said to one another,
"Surely no one has brought him something to eat?"
[34]Jesus said to them,
"My food is to do the will of him who sent me and to complete his work.
[35]Do you not say, 'Four months more, then comes the harvest'?
But I tell you, look around you,
and see how the fields are ripe for harvesting.
[36]The reaper is already receiving wages
and is gathering fruit for eternal life,
so that sower and reaper may rejoice together.
[37]For here the saying holds true,
'One sows and another reaps.'
[38]I sent you to reap that for which you did not labor.
Others have labored, and you have entered into their labor."

[39]Many Samaritans from that city believed in him
because of the woman's testimony,
"He told me everything I have ever done."
[40]So when the Samaritans came to him, they asked him to stay with them;
and he stayed there two days.
[41]And many more believed because of his word.
[42]They said to the woman,
"It is no longer because of what you said that we believe,
for we have heard for ourselves,
and we know that this is truly the Savior of the world."

The gospel of the Lord.

Fourth Sunday in Lent

FIRST READING: 1 Samuel 16:1-13

A reading from First Samuel.

¹The LORD said to Samuel,
"How long will you grieve over Saul?
I have rejected him from being king over Israel.
Fill your horn with oil and set out;
I will send you to Jesse the Bethlehemite,
for I have provided for myself a king among his sons."
²Samuel said, "How can I go?
If Saul hears of it, he will kill me."
And the LORD said,
"Take a heifer with you, and say,
'I have come to sacrifice to the LORD.'
³Invite Jesse to the sacrifice, and I will show you what you shall do;
and you shall anoint for me the one whom I name to you."

⁴Samuel did what the LORD commanded, and came to Bethlehem.
The elders of the city came to meet him trembling, and said,
"Do you come peaceably?"
⁵He said,
"Peaceably; I have come to sacrifice to the LORD;
sanctify yourselves and come with me to the sacrifice."
And he sanctified Jesse and his sons and invited them to the sacrifice.

⁶When they came, he looked on Eliab and thought,
"Surely the LORD's anointed is now before the LORD."
⁷But the LORD said to Samuel,
"Do not look on his appearance or on the height of his stature,
because I have rejected him;
for the LORD does not see as mortals see;
they look on the outward appearance,
but the LORD looks on the heart."
⁸Then Jesse called Abinadab, and made him pass before Samuel.
He said, "Neither has the LORD chosen this one."
⁹Then Jesse made Shammah pass by.
And he said,
"Neither has the LORD chosen this one."

FIRST READING   *Bethlehemite = BETH-leh-myt   heifer = HEF-er   Eliab = eh-LY-ub   Abinadab = uh-BIN-uh-dab   Shammah = SHAM-uh   Ramah = RAY-muh*
"The Lord does not see as mortals see." This is the author's message in the reading. It is a wonderful story that demands energy and enthusiasm in the telling. The names of the some of the sons of Jesse provide their own challenge. Try to be as confident about your pronunciation of their names as of the names of your own friends. Take the time to develop that familiarity.

¹⁰Jesse made seven of his sons pass before Samuel,
and Samuel said to Jesse,
"The Lord has not chosen any of these."

¹¹Samuel said to Jesse,
"Are all your sons here?"
And he said,
"There remains yet the youngest, but he is keeping the sheep."
And Samuel said to Jesse,
"Send and bring him; for we will not sit down until he comes here."
¹²He sent and brought him in.
Now he was ruddy, and had beautiful eyes, and was handsome.
The Lord said,
"Rise and anoint him; for this is the one."
¹³Then Samuel took the horn of oil,
and anointed him in the presence of his brothers;
and the spirit of the Lord came mightily upon David from that day forward.
Samuel then set out and went to Ramah.

The word of the Lord.   *or*   Word of God, word of life.

PSALMODY: Psalm 23

SECOND READING: Ephesians 5:8-14

A reading from Ephesians.

⁸Once you were darkness, but now in the Lord you are light.
Live as children of light—
⁹for the fruit of the light is found in all that is good and right and true.
¹⁰Try to find out what is pleasing to the Lord.
¹¹Take no part in the unfruitful works of darkness, but instead expose them.
¹²For it is shameful even to mention what such people do secretly;
¹³but everything exposed by the light becomes visible,
¹⁴for everything that becomes visible is light.

Therefore it says,
    "Sleeper, awake!
    Rise from the dead, and Christ will shine on you."

The word of the Lord.   *or*   Word of God, word of life.

SECOND READING   *Ephesians = eh-FEE-zhunz*
This brief text is deceptively difficult. Perhaps a helpful handle is realizing that the author talks not about being *in* the darkness but about *being* darkness and—Christ having shone on us—being light. The reader may find it helpful in understanding the thrust of verse 14 to take a look at Isaiah 60:1, 1 Timothy 3:16, and John 11:9-10. To be light is to be utterly transformed, to rise to a life of newness.

GOSPEL: John 9:1-41

The holy gospel according to John.

[1]As ⌜Jesus⌝ walked along, he saw a man blind from birth.
[2]His disciples asked him,
"Rabbi, who sinned, this man or his parents, that he was born blind?"
[3]Jesus answered,
"Neither this man nor his parents sinned;
he was born blind so that God's works might be revealed in him.
[4]We must work the works of him who sent me while it is day;
night is coming when no one can work.
[5]As long as I am in the world, I am the light of the world."

[6]When he had said this, he spat on the ground and made mud with the saliva
and spread the mud on the man's eyes, [7]saying to him,
"Go, wash in the pool of Siloam" (which means Sent).
Then he went and washed and came back able to see.

[8]The neighbors and those who had seen him before as a beggar began to ask,
"Is this not the man who used to sit and beg?"
[9]Some were saying, "It is he."
Others were saying, "No, but it is someone like him."
He kept saying, "I am the man."
[10]But they kept asking him, "Then how were your eyes opened?"
[11]He answered,
"The man called Jesus made mud, spread it on my eyes,
and said to me, 'Go to Siloam and wash.'
Then I went and washed and received my sight."
[12]They said to him, "Where is he?"
He said, "I do not know."

[13]They brought to the Pharisees the man who had formerly been blind.
[14]Now it was a sabbath day when Jesus made the mud and opened his eyes.
[15]Then the Pharisees also began to ask him how he had received his sight.
He said to them,
"He put mud on my eyes. Then I washed, and now I see."
[16]Some of the Pharisees said,
"This man is not from God, for he does not observe the sabbath."
But others said,
"How can a man who is a sinner perform such signs?"
And they were divided.

GOSPEL   *Siloam = sy-LOH-um*
This long story is loaded with dialogue. Invest significant time in determining the tone and tempo of each dramatic sequence. Rediscover the intrigue and tension the evangelist has so carefully developed in the story's telling. Bring the story to life. Help the hearers see the Son of Man.

¹⁷So they said again to the blind man,
"What do you say about him? It was your eyes he opened."
He said, "He is a prophet."

¹⁸The Jews did not believe that he had been blind and had received his sight
until they called the parents of the man who had received his sight
¹⁹and asked them,
"Is this your son, who you say was born blind?
How then does he now see?"
²⁰His parents answered,
"We know that this is our son, and that he was born blind;
²¹but we do not know how it is that now he sees,
nor do we know who opened his eyes.
Ask him; he is of age.
He will speak for himself."
²²His parents said this because they were afraid of the Jews;
for the Jews had already agreed
that anyone who confessed Jesus to be the Messiah
would be put out of the synagogue.
²³Therefore his parents said, "He is of age; ask him."

²⁴So for the second time they called the man who had been blind,
and they said to him,
"Give glory to God! We know that this man is a sinner."
²⁵He answered,
"I do not know whether he is a sinner.
One thing I do know, that though I was blind, now I see."
²⁶They said to him,
"What did he do to you? How did he open your eyes?"
²⁷He answered them,
"I have told you already, and you would not listen.
Why do you want to hear it again?
Do you also want to become his disciples?"
²⁸Then they reviled him, saying,
"You are his disciple, but we are disciples of Moses.
²⁹We know that God has spoken to Moses,
but as for this man, we do not know where he comes from."
³⁰The man answered,
"Here is an astonishing thing!
You do not know where he comes from, and yet he opened my eyes.
³¹We know that God does not listen to sinners,
but he does listen to one who worships him and obeys his will. ▸

[32]Never since the world began
has it been heard that anyone opened the eyes of a person born blind.
[33]If this man were not from God, he could do nothing."
[34]They answered him,
"You were born entirely in sins,
and are you trying to teach us?"
And they drove him out.

[35]Jesus heard that they had driven him out,
and when he found him, he said,
"Do you believe in the Son of Man?"
[36]He answered, "And who is he, sir?
Tell me, so that I may believe in him."
[37]Jesus said to him, "You have seen him,
and the one speaking with you is he."
[38]He said, "Lord, I believe."
And he worshiped him.
[39]Jesus said,
"I came into this world for judgment
so that those who do not see may see,
and those who do see may become blind."
[40]Some of the Pharisees near him heard this and said to him,
"Surely we are not blind, are we?"
[41]Jesus said to them,
"If you were blind, you would not have sin.
But now that you say, 'We see,' your sin remains."

The gospel of the Lord.

✠ FIFTH SUNDAY IN LENT

FIRST READING: Ezekiel 37:1-14

A reading from Ezekiel.

[1]The hand of the LORD came upon me,
and he brought me out by the spirit of the LORD
and set me down in the middle of a valley;
it was full of bones.
[2]He led me all around them;
there were very many lying in the valley, and they were very dry.
[3]He said to me,
"Mortal, can these bones live?"
I answered, "O Lord GOD, you know."

[4]Then he said to me,
"Prophesy to these bones, and say to them:
O dry bones, hear the word of the LORD.
[5]Thus says the Lord GOD to these bones:
I will cause breath to enter you, and you shall live.
[6]I will lay sinews on you,
and will cause flesh to come upon you, and cover you with skin,
and put breath in you, and you shall live;
and you shall know that I am the LORD."

[7]So I prophesied as I had been commanded;
and as I prophesied, suddenly there was a noise, a rattling,
and the bones came together, bone to its bone.
[8]I looked, and there were sinews on them,
and flesh had come upon them, and skin had covered them;
but there was no breath in them.
[9]Then he said to me,
"Prophesy to the breath, prophesy, mortal, and say to the breath:
Thus says the Lord GOD:
Come from the four winds, O breath,
and breathe upon these slain, that they may live."
[10]I prophesied as he commanded me,
and the breath came into them,
and they lived, and stood on their feet, a vast multitude. ▸

FIRST READING   *Ezekiel = eh-ZEE-kee-el   prophesy = PROF-uh-sigh*
This dramatic vision of the prophet requires a double portion of energy and enthusiasm for the telling of the story. Before the reader can help us to imagine a valley full of bones, the reader must visualize such a frightening sight. Then share the vision with us with a sense of mystery, wonder, and power. Note carefully that prophesy is a verb, pronounced as shown above.

¹¹Then he said to me,
"Mortal, these bones are the whole house of Israel.
They say, 'Our bones are dried up, and our hope is lost;
we are cut off completely.'
¹²Therefore prophesy, and say to them,
Thus says the Lord GOD:
I am going to open your graves,
and bring you up from your graves, O my people;
and I will bring you back to the land of Israel.
¹³And you shall know that I am the LORD, when I open your graves,
and bring you up from your graves, O my people.
¹⁴I will put my spirit within you, and you shall live,
and I will place you on your own soil;
then you shall know that I, the LORD, have spoken and will act,"
says the LORD.

The word of the Lord.   *or*   Word of God, word of life.

PSALMODY: Psalm 130

SECOND READING: Romans 8:6-11

A reading from Romans.

⁶To set the mind on the flesh is death,
but to set the mind on the Spirit is life and peace.
⁷For this reason the mind that is set on the flesh is hostile to God;
it does not submit to God's law—indeed it cannot,
⁸and those who are in the flesh cannot please God.

⁹But you are not in the flesh;
you are in the Spirit, since the Spirit of God dwells in you.
Anyone who does not have the Spirit of Christ does not belong to him.
¹⁰But if Christ is in you, though the body is dead because of sin,
the Spirit is life because of righteousness.
¹¹If the Spirit of him who raised Jesus from the dead dwells in you,
he who raised Christ from the dead
will give life to your mortal bodies also
through his Spirit that dwells in you.

The word of the Lord.   *or*   Word of God, word of life.

SECOND READING
The reader may be helped in connecting this reading with the first reading to know that in Hebrew the word for breath and the word for spirit are the same. If one recalls the text in Genesis (2:7) that "God . . . breathed [into the form made from the dust of the ground] . . . and the man became a living being," one can perhaps more readily understand the point the author of Romans is making—that it is the breath/spirit of God that gives life to us.

GOSPEL: John 11:1-45

The holy gospel according to John.

[1]Now a certain man was ill, Lazarus of Bethany,
the village of Mary and her sister Martha.
[2]Mary was the one who anointed the Lord with perfume
and wiped his feet with her hair;
her brother Lazarus was ill.

[3]So the sisters sent a message to Jesus,
"Lord, he whom you love is ill."
[4]But when Jesus heard it, he said,
"This illness does not lead to death;
rather it is for God's glory,
so that the Son of God may be glorified through it."
[5]Accordingly, though Jesus loved Martha and her sister and Lazarus,
[6]after having heard that Lazarus was ill,
he stayed two days longer in the place where he was.

[7]Then after this he said to the disciples,
"Let us go to Judea again."
[8]The disciples said to him,
"Rabbi, the Jews were just now trying to stone you,
and are you going there again?"
[9]Jesus answered, "Are there not twelve hours of daylight?
Those who walk during the day do not stumble,
because they see the light of this world.
[10]But those who walk at night stumble,
because the light is not in them."
[11]After saying this, he told them,
"Our friend Lazarus has fallen asleep,
but I am going there to awaken him."
[12]The disciples said to him,
"Lord, if he has fallen asleep, he will be all right."
[13]Jesus, however, had been speaking about his death,
but they thought that he was referring merely to sleep.
[14]Then Jesus told them plainly, "Lazarus is dead.
[15]For your sake I am glad I was not there, so that you may believe.
But let us go to him." ▸

GOSPEL   *Lazarus = LAZ-uh-rus*
A significant part of the challenge of this reading is its length. Avoid the temptation to rush through it.
The assembly has gathered specifically to hear the gospel. Delight in every detail. Allow the drama time to
unfold.

¹⁶Thomas, who was called the Twin, said to his fellow disciples,
"Let us also go, that we may die with him."

¹⁷When Jesus arrived,
he found that Lazarus had already been in the tomb four days.

¹⁸Now Bethany was near Jerusalem, some two miles away,
¹⁹and many of the Jews had come to Martha and Mary
to console them about their brother.

²⁰When Martha heard that Jesus was coming,
she went and met him, while Mary stayed at home.
²¹Martha said to Jesus,
"Lord, if you had been here, my brother would not have died.
²²But even now I know that God will give you whatever you ask of him."
²³Jesus said to her, "Your brother will rise again."
²⁴Martha said to him,
"I know that he will rise again in the resurrection on the last day."
²⁵Jesus said to her,
"I am the resurrection and the life.
Those who believe in me, even though they die, will live,
²⁶and everyone who lives and believes in me will never die.
Do you believe this?"
²⁷She said to him,
"Yes, Lord, I believe that you are the Messiah,
the Son of God, the one coming into the world."

²⁸When she had said this,
she went back and called her sister Mary, and told her privately,
"The Teacher is here and is calling for you."
²⁹And when she heard it, she got up quickly and went to him.

³⁰Now Jesus had not yet come to the village,
but was still at the place where Martha had met him.
³¹The Jews who were with her in the house, consoling her,
saw Mary get up quickly and go out.
They followed her
because they thought that she was going to the tomb to weep there.
³²When Mary came where Jesus was and saw him,
she knelt at his feet and said to him,
"Lord, if you had been here, my brother would not have died."

[33]When Jesus saw her weeping,
and the Jews who came with her also weeping,
he was greatly disturbed in spirit and deeply moved.
[34]He said, "Where have you laid him?"
They said to him, "Lord, come and see."
[35]Jesus began to weep.
[36]So the Jews said, "See how he loved him!"
[37]But some of them said,
"Could not he who opened the eyes of the blind man
have kept this man from dying?"

[38]Then Jesus, again greatly disturbed, came to the tomb.
It was a cave, and a stone was lying against it.
[39]Jesus said, "Take away the stone."
Martha, the sister of the dead man, said to him,
"Lord, already there is a stench because he has been dead four days."
[40]Jesus said to her,
"Did I not tell you that if you believed, you would see the glory of God?"

[41]So they took away the stone.
And Jesus looked upward and said,
"Father, I thank you for having heard me.
[42]I knew that you always hear me,
but I have said this for the sake of the crowd standing here,
so that they may believe that you sent me."
[43]When he had said this,
he cried with a loud voice, "Lazarus, come out!"
[44]The dead man came out,
his hands and feet bound with strips of cloth,
and his face wrapped in a cloth.
Jesus said to them, "Unbind him, and let him go."

[45]Many of the Jews therefore,
who had come with Mary and had seen what Jesus did,
believed in him.

The gospel of the Lord.

SUNDAY OF THE PASSION
PALM SUNDAY

Procession with Palms

PROCESSIONAL GOSPEL: Matthew 21:1-11

The holy gospel according to Matthew.

[1]When they had come near Jerusalem
and had reached Bethphage, at the Mount of Olives,
Jesus sent two disciples, [2]saying to them,
"Go into the village ahead of you,
and immediately you will find a donkey tied, and a colt with her;
untie them and bring them to me.
[3]If anyone says anything to you, just say this,
'The Lord needs them.'
And he will send them immediately."
[4]This took place to fulfill what had been spoken through the prophet,
saying,

> [5]"Tell the daughter of Zion,
> Look, your king is coming to you,
> humble, and mounted on a donkey,
> and on a colt, the foal of a donkey."

[6]The disciples went and did as Jesus had directed them;
[7]they brought the donkey and the colt,
and put their cloaks on them, and he sat on them.
[8]A very large crowd spread their cloaks on the road,
and others cut branches from the trees and spread them on the road.
[9]The crowds that went ahead of him and that followed were shouting,

> "Hosanna to the Son of David!
> Blessed is the one who comes in the name of the Lord!
> Hosanna in the highest heaven!"

[10]When he entered Jerusalem, the whole city was in turmoil, asking,
"Who is this?"
[11]The crowds were saying,
"This is the prophet Jesus from Nazareth in Galilee."

The gospel of the Lord.

PROCESSIONAL GOSPEL   *Bethphage = BETH-fuh-juh*
The richest reading of this little story will distinguish between the voices of Jesus, the prophet, and the crowds. Those subtle distinctions require forethought and adequate rehearsal time. Invest in both. Let this account of our Lord's grand entrance be a festive prelude to the later reading of the passion.

FIRST READING: Isaiah 50:4-9a

A reading from Isaiah.

⁴The Lord GOD has given me
   the tongue of a teacher,
that I may know how to sustain
   the weary with a word.
Morning by morning he wakens—
   wakens my ear
   to listen as those who are taught.
⁵The Lord GOD has opened my ear,
   and I was not rebellious,
   I did not turn backward.
⁶I gave my back to those who struck me,
   and my cheeks to those who pulled out the beard;
I did not hide my face
   from insult and spitting.

⁷The Lord GOD helps me;
   therefore I have not been disgraced;
therefore I have set my face like flint,
   and I know that I shall not be put to shame;
   ⁸he who vindicates me is near.
Who will contend with me?
   Let us stand up together.
Who are my adversaries?
   Let them confront me.
⁹It is the Lord GOD who helps me;
   who will declare me guilty?

The word of the Lord.   *or*   Word of God, word of life.

PSALMODY: Psalm 31:9–16

FIRST READING   *Isaiah = eye-ZAY-uh*
One might be helped to think about this reading as a poem. Be sensitive to the images painted in these verses and help the hearer to see them. The congregation is intended to hear in these words the voice of Jesus as he sets his face toward Jerusalem and his impending passion. Verse 8 is of particular interest and provides a particular challenge. The speaker asks a question in two different ways. They are rhetorical questions, though, so don't raise your pitch at the end of them. And be certain to provide an adequate pause between "together" and the next question so that the hearer can follow the dialogue.

SECOND READING: Philippians 2:5-11

A reading from Philippians.

⁵Let the same mind be in you that was in Christ Jesus,
 ⁶who, though he was in the form of God,
   did not regard equality with God
   as something to be exploited,
 ⁷but emptied himself,
   taking the form of a slave,
   being born in human likeness.
 And being found in human form,
   ⁸he humbled himself
   and became obedient to the point of death —
   even death on a cross.

 ⁹Therefore God also highly exalted him
   and gave him the name
   that is above every name,
 ¹⁰so that at the name of Jesus
   every knee should bend,
   in heaven and on earth and under the earth,
 ¹¹and every tongue should confess
   that Jesus Christ is Lord,
   to the glory of God the Father.

The word of the Lord.   *or*   Word of God, word of life.

SECOND READING   *Philippians = fih-LIP-ee-unz*
This text is widely known. That can be both a blessing and a bane. Do not approach the reading task casually. Live with the text a little this week and allow it to address you. The author attempts to describe the mind of Christ in verses 6 and 7. He describes the Father's rewarding of the Son in verses 9–11. But the topic sentence is verse 5, where he urges both the reader and the hearer to "let the same mind be in you." Bring appropriate urgency to this holy instruction.

GOSPEL: Matthew 26:14—27:66

Or Matthew 27:11-54, following on p. 111

The passion of our Lord Jesus Christ according to Matthew.

[14]One of the twelve, who was called Judas Iscariot,
went to the chief priests [15]and said,
"What will you give me if I betray him to you?"
They paid him thirty pieces of silver.
[16]And from that moment he began to look for an opportunity to betray him.

[17]On the first day of Unleavened Bread the disciples came to Jesus, saying,
"Where do you want us to make the preparations for you to eat the Passover?"
[18]He said,
"Go into the city to a certain man, and say to him,
'The Teacher says, My time is near;
I will keep the Passover at your house with my disciples.'"
[19]So the disciples did as Jesus had directed them,
and they prepared the Passover meal.

[20]When it was evening, he took his place with the twelve;
[21]and while they were eating, he said,
"Truly I tell you, one of you will betray me."
[22]And they became greatly distressed
and began to say to him one after another,
"Surely not I, Lord?"
[23]He answered,
"The one who has dipped his hand into the bowl with me will betray me.
[24]The Son of Man goes as it is written of him,
but woe to that one by whom the Son of Man is betrayed!
It would have been better for that one not to have been born."
[25]Judas, who betrayed him, said,
"Surely not I, Rabbi?"
He replied, "You have said so."

[26]While they were eating, Jesus took a loaf of bread,
and after blessing it he broke it,
gave it to the disciples, and said,
"Take, eat; this is my body."
[27]Then he took a cup,
and after giving thanks he gave it to them, saying, ▸

GOSPEL *Iscariot = is-CAR-ee-ut Gethsemane = geth-SEM-uh-nee Zebedee = ZEB-uh-dee Caiaphas = KAY-uh-fus prophesy = PROF-uh-sy Jeremiah = jehr-uh-MY-uh Barabbas = buh-RAB-us Cyrene = sy-REE-nuh Eli, lema sabachthani = EL-ee LEM-uh suh-BAHK-thun-ee Arimathea = ar-ih-muh-THEE-uh*
Sadly, a significant segment of the assembly will be exposed to the passion account only once this year. That may be the best argument for reading Matthew's telling in its entirety. If this once is to be the best it can be, the reader will want to be devotionally steeped in the story and have read it aloud any number of times in advance. Practice makes the difference between passable and persuasive. Consider the merit of a substantial pause (and even bowing deeply at the reading desk) following 27:50, when Jesus "breathed his last."

"Drink from it, all of you;
²⁸for this is my blood of the covenant,
which is poured out for many for the forgiveness of sins.
²⁹I tell you, I will never again drink of this fruit of the vine
until that day when I drink it new with you in my Father's kingdom."

³⁰When they had sung the hymn, they went out to the Mount of Olives.

³¹Then Jesus said to them,
"You will all become deserters because of me this night; for it is written,
   'I will strike the shepherd,
      and the sheep of the flock will be scattered.'
³²But after I am raised up, I will go ahead of you to Galilee."
³³Peter said to him,
"Though all become deserters because of you, I will never desert you."
³⁴Jesus said to him,
"Truly I tell you, this very night, before the cock crows,
you will deny me three times."
³⁵Peter said to him,
"Even though I must die with you, I will not deny you."
And so said all the disciples.

³⁶Then Jesus went with them to a place called Gethsemane;
and he said to his disciples,
"Sit here while I go over there and pray."
³⁷He took with him Peter and the two sons of Zebedee,
and began to be grieved and agitated.
³⁸Then he said to them,
"I am deeply grieved, even to death;
remain here, and stay awake with me."
³⁹And going a little farther, he threw himself on the ground and prayed,
"My Father, if it is possible, let this cup pass from me;
yet not what I want but what you want."
⁴⁰Then he came to the disciples and found them sleeping;
and he said to Peter,
"So, could you not stay awake with me one hour?
⁴¹Stay awake and pray that you may not come into the time of trial;
the spirit indeed is willing, but the flesh is weak."
⁴²Again he went away for the second time and prayed,
"My Father, if this cannot pass unless I drink it, your will be done."
⁴³Again he came and found them sleeping, for their eyes were heavy.

⁴⁴So leaving them again, he went away and prayed for the third time,
saying the same words.
⁴⁵Then he came to the disciples and said to them,
"Are you still sleeping and taking your rest?
See, the hour is at hand,
and the Son of Man is betrayed into the hands of sinners.
⁴⁶Get up, let us be going. See, my betrayer is at hand."

⁴⁷While he was still speaking, Judas, one of the twelve, arrived;
with him was a large crowd with swords and clubs,
from the chief priests and the elders of the people.
⁴⁸Now the betrayer had given them a sign, saying,
"The one I will kiss is the man; arrest him."
⁴⁹At once he came up to Jesus and said,
"Greetings, Rabbi!" and kissed him.
⁵⁰Jesus said to him, "Friend, do what you are here to do."
Then they came and laid hands on Jesus and arrested him.
⁵¹Suddenly, one of those with Jesus put his hand on his sword,
drew it, and struck the slave of the high priest, cutting off his ear.
⁵²Then Jesus said to him,
"Put your sword back into its place;
for all who take the sword will perish by the sword.
⁵³Do you think that I cannot appeal to my Father,
and he will at once send me more than twelve legions of angels?
⁵⁴But how then would the scriptures be fulfilled,
which say it must happen in this way?"
⁵⁵At that hour Jesus said to the crowds,
"Have you come out with swords and clubs to arrest me
as though I were a bandit?
Day after day I sat in the temple teaching, and you did not arrest me.
⁵⁶But all this has taken place,
so that the scriptures of the prophets may be fulfilled."
Then all the disciples deserted him and fled.

⁵⁷Those who had arrested Jesus took him to Caiaphas the high priest,
in whose house the scribes and the elders had gathered.
⁵⁸But Peter was following him at a distance,
as far as the courtyard of the high priest;
and going inside, he sat with the guards in order to see how this would end. ▸

⁵⁹Now the chief priests and the whole council
were looking for false testimony against Jesus
so that they might put him to death,
⁶⁰but they found none, though many false witnesses came forward.
At last two came forward ⁶¹and said,
"This fellow said,
'I am able to destroy the temple of God and to build it in three days.'"
⁶²The high priest stood up and said,
"Have you no answer? What is it that they testify against you?"
⁶³But Jesus was silent.
Then the high priest said to him,
"I put you under oath before the living God,
tell us if you are the Messiah, the Son of God."
⁶⁴Jesus said to him, "You have said so. But I tell you,
    From now on you will see the Son of Man
        seated at the right hand of Power
        and coming on the clouds of heaven."
⁶⁵Then the high priest tore his clothes and said,
"He has blasphemed! Why do we still need witnesses?
You have now heard his blasphemy. ⁶⁶What is your verdict?"
They answered, "He deserves death."
⁶⁷Then they spat in his face and struck him;
and some slapped him, ⁶⁸saying,
"Prophesy to us, you Messiah! Who is it that struck you?"

⁶⁹Now Peter was sitting outside in the courtyard.
A servant-girl came to him and said,
"You also were with Jesus the Galilean."
⁷⁰But he denied it before all of them, saying,
"I do not know what you are talking about."
⁷¹When he went out to the porch, another servant-girl saw him,
and she said to the bystanders, "This man was with Jesus of Nazareth."
⁷²Again he denied it with an oath, "I do not know the man."
⁷³After a little while the bystanders came up and said to Peter,
"Certainly you are also one of them, for your accent betrays you."
⁷⁴Then he began to curse, and he swore an oath,
"I do not know the man!"
At that moment the cock crowed.
⁷⁵Then Peter remembered what Jesus had said:
"Before the cock crows, you will deny me three times."
And he went out and wept bitterly.

²⁷:¹When morning came, all the chief priests and the elders of the people
conferred together against Jesus in order to bring about his death.
²They bound him, led him away, and handed him over to Pilate the governor.

³When Judas, his betrayer, saw that Jesus was condemned, he repented
and brought back the thirty pieces of silver to the chief priests and the elders.
⁴He said, "I have sinned by betraying innocent blood."
But they said, "What is that to us? See to it yourself."
⁵Throwing down the pieces of silver in the temple, he departed;
and he went and hanged himself.
⁶But the chief priests, taking the pieces of silver, said,
"It is not lawful to put them into the treasury, since they are blood money."
⁷After conferring together,
they used them to buy the potter's field as a place to bury foreigners.
⁸For this reason that field has been called the Field of Blood to this day.
⁹Then was fulfilled what had been spoken through the prophet Jeremiah,
"And they took the thirty pieces of silver,
the price of the one on whom a price had been set,
on whom some of the people of Israel had set a price,
¹⁰and they gave them for the potter's field, as the Lord commanded me."

¹¹Now Jesus stood before the governor; and the governor asked him,
"Are you the King of the Jews?"
Jesus said, "You say so."
¹²But when he was accused by the chief priests and elders,
he did not answer.
¹³Then Pilate said to him,
"Do you not hear how many accusations they make against you?"
¹⁴But he gave him no answer, not even to a single charge,
so that the governor was greatly amazed.

¹⁵Now at the festival
the governor was accustomed to release a prisoner for the crowd,
anyone whom they wanted.
¹⁶At that time they had a notorious prisoner, called Jesus Barabbas.
¹⁷So after they had gathered, Pilate said to them,
"Whom do you want me to release for you,
Jesus Barabbas or Jesus who is called the Messiah?"
¹⁸For he realized that it was out of jealousy that they had handed him over.
¹⁹While he was sitting on the judgment seat, his wife sent word to him,
"Have nothing to do with that innocent man,
for today I have suffered a great deal because of a dream about him." ▸

[20]Now the chief priests and the elders persuaded the crowds to ask for Barabbas and to have Jesus killed.
[21]The governor again said to them,
"Which of the two do you want me to release for you?"
And they said, "Barabbas."
[22]Pilate said to them,
"Then what should I do with Jesus who is called the Messiah?"
All of them said, "Let him be crucified!"
[23]Then he asked, "Why, what evil has he done?"
But they shouted all the more, "Let him be crucified!"
[24]So when Pilate saw that he could do nothing,
but rather that a riot was beginning,
he took some water and washed his hands before the crowd, saying,
"I am innocent of this man's blood; see to it yourselves."
[25]Then the people as a whole answered,
"His blood be on us and on our children!"
[26]So he released Barabbas for them;
and after flogging Jesus, he handed him over to be crucified.

[27]Then the soldiers of the governor took Jesus into the governor's headquarters,
and they gathered the whole cohort around him.
[28]They stripped him and put a scarlet robe on him,
[29]and after twisting some thorns into a crown, they put it on his head.
They put a reed in his right hand
and knelt before him and mocked him, saying,
"Hail, King of the Jews!"
[30]They spat on him, and took the reed and struck him on the head.
[31]After mocking him,
they stripped him of the robe and put his own clothes on him.
Then they led him away to crucify him.

[32]As they went out, they came upon a man from Cyrene named Simon;
they compelled this man to carry his cross.
[33]And when they came to a place called Golgotha
(which means Place of a Skull),
[34]they offered him wine to drink, mixed with gall;
but when he tasted it, he would not drink it.
[35]And when they had crucified him,
they divided his clothes among themselves by casting lots;
[36]then they sat down there and kept watch over him.
[37]Over his head they put the charge against him, which read,
"This is Jesus, the King of the Jews."

³⁸Then two bandits were crucified with him,
one on his right and one on his left.
³⁹Those who passed by derided him, shaking their heads ⁴⁰and saying,
"You who would destroy the temple and build it in three days, save yourself!
If you are the Son of God, come down from the cross."
⁴¹In the same way the chief priests also, along with the scribes and elders,
were mocking him, saying,
⁴²"He saved others; he cannot save himself.
He is the King of Israel; let him come down from the cross now,
and we will believe in him.
⁴³He trusts in God; let God deliver him now, if he wants to;
for he said, 'I am God's Son.'"
⁴⁴The bandits who were crucified with him also taunted him in the same way.

⁴⁵From noon on,
darkness came over the whole land until three in the afternoon.
⁴⁶And about three o'clock Jesus cried with a loud voice,
"Eli, Eli, lema sabachthani?" that is,
"My God, my God, why have you forsaken me?"
⁴⁷When some of the bystanders heard it, they said,
"This man is calling for Elijah."
⁴⁸At once one of them ran and got a sponge,
filled it with sour wine, put it on a stick,
and gave it to him to drink.
⁴⁹But the others said,
"Wait, let us see whether Elijah will come to save him."
⁵⁰Then Jesus cried again with a loud voice and breathed his last.

⁵¹At that moment the curtain of the temple was torn in two, from top to bottom.
The earth shook, and the rocks were split.
⁵²The tombs also were opened,
and many bodies of the saints who had fallen asleep were raised.
⁵³After his resurrection they came out of the tombs
and entered the holy city and appeared to many. ▸

[54]Now when the centurion and those with him,
who were keeping watch over Jesus,
saw the earthquake and what took place, they were terrified and said,
"Truly this man was God's Son!"

[55]Many women were also there, looking on from a distance;
they had followed Jesus from Galilee and had provided for him.
[56]Among them were Mary Magdalene, and Mary the mother of James and Joseph,
and the mother of the sons of Zebedee.

[57]When it was evening, there came a rich man from Arimathea, named Joseph,
who was also a disciple of Jesus.
[58]He went to Pilate and asked for the body of Jesus;
then Pilate ordered it to be given to him.
[59]So Joseph took the body and wrapped it in a clean linen cloth
[60]and laid it in his own new tomb, which he had hewn in the rock.
He then rolled a great stone to the door of the tomb and went away.
[61]Mary Magdalene and the other Mary were there, sitting opposite the tomb.

[62]The next day, that is, after the day of Preparation,
the chief priests and the Pharisees gathered before Pilate [63]and said,
"Sir, we remember what that impostor said while he was still alive,
'After three days I will rise again.'
[64]Therefore command the tomb to be made secure until the third day;
otherwise his disciples may go and steal him away,
and tell the people, 'He has been raised from the dead,'
and the last deception would be worse than the first."
[65]Pilate said to them,
"You have a guard of soldiers; go, make it as secure as you can."
[66]So they went with the guard and made the tomb secure by sealing the stone.

The gospel of the Lord.

OR: Matthew 27:11-54

The passion of our Lord Jesus Christ according to Matthew.

[11]Now Jesus stood before the governor; and the governor asked him,
"Are you the King of the Jews?"
Jesus said, "You say so."
[12]But when he was accused by the chief priests and elders,
he did not answer.
[13]Then Pilate said to him,
"Do you not hear how many accusations they make against you?"
[14]But he gave him no answer, not even to a single charge,
so that the governor was greatly amazed.
[15]Now at the festival
the governor was accustomed to release a prisoner for the crowd,
anyone whom they wanted.
[16]At that time they had a notorious prisoner, called Jesus Barabbas.
[17]So after they had gathered, Pilate said to them,
"Whom do you want me to release for you,
Jesus Barabbas or Jesus who is called the Messiah?"
[18]For he realized that it was out of jealousy that they had handed him over.
[19]While he was sitting on the judgment seat, his wife sent word to him,
"Have nothing to do with that innocent man,
for today I have suffered a great deal because of a dream about him."
[20]Now the chief priests and the elders persuaded the crowds to ask for Barabbas
and to have Jesus killed.
[21]The governor again said to them,
"Which of the two do you want me to release for you?"
And they said, "Barabbas."
[22]Pilate said to them,
"Then what should I do with Jesus who is called the Messiah?"
All of them said, "Let him be crucified!"
[23]Then he asked, "Why, what evil has he done?"
But they shouted all the more, "Let him be crucified!"

[24]So when Pilate saw that he could do nothing,
but rather that a riot was beginning,
he took some water and washed his hands before the crowd, saying,
"I am innocent of this man's blood; see to it yourselves." ▸

²⁵Then the people as a whole answered,
"His blood be on us and on our children!"
²⁶So he released Barabbas for them;
and after flogging Jesus, he handed him over to be crucified.

²⁷Then the soldiers of the governor took Jesus into the governor's headquarters,
and they gathered the whole cohort around him.
²⁸They stripped him and put a scarlet robe on him,
²⁹and after twisting some thorns into a crown, they put it on his head.
They put a reed in his right hand
and knelt before him and mocked him, saying,
"Hail, King of the Jews!"
³⁰They spat on him, and took the reed and struck him on the head.
³¹After mocking him,
they stripped him of the robe and put his own clothes on him.
Then they led him away to crucify him.

³²As they went out, they came upon a man from Cyrene named Simon;
they compelled this man to carry his cross.
³³And when they came to a place called Golgotha
(which means Place of a Skull),
³⁴they offered him wine to drink, mixed with gall;
but when he tasted it, he would not drink it.
³⁵And when they had crucified him,
they divided his clothes among themselves by casting lots;
³⁶then they sat down there and kept watch over him.
³⁷Over his head they put the charge against him, which read,
"This is Jesus, the King of the Jews."

³⁸Then two bandits were crucified with him,
one on his right and one on his left.
³⁹Those who passed by derided him, shaking their heads ⁴⁰and saying,
"You who would destroy the temple and build it in three days, save yourself!
If you are the Son of God, come down from the cross."
⁴¹In the same way the chief priests also, along with the scribes and elders,
were mocking him, saying,
⁴²"He saved others; he cannot save himself.
He is the King of Israel; let him come down from the cross now,
and we will believe in him.

⁴³He trusts in God; let God deliver him now, if he wants to;
for he said, 'I am God's Son.'"
⁴⁴The bandits who were crucified with him also taunted him in the same way.

⁴⁵From noon on, darkness came over the whole land
until three in the afternoon.
⁴⁶And about three o'clock Jesus cried with a loud voice,
"Eli, Eli, lema sabachthani?" that is,
"My God, my God, why have you forsaken me?"
⁴⁷When some of the bystanders heard it, they said,
"This man is calling for Elijah."
⁴⁸At once one of them ran and got a sponge,
filled it with sour wine, put it on a stick,
and gave it to him to drink.
⁴⁹But the others said,
"Wait, let us see whether Elijah will come to save him."
⁵⁰Then Jesus cried again with a loud voice and breathed his last.

⁵¹At that moment the curtain of the temple was torn in two, from top to bottom.
The earth shook, and the rocks were split.
⁵²The tombs also were opened,
and many bodies of the saints who had fallen asleep were raised.
⁵³After his resurrection they came out of the tombs
and entered the holy city and appeared to many.

⁵⁴Now when the centurion and those with him,
who were keeping watch over Jesus,
saw the earthquake and what took place, they were terrified and said,
"Truly this man was God's Son!"

The gospel of the Lord.

MONDAY IN HOLY WEEK

FIRST READING: Isaiah 42:1-9

A reading from Isaiah.

¹Here is my servant, whom I uphold,
    my chosen, in whom my soul delights;
I have put my spirit upon him;
    he will bring forth justice to the nations.
²He will not cry or lift up his voice,
    or make it heard in the street;
³a bruised reed he will not break,
    and a dimly burning wick he will not quench;
    he will faithfully bring forth justice.
⁴He will not grow faint or be crushed
    until he has established justice in the earth;
    and the coastlands wait for his teaching.

⁵Thus says God, the LORD,
    who created the heavens and stretched them out,
    who spread out the earth and what comes from it,
who gives breath to the people upon it
    and spirit to those who walk in it:
⁶I am the LORD, I have called you in righteousness,
    I have taken you by the hand and kept you;
I have given you as a covenant to the people,
    a light to the nations,
    ⁷to open the eyes that are blind,
to bring out the prisoners from the dungeon,
    from the prison those who sit in darkness.
⁸I am the LORD, that is my name;
    my glory I give to no other,
    nor my praise to idols.
⁹See, the former things have come to pass,
    and new things I now declare;
before they spring forth, I tell you of them.

The word of the Lord.   *or*   Word of God, word of life.

FIRST READING   *Isaiah = eye-ZAY-uh*
When carefully read, the people in the pews will see a portrait of Jesus in these verses. The faithful reader will invest some time in getting a clear sense of the images in verses 3 and 4 before sharing them with the assembly. The tone of the reading changes at verse 5, when God is identified in expansive and glorious phrases. Revel in them.

PSALMODY: Psalm 36:5-11

SECOND READING: Hebrews 9:11-15

A reading from Hebrews.

¹¹When Christ came as a high priest of the good things that have come,
then through the greater and perfect tent
(not made with hands, that is, not of this creation),
¹²he entered once for all into the Holy Place,
not with the blood of goats and calves,
but with his own blood, thus obtaining eternal redemption.

¹³For if the blood of goats and bulls,
with the sprinkling of the ashes of a heifer,
sanctifies those who have been defiled so that their flesh is purified,
¹⁴how much more will the blood of Christ,
who through the eternal Spirit offered himself without blemish to God,
purify our conscience from dead works to worship the living God!

¹⁵For this reason he is the mediator of a new covenant,
so that those who are called may receive the promised eternal inheritance,
because a death has occurred
that redeems them from the transgressions under the first covenant.

The word of the Lord.   *or*   Word of God, word of life.

SECOND READING   *heifer = HEF-er*
Three carefully constructed sentences containing the holy truth of this Holy Week beg the reader to slow down. The text calls for a careful reading, accented with conviction.

GOSPEL: John 12:1-11

The holy gospel according to John.

[1]Six days before the Passover Jesus came to Bethany,
the home of Lazarus, whom he had raised from the dead.
[2]There they gave a dinner for him.
Martha served, and Lazarus was one of those at the table with him.
[3]Mary took a pound of costly perfume made of pure nard,
anointed Jesus' feet, and wiped them with her hair.
The house was filled with the fragrance of the perfume.

[4]But Judas Iscariot, one of his disciples
(the one who was about to betray him), said,
[5]"Why was this perfume not sold for three hundred denarii
and the money given to the poor?"
[6](He said this not because he cared about the poor,
but because he was a thief;
he kept the common purse and used to steal what was put into it.)
[7]Jesus said,
"Leave her alone.
She bought it so that she might keep it for the day of my burial.
[8]You always have the poor with you,
but you do not always have me."

[9]When the great crowd of the Jews learned that he was there,
they came not only because of Jesus
but also to see Lazarus, whom he had raised from the dead.
[10]So the chief priests planned to put Lazarus to death as well,
[11]since it was on account of him that many of the Jews were deserting
and were believing in Jesus.

The gospel of the Lord.

GOSPEL   *Lazarus = LAZ-uh-rus Iscariot = is-CAR-ee-ut denarii = deh-NAR-ee-eye*
"You do not always have me" ought to give the hearer pause on Monday in Holy Week. Allow the first seven
and a half verses build to that understated reality. Shift vocal gears for verses 9–11, which provide a kind of
fascinating footnote to the Bethany dinner story.

TUESDAY IN HOLY WEEK

FIRST READING: Isaiah 49:1-7

A reading from Isaiah.

¹Listen to me, O coastlands,
    pay attention, you peoples from far away!
The Lord called me before I was born,
    while I was in my mother's womb he named me.
²He made my mouth like a sharp sword,
    in the shadow of his hand he hid me;
he made me a polished arrow,
    in his quiver he hid me away.
³And he said to me, "You are my servant,
    Israel, in whom I will be glorified."
⁴But I said, "I have labored in vain,
    I have spent my strength for nothing and vanity;
yet surely my cause is with the Lord,
    and my reward with my God."

⁵And now the Lord says,
    who formed me in the womb to be his servant,
to bring Jacob back to him,
    and that Israel might be gathered to him,
for I am honored in the sight of the Lord,
    and my God has become my strength—
⁶he says,
"It is too light a thing that you should be my servant
    to raise up the tribes of Jacob
    and to restore the survivors of Israel;
I will give you as a light to the nations,
    that my salvation may reach to the end of the earth."

⁷Thus says the Lord,
    the Redeemer of Israel and his Holy One,
to one deeply despised, abhorred by the nations,
    the slave of rulers, ▸

FIRST READING   *Isaiah = eye-ZAY-uh*
The servant who is given voice in this rich text will look like Jesus to much of the assembly. Search for the voice of Jesus for the reading of it. Several of the sentences are lengthy and circuitous. Reading the text aloud more than once in preparation will help the hearer sense more fully the hope that it contains.

"Kings shall see and stand up,
    princes, and they shall prostrate themselves,
because of the LORD, who is faithful,
    the Holy One of Israel, who has chosen you."

The word of the Lord.   *or*   Word of God, word of life.

PSALMODY: Psalm 71:1-14

SECOND READING: 1 Corinthians 1:18-31

A reading from First Corinthians.

[18]The message about the cross is foolishness to those who are perishing,
but to us who are being saved it is the power of God.
[19]For it is written,
    "I will destroy the wisdom of the wise,
        and the discernment of the discerning I will thwart."
[20]Where is the one who is wise?
Where is the scribe?
Where is the debater of this age?
Has not God made foolish the wisdom of the world?

[21]For since, in the wisdom of God,
the world did not know God through wisdom,
God decided, through the foolishness of our proclamation,
to save those who believe.
[22]For Jews demand signs and Greeks desire wisdom,
[23]but we proclaim Christ crucified,
a stumbling block to Jews and foolishness to Gentiles,
[24]but to those who are the called, both Jews and Greeks,
Christ the power of God and the wisdom of God.
[25]For God's foolishness is wiser than human wisdom,
and God's weakness is stronger than human strength.

[26]Consider your own call, brothers and sisters:
not many of you were wise by human standards,
not many were powerful,
not many were of noble birth.

SECOND READING
This magnificent reading provides the reader with an excellent opportunity to explore the merits of varying the pace of the delivery for added impact. As an example: slow down for the rhetorical questions in verse 20. Explore the possibility of delivering verse 23a ("but we proclaim Christ crucified") at a much more deliberate pace than the verses preceding and following it. "Sitting with the text"—attempting to hear the text—during the days before it is to be read will expose other ways to pace it.

²⁷But God chose what is foolish in the world to shame the wise;
God chose what is weak in the world to shame the strong;
²⁸God chose what is low and despised in the world,
things that are not,
to reduce to nothing things that are,
²⁹so that no one might boast in the presence of God.

³⁰He is the source of your life in Christ Jesus,
who became for us wisdom from God,
and righteousness and sanctification and redemption,
³¹in order that, as it is written,
"Let the one who boasts, boast in the Lord."

The word of the Lord.   *or*   Word of God, word of life.

GOSPEL: John 12:20-36

The holy gospel according to John.

²⁰Now among those who went up to worship at the festival were some Greeks.
²¹They came to Philip, who was from Bethsaida in Galilee,
and said to him, "Sir, we wish to see Jesus."
²²Philip went and told Andrew;
then Andrew and Philip went and told Jesus.
²³Jesus answered them,
"The hour has come for the Son of Man to be glorified.
²⁴Very truly, I tell you,
unless a grain of wheat falls into the earth and dies,
it remains just a single grain;
but if it dies, it bears much fruit.
²⁵Those who love their life lose it,
and those who hate their life in this world will keep it for eternal life.
²⁶Whoever serves me must follow me,
and where I am, there will my servant be also.
Whoever serves me, the Father will honor.

²⁷"Now my soul is troubled.
And what should I say—'Father, save me from this hour'?
No, it is for this reason that I have come to this hour.
²⁸Father, glorify your name." ▸

GOSPEL   *Bethsaida = beth-SAY-uh-duh*
Taking adequate time to ponder the meaning of the various images and phrases, as well as their relationship
to one another, is absolutely essential if one hopes for a coherent reading. There is a noticeable absence
of transitions between many of the thoughts. Map out helpful pause points and honor them. Allow the
assembly sufficient time to absorb the complexity of the gospel.

Then a voice came from heaven,
"I have glorified it, and I will glorify it again."
[29]The crowd standing there heard it and said that it was thunder.
Others said, "An angel has spoken to him."
[30]Jesus answered,
"This voice has come for your sake, not for mine.
[31]Now is the judgment of this world;
now the ruler of this world will be driven out.
[32]And I, when I am lifted up from the earth,
will draw all people to myself."
[33]He said this to indicate the kind of death he was to die.
[34]The crowd answered him,
"We have heard from the law that the Messiah remains forever.
How can you say that the Son of Man must be lifted up?
Who is this Son of Man?"
[35]Jesus said to them,
"The light is with you for a little longer.
Walk while you have the light,
so that the darkness may not overtake you.
If you walk in the darkness, you do not know where you are going.
[36]While you have the light, believe in the light,
so that you may become children of light."

After Jesus had said this, he departed and hid from them.

The gospel of the Lord.

✝ Wednesday in Holy Week

FIRST READING: Isaiah 50:4-9a

A reading from Isaiah.

⁴The Lord GOD has given me the tongue of a teacher,
that I may know how to sustain the weary with a word.
Morning by morning he wakens—
    wakens my ear
    to listen as those who are taught.
⁵The Lord GOD has opened my ear,
    and I was not rebellious,
    I did not turn backward.
⁶I gave my back to those who struck me,
    and my cheeks to those who pulled out the beard;
I did not hide my face from insult and spitting.

⁷The Lord GOD helps me;
    therefore I have not been disgraced;
therefore I have set my face like flint,
    and I know that I shall not be put to shame;
    ⁸he who vindicates me is near.
Who will contend with me?
    Let us stand up together.
Who are my adversaries?
    Let them confront me.
⁹It is the Lord GOD who helps me;
    who will declare me guilty?

The word of the Lord.   *or*   Word of God, word of life.

PSALMODY: Psalm 70

FIRST READING   *Isaiah = eye-ZAY-uh*
Rushing ruins poetry. This text demands that the reader provide time for the hearer to absorb the images and their relationship to one another (verses 4-6). The combative "Come and get me!" dialogue in verse 8 seeks a bold, expansive delivery. Verse 9 stands alone as a kind of confessional conclusion.

SECOND READING: Hebrews 12:1-3

A reading from Hebrews.

[1]Since we are surrounded by so great a cloud of witnesses,
let us also lay aside every weight and the sin that clings so closely,
and let us run with perseverance the race that is set before us,
[2]looking to Jesus the pioneer and perfecter of our faith,
who for the sake of the joy that was set before him
endured the cross, disregarding its shame,
and has taken his seat at the right hand of the throne of God.

[3]Consider him who endured such hostility against himself from sinners,
so that you may not grow weary or lose heart.

The word of the Lord.   *or*   Word of God, word of life.

SECOND READING
"Consider him" is the imperative of the author in verse 3. Read this marvelous little reading at a considered pace. Rarely will the assembly critique a reading of the scripture as "too slow."

GOSPEL: John 13:21-32

The holy gospel according to John.

[21]Jesus was troubled in spirit, and declared,
"Very truly, I tell you, one of you will betray me."
[22]The disciples looked at one another,
uncertain of whom he was speaking.

[23]One of his disciples—the one whom Jesus loved—was reclining next to him;
[24]Simon Peter therefore motioned to him
to ask Jesus of whom he was speaking.
[25]So while reclining next to Jesus, he asked him,
"Lord, who is it?"
[26]Jesus answered,
"It is the one to whom I give this piece of bread
when I have dipped it in the dish."
So when he had dipped the piece of bread,
he gave it to Judas son of Simon Iscariot.
[27]After he received the piece of bread, Satan entered into him.
Jesus said to him,
"Do quickly what you are going to do."
[28]Now no one at the table knew why he said this to him.
[29]Some thought that, because Judas had the common purse,
Jesus was telling him, "Buy what we need for the festival";
or, that he should give something to the poor.
[30]So, after receiving the piece of bread, he immediately went out.
And it was night.

[31]When he had gone out, Jesus said,
"Now the Son of Man has been glorified,
and God has been glorified in him.
[32]If God has been glorified in him,
God will also glorify him in himself and will glorify him at once."

The gospel of the Lord.

GOSPEL   *Iscariot = is-CAR-ee-ut*
The reading itself ought to sound "troubled in spirit." It is a sharply defined portrait of the disturbing events at our Lord's last meal. The reader will profit from visualizing the events and then making every effort to help the assembly see them as well. Point up the simple details by providing them with "vocal parentheses," treating them as a kind of aside. For example: "Simon Peter therefore motioned to him to ask Jesus . . ." and "Now no one at the table knew why he said this . . . ."

The Three Days

MAUNDY THURSDAY

FIRST READING: Exodus 12:1-4 [5-10] 11-14

A reading from Exodus.

¹The LORD said to Moses and Aaron in the land of Egypt:
²This month shall mark for you the beginning of months;
it shall be the first month of the year for you.
³Tell the whole congregation of Israel
that on the tenth of this month they are to take a lamb for each family,
a lamb for each household.
⁴If a household is too small for a whole lamb,
it shall join its closest neighbor in obtaining one;
the lamb shall be divided in proportion to the number of people who eat of it.

[⁵Your lamb shall be without blemish, a year-old male;
you may take it from the sheep or from the goats.
⁶You shall keep it until the fourteenth day of this month;
then the whole assembled congregation of Israel shall slaughter it at twilight.
⁷They shall take some of the blood and put it on the two doorposts
and the lintel of the houses in which they eat it.
⁸They shall eat the lamb that same night;
they shall eat it roasted over the fire
with unleavened bread and bitter herbs.
⁹Do not eat any of it raw or boiled in water,
but roasted over the fire, with its head, legs, and inner organs.
¹⁰You shall let none of it remain until the morning;
anything that remains until the morning you shall burn.]

¹¹This is how you shall eat it:
your loins girded, your sandals on your feet, and your staff in your hand;
and you shall eat it hurriedly.
It is the passover of the LORD.
¹²For I will pass through the land of Egypt that night,
and I will strike down every firstborn in the land of Egypt,
both human beings and animals;
on all the gods of Egypt I will execute judgments:
I am the LORD.
¹³The blood shall be a sign for you on the houses where you live: ▸

FIRST READING
This is God's instructional introduction of the Seder for Moses and Aaron and all the people (at which meal, more than a thousand years later, Jesus would instruct the Twelve in the meal of remembrance we now call holy communion). In preparation, look carefully at the division of the lines of texts. Not every line ought to end with a pause. It is of particular importance that the sentences are clearly communicated. That's especially critical for those detailing the preparation of the lamb in verses 5–10; it is a recipe, after all. Three simple statements stand out, and a good reading will help the hearer focus on them: Verse 11b: "It is the passover of the LORD." Verse 12b: "I am the LORD." Verse 14a: "This day shall be a day of remembrance for you." Kick those up a notch!

when I see the blood, I will pass over you,
and no plague shall destroy you when I strike the land of Egypt.
[14]This day shall be a day of remembrance for you.
You shall celebrate it as a festival to the LORD;
throughout your generations you shall observe it as a perpetual ordinance.

The word of the Lord.   *or*   Word of God, word of life.

PSALMODY: Psalm 116:1-2, 12-19

SECOND READING: 1 Corinthians 11:23-26

A reading from First Corinthians.

[23]For I received from the Lord what I also handed on to you,
that the Lord Jesus on the night when he was betrayed
took a loaf of bread,
[24]and when he had given thanks, he broke it and said,
"This is my body that is for you.
Do this in remembrance of me."
[25]In the same way he took the cup also, after supper, saying,
"This cup is the new covenant in my blood.
Do this, as often as you drink it, in remembrance of me."

[26]For as often as you eat this bread and drink the cup,
you proclaim the Lord's death until he comes.

The word of the Lord.   *or*   Word of God, word of life.

SECOND READING
This is a night like no other. These are the words of institution of the Lord's supper. In Latin they are simply referred to as "the words" (verba). This is a most magnificent summary, not only of the *what* of the meal ("my body . . . for you," "my blood") but of the *why*: ("Do this . . . in remembrance of me," " . . . proclaim the Lord's death until he comes"). The reading calls for both a sense of reverence and a sense of mystery.

GOSPEL: John 13:1-17, 31b-35

The holy gospel according to John.

¹Now before the festival of the Passover,
Jesus knew that his hour had come to depart from this world
and go to the Father.
Having loved his own who were in the world,
he loved them to the end.
²The devil had already put it into the heart of Judas son of Simon Iscariot
to betray him.

And during supper ³Jesus,
knowing that the Father had given all things into his hands,
and that he had come from God and was going to God,
⁴got up from the table,
took off his outer robe, and tied a towel around himself.
⁵Then he poured water into a basin
and began to wash the disciples' feet
and to wipe them with the towel that was tied around him.
⁶He came to Simon Peter, who said to him,
"Lord, are you going to wash my feet?"
⁷Jesus answered,
"You do not know now what I am doing,
but later you will understand."
⁸Peter said to him,
"You will never wash my feet."
Jesus answered,
"Unless I wash you, you have no share with me."
⁹Simon Peter said to him,
"Lord, not my feet only but also my hands and my head!"
¹⁰Jesus said to him,
"One who has bathed does not need to wash, except for the feet,
but is entirely clean.
And you are clean, though not all of you."
¹¹For he knew who was to betray him;
for this reason he said, "Not all of you are clean."

¹²After he had washed their feet, had put on his robe,
and had returned to the table, he said to them,
"Do you know what I have done to you? ▸

GOSPEL
The power of the gospel is diminished by too few pauses in most readings in the assembly. This reading cries out for substantive pauses between verses 2a and 2b, verses 11 and 12, verses 12 and 13, verses 17 and 31b, and verses 33 and 34. The scene will grow in vividness if the reader allows a moment for Jesus to move from one part of the room to another—from one activity to another—and if the reader allows time for thoughts to form in the mind of our Lord.

¹³You call me Teacher and Lord—
and you are right, for that is what I am.
¹⁴So if I, your Lord and Teacher, have washed your feet,
you also ought to wash one another's feet.
¹⁵For I have set you an example,
that you also should do as I have done to you.
¹⁶Very truly, I tell you,
servants are not greater than their master,
nor are messengers greater than the one who sent them.
¹⁷If you know these things,
you are blessed if you do them.

³¹ᵇ"Now the Son of Man has been glorified,
and God has been glorified in him.
³²If God has been glorified in him,
God will also glorify him in himself and will glorify him at once.
³³Little children, I am with you only a little longer.
You will look for me;
and as I said to the Jews so now I say to you,
'Where I am going, you cannot come.'

³⁴"I give you a new commandment,
that you love one another.
Just as I have loved you, you also should love one another.
³⁵By this everyone will know that you are my disciples,
if you have love for one another."

The gospel of the Lord.

✝ Good Friday

FIRST READING: Isaiah 52:13—53:12

A reading from Isaiah.

[13]See, my servant shall prosper;
   he shall be exalted and lifted up,
   and shall be very high.
[14]Just as there were many who were astonished at him
   —so marred was his appearance, beyond human semblance,
   and his form beyond that of mortals—
[15]so he shall startle many nations;
   kings shall shut their mouths because of him;
for that which had not been told them they shall see,
   and that which they had not heard they shall contemplate.

[53:1]Who has believed what we have heard?
   And to whom has the arm of the LORD been revealed?
[2]For he grew up before him like a young plant,
   and like a root out of dry ground;
he had no form or majesty that we should look at him,
   nothing in his appearance that we should desire him.
[3]He was despised and rejected by others;
   a man of suffering and acquainted with infirmity;
and as one from whom others hide their faces
   he was despised, and we held him of no account.

[4]Surely he has borne our infirmities
   and carried our diseases;
yet we accounted him stricken,
   struck down by God, and afflicted.
[5]But he was wounded for our transgressions,
   crushed for our iniquities;
upon him was the punishment that made us whole,
   and by his bruises we are healed.
[6]All we like sheep have gone astray;
   we have all turned to our own way,
and the LORD has laid on him
   the iniquity of us all. ▸

FIRST READING   *Isaiah = eye-ZAY-uh*
A thoughtful, contemplative reading will most help the assembly. Allow a depth of sorrow, of mystery, of wonder to permeate the reading.

⁷He was oppressed, and he was afflicted,
    yet he did not open his mouth;
like a lamb that is led to the slaughter,
    and like a sheep that before its shearers is silent,
    so he did not open his mouth.
⁸By a perversion of justice he was taken away.
    Who could have imagined his future?
For he was cut off from the land of the living,
    stricken for the transgression of my people.
⁹They made his grave with the wicked
    and his tomb with the rich,
although he had done no violence,
    and there was no deceit in his mouth.

¹⁰Yet it was the will of the LORD to crush him with pain.
When you make his life an offering for sin,
    he shall see his offspring, and shall prolong his days;
through him the will of the LORD shall prosper.
    ¹¹Out of his anguish he shall see light;
he shall find satisfaction through his knowledge.
    The righteous one, my servant, shall make many righteous,
    and he shall bear their iniquities.
¹²Therefore I will allot him a portion with the great,
    and he shall divide the spoil with the strong;
because he poured out himself to death,
    and was numbered with the transgressors;
yet he bore the sin of many,
    and made intercession for the transgressors.

The word of the Lord.   *or*   Word of God, word of life.

PSALMODY: Psalm 22

SECOND READING: Hebrews 10:16-25

Or Hebrews 4:14-16; 5:7-9, following

A reading from Hebrews.

⌈After the Holy Spirit says,⌉
  16"This is the covenant that I will make with them
  after those days, says the Lord:
  I will put my laws in their hearts,
  and I will write them on their minds,"
17he also adds,
  "I will remember their sins and their lawless deeds no more."
18Where there is forgiveness of these,
there is no longer any offering for sin.

19Therefore, my friends,
since we have confidence to enter the sanctuary by the blood of Jesus,
20by the new and living way that he opened for us through the curtain
(that is, through his flesh),
21and since we have a great priest over the house of God,
22let us approach with a true heart in full assurance of faith,
with our hearts sprinkled clean from an evil conscience
and our bodies washed with pure water.
23Let us hold fast to the confession of our hope without wavering,
for he who has promised is faithful.
24And let us consider how to provoke one another to love and good deeds,
25not neglecting to meet together, as is the habit of some,
but encouraging one another,
and all the more as you see the Day approaching.

The word of the Lord.   *or*   Word of God, word of life.

SECOND READING (Hebrews 10)
Allow the initial quotations "settling time" in the mind of the hearer, and follow them with a fervent invitation to "enter" "approach" "hold fast" and "consider how to provoke one another to love and good deeds." Read fervently.

OR: Hebrews 4:14-16; 5:7-9

A reading from Hebrews.

¹⁴Since we have a great high priest
who has passed through the heavens,
Jesus, the Son of God,
let us hold fast to our confession.
¹⁵For we do not have a high priest
who is unable to sympathize with our weaknesses,
but we have one who in every respect has been tested as we are,
yet without sin.
¹⁶Let us therefore approach the throne of grace with boldness,
so that we may receive mercy and find grace
to help in time of need.

⁵ː⁷In the days of his flesh, Jesus offered up prayers and supplications,
with loud cries and tears,
to the one who was able to save him from death,
and he was heard because of his reverent submission.
⁸Although he was a Son,
he learned obedience through what he suffered;
⁹and having been made perfect,
he became the source of eternal salvation for all who obey him.

The word of the Lord.   *or*   Word of God, word of life.

SECOND READING (Hebrews 4, 5)
Genuine warmth in this invitation (verses 14-16) to "hold fast to our confession" will be welcome in the darkness of this hour of contemplation. The invitation is actually the first of two little readings. The second (verses 5:7-9) is a hopeful synopsis of the agonies Christ endured and on which we are focused on this day. Separate the two with a solid pause. The hour calls for a muted, contemplative voice.

GOSPEL: John 18:1—19:42

The passion of our Lord Jesus Christ according to John.

¹ ⌈Jesus⌉ went out with his disciples across the Kidron valley
to a place where there was a garden, which he and his disciples entered.
²Now Judas, who betrayed him, also knew the place,
because Jesus often met there with his disciples.
³So Judas brought a detachment of soldiers together
with police from the chief priests and the Pharisees,
and they came there with lanterns and torches and weapons.
⁴Then Jesus, knowing all that was to happen to him,
came forward and asked them,
"Whom are you looking for?"
⁵They answered, "Jesus of Nazareth."
Jesus replied, "I am he."
Judas, who betrayed him, was standing with them.
⁶When Jesus said to them, "I am he,"
they stepped back and fell to the ground.
⁷Again he asked them, "Whom are you looking for?"
 And they said, "Jesus of Nazareth."
⁸Jesus answered, "I told you that I am he.
So if you are looking for me, let these men go."
⁹This was to fulfill the word that he had spoken,
"I did not lose a single one of those whom you gave me."
¹⁰Then Simon Peter, who had a sword, drew it,
struck the high priest's slave, and cut off his right ear.
The slave's name was Malchus.
¹¹Jesus said to Peter,
"Put your sword back into its sheath.
Am I not to drink the cup that the Father has given me?"

¹²So the soldiers, their officer, and the Jewish police
arrested Jesus and bound him.
¹³First they took him to Annas,
who was the father-in-law of Caiaphas, the high priest that year.
¹⁴Caiaphas was the one who had advised the Jews
that it was better to have one person die for the people. ▸

GOSPEL *Malchus = MAL-kus Caiaphas = KAY-uh-fus Barabbas = buh-RAB-us Gabbatha = GAB-uh-thuh hyssop = HISS-up Arimathea = ar-ih-muh-THEE-uh*
There is no substitute for investing oneself in prayer and in devotional consideration of John's telling of the passion during the days of Holy Week—nor for reading the gospel more than once, aloud. The assembly has gathered expressly to hear these words. There is no hurry. However the various episodes will require varied approaches in pace and volume. Consider pausing, with folded hands, and stepping back from the reading desk for a moment following the description of our Lord's death in 19:30.

¹⁵Simon Peter and another disciple followed Jesus.
Since that disciple was known to the high priest,
he went with Jesus into the courtyard of the high priest,
¹⁶but Peter was standing outside at the gate.
So the other disciple, who was known to the high priest,
went out, spoke to the woman who guarded the gate,
and brought Peter in.
¹⁷The woman said to Peter,
"You are not also one of this man's disciples, are you?"
He said, "I am not."
¹⁸Now the slaves and the police had made a charcoal fire because it was cold,
and they were standing around it and warming themselves.
Peter also was standing with them and warming himself.

¹⁹Then the high priest questioned Jesus about his disciples
and about his teaching.
²⁰Jesus answered, "I have spoken openly to the world;
I have always taught in synagogues and in the temple,
where all the Jews come together.
I have said nothing in secret.
²¹Why do you ask me?
Ask those who heard what I said to them; they know what I said."
²²When he had said this,
one of the police standing nearby struck Jesus on the face, saying,
"Is that how you answer the high priest?"
²³Jesus answered, "If I have spoken wrongly, testify to the wrong.
But if I have spoken rightly, why do you strike me?"
²⁴Then Annas sent him bound to Caiaphas the high priest.

²⁵Now Simon Peter was standing and warming himself.
They asked him, "You are not also one of his disciples, are you?"
He denied it and said, "I am not."
²⁶One of the slaves of the high priest,
a relative of the man whose ear Peter had cut off, asked,
"Did I not see you in the garden with him?"
²⁷Again Peter denied it, and at that moment the cock crowed.

²⁸Then they took Jesus from Caiaphas to Pilate's headquarters.
It was early in the morning.
They themselves did not enter the headquarters,
so as to avoid ritual defilement
and to be able to eat the Passover.

²⁹So Pilate went out to them and said,
"What accusation do you bring against this man?"
³⁰They answered, "If this man were not a criminal,
we would not have handed him over to you."
³¹Pilate said to them,
"Take him yourselves and judge him according to your law."
The Jews replied,
"We are not permitted to put anyone to death."
³²(This was to fulfill what Jesus had said
when he indicated the kind of death he was to die.)

³³Then Pilate entered the headquarters again,
summoned Jesus, and asked him,
"Are you the King of the Jews?"
³⁴Jesus answered,
"Do you ask this on your own, or did others tell you about me?"
³⁵Pilate replied, "I am not a Jew, am I?
Your own nation and the chief priests have handed you over to me.
What have you done?"
³⁶Jesus answered,
"My kingdom is not from this world.
If my kingdom were from this world,
my followers would be fighting
to keep me from being handed over to the Jews.
But as it is, my kingdom is not from here."
³⁷Pilate asked him, "So you are a king?"
Jesus answered,
"You say that I am a king.
For this I was born, and for this I came into the world,
to testify to the truth.
Everyone who belongs to the truth listens to my voice."
³⁸Pilate asked him, "What is truth?"

After he had said this, he went out to the Jews again and told them,
"I find no case against him.
³⁹But you have a custom that I release someone for you at the Passover.
Do you want me to release for you the King of the Jews?"
⁴⁰They shouted in reply,
"Not this man, but Barabbas!"
Now Barabbas was a bandit. ▸

^{19:1}Then Pilate took Jesus and had him flogged.
²And the soldiers wove a crown of thorns and put it on his head,
and they dressed him in a purple robe.
³They kept coming up to him, saying,
"Hail, King of the Jews!" and striking him on the face.
⁴Pilate went out again and said to them,
"Look, I am bringing him out to you
to let you know that I find no case against him."
⁵So Jesus came out, wearing the crown of thorns and the purple robe.
Pilate said to them, "Here is the man!"
⁶When the chief priests and the police saw him, they shouted,
"Crucify him! Crucify him!"
Pilate said to them,
"Take him yourselves and crucify him; I find no case against him."
⁷The Jews answered him,
"We have a law, and according to that law
he ought to die because he has claimed to be the Son of God."

⁸Now when Pilate heard this, he was more afraid than ever.
⁹He entered his headquarters again and asked Jesus,
"Where are you from?"
But Jesus gave him no answer.
¹⁰Pilate therefore said to him,
"Do you refuse to speak to me?
Do you not know that I have power to release you, and power to crucify you?"
¹¹Jesus answered him,
"You would have no power over me unless it had been given you from above;
therefore the one who handed me over to you is guilty of a greater sin."
¹²From then on Pilate tried to release him,
but the Jews cried out,
"If you release this man, you are no friend of the emperor.
Everyone who claims to be a king sets himself against the emperor."

¹³When Pilate heard these words, he brought Jesus outside
and sat on the judge's bench at a place called The Stone Pavement,
or in Hebrew Gabbatha.
¹⁴Now it was the day of Preparation for the Passover; and it was about noon.
He said to the Jews, "Here is your King!"
¹⁵They cried out,
"Away with him! Away with him! Crucify him!"
Pilate asked them, "Shall I crucify your King?"

The chief priests answered,
"We have no king but the emperor."
[16]Then he handed him over to them to be crucified.

So they took Jesus; [17]and carrying the cross by himself,
he went out to what is called The Place of the Skull,
which in Hebrew is called Golgotha.
[18]There they crucified him,
and with him two others, one on either side, with Jesus between them.
[19]Pilate also had an inscription written and put on the cross.
It read, "Jesus of Nazareth, the King of the Jews."
[20]Many of the Jews read this inscription,
because the place where Jesus was crucified was near the city;
and it was written in Hebrew, in Latin, and in Greek.
[21]Then the chief priests of the Jews said to Pilate,
"Do not write, 'The King of the Jews,' but,
'This man said, I am King of the Jews.'"
[22]Pilate answered,
"What I have written I have written."
[23]When the soldiers had crucified Jesus,
they took his clothes and divided them into four parts, one for each soldier.
They also took his tunic;
now the tunic was seamless, woven in one piece from the top.
[24]So they said to one another,
"Let us not tear it, but cast lots for it to see who will get it."
This was to fulfill what the scripture says,
    "They divided my clothes among themselves,
    and for my clothing they cast lots."
[25]And that is what the soldiers did.
Meanwhile, standing near the cross of Jesus were his mother,
and his mother's sister, Mary the wife of Clopas, and Mary Magdalene.
[26]When Jesus saw his mother
and the disciple whom he loved standing beside her,
he said to his mother, "Woman, here is your son."
[27]Then he said to the disciple, "Here is your mother."
And from that hour the disciple took her into his own home.

[28]After this, when Jesus knew that all was now finished,
he said (in order to fulfill the scripture),
"I am thirsty." ▸

²⁹A jar full of sour wine was standing there.
So they put a sponge full of the wine on a branch of hyssop
and held it to his mouth.
³⁰When Jesus had received the wine, he said,
"It is finished."
Then he bowed his head and gave up his spirit.

³¹Since it was the day of Preparation,
the Jews did not want the bodies left on the cross during the sabbath,
especially because that sabbath was a day of great solemnity.
So they asked Pilate to have the legs of the crucified men broken
and the bodies removed.
³²Then the soldiers came and broke the legs of the first
and of the other who had been crucified with him.
³³But when they came to Jesus and saw that he was already dead,
they did not break his legs.
³⁴Instead, one of the soldiers pierced his side with a spear,
and at once blood and water came out.
³⁵(He who saw this has testified so that you also may believe.
His testimony is true, and he knows that he tells the truth.)
³⁶These things occurred so that the scripture might be fulfilled,
"None of his bones shall be broken."
³⁷And again another passage of scripture says,
"They will look on the one whom they have pierced."

³⁸After these things, Joseph of Arimathea, who was a disciple of Jesus,
though a secret one because of his fear of the Jews,
asked Pilate to let him take away the body of Jesus.
Pilate gave him permission; so he came and removed his body.
³⁹Nicodemus, who had at first come to Jesus by night, also came,
bringing a mixture of myrrh and aloes, weighing about a hundred pounds.
⁴⁰They took the body of Jesus and wrapped it with the spices in linen cloths,
according to the burial custom of the Jews.
⁴¹Now there was a garden in the place where he was crucified,
and in the garden there was a new tomb in which no one had ever been laid.
⁴²And so, because it was the Jewish day of Preparation,
and the tomb was nearby, they laid Jesus there.

The gospel of the Lord.

Saturday in Holy Week

(for services other than the Vigil of Easter)

FIRST READING: Job 14:1-14
Or Lamentations 3:1-9, 19-24, following

A reading from Job.

¹"A mortal, born of woman, few of days and full of trouble,
²comes up like a flower and withers,
   flees like a shadow and does not last.
³Do you fix your eyes on such a one?
   Do you bring me into judgment with you?
⁴Who can bring a clean thing out of an unclean?
   No one can.
⁵Since their days are determined,
   and the number of their months is known to you,
   and you have appointed the bounds that they cannot pass,
⁶look away from them, and desist,
   that they may enjoy, like laborers, their days.

⁷"For there is hope for a tree,
   if it is cut down,that it will sprout again,
   and that its shoots will not cease.
⁸Though its root grows old in the earth,
   and its stump dies in the ground,
⁹yet at the scent of water it will bud
   and put forth branches like a young plant.
¹⁰But mortals die, and are laid low;
   humans expire, and where are they?
¹¹As waters fail from a lake,
   and a river wastes away and dries up,
¹²so mortals lie down and do not rise again;
   until the heavens are no more, they will not awake
   or be roused out of their sleep.
¹³O that you would hide me in Sheol,
   that you would conceal me until your wrath is past,
   that you would appoint me a set time, and remember me!
¹⁴If mortals die, will they live again?
   All the days of my service I would wait
   until my release should come."

The word of the Lord.   *or*   Word of God, word of life.

FIRST READING (Job) *Sheol = sheh-OHL*
Job's address to God will be unfamiliar to many in the assembly and, coming as it does in the middle of a longer story, it will not be easily understood. It will profit from careful preparation. There is a sense of deep despair that ought to saturate any reading of this poem.

OR: Lamentations 3:1-9, 19-24

A reading from Lamentations.

¹I am one who has seen affliction
    under the rod of God's wrath;
²he has driven and brought me
    into darkness without any light;
³against me alone he turns his hand,
    again and again, all day long.

⁴He has made my flesh and my skin waste away,
    and broken my bones;
⁵he has besieged and enveloped me
    with bitterness and tribulation;
⁶he has made me sit in darkness
    like the dead of long ago.

⁷He has walled me about so that I cannot escape;
    he has put heavy chains on me;
⁸though I call and cry for help,
    he shuts out my prayer;
⁹he has blocked my ways with hewn stones,
    he has made my paths crooked.

¹⁹The thought of my affliction and my homelessness
    is wormwood and gall!
²⁰My soul continually thinks of it
    and is bowed down within me.
²¹But this I call to mind,
    and therefore I have hope:

²²The steadfast love of the LORD never ceases,
    his mercies never come to an end;
²³they are new every morning;
    great is your faithfulness.
²⁴"The LORD is my portion," says my soul,
    "therefore I will hope in him."

The word of the Lord.   *or*   Word of God, word of life.

FIRST READING (Lamentations)
The tone of utter despair that permeates the first two-thirds of the text turns suddenly between verses 20 and 21. That turning demands a substantial pause. Attempt to give voice to the glimmer of hope in verses 22–24. A tentative note is the right note for this day.

PSALMODY: Psalm 31:1-4, 15-16

SECOND READING: 1 Peter 4:1-8

A reading from First Peter.

¹Since therefore Christ suffered in the flesh,
arm yourselves also with the same intention
(for whoever has suffered in the flesh has finished with sin),
²so as to live for the rest of your earthly life
no longer by human desires but by the will of God.
³You have already spent enough time in doing what the Gentiles like to do,
living in licentiousness, passions, drunkenness,
revels, carousing, and lawless idolatry.
⁴They are surprised that you no longer join them
in the same excesses of dissipation, and so they blaspheme.

⁵But they will have to give an accounting to him who stands ready
to judge the living and the dead.
⁶For this is the reason the gospel was proclaimed even to the dead,
so that, though they had been judged in the flesh as everyone is judged,
they might live in the spirit as God does.

⁷The end of all things is near;
therefore be serious and discipline yourselves for the sake of your prayers.
⁸Above all, maintain constant love for one another,
for love covers a multitude of sins.

The word of the Lord.   *or*   Word of God, word of life.

GOSPEL: Matthew 27:57-66
OR JOHN 19:38-42, following

The holy gospel according to Matthew.

⁵⁷When it was evening,
there came a rich man from Arimathea, named Joseph,
who was also a disciple of Jesus.
⁵⁸He went to Pilate and asked for the body of Jesus;
then Pilate ordered it to be given to him. ▸

SECOND READING   *licentiousness = ly-SEN-chus-ness*
This bit of instruction from the pastor to the people has a considered edge to it. Do not beat the hearers over the head, but give them a sense of the author's earnest admonition. Verse 6 is a jewel and the clear reason for the text's inclusion in the lectionary. Do not allow it to slip by unnoticed.

GOSPEL (Matthew)   *Arimathea = ar-ih-muh-THEE-uh*
The compassion and caring of Joseph of Arimathea is part one of three parts in this gospel. The picture of the two Marys, alone, opposite the tomb is the second and most poignant. Allow verse 61 to stand absolutely alone. The pathos is raw. Pause significantly before and after that sentence. The futile preparation of the chief priests and Pharisees is part three and sharpens the appetite for the gospel of the Resurrection of Our Lord.

⁵⁹So Joseph took the body and wrapped it in a clean linen cloth
⁶⁰and laid it in his own new tomb, which he had hewn in the rock.
He then rolled a great stone to the door of the tomb and went away.
⁶¹Mary Magdalene and the other Mary were there, sitting opposite the tomb.

⁶²The next day, that is, after the day of Preparation,
the chief priests and the Pharisees gathered before Pilate ⁶³and said,
"Sir, we remember what that impostor said while he was still alive,
'After three days I will rise again.'
⁶⁴Therefore command the tomb to be made secure until the third day;
otherwise his disciples may go and steal him away,
and tell the people, 'He has been raised from the dead,'
and the last deception would be worse than the first."
⁶⁵Pilate said to them,
"You have a guard of soldiers;
go, make it as secure as you can."
⁶⁶So they went with the guard and made the tomb secure by sealing the stone.

The gospel of the Lord.

OR: John 19:38-42

The holy gospel according to John.

³⁸Joseph of Arimathea, who was a disciple of Jesus,
though a secret one because of his fear of the Jews,
asked Pilate to let him take away the body of Jesus.
Pilate gave him permission; so he came and removed his body.
³⁹Nicodemus, who had at first come to Jesus by night, also came,
bringing a mixture of myrrh and aloes, weighing about a hundred pounds.
⁴⁰They took the body of Jesus
and wrapped it with the spices in linen cloths,
according to the burial custom of the Jews.
⁴¹Now there was a garden in the place where he was crucified,
and in the garden there was a new tomb in which no one had ever been laid.
⁴²And so, because it was the Jewish day of Preparation,
and the tomb was nearby, they laid Jesus there.

The gospel of the Lord.

GOSPEL (JOHN) *Arimathea = ar-ih-muh-THEE-uh*
A simple, solemn, and somber tone will help the assembly feel the moment.

Resurrection of Our Lord

Vigil of Easter

FIRST READING: Genesis 1:1—2:4a

CREATION

A reading from Genesis.

[1]In the beginning when God created the heavens and the earth,
[2]the earth was a formless void and darkness covered the face of the deep,
while a wind from God swept over the face of the waters.
[3]Then God said,
"Let there be light"; and there was light.
[4]And God saw that the light was good;
and God separated the light from the darkness.
[5]God called the light Day, and the darkness he called Night.
And there was evening and there was morning, the first day.

[6]And God said,
"Let there be a dome in the midst of the waters,
and let it separate the waters from the waters."
[7]So God made the dome
and separated the waters that were under the dome
from the waters that were above the dome.
And it was so.
[8]God called the dome Sky.
And there was evening and there was morning, the second day.

[9]And God said,
"Let the waters under the sky be gathered together into one place,
and let the dry land appear."
And it was so.
[10]God called the dry land Earth,
and the waters that were gathered together he called Seas.
And God saw that it was good.
[11]Then God said,
"Let the earth put forth vegetation: plants yielding seed,
and fruit trees of every kind on earth that bear fruit with the seed in it."
And it was so. ▸

---

1 GENESIS 1:1—2:4a
Read the story as though telling it for the first time to those who had never heard it. Bring to the reading every available ounce of energy. Take delight in God's every choice for names for the dome, the dry land, the waters and the lights. Help the assembly marvel at the wonder of it all.

¹²The earth brought forth vegetation:
plants yielding seed of every kind,
and trees of every kind bearing fruit with the seed in it.
And God saw that it was good.
¹³And there was evening and there was morning, the third day.

¹⁴And God said,
"Let there be lights in the dome of the sky
to separate the day from the night;
and let them be for signs and for seasons and for days and years,
¹⁵and let them be lights in the dome of the sky to give light upon the earth."
And it was so.
¹⁶God made the two great lights—the greater light to rule the day
and the lesser light to rule the night—and the stars.
¹⁷God set them in the dome of the sky to give light upon the earth,
¹⁸to rule over the day and over the night,
and to separate the light from the darkness.
And God saw that it was good.
¹⁹And there was evening and there was morning, the fourth day.

²⁰And God said,
"Let the waters bring forth swarms of living creatures,
and let birds fly above the earth across the dome of the sky."
²¹So God created the great sea monsters
and every living creature that moves,
of every kind, with which the waters swarm,
and every winged bird of every kind.
And God saw that it was good.
²²God blessed them, saying,
"Be fruitful and multiply and fill the waters in the seas,
and let birds multiply on the earth."
²³And there was evening and there was morning, the fifth day.

²⁴And God said,
"Let the earth bring forth living creatures of every kind:
cattle and creeping things and wild animals of the earth of every kind."
And it was so.
²⁵God made the wild animals of the earth of every kind,
and the cattle of every kind,
and everything that creeps upon the ground of every kind.
And God saw that it was good.

²⁶Then God said,
"Let us make humankind in our image, according to our likeness;
and let them have dominion over the fish of the sea,
and over the birds of the air,
and over the cattle, and over all the wild animals of the earth,
and over every creeping thing that creeps upon the earth."
    ²⁷So God created humankind in his image,
        in the image of God he created them;
        male and female he created them.
²⁸God blessed them, and God said to them,
"Be fruitful and multiply,
and fill the earth and subdue it;
and have dominion over the fish of the sea
and over the birds of the air
and over every living thing that moves upon the earth."
²⁹God said,
"See, I have given you every plant yielding seed
that is upon the face of all the earth,
and every tree with seed in its fruit;
you shall have them for food.
³⁰And to every beast of the earth,
and to every bird of the air,
and to everything that creeps on the earth,
everything that has the breath of life,
I have given every green plant for food."
And it was so.
³¹God saw everything that he had made, and indeed, it was very good.
And there was evening and there was morning, the sixth day.

²:¹Thus the heavens and the earth were finished, and all their multitude.
²And on the seventh day God finished the work that he had done,
and he rested on the seventh day from all the work that he had done.
³So God blessed the seventh day and hallowed it,
because on it God rested from all the work that he had done in creation.
⁴These are the generations of the heavens and the earth
when they were created.

The word of the Lord.   *or*   Word of God, word of life.

RESPONSE: Psalm 136:1-9, 23-26

SECOND READING: Genesis 7:1-5, 11-18; 8:6-18; 9:8-13
FLOOD

A reading from Genesis.

[1]The LORD said to Noah,
"Go into the ark, you and all your household,
for I have seen that you alone are righteous before me in this generation.
[2]Take with you seven pairs of all clean animals,
the male and its mate;
and a pair of the animals that are not clean,
the male and its mate;
[3]and seven pairs of the birds of the air also, male and female,
to keep their kind alive on the face of all the earth.
[4]For in seven days I will send rain on the earth
for forty days and forty nights;
and every living thing that I have made
I will blot out from the face of the ground."
[5]And Noah did all that the LORD had commanded him.

[11]In the six hundredth year of Noah's life,
in the second month, on the seventeenth day of the month,
on that day all the fountains of the great deep burst forth,
and the windows of the heavens were opened.
[12]The rain fell on the earth forty days and forty nights.
[13]On the very same day Noah with his sons,
Shem and Ham and Japheth,
and Noah's wife and the three wives of his sons entered the ark,
[14]they and every wild animal of every kind,
and all domestic animals of every kind,
and every creeping thing that creeps on the earth,
and every bird of every kind—every bird, every winged creature.
[15]They went into the ark with Noah,
two and two of all flesh in which there was the breath of life.
[16]And those that entered, male and female of all flesh,
went in as God had commanded him;
and the LORD shut him in.

---

2 GENESIS 7:1-5, 11-18; 8:6-18; 9:8-13 *Japheth = JAY-fith*
This is a cosmic event and demands a cosmic voice. Rarely has the assembly heard a reading that was "too loud" or "too slow." Every reader will do well to read half as fast and twice as loudly as first inclined.

[17]The flood continued forty days on the earth;
and the waters increased,
and bore up the ark, and it rose high above the earth.
[18]The waters swelled and increased greatly on the earth;
and the ark floated on the face of the waters.

[8:6]At the end of forty days
Noah opened the window of the ark that he had made
[7]and sent out the raven;
and it went to and fro until the waters were dried up from the earth.
[8]Then he sent out the dove from him,
to see if the waters had subsided from the face of the ground;
[9]but the dove found no place to set its foot,
and it returned to him to the ark,
for the waters were still on the face of the whole earth.
So he put out his hand and took it
and brought it into the ark with him.
[10]He waited another seven days,
and again he sent out the dove from the ark;
[11]and the dove came back to him in the evening,
and there in its beak was a freshly plucked olive leaf;
so Noah knew that the waters had subsided from the earth.
[12]Then he waited another seven days, and sent out the dove;
and it did not return to him any more.

[13]In the six hundred first year,
in the first month, on the first day of the month,
the waters were dried up from the earth;
and Noah removed the covering of the ark,
and looked, and saw that the face of the ground was drying.
[14]In the second month, on the twenty-seventh day of the month,
the earth was dry.
[15]Then God said to Noah,
[16]"Go out of the ark, you and your wife,
and your sons and your sons' wives with you.
[17]Bring out with you every living thing that is with you of all flesh—
birds and animals and every creeping thing that creeps on the earth—
so that they may abound on the earth,
and be fruitful and multiply on the earth."
[18]So Noah went out with his sons and his wife and his sons' wives. ▸

⁹:⁸Then God said to Noah and to his sons with him,

⁹"As for me,

I am establishing my covenant with you and your descendants after you,

¹⁰and with every living creature that is with you,

the birds, the domestic animals,

and every animal of the earth with you,

as many as came out of the ark.

¹¹I establish my covenant with you,

that never again shall all flesh be cut off by the waters of a flood,

and never again shall there be a flood to destroy the earth."

¹²God said,

"This is the sign of the covenant that I make

between me and you and every living creature that is with you,

for all future generations:

¹³I have set my bow in the clouds,

and it shall be a sign of the covenant between me and the earth."

The word of the Lord.   *or*   Word of God, word of life.

RESPONSE: Psalm 46

THIRD READING: Genesis 22:1-18
TESTING OF ABRAHAM

A reading from Genesis.

¹God tested Abraham.

He said to him, "Abraham!"

And he said, "Here I am."

² ⌈God⌉ said,

"Take your son, your only son Isaac, whom you love, and go to the land of

Moriah, and offer him there as a burnt offering

on one of the mountains that I shall show you."

³So Abraham rose early in the morning,

saddled his donkey, and took two of his young men with him,

and his son Isaac;

he cut the wood for the burnt offering,

and set out and went to the place in the distance that God had shown him.

---

3 GENESIS 22:1-18 *Moriah = moh-RY-uh*
Handle this horrific story with care. Allow the first sentence of verse 1 to stand as the headline for the account. A measured reading in volume and pace will help allow the natural tension to develop. Provide the voice of Abraham adequate uncertainty even when—especially when—his statements appear certain. The agony of a man caught between two great loves will emerge.

⁴On the third day Abraham looked up and saw the place far away.
⁵Then Abraham said to his young men,
"Stay here with the donkey;
the boy and I will go over there;
we will worship, and then we will come back to you."

⁶Abraham took the wood of the burnt offering
and laid it on his son Isaac,
and he himself carried the fire and the knife.
So the two of them walked on together.
⁷Isaac said to his father Abraham, "Father!"
And he said, "Here I am, my son."
He said, "The fire and the wood are here,
but where is the lamb for a burnt offering?"
⁸Abraham said,
"God himself will provide the lamb for a burnt offering, my son."
So the two of them walked on together.

⁹When they came to the place that God had shown him,
Abraham built an altar there and laid the wood in order.
He bound his son Isaac,
and laid him on the altar, on top of the wood.
¹⁰Then Abraham reached out his hand
and took the knife to kill his son.
¹¹But the angel of the LORD called to him from heaven, and said,
"Abraham, Abraham!"
And he said, "Here I am."
¹²He said,
"Do not lay your hand on the boy or do anything to him;
for now I know that you fear God,
since you have not withheld your son, your only son, from me."

¹³And Abraham looked up and saw a ram, caught in a thicket by its horns.
Abraham went and took the ram
and offered it up as a burnt offering instead of his son.
¹⁴So Abraham called that place "The LORD will provide";
as it is said to this day,
"On the mount of the LORD it shall be provided." ▶

¹⁵The angel of the LORD called to Abraham a second time from heaven, ¹⁶and said,

"By myself I have sworn, says the LORD:
Because you have done this,
and have not withheld your son, your only son,
¹⁷I will indeed bless you,
and I will make your offspring as numerous as the stars of heaven
and as the sand that is on the seashore.
And your offspring shall possess the gate of their enemies,
¹⁸and by your offspring shall all the nations of the earth
gain blessing for themselves,
because you have obeyed my voice."

The word of the Lord.   *or*   Word of God, word of life.

RESPONSE: Psalm 16

FOURTH READING: Exodus 14:10-31; 15:20-21
DELIVERANCE AT THE RED SEA

A reading from Exodus.

¹⁰As Pharaoh drew near, the Israelites looked back,
and there were the Egyptians advancing on them.
In great fear the Israelites cried out to the LORD.
¹¹They said to Moses,
"Was it because there were no graves in Egypt
that you have taken us away to die in the wilderness?
What have you done to us, bringing us out of Egypt?
¹²Is this not the very thing we told you in Egypt,
'Let us alone and let us serve the Egyptians'?
For it would have been better for us to serve the Egyptians
than to die in the wilderness."
¹³But Moses said to the people,
"Do not be afraid, stand firm,
and see the deliverance that the LORD will accomplish for you today;
for the Egyptians whom you see today you shall never see again.

---

4   EXODUS 14:10-31; 15:20-21   *Pharaoh = FAIR-oh*
This reading may benefit from two very different sounds. Verses 10-18 might effectively be read as though to be heard over the sound of a raging river, a hysterical mob of escapees, and the chariots, horses, and battle cries of an approaching army. In verses 19-29 the sound might shift to that of an intense narration of the action by an observer. In any event, do not attempt to tame this wild account of the power of God.

¹⁴The LORD will fight for you,
 and you have only to keep still."

¹⁵Then the LORD said to Moses,
"Why do you cry out to me?
Tell the Israelites to go forward.
¹⁶But you lift up your staff,
and stretch out your hand over the sea and divide it,
that the Israelites may go into the sea on dry ground.
¹⁷Then I will harden the hearts of the Egyptians
so that they will go in after them;
and so I will gain glory for myself over Pharaoh and all his army,
his chariots, and his chariot drivers.
¹⁸And the Egyptians shall know that I am the LORD,
when I have gained glory for myself over Pharaoh,
his chariots, and his chariot drivers."

¹⁹The angel of God who was going before the Israelite army moved
and went behind them;
and the pillar of cloud moved from in front of them
and took its place behind them.
²⁰It came between the army of Egypt and the army of Israel.
And so the cloud was there with the darkness,
and it lit up the night;
one did not come near the other all night.

²¹Then Moses stretched out his hand over the sea.
The LORD drove the sea back by a strong east wind all night,
and turned the sea into dry land;
and the waters were divided.
²²The Israelites went into the sea on dry ground,
the waters forming a wall for them on their right and on their left.
²³The Egyptians pursued, and went into the sea after them,
all of Pharaoh's horses, chariots, and chariot drivers.
²⁴At the morning watch
the LORD in the pillar of fire and cloud
looked down upon the Egyptian army,
and threw the Egyptian army into panic.
²⁵He clogged their chariot wheels so that they turned with difficulty.
The Egyptians said,
"Let us flee from the Israelites,
for the LORD is fighting for them against Egypt." ▸

[26]Then the Lord said to Moses,
"Stretch out your hand over the sea,
so that the water may come back upon the Egyptians,
upon their chariots and chariot drivers."
[27]So Moses stretched out his hand over the sea,
and at dawn the sea returned to its normal depth.
As the Egyptians fled before it,
the Lord tossed the Egyptians into the sea.
[28]The waters returned and covered the chariots and the chariot drivers,
the entire army of Pharaoh that had followed them into the sea;
not one of them remained.
[29]But the Israelites walked on dry ground through the sea,
the waters forming a wall for them on their right and on their left.

[30]Thus the Lord saved Israel that day from the Egyptians;
and Israel saw the Egyptians dead on the seashore.
[31]Israel saw the great work that the Lord did against the Egyptians.
So the people feared the Lord
and believed in the Lord and in his servant Moses.

[15:20]Then the prophet Miriam, Aaron's sister, took a tambourine in her hand;
and all the women went out after her with tambourines and with dancing.
[21]And Miriam sang to them:
　　"Sing to the Lord, for he has triumphed gloriously;
　　horse and rider he has thrown into the sea."

The word of the Lord.　　　　*or*　　　　Word of God, word of life.

RESPONSE: Exodus 15:1b-13, 17-18

FIFTH READING: Isaiah 55:1-11
SALVATION FREELY OFFERED TO ALL

A reading from Isaiah.

[1]Ho, everyone who thirsts,
    come to the waters;
and you that have no money,
    come, buy and eat!
Come, buy wine and milk
    without money and without price.
[2]Why do you spend your money for that which is not bread,
    and your labor for that which does not satisfy?
Listen carefully to me, and eat what is good,
    and delight yourselves in rich food.

[3]Incline your ear, and come to me;
    listen, so that you may live.
I will make with you an everlasting covenant,
    my steadfast, sure love for David.
[4]See, I made him a witness to the peoples,
    a leader and commander for the peoples.
[5]See, you shall call nations that you do not know,
    and nations that do not know you shall run to you,
because of the LORD your God, the Holy One of Israel,
    for he has glorified you.

[6]Seek the LORD while he may be found,
    call upon him while he is near;
[7]let the wicked forsake their way,
    and the unrighteous their thoughts;
let them return to the LORD, that he may have mercy on them,
    and to our God, for he will abundantly pardon.
[8]For my thoughts are not your thoughts,
    nor are your ways my ways, says the LORD.
[9]For as the heavens are higher than the earth,
    so are my ways higher than your ways
    and my thoughts than your thoughts.

[10]For as the rain and the snow come down from heaven,
    and do not return there until they have watered the earth, ▸

---

5 ISAIAH 55:1-11 *Isaiah = eye-ZAY-uh*
This is the voice of God. A diminutive "Ho" (verse 1) simply will not do. Bring all the energy and authority possible to the reading. Be alert to the danger lurking in verse 11b. The word at the end of the third line is not *propose* but *purpose*. It is used here as a verb, not a noun, but is pronounced the same.

making it bring forth and sprout,
  giving seed to the sower and bread to the eater,
¹¹so shall my word be that goes out from my mouth;
  it shall not return to me empty,
but it shall accomplish that which I purpose,
  and succeed in the thing for which I sent it.

The word of the Lord.   *or*   Word of God, word of life.

RESPONSE: Isaiah 12:2-6

SIXTH READING: Proverbs 8:1-8, 19-21; 9:4b-6
THE WISDOM OF GOD   *Alternate Reading: Baruch 3:9-15, 32—4:4 (p. 501)*

A reading from Proverbs.

¹Does not wisdom call,
  and does not understanding raise her voice?
²On the heights, beside the way,
  at the crossroads she takes her stand;
³beside the gates in front of the town,
  at the entrance of the portals she cries out:
⁴"To you, O people, I call,
  and my cry is to all that live.
⁵O simple ones, learn prudence;
  acquire intelligence, you who lack it.
⁶Hear, for I will speak noble things,
  and from my lips will come what is right;
⁷for my mouth will utter truth;
  wickedness is an abomination to my lips.
⁸All the words of my mouth are righteous;
  there is nothing twisted or crooked in them.

¹⁹"My fruit is better than gold, even fine gold,
  and my yield than choice silver.
²⁰I walk in the way of righteousness,
  along the paths of justice,

---

6 PROVERBS 8:1-8, 19-21; 9:4b-6
This is wisdom personified—literally. Picture wisdom as a woman calling out from various locations. Then give her voice and relish the poetic images she offers. Pay close attention to the punctuation, and allow it to establish the pace of each verse. More than most readings perhaps (in part because the images are poetic), this one will suffer badly from inadequate preparation.

²¹endowing with wealth those who love me,
and filling their treasuries."

^{9:4b}To those without sense she says,
⁵"Come, eat of my bread
and drink of the wine I have mixed.
⁶Lay aside immaturity, and live,
and walk in the way of insight."

The word of the Lord.   *or*   Word of God, word of life.

RESPONSE: Psalm 19

SEVENTH READING: Ezekiel 36:24-28
A NEW HEART AND A NEW SPIRIT

A reading from Ezekiel.

⌐Thus says the Lord GOD:⌐
²⁴I will take you from the nations,
and gather you from all the countries,
and bring you into your own land.
²⁵I will sprinkle clean water upon you,
and you shall be clean from all your uncleannesses,
and from all your idols I will cleanse you.
²⁶A new heart I will give you,
and a new spirit I will put within you;
and I will remove from your body the heart of stone
and give you a heart of flesh.
²⁷I will put my spirit within you,
and make you follow my statutes and be careful to observe my ordinances.
²⁸Then you shall live in the land that I gave to your ancestors;
and you shall be my people, and I will be your God.

The word of the Lord.   *or*   Word of God, word of life.

RESPONSE: Psalm 42 and Psalm 43

---

7 EZEKIEL 36:24-28 *Ezekiel = eh-ZEEK-ee-el*
"Thus says the Lord God" forces the reader to seek the sound of the voice of God. Give each sentence a quiet strength; each promise, a blessed assurance. This is love like a rock.

EIGHTH READING: Ezekiel 37:1-14
VALLEY OF THE DRY BONES

A reading from Ezekiel.

¹The hand of the LORD came upon me,
and he brought me out by the spirit of the LORD
and set me down in the middle of a valley;
it was full of bones.
²He led me all around them;
there were very many lying in the valley, and they were very dry.
³He said to me,
"Mortal, can these bones live?"
I answered, "O Lord GOD, you know."

⁴Then he said to me,
"Prophesy to these bones, and say to them:
O dry bones, hear the word of the LORD.
⁵Thus says the Lord GOD to these bones:
I will cause breath to enter you, and you shall live.
⁶I will lay sinews on you,
and will cause flesh to come upon you, and cover you with skin,
and put breath in you, and you shall live;
and you shall know that I am the LORD."

⁷So I prophesied as I had been commanded;
and as I prophesied, suddenly there was a noise, a rattling,
and the bones came together, bone to its bone.
⁸I looked, and there were sinews on them,
and flesh had come upon them, and skin had covered them;
but there was no breath in them.
⁹Then he said to me,
"Prophesy to the breath, prophesy, mortal, and say to the breath:
Thus says the Lord GOD:
Come from the four winds, O breath,
and breathe upon these slain, that they may live."
¹⁰I prophesied as he commanded me,
and the breath came into them,
and they lived, and stood on their feet, a vast multitude.

---

8 EZEKIEL 37:1-14 *Ezekiel = eh-ZEEK-ee-el prophesy = PROF-uh-sigh*
The high drama, frightening sounds, and fantastic images of this account will be diminished if the reader
fails to distinguish between the verb *prophesy* and the noun *prophecy*. It is the verb that is used here. Get
that right, then let the reading rip!

¹¹Then he said to me,
"Mortal, these bones are the whole house of Israel.
They say, 'Our bones are dried up, and our hope is lost;
we are cut off completely.'
¹²Therefore prophesy, and say to them,
Thus says the Lord GOD:
I am going to open your graves,
and bring you up from your graves, O my people;
and I will bring you back to the land of Israel.
¹³And you shall know that I am the LORD,
when I open your graves,
and bring you up from your graves, O my people.
¹⁴I will put my spirit within you, and you shall live,
and I will place you on your own soil;
then you shall know that I, the LORD, have spoken and will act,"
says the LORD.

The word of the Lord.   *or*   Word of God, word of life.

RESPONSE: Psalm 143

NINTH READING: Zephaniah 3:14-20
THE GATHERING OF GOD'S PEOPLE

A reading from Zephaniah.

¹⁴Sing aloud, O daughter Zion;
    shout, O Israel!
Rejoice and exult with all your heart,
    O daughter Jerusalem!
¹⁵The LORD has taken away the judgments against you,
    he has turned away your enemies.
The king of Israel, the LORD, is in your midst;
    you shall fear disaster no more.
¹⁶On that day it shall be said to Jerusalem:
Do not fear, O Zion;
    do not let your hands grow weak. ▸

---

9 **ZEPHANIAH 3:14-20** *Zephaniah = zef-uh-NY-uh*
The voice of the prophet has the cadence of a sermon by the sainted Dr. Martin Luther King Jr. While the readings in this lectionary are laid out by sense lines, you need not necessarily pause at the end of every line. Read the text aloud a number of times before the assembly gathers. Capture its flow. Then rejoice and let the reading sing!

¹⁷The Lord, your God, is in your midst,
    a warrior who gives victory;
he will rejoice over you with gladness,
    he will renew you in his love;
he will exult over you with loud singing
    ¹⁸as on a day of festival.

I will remove disaster from you,
    so that you will not bear reproach for it.
¹⁹I will deal with all your oppressors
    at that time.
And I will save the lame
    and gather the outcast,
and I will change their shame into praise
    and renown in all the earth.
²⁰At that time I will bring you home,
    at the time when I gather you;
for I will make you renowned and praised
    among all the peoples of the earth,
when I restore your fortunes
    before your eyes, says the Lord.

The word of the Lord.   *or*   Word of God, word of life.

RESPONSE: Psalm 98

TENTH READING: Jonah 1:1—2:1
THE DELIVERANCE OF JONAH

A reading from Jonah.

¹Now the word of the Lord came to Jonah son of Amittai, saying,
²"Go at once to Nineveh, that great city, and cry out against it;
for their wickedness has come up before me."
³But Jonah set out to flee to Tarshish from the presence of the Lord.
He went down to Joppa and found a ship going to Tarshish;
so he paid his fare and went on board,
to go with them to Tarshish, away from the presence of the Lord.

---

10 JONAH 1:1—2:1 *Amittai = uh-MIT-eye*
This is a wonderfully detailed, dramatic story that will remind many of other storm-stilling stories in the Bible. Try hard to convey the sailors' fear of the storm and, later, of God. Lean into verse 17—it is a sign of the resurrection.

⁴But the LORD hurled a great wind upon the sea,
and such a mighty storm came upon the sea
that the ship threatened to break up.
⁵Then the mariners were afraid, and each cried to his god.
They threw the cargo that was in the ship into the sea, to lighten it for them.
Jonah, meanwhile, had gone down into the hold of the ship
and had lain down, and was fast asleep.
⁶The captain came and said to him,
"What are you doing sound asleep?
Get up, call on your god!
Perhaps the god will spare us a thought so that we do not perish."

⁷The sailors said to one another,
"Come, let us cast lots,
so that we may know on whose account this calamity has come upon us."
So they cast lots, and the lot fell on Jonah.
⁸Then they said to him,
"Tell us why this calamity has come upon us.
What is your occupation?
Where do you come from?
What is your country?
And of what people are you?"
⁹I am a Hebrew, he replied.
"I worship the LORD, the God of heaven,
who made the sea and the dry land."
¹⁰Then the men were even more afraid, and said to him,
"What is this that you have done!"
For the men knew that he was fleeing from the presence of the LORD,
because he had told them so.

¹¹Then they said to him,
"What shall we do to you, that the sea may quiet down for us?"
For the sea was growing more and more tempestuous.
¹²He said to them,
"Pick me up and throw me into the sea;
then the sea will quiet down for you;
for I know it is because of me that this great storm has come upon you."
¹³Nevertheless the men rowed hard to bring the ship back to land,
but they could not,
for the sea grew more and more stormy against them. ▸

¹⁴Then they cried out to the LORD,
"Please, O LORD, we pray,
do not let us perish on account of this man's life.
Do not make us guilty of innocent blood;
for you, O LORD, have done as it pleased you."
¹⁵So they picked Jonah up and threw him into the sea;
and the sea ceased from its raging.
¹⁶Then the men feared the LORD even more,
and they offered a sacrifice to the LORD and made vows.

¹⁷But the LORD provided a large fish to swallow up Jonah;
and Jonah was in the belly of the fish three days and three nights.

²:¹Then Jonah prayed to the LORD his God from the belly of the fish.

The word of the Lord.   *or*   Word of God, word of life.

RESPONSE: Jonah 2:2-3 [4-6] 7-9

ELEVENTH READING: Isaiah 61:1-4, 9-11
CLOTHED IN THE GARMENTS OF SALVATION

A reading from Isaiah.

The spirit of the Lord GOD is upon me,
    because the LORD has anointed me;
he has sent me to bring good news to the oppressed,
    to bind up the brokenhearted,
to proclaim liberty to the captives,
    and release to the prisoners;
²to proclaim the year of the LORD's favor,
    and the day of vengeance of our God;
    to comfort all who mourn;
³to provide for those who mourn in Zion—
    to give them a garland instead of ashes,
the oil of gladness instead of mourning,
    the mantle of praise instead of a faint spirit.
They will be called oaks of righteousness,
    the planting of the LORD, to display his glory.

---

11 ISAIAH 61:1-4, 9-11 *Isaiah = eye-ZAY-uh*
This is a proclamation of unalloyed joy. The greatest challenge will be pacing and tone so that there is some
ebb and flow to the reading. Again, practice will help.

⁴They shall build up the ancient ruins,
    they shall raise up the former devastations;
they shall repair the ruined cities,
    the devastations of many generations.

⁹Their descendants shall be known among the nations,
    and their offspring among the peoples;
all who see them shall acknowledge
    that they are a people whom the LORD has blessed.
¹⁰I will greatly rejoice in the LORD,
    my whole being shall exult in my God;
for he has clothed me with the garments of salvation,
    he has covered me with the robe of righteousness,
as a bridegroom decks himself with a garland,
    and as a bride adorns herself with her jewels.
¹¹For as the earth brings forth its shoots,
    and as a garden causes what is sown in it to spring up,
so the Lord GOD will cause righteousness and praise
    to spring up before all the nations.

The word of the Lord.   *or*   Word of God, word of life.

RESPONSE: Deuteronomy 32:1-4, 7, 36a, 43a

TWELFTH READING: Daniel 3:1-29
DELIVERANCE FROM THE FIERY FURNACE

A reading from Daniel.

¹King Nebuchadnezzar made a golden statue whose height was sixty cubits
and whose width was six cubits;
he set it up on the plain of Dura in the province of Babylon.
²Then King Nebuchadnezzar sent for the satraps,
the prefects, and the governors,
the counselors, the treasurers, the justices, the magistrates,
and all the officials of the provinces,
to assemble and come to the dedication of the statue
that King Nebuchadnezzar had set up. ▸

---

12 DANIEL 3:1-29 *Nebuchadnezzar = neb-uh-kud-NEZ-ur   satraps = SAY-traps   trigon = TRY-gon*
Chaldeans = kahl-DEE-unz   Shadrach = SHAD-rak   Meshach = ME-shak   Abednego = uh-BED-nih-go
This delightful account with its tongue-twisting, often repeated phrases, and frantic pace will give up its
wonders only to those who are ready to practice, practice, practice! The list of instruments, in particular,
has potential for humor. The whole has the feel of a holy children's story. Read it with energy, delight, and
unbounded enthusiasm.

³So the satraps, the prefects, and the governors,
the counselors, the treasurers, the justices, the magistrates,
and all the officials of the provinces,
assembled for the dedication of the statue
that King Nebuchadnezzar had set up.
When they were standing before the statue that Nebuchadnezzar had set up,
⁴the herald proclaimed aloud,
"You are commanded, O peoples, nations, and languages,
⁵that when you hear the sound of the horn, pipe, lyre,
trigon, harp, drum, and entire musical ensemble,
you are to fall down and worship the golden statue
that King Nebuchadnezzar has set up.
⁶Whoever does not fall down and worship
shall immediately be thrown into a furnace of blazing fire."
⁷Therefore, as soon as all the peoples heard the sound of the horn, pipe, lyre,
trigon, harp, drum, and entire musical ensemble,
all the peoples, nations, and languages fell down
and worshiped the golden statue that King Nebuchadnezzar had set up.

⁸Accordingly, at this time
certain Chaldeans came forward and denounced the Jews.
⁹They said to King Nebuchadnezzar,
"O king, live forever!
¹⁰You, O king, have made a decree,
that everyone who hears the sound of the horn, pipe, lyre,
trigon, harp, drum, and entire musical ensemble,
shall fall down and worship the golden statue,
¹¹and whoever does not fall down and worship
shall be thrown into a furnace of blazing fire.
¹²There are certain Jews
whom you have appointed over the affairs of the province of Babylon:
Shadrach, Meshach, and Abednego.
These pay no heed to you, O king.
They do not serve your gods
and they do not worship the golden statue that you have set up."

¹³Then Nebuchadnezzar in furious rage
commanded that Shadrach, Meshach, and Abednego be brought in;
so they brought those men before the king.

[14]Nebuchadnezzar said to them,
"Is it true, O Shadrach, Meshach, and Abednego,
that you do not serve my gods
and you do not worship the golden statue that I have set up?
[15]Now if you are ready when you hear the sound of the horn, pipe, lyre,
trigon, harp, drum, and entire musical ensemble
to fall down and worship the statue that I have made,
well and good.
But if you do not worship,
you shall immediately be thrown into a furnace of blazing fire,
and who is the god that will deliver you out of my hands?"

[16]Shadrach, Meshach, and Abednego answered the king,
"O Nebuchadnezzar,
we have no need to present a defense to you in this matter.
[17]If our God whom we serve is able to deliver us
from the furnace of blazing fire and out of your hand, O king,
let him deliver us.
[18]But if not, be it known to you, O king,
that we will not serve your gods
and we will not worship the golden statue that you have set up."

[19]Then Nebuchadnezzar was so filled with rage
against Shadrach, Meshach, and Abednego
that his face was distorted.
He ordered the furnace heated up seven times more than was customary,
[20]and ordered some of the strongest guards in his army
to bind Shadrach, Meshach, and Abednego
and to throw them into the furnace of blazing fire.
[21]So the men were bound, still wearing their tunics,
their trousers, their hats, and their other garments,
and they were thrown into the furnace of blazing fire.
[22]Because the king's command was urgent
and the furnace was so overheated,
the raging flames killed the men
who lifted Shadrach, Meshach, and Abednego.
[23]But the three men, Shadrach, Meshach, and Abednego,
fell down, bound, into the furnace of blazing fire. ▸

²⁴Then King Nebuchadnezzar was astonished and rose up quickly.
He said to his counselors,
"Was it not three men that we threw bound into the fire?"
They answered the king, "True, O king."
²⁵He replied, "But I see four men unbound,
walking in the middle of the fire,
and they are not hurt;
and the fourth has the appearance of a god."

²⁶Nebuchadnezzar then approached the door of the furnace of blazing fire
and said,
"Shadrach, Meshach, and Abednego,
servants of the Most High God,
come out! Come here!"
So Shadrach, Meshach, and Abednego came out from the fire.
²⁷And the satraps, the prefects, the governors,
and the king's counselors gathered together
and saw that the fire had not had any power over the bodies of those men;
the hair of their heads was not singed,
their tunics were not harmed,
and not even the smell of fire came from them.

²⁸Nebuchadnezzar said,
"Blessed be the God of Shadrach, Meshach, and Abednego,
who has sent his angel and delivered his servants who trusted in him.
They disobeyed the king's command and yielded up their bodies
rather than serve and worship any god except their own God.
²⁹Therefore I make a decree:
Any people, nation, or language that utters blasphemy
against the God of Shadrach, Meshach, and Abednego
shall be torn limb from limb,
and their houses laid in ruins;
for there is no other god who is able to deliver in this way."

The word of the Lord.　　　　*or*　　　　Word of God, word of life.

RESPONSE: Song of the Three 35-65

NEW TESTAMENT READING: Romans 6:3-11

A reading from Romans.

³Do you not know that all of us who have been baptized into Christ Jesus
were baptized into his death?
⁴Therefore we have been buried with him by baptism into death,
so that, just as Christ was raised from the dead by the glory of the Father,
so we too might walk in newness of life.

⁵For if we have been united with him in a death like his,
we will certainly be united with him in a resurrection like his.
⁶We know that our old self was crucified with him
so that the body of sin might be destroyed,
and we might no longer be enslaved to sin.
⁷For whoever has died is freed from sin.
⁸But if we have died with Christ,
we believe that we will also live with him.
⁹We know that Christ, being raised from the dead, will never die again;
death no longer has dominion over him.
¹⁰The death he died, he died to sin, once for all;
but the life he lives, he lives to God.

¹¹So you also must consider yourselves dead to sin
and alive to God in Christ Jesus.

The word of the Lord.   *or*   Word of God, word of life.

GOSPEL: John 20:1-18

The holy gospel according to John.

¹Early on the first day of the week, while it was still dark,
Mary Magdalene came to the tomb
and saw that the stone had been removed from the tomb.
²So she ran and went to Simon Peter and the other disciple,
the one whom Jesus loved, and said to them,
"They have taken the Lord out of the tomb,
and we do not know where they have laid him." ▸

NEW TESTAMENT READING
In these few verses St. Paul makes sense of all the preceding stories about drowning and dying,
faithlessness and repentance. A voice of loving admonition will bring this truth to vigilant hearts.

³Then Peter and the other disciple set out and went toward the tomb.
⁴The two were running together,
but the other disciple outran Peter and reached the tomb first.
⁵He bent down to look in and saw the linen wrappings lying there,
but he did not go in.
⁶Then Simon Peter came, following him, and went into the tomb.
He saw the linen wrappings lying there,
⁷and the cloth that had been on Jesus' head,
not lying with the linen wrappings but rolled up in a place by itself.
⁸Then the other disciple, who reached the tomb first,
also went in, and he saw and believed;
⁹for as yet they did not understand the scripture,
that he must rise from the dead.
¹⁰Then the disciples returned to their homes.

¹¹But Mary stood weeping outside the tomb.
As she wept, she bent over to look into the tomb;
¹²and she saw two angels in white,
sitting where the body of Jesus had been lying,
one at the head and the other at the feet.
¹³They said to her, "Woman, why are you weeping?"
She said to them,
"They have taken away my Lord, and I do not know where they have laid him."
¹⁴When she had said this, she turned around and saw Jesus standing there,
but she did not know that it was Jesus.
¹⁵Jesus said to her,
"Woman, why are you weeping? Whom are you looking for?"
Supposing him to be the gardener, she said to him,
"Sir, if you have carried him away,
tell me where you have laid him, and I will take him away."
¹⁶Jesus said to her, "Mary!"
She turned and said to him in Hebrew, "Rabbouni!" (which means Teacher).
¹⁷Jesus said to her,
"Do not hold on to me, because I have not yet ascended to the Father.
But go to my brothers and say to them,
'I am ascending to my Father and your Father,
to my God and your God.'"
¹⁸Mary Magdalene went and announced to the disciples,
"I have seen the Lord";
and she told them that he had said these things to her.

The gospel of the Lord.

GOSPEL   *Rabbouni = ruh-BOON-ih*
Allow the verbs to set the pace for this gospel. Verses 1-10, describing various races to the tomb, will be animated by a more rapid delivery than usual. This will contrast dramatically with a more considered pace as Mary stands weeping outside the tomb. In all this, bring the sounds of wonder and joy to the discovery of the empty tomb.

✠ RESURRECTION OF OUR LORD

Easter Day

FIRST READING: Acts 10:34-43

Or Jeremiah 31:1-6, following

A reading from Acts.

³⁴Peter began to speak to ⌈the people⌉:
"I truly understand that God shows no partiality,
³⁵but in every nation anyone who fears him and does what is right
is acceptable to him.

³⁶"You know the message he sent to the people of Israel,
preaching peace by Jesus Christ—
he is Lord of all.
³⁷That message spread throughout Judea,
beginning in Galilee after the baptism that John announced:
³⁸how God anointed Jesus of Nazareth with the Holy Spirit and with power;
how he went about doing good
and healing all who were oppressed by the devil,
for God was with him.
³⁹We are witnesses to all that he did both in Judea and in Jerusalem.
They put him to death by hanging him on a tree;
⁴⁰but God raised him on the third day
and allowed him to appear, ⁴¹not to all the people
but to us who were chosen by God as witnesses,
and who ate and drank with him after he rose from the dead.

⁴²"He commanded us to preach to the people
and to testify that he is the one ordained by God
as judge of the living and the dead.
⁴³All the prophets testify about him that everyone who believes in him
receives forgiveness of sins through his name."

The word of the Lord.   *or*   Word of God, word of life.

FIRST READING (Acts)
In this marvelous text, Peter summarizes the whole of salvation history in ten verses! Bring to it a profound sense of joy and wonder, and help the hearer to revel in the love of God as we have known it in Christ Jesus, our Lord.

OR: Jeremiah 31:1-6

A reading from Jeremiah.

¹At that time, says the LORD,
I will be the God of all the families of Israel,
and they shall be my people.
²Thus says the LORD:
The people who survived the sword found grace in the wilderness;
when Israel sought for rest,
³the LORD appeared to him from far away.
I have loved you with an everlasting love;
therefore I have continued my faithfulness to you.

⁴Again I will build you, and you shall be built, O virgin Israel!
Again you shall take your tambourines,
and go forth in the dance of the merrymakers.
⁵Again you shall plant vineyards on the mountains of Samaria;
the planters shall plant, and shall enjoy the fruit.
⁶For there shall be a day
when sentinels will call in the hill country of Ephraim:
"Come, let us go up to Zion, to the LORD our God."

The word of the Lord.   *or*   Word of God, word of life.

PSALMODY: Psalm 118:1-2, 14-24

SECOND READING: Colossians 3:1-4
OR ACTS 10:34-43, following

A reading from Colossians.

¹If you have been raised with Christ,
seek the things that are above,
where Christ is, seated at the right hand of God.
²Set your minds on things that are above,
not on things that are on earth,
³for you have died, and your life is hidden with Christ in God.
⁴When Christ who is your life is revealed,
then you also will be revealed with him in glory.

The word of the Lord.   *or*   Word of God, word of life.

FIRST READING (Jeremiah)   *Jeremiah = jehr-eh-MY-uh   Samaria = suh-MAIR-ee-uh   Ephraim = EEF-rih-um*
In a moving declaration of an everlasting love, the Lord God promises Israel a glorious future. For many it will be the first scripture of Easter. Bring all the strength and joy one can muster to this hope-full word.

SECOND READING (Colossians)   *Colossians = kuh-LOSH-uns*
We have died with Christ. We have been raised with Christ. We are "hidden with Christ in God." We will be "revealed with him in glory." The point is a simple one: the entire existence of the baptized—as well as our future—is wrapped up in Christ Jesus. The writer urges us to keep these truths in mind.

OR: Acts 10:34-43

A reading from Acts.

³⁴Peter began to speak to ⌜the people⌝:
"I truly understand that God shows no partiality,
³⁵but in every nation anyone who fears him and does what is right
is acceptable to him.

³⁶"You know the message he sent to the people of Israel,
preaching peace by Jesus Christ—
he is Lord of all.
³⁷That message spread throughout Judea,
beginning in Galilee after the baptism that John announced:
³⁸how God anointed Jesus of Nazareth with the Holy Spirit and with power;
how he went about doing good
and healing all who were oppressed by the devil,
for God was with him.
³⁹We are witnesses to all that he did both in Judea and in Jerusalem.
They put him to death by hanging him on a tree;
⁴⁰but God raised him on the third day
and allowed him to appear, ⁴¹not to all the people
but to us who were chosen by God as witnesses,
and who ate and drank with him after he rose from the dead.

⁴²"He commanded us to preach to the people
and to testify that he is the one ordained by God
as judge of the living and the dead.
⁴³All the prophets testify about him that everyone who believes in him
receives forgiveness of sins through his name."

The word of the Lord.   *or*   Word of God, word of life.

SECOND READING (Acts)
In this marvelous text, Peter summarizes the whole of salvation history in ten verses! Bring to it a profound sense of joy and wonder, and help the hearer to revel in the love of God as we have known it in Christ Jesus, our Lord.

GOSPEL: Matthew 28:1-10
OR JOHN 20:1-18, following

The holy gospel according to Matthew.

¹After the sabbath, as the first day of the week was dawning,
Mary Magdalene and the other Mary went to see the tomb.
²And suddenly there was a great earthquake;
for an angel of the Lord, descending from heaven,
came and rolled back the stone and sat on it.
³His appearance was like lightning, and his clothing white as snow.
⁴For fear of him the guards shook and became like dead men.
⁵But the angel said to the women,
"Do not be afraid;
I know that you are looking for Jesus who was crucified.
⁶He is not here; for he has been raised, as he said.
Come, see the place where he lay.
⁷Then go quickly and tell his disciples,
'He has been raised from the dead,
and indeed he is going ahead of you to Galilee; there you will see him.'
This is my message for you."

⁸So they left the tomb quickly with fear and great joy,
and ran to tell his disciples.
⁹Suddenly Jesus met them and said, "Greetings!"
And they came to him, took hold of his feet, and worshiped him.
¹⁰Then Jesus said to them,
"Do not be afraid;
go and tell my brothers to go to Galilee; there they will see me."

The gospel of the Lord.

OR: John 20:1-18

The holy gospel according to John.

¹Early on the first day of the week, while it was still dark,
Mary Magdalene came to the tomb
and saw that the stone had been removed from the tomb.

GOSPEL (Matthew)
This telling of the resurrection is rife with dramatic detail. The rolling tombstone touches off an earthquake; guards are dropping like dead men; and the angel's message (more detailed than any in scripture) ends with the delightfully redundant conclusion: "This is my message for you." Consideration about how to handle vocally each is essential. Take time to consider Jesus' one-word "Greetings!" to the Marys in verse 9a. The delight in this reading is in the details.

GOSPEL (John)
Allow the verbs to set the pace for this gospel. Verses 1–10, describing various races to the tomb, will be animated by a more rapid delivery than usual. This will contrast dramatically with a more considered pace as Mary stands weeping outside the tomb. In all this, bring the sounds of wonder and joy to the discovery of the empty tomb.

²So she ran and went to Simon Peter and the other disciple,
the one whom Jesus loved, and said to them,
"They have taken the Lord out of the tomb,
and we do not know where they have laid him."

³Then Peter and the other disciple set out and went toward the tomb.
⁴The two were running together,
but the other disciple outran Peter and reached the tomb first.
⁵He bent down to look in and saw the linen wrappings lying there,
but he did not go in.
⁶Then Simon Peter came, following him, and went into the tomb.
He saw the linen wrappings lying there,
⁷and the cloth that had been on Jesus' head,
not lying with the linen wrappings but rolled up in a place by itself.
⁸Then the other disciple, who reached the tomb first,
also went in, and he saw and believed;
⁹for as yet they did not understand the scripture,
that he must rise from the dead.
¹⁰Then the disciples returned to their homes.

¹¹But Mary stood weeping outside the tomb.
As she wept, she bent over to look into the tomb;
¹²and she saw two angels in white,
sitting where the body of Jesus had been lying,
one at the head and the other at the feet.
¹³They said to her, "Woman, why are you weeping?"
She said to them,
"They have taken away my Lord,
and I do not know where they have laid him."
¹⁴When she had said this, she turned around and saw Jesus standing there,
but she did not know that it was Jesus.
¹⁵Jesus said to her,
"Woman, why are you weeping? Whom are you looking for?"
Supposing him to be the gardener, she said to him,
"Sir, if you have carried him away,
tell me where you have laid him, and I will take him away."
¹⁶Jesus said to her, "Mary!"
She turned and said to him in Hebrew,
"Rabbouni!" (which means Teacher).
¹⁷Jesus said to her,
"Do not hold on to me, because I have not yet ascended to the Father.
But go to my brothers and say to them,
'I am ascending to my Father and your Father,
to my God and your God.'"
¹⁸Mary Magdalene went and announced to the disciples,
"I have seen the Lord";
and she told them that he had said these things to her.

The gospel of the Lord.

FIRST READING: Isaiah 25:6-9

A reading from Isaiah.

⁶On this mountain the LORD of hosts will make for all peoples
    a feast of rich food, a feast of well-aged wines,
    of rich food filled with marrow, of well-aged wines strained clear.
⁷And he will destroy on this mountain
    the shroud that is cast over all peoples,
    the sheet that is spread over all nations;
    he will swallow up death forever.
⁸Then the Lord GOD will wipe away the tears from all faces,
    and the disgrace of his people he will take away from all the earth,
    for the LORD has spoken.

⁹It will be said on that day,
    Lo, this is our God; we have waited for him, so that he might save us.
    This is the LORD for whom we have waited;
    let us be glad and rejoice in his salvation.

The word of the Lord.   *or*   Word of God, word of life.

PSALMODY: Psalm 114

SECOND READING: 1 Corinthians 5:6b-8

A reading from First Corinthians.

⁶ᵇDo you not know that a little yeast leavens the whole batch of dough?
⁷Clean out the old yeast so that you may be a new batch,
as you really are unleavened.
For our paschal lamb, Christ, has been sacrificed.
⁸Therefore, let us celebrate the festival,
not with the old yeast, the yeast of malice and evil,
but with the unleavened bread of sincerity and truth.

The word of the Lord.   *or*   Word of God, word of life.

FIRST READING   *Isaiah = eye-ZAY-uh*
This text hints at its own sound in its last line: "Let us be glad and rejoice." A skilled reader will be sensitive not only to the voice but also to the face that proclaims this good news. Joy and gladness ought to be heard and seen.

SECOND READING
In the context of this evening's celebration of the resurrection, this simple little word of encouragement using post-Passover/bakery images ought to sound upbeat and loving.

GOSPEL: Luke 24:13-49

The holy gospel according to Luke.

¹³Now on that same day ⌐when Jesus had appeared to Mary Magdalene,⌐
two ⌐disciples⌐ were going to a village called Emmaus,
about seven miles from Jerusalem,
¹⁴and talking with each other about all these things that had happened.
¹⁵While they were talking and discussing,
Jesus himself came near and went with them,
¹⁶but their eyes were kept from recognizing him.
¹⁷And he said to them,
"What are you discussing with each other while you walk along?"
They stood still, looking sad.
¹⁸Then one of them, whose name was Cleopas, answered him,
"Are you the only stranger in Jerusalem
who does not know the things that have taken place there in these days?"
¹⁹He asked them, "What things?"
They replied, "The things about Jesus of Nazareth,
who was a prophet mighty in deed and word before God and all the people,
²⁰and how our chief priests and leaders
handed him over to be condemned to death and crucified him.
²¹But we had hoped that he was the one to redeem Israel.
Yes, and besides all this,
it is now the third day since these things took place.
²²Moreover, some women of our group astounded us.
They were at the tomb early this morning,
²³and when they did not find his body there, they came back
and told us that they had indeed seen a vision of angels
who said that he was alive.
²⁴Some of those who were with us went to the tomb
and found it just as the women had said;
but they did not see him."

²⁵Then he said to them,
"Oh, how foolish you are,
and how slow of heart to believe all that the prophets have declared!
²⁶Was it not necessary that the Messiah should suffer these things
and then enter into his glory?"
²⁷Then beginning with Moses and all the prophets,
he interpreted to them the things about himself in all the scriptures. ▶

GOSPEL   *Cleopas = KLEE-uh-pus*
This is a lot of gospel! The issues demanding the reader's attention are several: (1) it is a long reading—avoid the tendency to hurry it; (2) the deep sadness and discouragement of the disciples must be given genuine voice; (3) the changes of scene will be clarified by substantial pauses in the reading; (4) the sound of the voice of Jesus will be varied depending on the circumstances, the surroundings, and the nature of the words themselves.

²⁸As they came near the village to which they were going,
he walked ahead as if he were going on.
²⁹But they urged him strongly, saying,
"Stay with us,
because it is almost evening and the day is now nearly over."
So he went in to stay with them.
³⁰When he was at the table with them,
he took bread, blessed and broke it, and gave it to them.
³¹Then their eyes were opened, and they recognized him;
and he vanished from their sight.
³²They said to each other,
"Were not our hearts burning within us
while he was talking to us on the road,
while he was opening the scriptures to us?"

³³That same hour they got up and returned to Jerusalem;
and they found the eleven and their companions gathered together.
³⁴They were saying,
"The Lord has risen indeed, and he has appeared to Simon!"
³⁵Then they told what had happened on the road,
and how he had been made known to them in the breaking of the bread.

³⁶While they were talking about this,
Jesus himself stood among them and said to them,
"Peace be with you."
³⁷They were startled and terrified,
and thought that they were seeing a ghost.
³⁸He said to them,
"Why are you frightened, and why do doubts arise in your hearts?
³⁹Look at my hands and my feet; see that it is I myself.
Touch me and see;
for a ghost does not have flesh and bones as you see that I have."
⁴⁰And when he had said this, he showed them his hands and his feet.
⁴¹While in their joy they were disbelieving and still wondering,
he said to them,
"Have you anything here to eat?"
⁴²They gave him a piece of broiled fish,
⁴³and he took it and ate in their presence.

[44]Then he said to them,
"These are my words that I spoke to you while I was still with you—
that everything written about me
in the law of Moses, the prophets, and the psalms must be fulfilled."
[45]Then he opened their minds to understand the scriptures,
[46]and he said to them,
"Thus it is written,
that the Messiah is to suffer and to rise from the dead on the third day,
[47]and that repentance and forgiveness of sins
is to be proclaimed in his name to all nations, beginning from Jerusalem.
[48]You are witnesses of these things.
[49]And see, I am sending upon you what my Father promised;
so stay here in the city until you have been clothed with power from on high."

The gospel of the Lord.

Easter

✠ Easter Monday

FIRST READING: Daniel 12:1-3

A reading from Daniel.

¹At that time Michael, the great prince,
the protector of your people, shall arise.
There shall be a time of anguish,
such as has never occurred since nations first came into existence.
But at that time your people shall be delivered,
everyone who is found written in the book.
²Many of those who sleep in the dust of the earth shall awake,
some to everlasting life,
and some to shame and everlasting contempt.
³Those who are wise shall shine like the brightness of the sky,
and those who lead many to righteousness,
like the stars forever and ever.

The word of the Lord.   *or*   Word of God, word of life.

PSALMODY: Psalm 16:8-11

SECOND READING: Acts 2:14, 22b-32

A reading from Acts.

¹⁴Peter, standing with the eleven, raised his voice and addressed ⌜the crowd,⌝
"Men of Judea and all who live in Jerusalem,
let this be known to you, and listen to what I say.
²²ᵇJesus of Nazareth, a man attested to you by God
with deeds of power, wonders, and signs
that God did through him among you,
as you yourselves know— ▸

FIRST READING
This account begins with a sense of foreboding: what will the end times bring? But then it segues into a joy appropriate to this season of resurrection. Make verse 3 sparkle like the stars.

SECOND READING   *Hades = HAY-deez*
The first readings in the weeks of Easter come from the story of the early church in Acts, not from the Hebrew scripture (Old Testament). Here St. Peter interprets the words of King David in Psalm 16 as having reference to Christ. The text demands from the reader a sense of wonder and awe.

²³this man, handed over to you
according to the definite plan and foreknowledge of God,
you crucified and killed by the hands of those outside the law.
²⁴But God raised him up,
having freed him from death,
because it was impossible for him to be held in its power.

²⁵"For David says concerning him,
　'I saw the Lord always before me,
　　for he is at my right hand so that I will not be shaken;
　²⁶therefore my heart was glad, and my tongue rejoiced;
　　moreover my flesh will live in hope.
　²⁷For you will not abandon my soul to Hades,
　　or let your Holy One experience corruption.
　²⁸You have made known to me the ways of life;
　　you will make me full of gladness with your presence.'

²⁹"Fellow Israelites,
I may say to you confidently of our ancestor David
that he both died and was buried,
and his tomb is with us to this day.
³⁰Since he was a prophet,
he knew that God had sworn with an oath to him
that he would put one of his descendants on his throne.
³¹Foreseeing this,
David spoke of the resurrection of the Messiah, saying,
　'He was not abandoned to Hades,
　　nor did his flesh experience corruption.'
³²This Jesus God raised up, and of that all of us are witnesses."

The word of the Lord.　　　*or*　　　Word of God, word of life.

GOSPEL: Matthew 28:9-15a

The holy gospel according to Matthew.

⁹Suddenly Jesus met ⌜Mary Magdalene and the other Mary⌝
and said, "Greetings!"
And they came to him, took hold of his feet, and worshiped him.
¹⁰Then Jesus said to them,
"Do not be afraid;
go and tell my brothers to go to Galilee; there they will see me."

¹¹While they were going, some of the guard went into the city
and told the chief priests everything that had happened.
¹²After the priests had assembled with the elders,
they devised a plan to give a large sum of money to the soldiers,
¹³telling them, "You must say,
'His disciples came by night and stole him away while we were asleep.'
¹⁴If this comes to the governor's ears,
we will satisfy him and keep you out of trouble."
¹⁵So they took the money and did as they were directed.

The gospel of the Lord.

GOSPEL
This is the only time this brief account appears in the lectionary. The deviousness of the leaders' plan should be heard in the tone of the reading.

Second Sunday of Easter

FIRST READING: Acts 2:14a, 22-32

A reading from Acts.

¹⁴ᵃPeter, standing with the eleven, raised his voice and addressed ⌈the crowd⌉:

²²"You that are Israelites, listen to what I have to say:
Jesus of Nazareth, a man attested to you by God
with deeds of power, wonders, and signs
that God did through him among you,
as you yourselves know—
²³this man, handed over to you
according to the definite plan and foreknowledge of God,
you crucified and killed by the hands of those outside the law.
²⁴But God raised him up, having freed him from death,
because it was impossible for him to be held in its power.

²⁵"For David says concerning him,
  'I saw the Lord always before me,
    for he is at my right hand so that I will not be shaken;
  ²⁶therefore my heart was glad, and my tongue rejoiced;
    moreover my flesh will live in hope.
  ²⁷For you will not abandon my soul to Hades,
    or let your Holy One experience corruption.
  ²⁸You have made known to me the ways of life;
    you will make me full of gladness with your presence.'

²⁹"Fellow Israelites,
I may say to you confidently of our ancestor David
that he both died and was buried, and his tomb is with us to this day.
³⁰Since he was a prophet,
he knew that God had sworn with an oath to him
that he would put one of his descendants on his throne.
³¹Foreseeing this, David spoke of the resurrection of the Messiah, saying,
  'He was not abandoned to Hades, nor did his flesh experience corruption.'
³²This Jesus God raised up, and of that all of us are witnesses."

The word of the Lord.   *or*   Word of God, word of life.

FIRST READING   *Hades = HAY-deez*
The first readings in the weeks of Easter come from the story of the early church in Acts, not from the Hebrew scripture (Old Testament). Here St. Peter interprets the words of King David in Psalm 16 as having reference to the Lord Jesus. Peter not only suggests that David sees in Jesus (who "was descended from the house and family of David"—Luke 2) the promised King of the Jews, but anticipates the resurrection in the words of the psalm. The text demands from the reader a sense of wonder and awe.

PSALMODY: Psalm 16

SECOND READING: 1 Peter 1:3-9

A reading from First Peter.

³Blessed be the God and Father of our Lord Jesus Christ!
By his great mercy he has given us a new birth
into a living hope through the resurrection of Jesus Christ from the dead,
⁴and into an inheritance that is imperishable, undefiled, and unfading,
kept in heaven for you,
⁵who are being protected by the power of God
through faith for a salvation ready to be revealed in the last time.
⁶In this you rejoice,
even if now for a little while you have had to suffer various trials,
⁷so that the genuineness of your faith—
being more precious than gold that, though perishable, is tested by fire—
may be found to result in praise and glory and honor
when Jesus Christ is revealed.

⁸Although you have not seen him, you love him;
and even though you do not see him now,
you believe in him and rejoice with an indescribable and glorious joy,
⁹for you are receiving the outcome of your faith,
the salvation of your souls.

The word of the Lord.   *or*   Word of God, word of life.

GOSPEL: John 20:19-31

The holy gospel according to John.

¹⁹When it was evening on that day, the first day of the week,
and the doors of the house where the disciples had met
were locked for fear of the Jews,
Jesus came and stood among them and said,
"Peace be with you." ▸

SECOND READING

Here are just four sentences—which makes the reading compact and complex. The words carry a message of lasting hope. In a sense they are an effort to keep Easter alive in the consciousness of the faithful, even in the midst of difficult days. The reader will do well to take time with the text, taking advantage of every period, comma, and semicolon to make the meaning clear. Make the pauses work for reader and hearer both. Give each thought adequate opportunity to sink in.

GOSPEL

Caution: Rushing this story will diminish its impact. The story stretches over a full week. Help the hearer to feel the passage of time. Provide significant pauses between Jesus' word of peace, his "breathing on them" (verse 22), and his invitation to Thomas (verse 27). The summary paragraph (verses 30–31) will helpfully be separated from the narrative by a healthy pause.

²⁰After he said this, he showed them his hands and his side.
Then the disciples rejoiced when they saw the Lord.
²¹Jesus said to them again,
"Peace be with you.
As the Father has sent me, so I send you."
²²When he had said this, he breathed on them and said to them,
"Receive the Holy Spirit.
²³If you forgive the sins of any, they are forgiven them;
if you retain the sins of any, they are retained."

²⁴But Thomas (who was called the Twin), one of the twelve,
was not with them when Jesus came.
²⁵So the other disciples told him, "We have seen the Lord."
But he said to them,
"Unless I see the mark of the nails in his hands,
and put my finger in the mark of the nails and my hand in his side,
I will not believe."

²⁶A week later his disciples were again in the house,
and Thomas was with them.
Although the doors were shut,
Jesus came and stood among them and said,
"Peace be with you."
²⁷Then he said to Thomas,
"Put your finger here and see my hands.
Reach out your hand and put it in my side.
Do not doubt but believe."
²⁸Thomas answered him,
"My Lord and my God!"
²⁹Jesus said to him,
"Have you believed because you have seen me?
Blessed are those who have not seen and yet have come to believe."

³⁰Now Jesus did many other signs in the presence of his disciples,
which are not written in this book.
³¹But these are written so that you may come to believe
that Jesus is the Messiah, the Son of God,
and that through believing you may have life in his name.

The gospel of the Lord.

THIRD SUNDAY OF EASTER

FIRST READING: Acts 2:14a, 36-41

A reading from Acts.

^{14a}Peter, standing with the eleven, raised his voice and addressed ⌜the crowd⌝:

³⁶"Let the entire house of Israel know with certainty
that God has made him both Lord and Messiah,
this Jesus whom you crucified."

³⁷Now when they heard this,
they were cut to the heart and said to Peter and to the other apostles,
"Brothers, what should we do?"
³⁸Peter said to them,
"Repent, and be baptized every one of you
in the name of Jesus Christ
so that your sins may be forgiven;
and you will receive the gift of the Holy Spirit.
³⁹For the promise is for you, for your children,
and for all who are far away,
everyone whom the Lord our God calls to him."
⁴⁰And he testified with many other arguments and exhorted them, saying,
"Save yourselves from this corrupt generation."
⁴¹So those who welcomed his message were baptized,
and that day about three thousand persons were added.

The word of the Lord.   *or*   Word of God, word of life.

PSALMODY: Psalm 116:1-4, 12-19

FIRST READING
This is a continuation of Peter's address from last Sunday and speaks to the reaction of those who heard him. It is straightforward, but the reader may want to segment the thoughts of the final paragraph in this manner: verse 37; 38-39; 40; 41. Treating those five verses as four separate thoughts may help both reader and hearer better follow the sequence. Then preach it—or at least help the assembly to hear Peter preaching it!

SECOND READING: 1 Peter 1:17-23

A reading from First Peter.

[17]If you invoke as Father
the one who judges all people impartially according to their deeds,
live in reverent fear during the time of your exile.
[18]You know that you were ransomed from the futile ways
inherited from your ancestors,
not with perishable things like silver or gold,
[19]but with the precious blood of Christ,
like that of a lamb without defect or blemish.
[20]He was destined before the foundation of the world,
but was revealed at the end of the ages for your sake.
[21]Through him you have come to trust in God,
who raised him from the dead and gave him glory,
so that your faith and hope are set on God.

[22]Now that you have purified your souls by your obedience to the truth
so that you have genuine mutual love,
love one another deeply from the heart.
[23]You have been born anew,
not of perishable but of imperishable seed,
through the living and enduring word of God.

The word of the Lord.   *or*   Word of God, word of life.

SECOND READING

Do not let the brevity of these readings lull you into an "Oh, this is simple!" laziness. These seven verses are actually quite complicated, and the people will need all the help the reader might provide. The theme is: Live like people who have been redeemed by the blood of Christ. Verse 22 is the topic sentence. Think of it this way: "Love one another deeply from the heart, now that you have purified your souls by your obedience to the truth, so that you have genuine mutual love." Practice hard and then take it slow, good reader!

GOSPEL: Luke 24:13-35

The holy gospel according to Luke.

¹³Now on that same day ⌐when Jesus had appeared to Mary Magdalene,⌐
two ⌐disciples⌐ were going to a village called Emmaus,
about seven miles from Jerusalem,
¹⁴and talking with each other about all these things that had happened.
¹⁵While they were talking and discussing,
Jesus himself came near and went with them,
¹⁶but their eyes were kept from recognizing him.
¹⁷And he said to them,
"What are you discussing with each other while you walk along?"
They stood still, looking sad.
¹⁸Then one of them, whose name was Cleopas, answered him,
"Are you the only stranger in Jerusalem
who does not know the things that have taken place there in these days?"
¹⁹He asked them, "What things?"
They replied, "The things about Jesus of Nazareth,
who was a prophet mighty in deed and word before God and all the people,
²⁰and how our chief priests and leaders
handed him over to be condemned to death and crucified him.
²¹But we had hoped that he was the one to redeem Israel.
Yes, and besides all this,
it is now the third day since these things took place.
²²Moreover, some women of our group astounded us.
They were at the tomb early this morning,
²³and when they did not find his body there, they came back
and told us that they had indeed seen a vision of angels
who said that he was alive.
²⁴Some of those who were with us went to the tomb
and found it just as the women had said;
but they did not see him."

²⁵Then he said to them,
"Oh, how foolish you are,
and how slow of heart to believe all that the prophets have declared!
²⁶Was it not necessary that the Messiah should suffer these things
and then enter into his glory?"
²⁷Then beginning with Moses and all the prophets,
he interpreted to them the things about himself in all the scriptures. ▸

GOSPEL   *Cleopas = KLEE-uh-pus*
Bringing the sound of weariness and deep sadness to the voices of the disciples on the road will provide a
meaningful contrast to their resurrected spirits and renewed energy in verses 32 and 33. Slow the delivery
of their speech (verses 18–24). Allow the modest raising of hopes in verses 22 and 23 to be dashed by the
acknowledgment in 24 that "they did not see him." The reader enriches the experience for the hearer by
telling the story as though unaware of how it ends.

^{28}As they came near the village to which they were going,
he walked ahead as if he were going on.
^{29}But they urged him strongly, saying,
"Stay with us,
because it is almost evening and the day is now nearly over."
So he went in to stay with them.

^{30}When he was at the table with them,
he took bread, blessed and broke it, and gave it to them.
^{31}Then their eyes were opened, and they recognized him;
and he vanished from their sight.
^{32}They said to each other,
"Were not our hearts burning within us
while he was talking to us on the road,
while he was opening the scriptures to us?"
^{33}That same hour they got up and returned to Jerusalem;
and they found the eleven and their companions gathered together.
^{34}They were saying,
"The Lord has risen indeed, and he has appeared to Simon!"
^{35}Then they told what had happened on the road,
and how he had been made known to them in the breaking of the bread.

The gospel of the Lord.

Fourth Sunday of Easter

FIRST READING: Acts 2:42-47

A reading from Acts.

⌐42⌐The baptized⌐ devoted themselves to the apostles' teaching and fellowship,
to the breaking of bread and the prayers.
⁴³Awe came upon everyone,
because many wonders and signs were being done by the apostles.
⁴⁴All who believed were together and had all things in common;
⁴⁵they would sell their possessions and goods
and distribute the proceeds to all, as any had need.
⁴⁶Day by day, as they spent much time together in the temple,
they broke bread at home and ate their food with glad and generous hearts,
⁴⁷praising God and having the goodwill of all the people.
And day by day the Lord added to their number those who were being saved.

The word of the Lord. *or* Word of God, word of life.

PSALMODY: Psalm 23

SECOND READING: 1 Peter 2:19-25

A reading from First Peter.

¹⁹It is a credit to you if, being aware of God,
you endure pain while suffering unjustly.
²⁰If you endure when you are beaten for doing wrong, what credit is that?
But if you endure when you do right and suffer for it,
you have God's approval.
²¹For to this you have been called,
because Christ also suffered for you, leaving you an example,
so that you should follow in his steps.

²²"He committed no sin,
and no deceit was found in his mouth."
²³When he was abused, he did not return abuse;
when he suffered, he did not threaten; ▸

FIRST READING
This is Luke's marvelous description of what the church should look like. The reader will help the hearer perhaps by remembering "then" but thinking "now." Even as you share what the early church looked like, concentrate on helping the hearer to understand that this is exactly what the church—and what our congregation!—should look like and can look like.

SECOND READING
This is one of the most beautiful pericopes in the entire three-year cycle. And yet, with its instruction to bear unjust suffering patiently, it is one of the most difficult for people to hear and to hold. Live with the text this week in preparation for reading it. Use it as a focus for personal devotion every day this week. Let it sink in, in your life. Then share it, in all its beauty and high expectation, with those who gather to hear the word on Sunday.

but he entrusted himself to the one who judges justly.
²⁴He himself bore our sins in his body on the cross,
so that, free from sins, we might live for righteousness;
by his wounds you have been healed.
²⁵For you were going astray like sheep,
but now you have returned to the shepherd and guardian of your souls.

The word of the Lord.   *or*   Word of God, word of life.

GOSPEL: John 10:1-10

The holy gospel according to John.

⌐Jesus said:¬
¹"Very truly, I tell you,
anyone who does not enter the sheepfold by the gate
but climbs in by another way is a thief and a bandit.
²The one who enters by the gate is the shepherd of the sheep.
³The gatekeeper opens the gate for him, and the sheep hear his voice.
He calls his own sheep by name and leads them out.
⁴When he has brought out all his own, he goes ahead of them,
and the sheep follow him because they know his voice.
⁵They will not follow a stranger,
but they will run from him
because they do not know the voice of strangers."

⁶Jesus used this figure of speech with them,
but they did not understand what he was saying to them.
⁷So again Jesus said to them,
"Very truly, I tell you, I am the gate for the sheep.
⁸All who came before me are thieves and bandits;
but the sheep did not listen to them.
⁹I am the gate.
Whoever enters by me will be saved,
and will come in and go out and find pasture.
¹⁰The thief comes only to steal and kill and destroy.
I came that they may have life, and have it abundantly."

The gospel of the Lord.

GOSPEL

While "I am the gate" may not be the flashiest metaphor invoked by our Lord, this wonderful little teaching moment leads to one of Jesus' most encouraging declarations: "I came that they may have life, and have it abundantly." An intensity in the reading from the very start may provide the most productive path to its marvelous conclusion.

FIFTH SUNDAY OF EASTER

FIRST READING: Acts 7:55-60

A reading from Acts.

⁵⁵Filled with the Holy Spirit,
⌐Stephen⌐ gazed into heaven and saw the glory of God
and Jesus standing at the right hand of God.
⁵⁶"Look," he said,
"I see the heavens opened
and the Son of Man standing at the right hand of God!"
⁵⁷But they covered their ears,
and with a loud shout all rushed together against him.
⁵⁸Then they dragged him out of the city and began to stone him;
and the witnesses laid their coats at the feet of a young man named Saul.
⁵⁹While they were stoning Stephen, he prayed,
"Lord Jesus, receive my spirit."
⁶⁰Then he knelt down and cried out in a loud voice,
"Lord, do not hold this sin against them."
When he had said this, he died.

The word of the Lord.   *or*   Word of God, word of life.

PSALMODY: Psalm 31:1-5, 15-16

FIRST READING

The story of St. Stephen, traditionally understood to be the first martyr of the church, is simple and straightforward. It has a quiet strength about it and need not be overdramatized by the reader. His quiet confidence in the power of God, even in the face of death, ("I see the heavens opened and the Son of Man standing at the right hand of God!") is of the essence. Stephen's prayers, "Lord, do not hold this sin against them," and "Lord Jesus, receive my spirit," echo the words of Jesus on the cross and anticipate the psalm appointed for this Sunday (31:5), "Into your hands I commend my spirit." Be certain to pause after "the glory of God" in verse 55. It is not "the glory of God and Jesus" he saw, but (1) the glory of God and (2) Jesus standing at the right hand of God.

SECOND READING: 1 Peter 2:2-10

A reading from First Peter.

[2]Like newborn infants, long for the pure, spiritual milk,
so that by it you may grow into salvation—
[3]if indeed you have tasted that the Lord is good.

[4]Come to him, a living stone,
though rejected by mortals yet chosen and precious in God's sight,
and [5]like living stones, let yourselves be built into a spiritual house,
to be a holy priesthood,
to offer spiritual sacrifices acceptable to God through Jesus Christ.
[6]For it stands in scripture:
  "See, I am laying in Zion a stone,
    a cornerstone chosen and precious;
  and whoever believes in him will not be put to shame."
[7]To you then who believe, he is precious;
but for those who do not believe,
  "The stone that the builders rejected
    has become the very head of the corner,"
[8]and "A stone that makes them stumble,
    and a rock that makes them fall."
They stumble because they disobey the word, as they were destined to do.

[9]But you are a chosen race, a royal priesthood, a holy nation,
God's own people,
in order that you may proclaim the mighty acts
of him who called you out of darkness into his marvelous light.
[10]Once you were not a people,
but now you are God's people;
once you had not received mercy,
but now you have received mercy.

The word of the Lord.   *or*   Word of God, word of life.

SECOND READING

This reading is a bit complicated because the author refers both to Jesus and to us as "living stones." Nowhere is that more evident than in verses 4 and 5: "Come to him (Jesus), a living stone, though rejected by mortals yet chosen and precious in God's sight, and (you) like living stones, let yourselves be built into a spiritual house." The text itself is a wonderful declaration of what it means to be a baptized person. Share that joy with the hearers!

GOSPEL: John 14:1-14

The holy gospel according to John.

⌐Jesus said to the disciples:⌐
[1]"Do not let your hearts be troubled. Believe in God, believe also in me.
[2]In my Father's house there are many dwelling places.
If it were not so, would I have told you that I go to prepare a place for you?
[3]And if I go and prepare a place for you,
I will come again and will take you to myself,
so that where I am, there you may be also.
[4]And you know the way to the place where I am going."

[5]Thomas said to him,
"Lord, we do not know where you are going.
How can we know the way?"
[6]Jesus said to him, "I am the way, and the truth, and the life.
No one comes to the Father except through me.
[7]If you know me, you will know my Father also.
From now on you do know him and have seen him."

[8]Philip said to him,
"Lord, show us the Father, and we will be satisfied."
[9]Jesus said to him,
"Have I been with you all this time, Philip,
and you still do not know me?
Whoever has seen me has seen the Father.
How can you say, 'Show us the Father'?
[10]Do you not believe that I am in the Father and the Father is in me?
The words that I say to you I do not speak on my own;
but the Father who dwells in me does his works.
[11]Believe me that I am in the Father and the Father is in me;
but if you do not, then believe me because of the works themselves.

[12]"Very truly, I tell you,
the one who believes in me will also do the works that I do and,
in fact, will do greater works than these,
because I am going to the Father.
[13]I will do whatever you ask in my name,
so that the Father may be glorified in the Son.
[14]If in my name you ask me for anything, I will do it."

The gospel of the Lord.

GOSPEL
A well-rehearsed reading might contrast a deep affection in our Lord's voice (verses 1–7) with something akin to frustration (if not some irritation) in verses 9–11. A deep breath might precede the concluding verses, 12–14.

✠ Sixth Sunday of Easter

FIRST READING: Acts 17:22-31

A reading from Acts.

²²Paul stood in front of the Areopagus and said,
"Athenians, I see how extremely religious you are in every way.
²³For as I went through the city
and looked carefully at the objects of your worship,
I found among them an altar with the inscription, 'To an unknown god.'
What therefore you worship as unknown, this I proclaim to you.
²⁴The God who made the world and everything in it,
he who is Lord of heaven and earth,
does not live in shrines made by human hands,
²⁵nor is he served by human hands, as though he needed anything,
since he himself gives to all mortals life and breath and all things.

²⁶"From one ancestor he made all nations to inhabit the whole earth,
and he allotted the times of their existence
and the boundaries of the places where they would live,
²⁷so that they would search for God
and perhaps grope for him and find him—
though indeed he is not far from each one of us.
²⁸For 'In him we live and move and have our being';
as even some of your own poets have said,
   'For we too are his offspring.'

²⁹"Since we are God's offspring,
we ought not to think that the deity is like gold, or silver, or stone,
an image formed by the art and imagination of mortals.
³⁰While God has overlooked the times of human ignorance,
now he commands all people everywhere to repent,
³¹because he has fixed a day
on which he will have the world judged in righteousness
by a man whom he has appointed,
and of this he has given assurance to all by raising him from the dead."

The word of the Lord.   *or*   Word of God, word of life.

FIRST READING   *Areopagus = ar-ih-OP-uh-gus   Athenians = uh-THEEN-ee-unz*
St. Paul is making a speech to a group of very bright people. They had altars to gods of many names. Just
to play it safe, they had an altar dedicated to "an unknown god." Paul says he is going to tell them about the
God whose name they do not know. Then he proceeds to explain the God we know, from Adam and Eve right
on through Jesus' resurrection, including us in the picture. That is the good news of Easter. Give this high-
powered sermon the energy and urgency it demands!

PSALMODY: Psalm 66:8-20

SECOND READING: 1 Peter 3:13-22

A reading from First Peter.

¹³Who will harm you if you are eager to do what is good?
¹⁴But even if you do suffer for doing what is right, you are blessed.
Do not fear what they fear, and do not be intimidated,
¹⁵but in your hearts sanctify Christ as Lord.
Always be ready to make your defense to anyone
who demands from you an accounting for the hope that is in you;
¹⁶yet do it with gentleness and reverence.
Keep your conscience clear, so that, when you are maligned,
those who abuse you for your good conduct in Christ may be put to shame.
¹⁷For it is better to suffer for doing good, if suffering should be God's will,
than to suffer for doing evil.
¹⁸For Christ also suffered for sins once for all,
the righteous for the unrighteous,
in order to bring you to God.
He was put to death in the flesh, but made alive in the spirit,
¹⁹in which also he went and made a proclamation to the spirits in prison,
²⁰who in former times did not obey,
when God waited patiently in the days of Noah,
during the building of the ark,
in which a few, that is, eight persons, were saved through water.

²¹And baptism, which this prefigured, now saves you—
not as a removal of dirt from the body,
but as an appeal to God for a good conscience,
through the resurrection of Jesus Christ,
²²who has gone into heaven and is at the right hand of God,
with angels, authorities, and powers made subject to him.

The word of the Lord.   *or*   Word of God, word of life.

SECOND READING
This is a tough little reading. The words are simple, but the thoughts are complex. That makes it doubly important to read slowly. The author says that even if one suffers for doing the right thing, one ought to hold onto Jesus as the source of hope. Jesus too suffered injustice "in order to bring you to God." The risen Christ has proclaimed (in the resurrection) the power of God to the spirits of evil. Christ has returned to heaven and rules over all. Deliver the letter as it was written: with boldness and confidence!

GOSPEL: John 14:15-21

The holy gospel according to John.

⌈Jesus said to the disciples:⌉
¹⁵"If you love me, you will keep my commandments.
¹⁶And I will ask the Father,
and he will give you another Advocate, to be with you forever.
¹⁷This is the Spirit of truth, whom the world cannot receive,
because it neither sees him nor knows him.
You know him, because he abides with you, and he will be in you.

¹⁸"I will not leave you orphaned; I am coming to you.
¹⁹In a little while the world will no longer see me,
but you will see me;
because I live, you also will live.
²⁰On that day you will know that I am in my Father,
and you in me, and I in you.
²¹They who have my commandments and keep them are those who love me;
and those who love me will be loved by my Father,
and I will love them and reveal myself to them."

The gospel of the Lord.

GOSPEL
Too often the words of Jesus are read as though they were written in a script. This deeply touching sequence of teachings and promises might profit by a more hesitant delivery, allowing the assembly to sense our Lord's working at what he wishes to say next.

✝ ASCENSION OF OUR LORD

FIRST READING: Acts 1:1-11

A reading from Acts.

⌐Luke writes:⌐
¹In the first book, Theophilus,
I wrote about all that Jesus did and taught from the beginning
²until the day when he was taken up to heaven,
after giving instructions through the Holy Spirit
to the apostles whom he had chosen.
³After his suffering he presented himself alive to them
by many convincing proofs,
appearing to them during forty days
and speaking about the kingdom of God.
⁴While staying with them, he ordered them not to leave Jerusalem,
but to wait there for the promise of the Father.
"This," he said, "is what you have heard from me;
⁵for John baptized with water,
but you will be baptized with the Holy Spirit not many days from now."

⁶So when they had come together, they asked him,
"Lord, is this the time when you will restore the kingdom to Israel?"
⁷He replied,
"It is not for you to know the times or periods
that the Father has set by his own authority.
⁸But you will receive power when the Holy Spirit has come upon you;
and you will be my witnesses
in Jerusalem, in all Judea and Samaria, and to the ends of the earth."
⁹When he had said this, as they were watching,
he was lifted up, and a cloud took him out of their sight.

¹⁰While he was going and they were gazing up toward heaven,
suddenly two men in white robes stood by them.
¹¹They said, "Men of Galilee,
why do you stand looking up toward heaven?
This Jesus, who has been taken up from you into heaven,
will come in the same way as you saw him go into heaven."

The word of the Lord.   *or*   Word of God, word of life.

FIRST READING   *Theophilus = thee-OFF-il-us*
The reader might wish to throw caution to the wind here and begin the reading with verse 1 rather than the proposed clarification of authorship, "Luke writes." Launch into the reading with all the energy invested in writing to a dear friend. Then allow the story to unfold to the wonder and mystery of verse 9. Set that verse apart from all the others. Verses 10 and 11 might provide a kind of ironic epitaph.

PSALMODY: Psalm 47 or Psalm 93

SECOND READING: Ephesians 1:15-23

A reading from Ephesians.

[15]I have heard of your faith in the Lord Jesus
and your love toward all the saints,
and for this reason [16]I do not cease to give thanks for you
as I remember you in my prayers.
[17]I pray that the God of our Lord Jesus Christ, the Father of glory,
may give you a spirit of wisdom and revelation as you come to know him,
[18]so that, with the eyes of your heart enlightened,
you may know what is the hope to which he has called you,
what are the riches of his glorious inheritance among the saints,
[19]and what is the immeasurable greatness of his power for us who believe,
according to the working of his great power.

[20]God put this power to work in Christ when he raised him from the dead
and seated him at his right hand in the heavenly places,
[21]far above all rule and authority and power and dominion,
and above every name that is named,
not only in this age but also in the age to come.
[22]And he has put all things under his feet
and has made him the head over all things for the church,
[23]which is his body, the fullness of him who fills all in all.

The word of the Lord.   *or*   Word of God, word of life.

SECOND READING   *Ephesians = eh-FEE-zhunz*
This reading too will profit from the energy associated with an enthusiastic letter writer. With that initial direction, consider this word of caution: these sentences are long, loaded, and nuanced. The wise reader will map them out mentally before beginning to read them aloud and will want to read them aloud more than once in preparing to share them with the assembly.

GOSPEL: Luke 24:44-53

The holy gospel according to Luke.

⁴⁴ ⌐Jesus said to the eleven and those with them,⌐
"These are my words that I spoke to you while I was still with you—
that everything written about me
in the law of Moses, the prophets, and the psalms must be fulfilled."
⁴⁵Then he opened their minds to understand the scriptures,
⁴⁶and he said to them,
"Thus it is written, that the Messiah is to suffer
and to rise from the dead on the third day,
⁴⁷and that repentance and forgiveness of sins
is to be proclaimed in his name to all nations,
beginning from Jerusalem.
⁴⁸You are witnesses of these things.
⁴⁹And see, I am sending upon you what my Father promised;
so stay here in the city until you have been clothed with power from on high."

⁵⁰Then he led them out as far as Bethany,
and, lifting up his hands, he blessed them.
⁵¹While he was blessing them, he withdrew from them
and was carried up into heaven.
⁵²And they worshiped him, and returned to Jerusalem with great joy;
⁵³and they were continually in the temple blessing God.

The gospel of the Lord.

GOSPEL
Allow a sense of awe to color every aspect of this reading—not merely at the aerodynamics of the ascension, but at Jesus' opening of minds, at the implications of being witnesses, and at the conferral of the apostolic mission. Color it all with awe, and with great joy.

SEVENTH SUNDAY OF EASTER

FIRST READING: Acts 1:6-14

A reading from Acts.

⁶When ⌜the apostles⌝ had come together, they asked ⌜Jesus,⌝
"Lord, is this the time when you will restore the kingdom to Israel?"
⁷He replied,
"It is not for you to know the times or periods
that the Father has set by his own authority.
⁸But you will receive power when the Holy Spirit has come upon you;
and you will be my witnesses
in Jerusalem, in all Judea and Samaria, and to the ends of the earth."

⁹When he had said this, as they were watching,
he was lifted up, and a cloud took him out of their sight.
¹⁰While he was going and they were gazing up toward heaven,
suddenly two men in white robes stood by them.
¹¹They said,
"Men of Galilee, why do you stand looking up toward heaven?
This Jesus, who has been taken up from you into heaven,
will come in the same way as you saw him go into heaven."

¹²Then they returned to Jerusalem from the mount called Olivet,
which is near Jerusalem, a sabbath day's journey away.
¹³When they had entered the city,
they went to the room upstairs where they were staying,
Peter, and John, and James, and Andrew, Philip and Thomas,
Bartholomew and Matthew, James son of Alphaeus,
and Simon the Zealot, and Judas son of James.
¹⁴All these were constantly devoting themselves to prayer,
together with certain women,
including Mary the mother of Jesus, as well as his brothers.

The word of the Lord.   *or*   Word of God, word of life.

PSALMODY: Psalm 68:1-10, 32-35

FIRST READING   *Alphaeus = al-FEE-us   Zealot = ZEL-ut*
The story is the well-known one of the ascension of our Lord. Verses 6-11 demand a sense of awe and majesty in their reading. Verses 12–14 detail who was present in the aftermath—the eleven disciples, Mary the mother of Jesus, and "certain women"—and appears to be Luke's way of anchoring the moment in history. The other point of this part of the text is that they were "constantly devoting themselves to prayer," which is the principal work of the people of God. Do not just tell the story—proclaim it! Let the hearer know from beginning to end that this is the gospel truth!

SECOND READING: 1 Peter 4:12-14; 5:6-11

A reading from First Peter.

[12]Beloved, do not be surprised at the fiery ordeal
that is taking place among you to test you,
as though something strange were happening to you.
[13]But rejoice insofar as you are sharing Christ's sufferings,
so that you may also be glad and shout for joy when his glory is revealed.
[14]If you are reviled for the name of Christ, you are blessed,
because the spirit of glory, which is the Spirit of God,
is resting on you.

[5:6]Humble yourselves therefore under the mighty hand of God,
so that he may exalt you in due time.
[7]Cast all your anxiety on him, because he cares for you.
[8]Discipline yourselves, keep alert.
Like a roaring lion your adversary the devil prowls around,
looking for someone to devour.
[9]Resist him, steadfast in your faith,
for you know that your brothers and sisters in all the world
are undergoing the same kinds of suffering.

[10]And after you have suffered for a little while,
the God of all grace, who has called you to his eternal glory in Christ,
will himself restore, support, strengthen, and establish you.
[11]To him be the power forever and ever. Amen.

The word of the Lord.   *or*   Word of God, word of life.

SECOND READING
Peter's words are, obviously, addressed to a people in pain. Their suffering for the faith was apparently significant. But these words are addressed to the people of faith in the pew on Easter 7 as well. They are an invitation to translate or understand the suffering, pain, or difficulty which we may be experiencing as "sharing Christ's suffering." They invite us to understand our suffering as holy work and to know that our pain will not last forever. This is an encouraging word the reader is called to share. It is best summarized in the sentence "Cast all your anxiety on him (God), because he cares for you." Sound encouraging in the reading.

GOSPEL: John 17:1-11

The holy gospel according to John.

¹After Jesus had spoken these words ⌐to his disciples,⌐
he looked up to heaven and said,
"Father, the hour has come;
glorify your Son so that the Son may glorify you,
²since you have given him authority over all people,
to give eternal life to all whom you have given him.
³And this is eternal life,
that they may know you, the only true God,
and Jesus Christ whom you have sent.
⁴I glorified you on earth
by finishing the work that you gave me to do.
⁵So now, Father, glorify me in your own presence
with the glory that I had in your presence before the world existed.

⁶"I have made your name known to those whom you gave me from the world.
They were yours, and you gave them to me,
and they have kept your word.
⁷Now they know that everything you have given me is from you;
⁸for the words that you gave to me I have given to them,
and they have received them
and know in truth that I came from you;
and they have believed that you sent me.
⁹I am asking on their behalf;
I am not asking on behalf of the world,
but on behalf of those whom you gave me, because they are yours.
¹⁰All mine are yours, and yours are mine;
and I have been glorified in them.

¹¹"And now I am no longer in the world,
but they are in the world,
and I am coming to you.
Holy Father, protect them in your name that you have given me,
so that they may be one, as we are one."

The gospel of the Lord.

GOSPEL
The Son's impassioned plea to the Father demands a genuine intensity on the part of the reader.
This does not necessarily demand a raised voice—but it does require an invested heart. Help the assembly
to hear the intensity of our Lord's love for his friends in the fervor of his prayer.

VIGIL OF PENTECOST

FIRST READING: Exodus 19:1-9
OR ACTS 2:1-11, following

A reading from Exodus.

¹On the third new moon after the Israelites had gone out of the land of Egypt,
on that very day, they came into the wilderness of Sinai.
²They had journeyed from Rephidim,
entered the wilderness of Sinai, and camped in the wilderness;
Israel camped there in front of the mountain.

³Then Moses went up to God;
the LORD called to him from the mountain, saying,
"Thus you shall say to the house of Jacob, and tell the Israelites:
⁴You have seen what I did to the Egyptians,
and how I bore you on eagles' wings and brought you to myself.
⁵Now therefore, if you obey my voice and keep my covenant,
you shall be my treasured possession out of all the peoples.
Indeed, the whole earth is mine,
⁶but you shall be for me a priestly kingdom and a holy nation.
These are the words that you shall speak to the Israelites."

⁷So Moses came, summoned the elders of the people,
and set before them all these words that the LORD had commanded him.
⁸The people all answered as one:
"Everything that the LORD has spoken we will do."
Moses reported the words of the people to the LORD.
⁹Then the LORD said to Moses,
"I am going to come to you in a dense cloud,
in order that the people may hear when I speak with you
and so trust you ever after."

The word of the Lord.   *or*   Word of God, word of life.

FIRST READING (Exodus)   *Sinai = SY-ny   Rephidim = REF-uh-dim*
The text is loaded with significant comings and goings, culminating in God's promise to come to Moses "in a dense cloud." Point the various arrivals and departures with pauses. Allow the hearer adequate time to follow the action.

OR: Acts 2:1-11

A reading from Acts.

¹When the day of Pentecost had come,
⌈the apostles⌉ were all together in one place.
²And suddenly from heaven there came a sound like the rush of a violent wind,
and it filled the entire house where they were sitting.
³Divided tongues, as of fire, appeared among them,
and a tongue rested on each of them.
⁴All of them were filled with the Holy Spirit
and began to speak in other languages, as the Spirit gave them ability.

⁵Now there were devout Jews from every nation under heaven
living in Jerusalem.
⁶And at this sound the crowd gathered and was bewildered,
because each one heard them speaking in the native language of each.
⁷Amazed and astonished, they asked,
"Are not all these who are speaking Galileans?
⁸And how is it that we hear, each of us, in our own native language?
⁹Parthians, Medes, Elamites,
and residents of Mesopotamia, Judea and Cappadocia, Pontus and Asia,
¹⁰Phrygia and Pamphylia, Egypt and the parts of Libya belonging to Cyrene,
and visitors from Rome, both Jews and proselytes, ¹¹Cretans and Arabs—
in our own languages we hear them speaking about God's deeds of power."

The word of the Lord.   *or*   Word of God, word of life.

PSALMODY: Psalm 33:12-22 or Psalm 130

SECOND READING: Romans 8:14-17, 22-27

A reading from Romans.

¹⁴All who are led by the Spirit of God are children of God.
¹⁵For you did not receive a spirit of slavery to fall back into fear,
but you have received a spirit of adoption.
When we cry, "Abba! Father!"
¹⁶it is that very Spirit bearing witness with our spirit
that we are children of God,

FIRST READING (Acts) *Mesopotamia = mes-oh-poh-TAY-mee-uh   Cappadocia = kap-uh-DOH-shee-uh
Phrygia = FRIJ-yuh   Pamphylia = pam-FIL-yuh   Cyrene = sy-REE-nuh*
This reading provides two distinct and significant challenges for the reader. The most apparent is the list of
less-than-familiar cities and regions. The other is the overwhelming noise that fills the entire house. The story
demands more energy and volume than most. It will also be helped if the reader is so utterly confident in the
pronunciations that the geographic sites can tumble out in something of an ecstatic rush. The well prepared
reader will have practiced long and hard.

¹⁷and if children, then heirs,
heirs of God and joint heirs with Christ—
if, in fact, we suffer with him
so that we may also be glorified with him.

²²We know that the whole creation has been groaning in labor pains until now;
²³and not only the creation,
but we ourselves, who have the first fruits of the Spirit,
groan inwardly while we wait for adoption, the redemption of our bodies.
²⁴For in hope we were saved.
Now hope that is seen is not hope.
For who hopes for what is seen?
²⁵But if we hope for what we do not see, we wait for it with patience.

²⁶Likewise the Spirit helps us in our weakness;
for we do not know how to pray as we ought,
but that very Spirit intercedes with sighs too deep for words.
²⁷And God, who searches the heart,
knows what is the mind of the Spirit,
because the Spirit intercedes for the saints according to the will of God.

The word of the Lord.   *or*   Word of God, word of life.

GOSPEL: John 7:37-39

The holy gospel according to John.

³⁷On the last day of the festival ⌐of Booths,⌐ the great day,
while Jesus was standing ⌐in the temple,⌐ he cried out,
"Let anyone who is thirsty come to me,
³⁸and let the one who believes in me drink.
As the scripture has said,
'Out of the believer's heart shall flow rivers of living water.'"
³⁹Now he said this about the Spirit,
which believers in him were to receive;
for as yet there was no Spirit,
because Jesus was not yet glorified.

The gospel of the Lord.

SECOND READING
This is a complex little reading. While the entire text speaks about the work of the Spirit, the thoughts are somewhat disjointed and the shape of the sentences is not always simple. Nothing will serve the lector so well as to "live with the text" during the week by employing it as the centerpiece of one's daily devotions.

GOSPEL
"He cried out." So says the text. Bringing that description to voice is the challenge. Is this a hopeful, ecstatic prophecy? Test the reading in rehearsal at a variety of decibels until it sounds right. Separate the explanation offered in verse 39 from the rest of the text with a pause and a change in volume.

FIRST READING: Acts 2:1-21
O<small>R</small> N<small>UMBERS</small> 11:24-30, following

A reading from Acts.

¹When the day of Pentecost had come,
⌐the apostles⌐ were all together in one place.
²And suddenly from heaven there came a sound
like the rush of a violent wind,
and it filled the entire house where they were sitting.
³Divided tongues, as of fire, appeared among them,
and a tongue rested on each of them.
⁴All of them were filled with the Holy Spirit
and began to speak in other languages, as the Spirit gave them ability.

⁵Now there were devout Jews from every nation under heaven
living in Jerusalem.
⁶And at this sound the crowd gathered and was bewildered,
because each one heard them speaking in the native language of each.
⁷Amazed and astonished, they asked,
"Are not all these who are speaking Galileans?
⁸And how is it that we hear, each of us, in our own native language?
⁹Parthians, Medes, Elamites,
and residents of Mesopotamia, Judea and Cappadocia, Pontus and Asia,
¹⁰Phrygia and Pamphylia, Egypt and the parts of Libya belonging to Cyrene,
and visitors from Rome, both Jews and proselytes, ¹¹Cretans and Arabs—
in our own languages we hear them speaking about God's deeds of power."

¹²All were amazed and perplexed, saying to one another,
"What does this mean?"
¹³But others sneered and said, "They are filled with new wine."

¹⁴But Peter, standing with the eleven, raised his voice and addressed them,
"Men of Judea and all who live in Jerusalem,
let this be known to you, and listen to what I say.
¹⁵Indeed, these are not drunk, as you suppose,
for it is only nine o'clock in the morning.

FIRST READING (Acts) *Mesopotamia = mes-oh-poh-TAY-mee-uh   Cappadocia = kap-uh-DOH-shee-uh
Phrygia = FRIJ-yuh   Pamphylia = pam-FIL-yuh   Cyrene = sy-REE-nuh*
This reading provides two distinct and significant challenges for the reader. The most apparent is the list
of less-than-familiar cities and regions. The other is the overwhelming noise that fills the entire house. The
story demands more energy and volume than most. It will also be helped if the reader is so utterly confident
in the pronunciations that the geographic sites can tumble out in something of an ecstatic rush. Also, note
that the word "prophesy" in verse 17 is a verb and pronounced *PROF-uh-sigh*. The well prepared reader will
have practiced long and hard.

¹⁶No, this is what was spoken through the prophet Joel:

  ¹⁷'In the last days it will be, God declares,
     that I will pour out my Spirit upon all flesh,
       and your sons and your daughters shall prophesy,
     and your young men shall see visions,
       and your old men shall dream dreams.
  ¹⁸Even upon my slaves, both men and women,
     in those days I will pour out my Spirit;
        and they shall prophesy.
  ¹⁹And I will show portents in the heaven above
     and signs on the earth below,
       blood, and fire, and smoky mist.
  ²⁰The sun shall be turned to darkness
     and the moon to blood,
       before the coming of the Lord's great and glorious day.
  ²¹Then everyone who calls on the name of the Lord shall be saved.' "

The word of the Lord.   *or*   Word of God, word of life.

OR: Numbers 11:24-30

A reading from Numbers.

²⁴Moses went out and told the people the words of the Lord;
and he gathered seventy elders of the people,
and placed them all around the tent.
²⁵Then the Lord came down in the cloud and spoke to him,
and took some of the spirit that was on him
and put it on the seventy elders;
and when the spirit rested upon them, they prophesied.
But they did not do so again.

²⁶Two men remained in the camp,
one named Eldad, and the other named Medad,
and the spirit rested on them;
they were among those registered,
but they had not gone out to the tent,
and so they prophesied in the camp.
²⁷And a young man ran and told Moses,
"Eldad and Medad are prophesying in the camp." ▸

FIRST READING (Numbers)   *Eldad = EL-dad Medad = MEE-dad*
Toward the end of verse 25, the word "once" is implied, but not present: ". . . they prophesied [once]."
Because of its absence, a healthy pause before reading, "But they did not do so again" is essential if verse
25 is to make sense to the hearer. Allow the whole text to celebrate the lighting of the Spirit of God on God's
people.

²⁸And Joshua son of Nun, the assistant of Moses, one of his chosen men, said,
"My lord Moses, stop them!"
²⁹But Moses said to him,
"Are you jealous for my sake?
Would that all the LORD's people were prophets,
and that the LORD would put his spirit on them!"
³⁰And Moses and the elders of Israel returned to the camp.

The word of the Lord.   *or*   Word of God, word of life.

PSALMODY: Psalm 104:24-34, 35b

SECOND READING: 1 Corinthians 12:3b-13
OR ACTS 2:1-21, following

A reading from First Corinthians.

³ᵇNo one can say "Jesus is Lord" except by the Holy Spirit.

⁴Now there are varieties of gifts, but the same Spirit;
⁵and there are varieties of services, but the same Lord;
⁶and there are varieties of activities,
but it is the same God who activates all of them in everyone.
⁷To each is given the manifestation of the Spirit for the common good.
⁸To one is given through the Spirit the utterance of wisdom,
and to another the utterance of knowledge according to the same Spirit,
⁹to another faith by the same Spirit,
to another gifts of healing by the one Spirit,
¹⁰to another the working of miracles,
to another prophecy,
to another the discernment of spirits,
to another various kinds of tongues,
to another the interpretation of tongues.
¹¹All these are activated by one and the same Spirit,
who allots to each one individually just as the Spirit chooses.

¹²For just as the body is one and has many members,
and all the members of the body, though many, are one body,
so it is with Christ.

SECOND READING (1 Corinthians)   *prophecy = PROF-uh-see*
This is a word of enormous encouragement to every baptized person. As with the first reading, this one
requires a sense of energy and joy—but an instructive pace (not too fast) with careful attention to diction.
Take a close look and work carefully at verses 8–10 and verse 12. This text takes some time for the hearer
adequately to absorb. Notice that here the word "prophecy" is the noun, not the verb as in the Acts reading.

¹³For in the one Spirit we were all baptized into one body—
Jews or Greeks, slaves or free—
and we were all made to drink of one Spirit.

The word of the Lord.   *or*   Word of God, word of life.

OR: Acts 2:1-21

A reading from Acts.

¹When the day of Pentecost had come,
⌐the apostles⌐ were all together in one place.
²And suddenly from heaven there came a sound like the rush of a violent wind,
and it filled the entire house where they were sitting.
³Divided tongues, as of fire, appeared among them,
and a tongue rested on each of them.
⁴All of them were filled with the Holy Spirit
and began to speak in other languages, as the Spirit gave them ability.
⁵Now there were devout Jews from every nation under heaven
living in Jerusalem.
⁶And at this sound the crowd gathered and was bewildered,
because each one heard them speaking in the native language of each.
⁷Amazed and astonished, they asked,
"Are not all these who are speaking Galileans?
⁸And how is it that we hear, each of us, in our own native language?
⁹Parthians, Medes, Elamites,
and residents of Mesopotamia, Judea and Cappadocia, Pontus and Asia,
¹⁰Phrygia and Pamphylia, Egypt and the parts of Libya belonging to Cyrene,
and visitors from Rome, both Jews and proselytes, ¹¹Cretans and Arabs—
in our own languages we hear them speaking about God's deeds of power."

¹²All were amazed and perplexed, saying to one another,
"What does this mean?"
¹³But others sneered and said, "They are filled with new wine."

¹⁴But Peter, standing with the eleven, raised his voice and addressed them,
"Men of Judea and all who live in Jerusalem,
let this be known to you, and listen to what I say.
¹⁵Indeed, these are not drunk, as you suppose,
for it is only nine o'clock in the morning. ▸

SECOND READING (Acts)
See notes for the first reading from Acts.

¹⁶No, this is what was spoken through the prophet Joel:
  ¹⁷'In the last days it will be, God declares,
  that I will pour out my Spirit upon all flesh,
    and your sons and your daughters shall prophesy,
  and your young men shall see visions,
    and your old men shall dream dreams.
  ¹⁸Even upon my slaves, both men and women,
    in those days I will pour out my Spirit;
      and they shall prophesy.
  ¹⁹And I will show portents in the heaven above
    and signs on the earth below,
      blood, and fire, and smoky mist.
  ²⁰The sun shall be turned to darkness
    and the moon to blood,
      before the coming of the Lord's great and glorious day.
  ²¹Then everyone who calls on the name of the Lord shall be saved.' "

The word of the Lord.   *or*   Word of God, word of life.

GOSPEL: John 20:19-23
Or John 7:37-39, following

The holy gospel according to John.

¹⁹When it was evening on that day, the first day of the week,
and the doors of the house where the disciples had met
were locked for fear of the Jews,
Jesus came and stood among them and said,
"Peace be with you."
²⁰After he said this, he showed them his hands and his side.
Then the disciples rejoiced when they saw the Lord.
²¹Jesus said to them again,
"Peace be with you.
As the Father has sent me, so I send you."

²²When he had said this, he breathed on them and said to them,
"Receive the Holy Spirit.
²³If you forgive the sins of any, they are forgiven them;
if you retain the sins of any, they are retained."

The gospel of the Lord.

GOSPEL (John 20)
The heart of this little story (when read on Pentecost) is found in the odd little phrase "he breathed on them."
A penetrating reading of the text will require some consideration of how one might illuminate or illustrate
this "lighting of the Spirit of God" in the articulation of that phrase.

OR: John 7:37-39

The holy gospel according to John.

³⁷On the last day of the festival ⌐of Booths⌐ the great day,
while Jesus was standing ⌐in the temple⌐ he cried out,
"Let anyone who is thirsty come to me,
³⁸and let the one who believes in me drink.
As the scripture has said,
'Out of the believer's heart shall flow rivers of living water.'"
³⁹Now he said this about the Spirit,
which believers in him were to receive;
for as yet there was no Spirit,
because Jesus was not yet glorified.

The gospel of the Lord.

GOSPEL (John 7)
This awkward little reading celebrates—by allusion to its absence!—the gift of the Spirit of God. It merits prayerful pondering, perhaps consultation of a commentary, and a deliberate delivery.

Time after Pentecost
COMPLEMENTARY SERIES

An alternative series with semicontinuous First Readings and Psalms begins on page 303.

The Holy Trinity
First Sunday after Pentecost

FIRST READING: Genesis 1:1—2:4a

A reading from Genesis.

¹In the beginning when God created the heavens and the earth,
²the earth was a formless void
and darkness covered the face of the deep,
while a wind from God swept over the face of the waters.
³Then God said,
"Let there be light"; and there was light.
⁴And God saw that the light was good;
and God separated the light from the darkness.
⁵God called the light Day,
and the darkness he called Night.
And there was evening and there was morning, the first day.

⁶And God said,
"Let there be a dome in the midst of the waters,
and let it separate the waters from the waters."
⁷So God made the dome and separated the waters that were under the dome
from the waters that were above the dome.
And it was so.
⁸God called the dome Sky.
And there was evening and there was morning, the second day.

⁹And God said,
"Let the waters under the sky be gathered together into one place,
and let the dry land appear."
And it was so.
¹⁰God called the dry land Earth,
and the waters that were gathered together he called Seas.
And God saw that it was good.
¹¹Then God said,
"Let the earth put forth vegetation:
plants yielding seed,
and fruit trees of every kind on earth that bear fruit with the seed in it."
And it was so. ▸

FIRST READING
Length and familiarity both pose dangers for the reader of this pericope. Take steps to address these dangers. (1) Steep yourself in the text. Rediscover it by re-reading it with some frequency in preparation for Sunday. (2) Notice that the repetition in the reading develops a cadence or rhythm that helps to carry the story along. (3) Finally, remember the day. This Sunday, The Holy Trinity, is, as it were, God's "Name Day." Today we celebrate the majesty and the mystery of God. Help us imagine the Father, the Son, and the Holy Spirit engaged in the wild and wonderful task of creation. An expansive act of creation demands an expansive reading!

¹²The earth brought forth vegetation:
plants yielding seed of every kind,
and trees of every kind bearing fruit with the seed in it.
And God saw that it was good.
¹³And there was evening and there was morning, the third day.

¹⁴And God said,
"Let there be lights in the dome of the sky
to separate the day from the night;
and let them be for signs and for seasons and for days and years,
¹⁵and let them be lights in the dome of the sky to give light upon the earth."
And it was so.
¹⁶God made the two great lights—
the greater light to rule the day
and the lesser light to rule the night—and the stars.
¹⁷God set them in the dome of the sky to give light upon the earth,
¹⁸to rule over the day and over the night,
and to separate the light from the darkness.
And God saw that it was good.
¹⁹And there was evening and there was morning, the fourth day.

²⁰And God said,
"Let the waters bring forth swarms of living creatures,
and let birds fly above the earth across the dome of the sky."
²¹So God created the great sea monsters
and every living creature that moves, of every kind,
with which the waters swarm,
and every winged bird of every kind.
And God saw that it was good.
²²God blessed them, saying,
"Be fruitful and multiply and fill the waters in the seas,
and let birds multiply on the earth."
²³And there was evening and there was morning, the fifth day.

²⁴And God said,
"Let the earth bring forth living creatures of every kind:
cattle and creeping things and wild animals of the earth of every kind."
And it was so.
²⁵God made the wild animals of the earth of every kind,
and the cattle of every kind,
and everything that creeps upon the ground of every kind.
And God saw that it was good.

^{26}Then God said,
"Let us make humankind in our image,
according to our likeness;
and let them have dominion over the fish of the sea,
and over the birds of the air,
and over the cattle, and over all the wild animals of the earth,
and over every creeping thing that creeps upon the earth."
  ^{27}So God created humankind in his image,
      in the image of God he created them;
      male and female he created them.
^{28}God blessed them, and God said to them,
"Be fruitful and multiply,
and fill the earth and subdue it;
and have dominion over the fish of the sea
and over the birds of the air
and over every living thing that moves upon the earth."
^{29}God said,
"See, I have given you every plant yielding seed
that is upon the face of all the earth,
and every tree with seed in its fruit;
you shall have them for food.
^{30}And to every beast of the earth,
and to every bird of the air,
and to everything that creeps on the earth,
everything that has the breath of life,
I have given every green plant for food."
And it was so.
^{31}God saw everything that he had made,
and indeed, it was very good.
And there was evening and there was morning, the sixth day.

$^{2:1}$Thus the heavens and the earth were finished,
and all their multitude.
^{2}And on the seventh day God finished the work that he had done,
and he rested on the seventh day from all the work that he had done.
^{3}So God blessed the seventh day and hallowed it,
because on it God rested from all the work that he had done in creation.

^{4}These are the generations of the heavens and the earth when they were created.

The word of the Lord.   *or*   Word of God, word of life.

PSALMODY: Psalm 8

SECOND READING: 2 Corinthians 13:11-13

A reading from Second Corinthians.

⌜Paul writes:⌝
[11]Finally, brothers and sisters, farewell.
Put things in order, listen to my appeal,
agree with one another, live in peace;
and the God of love and peace will be with you.
[12]Greet one another with a holy kiss.
All the saints greet you.

[13]The grace of the Lord Jesus Christ, the love of God,
and the communion of the Holy Spirit be with all of you.

The word of the Lord.   *or*   Word of God, word of life.

GOSPEL: Matthew 28:16-20

The holy gospel according to Matthew.

[16]Now the eleven disciples went to Galilee,
to the mountain to which Jesus had directed them.
[17]When they saw him, they worshiped him; but some doubted.

[18]And Jesus came and said to them,
"All authority in heaven and on earth has been given to me.
[19]Go therefore and make disciples of all nations,
baptizing them in the name of the Father and of the Son
and of the Holy Spirit,
[20]and teaching them to obey everything that I have commanded you.
And remember, I am with you always, to the end of the age."

The gospel of the Lord.

SECOND READING
This text is included because it is one of the early references to the Holy Trinity. Verse 13 is widely known as the Apostolic Greeting. It is the final lines of a letter to the church at Corinth. Watch the periods and commas, providing the pauses for which they call. Allow each sentence—each phrase—to stand alone as the final thoughts in a letter often do. Take your time.

GOSPEL
This is one of the Jesus' sayings that many in the assembly will know by heart. Combine authority and affection in a reading that sounds as though it comes from Jesus' heart.

FIRST READING: Isaiah 49:8-16a

A reading from Isaiah.

⁸Thus says the LORD:
In a time of favor I have answered you,
    on a day of salvation I have helped you;
I have kept you and given you
    as a covenant to the people,
to establish the land,
    to apportion the desolate heritages;
⁹saying to the prisoners, "Come out,"
    to those who are in darkness, "Show yourselves."
They shall feed along the ways,
    on all the bare heights shall be their pasture;
¹⁰they shall not hunger or thirst,
    neither scorching wind nor sun shall strike them down,
for he who has pity on them will lead them,
    and by springs of water will guide them.
¹¹And I will turn all my mountains into a road,
    and my highways shall be raised up.
¹²Lo, these shall come from far away,
    and lo, these from the north and from the west,
    and these from the land of Syene.

¹³Sing for joy, O heavens, and exult, O earth;
    break forth, O mountains, into singing!
For the LORD has comforted his people,
    and will have compassion on his suffering ones.

¹⁴But Zion said, "The LORD has forsaken me,
    my LORD has forgotten me."
¹⁵Can a woman forget her nursing child,
    or show no compassion for the child of her womb?
Even these may forget,
    yet I will not forget you.
¹⁶See, I have inscribed you on the palms of my hands.

The word of the Lord.   *or*   Word of God, word of life.

FIRST READING   *Isaiah = eye-ZAY-uh Syene = sy-EE-nih*
The early verses of the text, which celebrate the role and the action of "the servant," demand that the reader invest some time in a consideration of the whole 49th chapter if the reader's understanding is to develop into an intelligent reading. The three sentences of verses 15–16 are among the most poignant in scripture. Savor each one.

PSALMODY: Psalm 131

SECOND READING: 1 Corinthians 4:1-5

A reading from First Corinthians.

¹Think of us in this way,
as servants of Christ and stewards of God's mysteries.
²Moreover, it is required of stewards that they be found trustworthy.
³But with me it is a very small thing that I should be judged by you
or by any human court.
I do not even judge myself.
⁴I am not aware of anything against myself,
but I am not thereby acquitted.
It is the Lord who judges me.
⁵Therefore do not pronounce judgment before the time,
before the Lord comes,
who will bring to light the things now hidden in darkness
and will disclose the purposes of the heart.
Then each one will receive commendation from God.

The word of the Lord.   *or*   Word of God, word of life.

SECOND READING
Is there just a hint of arrogance in verse 4: "I am not aware of anything against myself"? Or is it apostolic confidence? A blending of the two tones may be the key to helping the assembly hear a very human Paul.

GOSPEL: Matthew 6:24-34

The holy gospel according to Matthew.

⌐Jesus said to the disciples:⌐
24"No one can serve two masters;
for a slave will either hate the one and love the other,
or be devoted to the one and despise the other.
You cannot serve God and wealth.

25"Therefore I tell you,
do not worry about your life,
what you will eat or what you will drink,
or about your body, what you will wear.
Is not life more than food, and the body more than clothing?
26Look at the birds of the air;
they neither sow nor reap nor gather into barns,
and yet your heavenly Father feeds them.
Are you not of more value than they?
27And can any of you by worrying
add a single hour to your span of life?
28And why do you worry about clothing?
Consider the lilies of the field, how they grow;
they neither toil nor spin,
29yet I tell you, even Solomon in all his glory
was not clothed like one of these.
30But if God so clothes the grass of the field,
which is alive today and tomorrow is thrown into the oven,
will he not much more clothe you—you of little faith?

31"Therefore do not worry, saying,
'What will we eat?' or 'What will we drink?' or 'What will we wear?'
32For it is the Gentiles who strive for all these things;
and indeed your heavenly Father knows that you need all these things.
33But strive first for the kingdom of God and his righteousness,
and all these things will be given to you as well.

34"So do not worry about tomorrow,
for tomorrow will bring worries of its own.
Today's trouble is enough for today."

The gospel of the Lord.

GOSPEL
Appropriately spaced pauses will allow the assembly to hear our Lord "think up" one phrase, one illustration after another in an attempt to teach his followers something about contentment. Do not merely read the text. Bring it to life.

FIRST READING: Deuteronomy 11:18-21, 26-28

A reading from Deuteronomy.

⌐Moses said to all Israel:⌐
[18]You shall put these words of mine in your heart and soul,
and you shall bind them as a sign on your hand,
and fix them as an emblem on your forehead.
[19]Teach them to your children,
talking about them when you are at home and when you are away,
when you lie down and when you rise.
[20]Write them on the doorposts of your house and on your gates,
[21]so that your days and the days of your children may be multiplied
in the land that the LORD swore to your ancestors to give them,
as long as the heavens are above the earth.

[26]See, I am setting before you today a blessing and a curse:
[27]the blessing, if you obey the commandments of the LORD your God
that I am commanding you today;
[28]and the curse, if you do not obey the commandments of the LORD your God,
but turn from the way that I am commanding you today,
to follow other gods that you have not known.

The word of the Lord.   *or*   Word of God, word of life.

PSALMODY: Psalm 31:1-5, 19-24

FIRST READING   *Deuteronomy = dew-ter-ON-uh-mee*
The wearing of phylacteries (small cubes made of animal skins, containing four quotations from the Hebrew scripture, attached to leather straps wrapped around the head and arm, worn by orthodox Jews during morning prayer) is anchored in this text. The practice is designed to recall that the words of God ought to control one's thinking and acting. This reading is Moses' urgent instruction to the people to recall and obey the commandments of the LORD. Pay close attention to the text's punctuation, and heed it. Punctuation marks are road signs for a cogent reading.

SECOND READING: Romans 1:16-17; 3:22b-28 [29-31]

A reading from Romans.

[16]I am not ashamed of the gospel;
it is the power of God for salvation to everyone who has faith,
to the Jew first and also to the Greek.
[17]For in it the righteousness of God is revealed through faith for faith;
as it is written,
"The one who is righteous will live by faith."

[3:22b]For there is no distinction,
[23]since all have sinned and fall short of the glory of God;
[24]they are now justified by his grace as a gift,
through the redemption that is in Christ Jesus,
[25]whom God put forward as a sacrifice of atonement by his blood,
effective through faith.
He did this to show his righteousness,
because in his divine forbearance
he had passed over the sins previously committed;
[26]it was to prove at the present time that he himself is righteous
and that he justifies the one who has faith in Jesus.
[27]Then what becomes of boasting? It is excluded.
By what law? By that of works?
No, but by the law of faith.
[28]For we hold that a person is justified by faith
apart from works prescribed by the law.

[[29]Or is God the God of Jews only?
Is he not the God of Gentiles also?
Yes, of Gentiles also, [30]since God is one;
and he will justify the circumcised on the ground of faith
and the uncircumcised through that same faith.
[31]Do we then overthrow the law by this faith?
By no means! On the contrary, we uphold the law.]

The word of the Lord.   *or*   Word of God, word of life.

SECOND READING
Practice this one, repeatedly, and read it slowly. This cutting jumps from the first chapter of the letter to the third in an effort to summarize its contents. Readings from Romans will occupy our attention all summer long. In simplest terms, the author says Gentiles and Jews alike are justified by faith in Jesus and that, having been justified, they desire to uphold the law. At the beginning of verse 30, stress "one," not "is." Paul is not saying that God is a Gentile, but that God is one God.

GOSPEL: Matthew 7:21-29

The holy gospel according to Matthew.

⌐Jesus said to the disciples:¬
²¹"Not everyone who says to me, 'Lord, Lord,'
will enter the kingdom of heaven,
but only the one who does the will of my Father in heaven.
²²On that day many will say to me,
'Lord, Lord, did we not prophesy in your name,
and cast out demons in your name,
and do many deeds of power in your name?'
²³Then I will declare to them,
'I never knew you; go away from me, you evildoers.'

²⁴"Everyone then who hears these words of mine and acts on them
will be like a wise man who built his house on rock.
²⁵The rain fell, the floods came, and the winds blew and beat on that house,
but it did not fall, because it had been founded on rock.
²⁶And everyone who hears these words of mine and does not act on them
will be like a foolish man who built his house on sand.
²⁷The rain fell, and the floods came,
and the winds blew and beat against that house, and it fell—
and great was its fall!"

²⁸Now when Jesus had finished saying these things,
the crowds were astounded at his teaching,
²⁹for he taught them as one having authority, and not as their scribes.

The gospel of the Lord.

GOSPEL   *prophesy = PROF-uh-sigh*
This simple bit of instruction urges the hearer to be attentive to the words of Jesus and to act on them. Help the assembly hear the dialogue in verses 21–23. Modest astonishment or disbelief in the voice of the pious plea might contrast well to the understated voice of Jesus: "I never knew you." Allow a kind of warmth to enfold the warning in verses 24 to 27. A healthy pause between verses 27 and 28 will ready the hearer for the powerful observation contained in the final verses.

FIRST READING: Hosea 5:15—6:6

A reading from Hosea.

¹⁵I will return again to my place
until they acknowledge their guilt and seek my face.
In their distress they will beg my favor:
^{6:1}"Come, let us return to the LORD;
for it is he who has torn, and he will heal us;
he has struck down, and he will bind us up.
²After two days he will revive us;
on the third day he will raise us up,
that we may live before him.
³Let us know, let us press on to know the LORD;
his appearing is as sure as the dawn;
he will come to us like the showers,
like the spring rains that water the earth."

⁴What shall I do with you, O Ephraim?
What shall I do with you, O Judah?
Your love is like a morning cloud,
like the dew that goes away early.
⁵Therefore I have hewn them by the prophets,
I have killed them by the words of my mouth,
and my judgment goes forth as the light.
⁶For I desire steadfast love and not sacrifice,
the knowledge of God rather than burnt offerings.

The word of the Lord.   *or*   Word of God, word of life.

PSALMODY: Psalm 50:7-15

FIRST READING   *Hosea = hoh-ZAY-uh   Ephraim = EEF-rih-um*
This is a strong, classic cutting from the prophet Hosea. The assembly needs to hear two voices in this text. 5:15 is the voice of God. 6:1-3 is the voice of God's people repenting, as God hopes they will. 6:4-6 is the voice of God again. As the reader, you need not change the sound of your voice, but you can help the congregation hear the change of voice by pausing at each shift of speaker and helping us to sense the determination in the voice of the people and the strength in the voice of God. Note the beautiful poetic contrast that speaks of God's faithfulness as the certainty of spring rain and speaks of Ephraim's love as "the dew that goes away early."

SECOND READING: Romans 4:13-25

A reading from Romans.

[13]The promise that he would inherit the world
did not come to Abraham or to his descendants through the law
but through the righteousness of faith.
[14]If it is the adherents of the law who are to be the heirs,
faith is null and the promise is void.
[15]For the law brings wrath;
but where there is no law, neither is there violation.

[16]For this reason it depends on faith,
in order that the promise may rest on grace
and be guaranteed to all his descendants,
not only to the adherents of the law
but also to those who share the faith of Abraham
(for he is the father of all of us,
[17]as it is written, "I have made you the father of many nations")—
in the presence of the God in whom he believed,
who gives life to the dead
and calls into existence the things that do not exist.

[18]Hoping against hope,
he believed that he would become "the father of many nations,"
according to what was said, "So numerous shall your descendants be."
[19]He did not weaken in faith when he considered his own body,
which was already as good as dead (for he was about a hundred years old),
or when he considered the barrenness of Sarah's womb.
[20]No distrust made him waver concerning the promise of God,
but he grew strong in his faith as he gave glory to God,
[21]being fully convinced that God was able to do what he had promised.
[22]Therefore his faith "was reckoned to him as righteousness."
[23]Now the words, "it was reckoned to him,"
were written not for his sake alone, [24]but for ours also.
It will be reckoned to us who believe in him
who raised Jesus our Lord from the dead,
[25]who was handed over to death for our trespasses
and was raised for our justification.

The word of the Lord.   *or*   Word of God, word of life.

SECOND READING
This is a determined, logical explication of the truth that our inheritance of God's promises rests on faith, not on our adherence to the law. The reading demands the voice of conviction. Long complex sentences require the reader to pay careful attention to commas and periods as well as to the logical sequence of thought, often interrupted by parenthetical expressions. It is not an easy reading. Take some time to let the text soak into the reader's soul during the week of preparation.

GOSPEL: Matthew 9:9-13, 18-26

The holy gospel according to Matthew.

[9]As Jesus was walking along,
he saw a man called Matthew sitting at the tax booth;
and he said to him, "Follow me."
And he got up and followed him.

[10]And as he sat at dinner in the house,
many tax collectors and sinners came
and were sitting with him and his disciples.
[11]When the Pharisees saw this, they said to his disciples,
"Why does your teacher eat with tax collectors and sinners?"
[12]But when he heard this, he said,
"Those who are well have no need of a physician,
but those who are sick.
[13]Go and learn what this means, 'I desire mercy, not sacrifice.'
For I have come to call not the righteous but sinners."

[18]While he was saying these things to them,
suddenly a leader of the synagogue came in and knelt before him, saying,
"My daughter has just died;
but come and lay your hand on her, and she will live."
[19]And Jesus got up and followed him, with his disciples.
[20]Then suddenly a woman
who had been suffering from hemorrhages for twelve years
came up behind him and touched the fringe of his cloak,
[21]for she said to herself,
"If I only touch his cloak, I will be made well."
[22]Jesus turned, and seeing her he said,
"Take heart, daughter; your faith has made you well."
And instantly the woman was made well.

[23]When Jesus came to the leader's house
and saw the flute players and the crowd making a commotion,
[24]he said, "Go away; for the girl is not dead but sleeping."
And they laughed at him.
[25]But when the crowd had been put outside,
he went in and took her by the hand, and the girl got up.
[26]And the report of this spread throughout that district.

The gospel of the Lord.

GOSPEL   *synagogue = SIN-uh-gog   hemorrhages = HEM-or-uh-juhz*
The challenge in this reading is that it tells four different stories, and the third is interrupted by the fourth.
A pause of significance between each of the paragraphs will be essential. A parenthetical pause coupled
with an increased sense of urgency—to help the assembly hear the insertion of the story of the bleeding
woman as an interruption—should precede verse 20. A final pause before verse 26 will help give that
concluding verse the sense that the report of all this "spread throughout that district."

Sunday, June 12–18 *(if after Holy Trinity)*
Time after Pentecost — Lectionary 11

FIRST READING: Exodus 19:2-8a

A reading from Exodus.

² ⌜The Israelites⌝ had journeyed from Rephidim,
entered the wilderness of Sinai, and camped in the wilderness;
Israel camped there in front of the mountain.
³Then Moses went up to God;
the LORD called to him from the mountain, saying,
"Thus you shall say to the house of Jacob, and tell the Israelites:
⁴You have seen what I did to the Egyptians,
and how I bore you on eagles' wings and brought you to myself.
⁵Now therefore, if you obey my voice and keep my covenant,
you shall be my treasured possession out of all the peoples.
Indeed, the whole earth is mine,
⁶but you shall be for me a priestly kingdom and a holy nation.
These are the words that you shall speak to the Israelites."

⁷So Moses came, summoned the elders of the people,
and set before them all these words that the LORD had commanded him.
⁸The people all answered as one:
"Everything that the LORD has spoken we will do."

The word of the Lord.   *or*   Word of God, word of life.

PSALMODY: Psalm 100

FIRST READING   *Rephidim = REF-uh-dim   Sinai = SY-ny*
This little story affirms the singular and specific relationship between Almighty God and the people of Israel.
The church understands a similar relationship to have been established between Almighty God and itself in
the sacrament of holy baptism. It is the responsibility of the reader to help the people in the pew sense that
this is their story. The power of God and the strength of the people's resolve require a commanding reading.

SECOND READING: Romans 5:1-8

A reading from Romans.

¹Since we are justified by faith,
we have peace with God through our Lord Jesus Christ,
²through whom we have obtained access to this grace in which we stand;
and we boast in our hope of sharing the glory of God.
³And not only that, but we also boast in our sufferings,
knowing that suffering produces endurance,
⁴and endurance produces character,
and character produces hope,
⁵and hope does not disappoint us,
because God's love has been poured into our hearts
through the Holy Spirit that has been given to us.

⁶For while we were still weak,
at the right time Christ died for the ungodly.
⁷Indeed, rarely will anyone die for a righteous person—
though perhaps for a good person someone might actually dare to die.
⁸But God proves his love for us
in that while we still were sinners Christ died for us.

The word of the Lord.   *or*   Word of God, word of life.

SECOND READING
The author illustrates that it is Christ Jesus who has established the relationship between God and humankind "while we still were sinners." Verses 3-5 are one sentence and require careful attention to the commas, so that the sentence builds to a climax at the end of verse 5 and not with the words "and hope does not disappoint us." These are two powerful little readings that will be more powerful still if the reader will dedicate some quiet time during the week in which to meditate on the truth they proclaim.

GOSPEL: Matthew 9:35—10:8 [9-23]

The holy gospel according to Matthew.

[35]Jesus went about all the cities and villages,
teaching in their synagogues,
and proclaiming the good news of the kingdom,
and curing every disease and every sickness.
[36]When he saw the crowds, he had compassion for them,
because they were harassed and helpless, like sheep without a shepherd.
[37]Then he said to his disciples,
"The harvest is plentiful, but the laborers are few;
[38]therefore ask the Lord of the harvest to send out laborers into his harvest."
[10:1]Then Jesus summoned his twelve disciples
and gave them authority over unclean spirits,
to cast them out, and to cure every disease and every sickness.

[2]These are the names of the twelve apostles:
first, Simon, also known as Peter, and his brother Andrew;
James son of Zebedee, and his brother John;
[3]Philip and Bartholomew; Thomas and Matthew the tax collector;
James son of Alphaeus, and Thaddaeus;
[4]Simon the Cananaean, and Judas Iscariot, the one who betrayed him.

[5]These twelve Jesus sent out with the following instructions:
"Go nowhere among the Gentiles, and enter no town of the Samaritans,
[6]but go rather to the lost sheep of the house of Israel.
[7]As you go, proclaim the good news,
'The kingdom of heaven has come near.'
[8]Cure the sick, raise the dead, cleanse the lepers, cast out demons.
You received without payment; give without payment.
[[9]Take no gold, or silver, or copper in your belts,
[10]no bag for your journey, or two tunics, or sandals, or a staff;
for laborers deserve their food.
[11]Whatever town or village you enter, find out who in it is worthy,
and stay there until you leave.
[12]As you enter the house, greet it.
[13]If the house is worthy, let your peace come upon it;
but if it is not worthy, let your peace return to you.
[14]If anyone will not welcome you or listen to your words,
shake off the dust from your feet as you leave that house or town.

GOSPEL   *synagogues = SIN-uh-gogz   Zebedee = ZEB-uh-dee   Alphaeus = al-FEE-us   Thaddaeus =*
THAD-ee-us   Cananaean = kay-nuh-NEE-un   Iscariot = is-CAR-ee-ut   Samaritans = suh-MAIR-it-uns
Gomorrah = guh-MOR-uh
The temptation is to abbreviate the gospel by reading the shorter option. Resist it if you are able. The
baptized will be helped in their daily proclamation of the gospel by these blunt warnings and terse
instructions. Avoid with equal conviction the temptation to rush the reading because it is lengthy. Allow
each imperative and every warning adequate opportunity to sink into the consciousness of the hearer.

¹⁵Truly I tell you,
it will be more tolerable for the land of Sodom and Gomorrah
on the day of judgment than for that town.

¹⁶"See, I am sending you out like sheep into the midst of wolves;
so be wise as serpents and innocent as doves.
¹⁷Beware of them, for they will hand you over to councils
and flog you in their synagogues;
¹⁸and you will be dragged before governors and kings because of me,
as a testimony to them and the Gentiles.
¹⁹When they hand you over,
do not worry about how you are to speak or what you are to say;
for what you are to say will be given to you at that time;
²⁰for it is not you who speak,
but the Spirit of your Father speaking through you.

²¹"Brother will betray brother to death, and a father his child,
and children will rise against parents and have them put to death;
²²and you will be hated by all because of my name.
But the one who endures to the end will be saved.
²³When they persecute you in one town, flee to the next;
for truly I tell you,
you will not have gone through all the towns of Israel
before the Son of Man comes."]

The gospel of the Lord.

FIRST READING: Jeremiah 20:7-13

A reading from Jeremiah.

[7]O LORD, you have enticed me, and I was enticed;
you have overpowered me, and you have prevailed.
I have become a laughingstock all day long;
everyone mocks me.
[8]For whenever I speak, I must cry out,
I must shout, "Violence and destruction!"
For the word of the LORD has become for me
a reproach and derision all day long.
[9]If I say, "I will not mention him, or speak any more in his name,"
then within me there is something like a burning fire shut up in my bones;
I am weary with holding it in, and I cannot.
[10]For I hear many whispering:
"Terror is all around!
Denounce him! Let us denounce him!"
All my close friends are watching for me to stumble.
"Perhaps he can be enticed,
and we can prevail against him, and take our revenge on him."

[11]But the LORD is with me like a dread warrior;
therefore my persecutors will stumble, and they will not prevail.
They will be greatly shamed, for they will not succeed.
Their eternal dishonor will never be forgotten.
[12]O LORD of hosts, you test the righteous,
you see the heart and the mind;
let me see your retribution upon them,
for to you I have committed my cause.

[13]Sing to the LORD; praise the LORD!
For he has delivered the life of the needy
from the hands of evildoers.

The word of the Lord.   *or*   Word of God, word of life.

FIRST READING   *Jeremiah = jehr-uh-MY-uh*
In this reading we get to listen in on the intimate conversation of the prophet Jeremiah and Almighty God. Jeremiah is having a hard time being a prophet. God keeps insisting that he announce bad news ("Violence and destruction!"). Bitterness and discouragement characterize verses 7–10. But in the pause between verses 10 and 11 the prophet's tone changes as he takes a deep breath, reaffirms the company of the LORD in this holy work, and recommits himself to the task. The invested reader might well take a deep breath at the same place.

PSALMODY: Psalm 69:7-10 [11-15] 16-18

SECOND READING: Romans 6:1b-11

A reading from Romans.

¹ᵇShould we continue in sin in order that grace may abound?
²By no means! How can we who died to sin go on living in it?
³Do you not know that all of us who have been baptized into Christ Jesus
were baptized into his death?
⁴Therefore we have been buried with him by baptism into death,
so that, just as Christ was raised from the dead by the glory of the Father,
so we too might walk in newness of life.

⁵For if we have been united with him in a death like his,
we will certainly be united with him in a resurrection like his.
⁶We know that our old self was crucified with him
so that the body of sin might be destroyed,
and we might no longer be enslaved to sin.
⁷For whoever has died is freed from sin.
⁸But if we have died with Christ,
we believe that we will also live with him.
⁹We know that Christ, being raised from the dead, will never die again;
death no longer has dominion over him.
¹⁰The death he died, he died to sin, once for all;
but the life he lives, he lives to God.
¹¹So you also must consider yourselves dead to sin
and alive to God in Christ Jesus.

The word of the Lord.   *or*   Word of God, word of life.

SECOND READING
Previously the writer has expounded on the marvel of grace. In this text the writer urges us to "die to sin" and explains how "dying with Christ" in baptism ought to signal an end to our enslavement to sin. This is another very familiar section of scripture. Do not take it for granted! Reading and re-reading it this week will lead the reader to greater understanding and deeper appreciation of its beauty. Invest it with the energy such holy truth deserves.

GOSPEL: Matthew 10:24-39

The holy gospel according to Matthew.

⌜Jesus said to the twelve:⌝
²⁴"A disciple is not above the teacher, nor a slave above the master;
²⁵it is enough for the disciple to be like the teacher,
and the slave like the master.
If they have called the master of the house Beelzebul,
how much more will they malign those of his household!

²⁶"So have no fear of them;
for nothing is covered up that will not be uncovered,
and nothing secret that will not become known.
²⁷What I say to you in the dark, tell in the light;
and what you hear whispered, proclaim from the housetops.
²⁸Do not fear those who kill the body but cannot kill the soul;
rather fear him who can destroy both soul and body in hell.
²⁹Are not two sparrows sold for a penny?
Yet not one of them will fall to the ground apart from your Father.
³⁰And even the hairs of your head are all counted.
³¹So do not be afraid; you are of more value than many sparrows.

³²"Everyone therefore who acknowledges me before others,
I also will acknowledge before my Father in heaven;
³³but whoever denies me before others,
I also will deny before my Father in heaven.
³⁴Do not think that I have come to bring peace to the earth;
I have not come to bring peace, but a sword.
³⁵For I have come to set a man against his father,
and a daughter against her mother,
and a daughter-in-law against her mother-in-law;
³⁶and one's foes will be members of one's own household.
³⁷Whoever loves father or mother more than me is not worthy of me;
and whoever loves son or daughter more than me is not worthy of me;
³⁸and whoever does not take up the cross and follow me is not worthy of me.
³⁹Those who find their life will lose it,
and those who lose their life for my sake will find it."

The gospel of the Lord.

GOSPEL *Beelzebul = bee-EL-zuh-bul*
These verses are loaded. The assembly will need time to appropriate them. A reading that brings the earnest intensity of a committed teacher will capture the spirit of the text. A reading that directs extra attention to the periods will help the hearer capture the meanings of the text. Decide well in advance which sentences are naturally grouped with other sentences and which ought to stand alone.

SUNDAY, JUNE 26–JULY 2
TIME AFTER PENTECOST — LECTIONARY 13

FIRST READING: Jeremiah 28:5-9

A reading from Jeremiah.

⁵The prophet Jeremiah spoke to the prophet Hananiah
in the presence of the priests
and all the people who were standing in the house of the LORD;
⁶and the prophet Jeremiah said,
"Amen! May the LORD do so;
may the LORD fulfill the words that you have prophesied,
and bring back to this place from Babylon
the vessels of the house of the LORD, and all the exiles.

⁷"But listen now to this word that I speak in your hearing
and in the hearing of all the people.
⁸The prophets who preceded you and me from ancient times
prophesied war, famine, and pestilence
against many countries and great kingdoms.
⁹As for the prophet who prophesies peace,
when the word of that prophet comes true,
then it will be known that the LORD has truly sent the prophet."

The word of the Lord.   *or*   Word of God, word of life.

PSALMODY: Psalm 89:1-4, 15-18

FIRST READING   *Jeremiah = jehr-uh-MY-uh   Hananiah = han-uh-NY-uh   Babylon = BAB-ih-lon*
A dispute among prophets! Jeremiah is responding to Hananiah's prophecy of the return of the people of Israel, who have been in exile in Babylon. In essence Jeremiah says, "I hope and pray that you are right." Previous prophets prophesied war and famine. People knew they were genuine prophets because war and famine followed. The conclusion Jeremiah draws in verse 9 is that we will know that the LORD has sent the prophet who prophesies peace when the prophecy becomes true. Give Jeremiah a voice of calm assurance—strength in the knowledge that God speaks through him.

SECOND READING: Romans 6:12-23

A reading from Romans.

[12]Do not let sin exercise dominion in your mortal bodies,
to make you obey their passions.
[13]No longer present your members to sin as instruments of wickedness,
but present yourselves to God
as those who have been brought from death to life,
and present your members to God as instruments of righteousness.
[14]For sin will have no dominion over you,
since you are not under law but under grace.

[15]What then? Should we sin because we are not under law but under grace?
By no means!
[16]Do you not know that if you present yourselves to anyone as obedient slaves,
you are slaves of the one whom you obey,
either of sin, which leads to death,
or of obedience, which leads to righteousness?
[17]But thanks be to God that you, having once been slaves of sin,
have become obedient from the heart
to the form of teaching to which you were entrusted,
[18]and that you, having been set free from sin,
have become slaves of righteousness.
[19]I am speaking in human terms because of your natural limitations.
For just as you once presented your members as slaves to impurity
and to greater and greater iniquity,
so now present your members as slaves to righteousness for sanctification.

[20]When you were slaves of sin,
you were free in regard to righteousness.
[21]So what advantage did you then get
from the things of which you now are ashamed?
The end of those things is death.
[22]But now that you have been freed from sin and enslaved to God,
the advantage you get is sanctification.
The end is eternal life.
[23]For the wages of sin is death,
but the free gift of God is eternal life in Christ Jesus our Lord.

The word of the Lord.   *or*   Word of God, word of life.

SECOND READING
This is a tough one! The writer contrasts being a slave to sin to being a slave to righteousness. It's a neat concept, but it will require some careful reading and re-reading to be certain the lector follows the argument and can help the hearer follow it. Again, pay careful attention to the punctuation. It will provide the hearer with the time needed to grasp the author's argument.

GOSPEL: Matthew 10:40-42

The holy gospel according to Matthew.

⌐Jesus said to the twelve:⌐
⁴⁰"Whoever welcomes you welcomes me,
and whoever welcomes me welcomes the one who sent me.
⁴¹Whoever welcomes a prophet in the name of a prophet
will receive a prophet's reward;
and whoever welcomes a righteous person in the name of a righteous person
will receive the reward of the righteous;
⁴²and whoever gives even a cup of cold water to one of these little ones
in the name of a disciple—
truly I tell you, none of these will lose their reward."

The gospel of the Lord.

GOSPEL
Everyone knows the Great Commission recorded at the end of Matthew's gospel. One might productively think of this little text as "Cold Water Commissioning." Jesus emphasizes the connection the disciples have with him and, in turn, with the Father. The reward, for even so small a gesture as a cup of cold water for a child, is certain. Stress the warm assurance in the last line.

SUNDAY, JULY 3–9
TIME AFTER PENTECOST — LECTIONARY 14

FIRST READING: Zechariah 9:9-12

A reading from Zechariah.

⁹Rejoice greatly, O daughter Zion!
　　Shout aloud, O daughter Jerusalem!
Lo, your king comes to you;
　　triumphant and victorious is he,
humble and riding on a donkey,
　　on a colt, the foal of a donkey.
¹⁰He will cut off the chariot from Ephraim
　　and the war horse from Jerusalem;
and the battle bow shall be cut off,
　　and he shall command peace to the nations;
his dominion shall be from sea to sea,
　　and from the River to the ends of the earth.

¹¹As for you also, because of the blood of my covenant with you,
　　I will set your prisoners free from the waterless pit.
¹²Return to your stronghold, O prisoners of hope;
　　today I declare that I will restore to you double.

The word of the Lord.　　　*or*　　　Word of God, word of life.

PSALMODY: Psalm 145:8-14

FIRST READING　　*Zechariah = zek-uh-RY-uh　Ephraim = EEF-rih-um*
These words of the prophet announce the beginning of the promised messiah's reign over the whole earth. (The reader will recognize them as being traditionally associated with Jesus' triumphant entry into Jerusalem on Palm Sunday.) These promises are reason for rejoicing. This holy declaration requires energy and strength. Read boldly.

SECOND READING: Romans 7:15-25a

A reading from Romans.

¹⁵I do not understand my own actions.
For I do not do what I want,
but I do the very thing I hate.
¹⁶Now if I do what I do not want, I agree that the law is good.
¹⁷But in fact it is no longer I that do it,
but sin that dwells within me.
¹⁸For I know that nothing good dwells within me, that is, in my flesh.
I can will what is right, but I cannot do it.
¹⁹For I do not do the good I want,
but the evil I do not want is what I do.
²⁰Now if I do what I do not want, it is no longer I that do it,
but sin that dwells within me.
²¹So I find it to be a law that when I want to do what is good,
evil lies close at hand.
²²For I delight in the law of God in my inmost self,
²³but I see in my members another law at war with the law of my mind,
making me captive to the law of sin that dwells in my members.

²⁴Wretched man that I am!
Who will rescue me from this body of death?
²⁵Thanks be to God through Jesus Christ our Lord!

The word of the Lord.   *or*   Word of God, word of life.

SECOND READING
Take note! This is a difficult little text. Approach it with care. Read it slowly and with careful attention to every word. St. Paul's point is that God's law directs us toward right behavior, but that we tend not to do the good that we want to do but rather the evil we hate. It is this reality that leads the writer and the hearer to the conclusion that our state is "wretched." A substantial pause before verse 24 is essential to establish the central question asked in the second half of that verse: "Who will rescue me from this body of death?" Another pause of substance might helpfully precede verse 25, which requires a voice firm with conviction born of deep faith: "Thanks be to God through Jesus Christ our Lord!" It is Jesus, and only Jesus, who can and does rescue us.

GOSPEL: Matthew 11:16-19, 25-30

The holy gospel according to Matthew.

⌐Jesus spoke to the crowd saying:⌐
[16]"To what will I compare this generation?
It is like children sitting in the marketplaces and calling to one another,
    [17]'We played the flute for you, and you did not dance;
        we wailed, and you did not mourn.'
[18]For John came neither eating nor drinking,
and they say, 'He has a demon';
[19]the Son of Man came eating and drinking, and they say,
'Look, a glutton and a drunkard, a friend of tax collectors and sinners!'
Yet wisdom is vindicated by her deeds."

[25]At that time Jesus said,
"I thank you, Father, Lord of heaven and earth,
because you have hidden these things from the wise and the intelligent
and have revealed them to infants;
[26]yes, Father, for such was your gracious will.
[27]All things have been handed over to me by my Father;
and no one knows the Son except the Father,
and no one knows the Father except the Son
and anyone to whom the Son chooses to reveal him.

[28]"Come to me, all you that are weary and are carrying heavy burdens,
and I will give you rest.
[29]Take my yoke upon you, and learn from me;
for I am gentle and humble in heart,
and you will find rest for your souls.
[30]For my yoke is easy, and my burden is light."

The gospel of the Lord.

GOSPEL
There are three very different sayings included in the gospel. Allow the hearer to sense their separateness. Pause, at length, between each. Each has its own sound. All are instructive and require the voice of the teacher. The first might have an edge to it. The second has a sense of confident gratitude. The third, perhaps, the sound of gentle invitation.

FIRST READING: Isaiah 55:10-13

A reading from Isaiah.

¹⁰For as the rain and the snow come down from heaven,
  and do not return there until they have watered the earth,
making it bring forth and sprout,
  giving seed to the sower and bread to the eater,
¹¹so shall my word be that goes out from my mouth;
  it shall not return to me empty,
but it shall accomplish that which I purpose,
  and succeed in the thing for which I sent it.

¹²For you shall go out in joy,
  and be led back in peace;
the mountains and the hills before you shall burst into song,
  and all the trees of the field shall clap their hands.
¹³Instead of the thorn shall come up the cypress;
  instead of the brier shall come up the myrtle;
and it shall be to the LORD for a memorial,
  for an everlasting sign that shall not be cut off.

The word of the Lord.   *or*   Word of God, word of life.

PSALMODY: Psalm 65:[1-8] 9-13

FIRST READING   *Isaiah = eye-ZAY-uh*
The "for as" in verse 10 parallels the "so shall" in verse 11. Use care, because the sentence is long and the images are many. The hearer will need time to see those images. Allow a sense of confidence and joy in God's ability to replace the "thorn" with the "cypress" and the "brier" with the "myrtle" to pervade the reading. The good growing things of the earth are an "everlasting sign" of God's power and God's care for God's people. (A word of warning about verse 11: the word at the end of the third line is *purpose*, not *propose*. We rarely use the word as a verb in common parlance. Don't let it throw you.)

SECOND READING: Romans 8:1-11

A reading from Romans.

[1]There is therefore now no condemnation for those who are in Christ Jesus.
[2]For the law of the Spirit of life in Christ Jesus
has set you free from the law of sin and of death.
[3]For God has done what the law, weakened by the flesh, could not do:
by sending his own Son in the likeness of sinful flesh,
and to deal with sin, he condemned sin in the flesh,
[4]so that the just requirement of the law might be fulfilled in us,
who walk not according to the flesh but according to the Spirit.
[5]For those who live according to the flesh
set their minds on the things of the flesh,
but those who live according to the Spirit
set their minds on the things of the Spirit.
[6]To set the mind on the flesh is death,
but to set the mind on the Spirit is life and peace.
[7]For this reason the mind that is set on the flesh is hostile to God;
it does not submit to God's law—indeed it cannot,
[8]and those who are in the flesh cannot please God.

[9]But you are not in the flesh; you are in the Spirit,
since the Spirit of God dwells in you.
Anyone who does not have the Spirit of Christ does not belong to him.
[10]But if Christ is in you, though the body is dead because of sin,
the Spirit is life because of righteousness.
[11]If the Spirit of him who raised Jesus from the dead dwells in you,
he who raised Christ from the dead will give life to your mortal bodies also
through his Spirit that dwells in you.

The word of the Lord.   *or*   Word of God, word of life.

SECOND READING

The stark contrast between "flesh" and "Spirit" runs through the whole of the reading. It is complex and not a little repetitive. Take one sentence, one clause, one thought at a time. Carefully observe the commas, semicolons, colons, and periods. Then read with confidence—this is good news! "If the Spirit of him who raised Jesus from the dead dwells in you" (and it does!), "he who raised Christ from the dead will give life to your mortal bodies also through his Spirit that dwells in you."

GOSPEL: Matthew 13:1-9, 18-23

The holy gospel according to Matthew.

[1]That same day Jesus went out of the house and sat beside the sea.
[2]Such great crowds gathered around him
that he got into a boat and sat there,
while the whole crowd stood on the beach.
[3]And he told them many things in parables, saying:
"Listen! A sower went out to sow.
[4]And as he sowed, some seeds fell on the path,
and the birds came and ate them up.
[5]Other seeds fell on rocky ground, where they did not have much soil,
and they sprang up quickly, since they had no depth of soil.
[6]But when the sun rose, they were scorched;
and since they had no root, they withered away.
[7]Other seeds fell among thorns, and the thorns grew up and choked them.
[8]Other seeds fell on good soil and brought forth grain,
some a hundredfold, some sixty, some thirty.
[9]Let anyone with ears listen!"

[18]"Hear then the parable of the sower.
[19]When anyone hears the word of the kingdom and does not understand it,
the evil one comes and snatches away what is sown in the heart;
this is what was sown on the path.
[20]As for what was sown on rocky ground,
this is the one who hears the word and immediately receives it with joy;
[21]yet such a person has no root, but endures only for a while,
and when trouble or persecution arises on account of the word,
that person immediately falls away.
[22]As for what was sown among thorns,
this is the one who hears the word,
but the cares of the world and the lure of wealth choke the word,
and it yields nothing.
[23]But as for what was sown on good soil,
this is the one who hears the word and understands it,
who indeed bears fruit and yields,
in one case a hundredfold, in another sixty, and in another thirty."

The gospel of the Lord.

GOSPEL
An animated telling of the parable to the crowd (verses 1–9), followed by a good healthy pause and a more instructive tone for its interpretation to the disciples (verses 18–23), will help hold the hearers' attention. Taking extra time in preparation to linger over the phrasing of familiar texts such as this leads not only to deeper understanding but new ways of voicing well-known words. Above all, avoid the temptation to hurry through a rich and instructive text we know so well.

SUNDAY, JULY 17–23
TIME AFTER PENTECOST — LECTIONARY 16

FIRST READING: Isaiah 44:6-8 *Alternate Reading: Wisdom 12:13, 16-19 (p. 503)*

A reading from Isaiah.

⁶Thus says the LORD, the King of Israel,
  and his Redeemer, the LORD of hosts:
I am the first and I am the last;
  besides me there is no god.
⁷Who is like me?
Let them proclaim it,
  let them declare and set it forth before me.
Who has announced from of old the things to come?
  Let them tell us what is yet to be.
⁸Do not fear, or be afraid;
  have I not told you from of old and declared it?
  You are my witnesses!
Is there any god besides me?
  There is no other rock; I know not one.

The word of the Lord.   *or*   Word of God, word of life.

PSALMODY: Psalm 86:11-17

SECOND READING: Romans 8:12-25

A reading from Romans.

¹²So then, brothers and sisters, we are debtors, not to the flesh,
to live according to the flesh—
¹³for if you live according to the flesh, you will die;
but if by the Spirit you put to death the deeds of the body, you will live.
¹⁴For all who are led by the Spirit of God are children of God.

FIRST READING   *Isaiah = eye-ZAY-uh*
This bold, repeated declaration of the sovereignty of Almighty God is designed to reassure God's people—Israel and the hearer. Do not rush the presentation. The questions are rhetorical. (God already knows the answer!) Pause after each question. Punch the answer. Let every declaration ring from the rafters. Let every phrase sing with the power of God.

SECOND READING
The reader will want to spend extra time with this text. To begin, one might read it devotionally several times through. Sit quietly with the text in hand and allow the words to be addressed to you. As children of God, we must be prepared to suffer with Christ, until that time when we share in his glory. The certainty (and the

¹⁵For you did not receive a spirit of slavery to fall back into fear,
but you have received a spirit of adoption.
When we cry, "Abba! Father!"
¹⁶it is that very Spirit bearing witness with our spirit
that we are children of God,
¹⁷and if children, then heirs,
heirs of God and joint heirs with Christ—
if, in fact, we suffer with him so that we may also be glorified with him.

¹⁸I consider that the sufferings of this present time
are not worth comparing with the glory about to be revealed to us.
¹⁹For the creation waits with eager longing
for the revealing of the children of God;
²⁰for the creation was subjected to futility,
not of its own will but by the will of the one who subjected it,
in hope ²¹that the creation itself will be set free from its bondage to decay
and will obtain the freedom of the glory of the children of God.
²²We know that the whole creation has been groaning in labor pains until now;
²³and not only the creation, but we ourselves,
who have the first fruits of the Spirit,
groan inwardly while we wait for adoption, the redemption of our bodies.

²⁴For in hope we were saved.
Now hope that is seen is not hope.
For who hopes for what is seen?
²⁵But if we hope for what we do not see, we wait for it with patience.

The word of the Lord.   *or*   Word of God, word of life.

GOSPEL: Matthew 13:24-30, 36-43

The holy gospel according to Matthew.

²⁴ ⌜Jesus⌝ put before ⌜the crowds⌝ another parable:
"The kingdom of heaven may be compared
to someone who sowed good seed in his field;
²⁵but while everybody was asleep,
an enemy came and sowed weeds among the wheat, and then went away.
²⁶So when the plants came up and bore grain,
then the weeds appeared as well. ▸

---

patience) with which we wait for the revelation of the rule of God is a gift to us from the Spirit of God.
A sense of confidence and certainty will help carry the meaning of the text to the assembly.

GOSPEL
A more animated telling of the parable (verses 24–30) can constructively contrast with a patient explanation of it (verses 36–43). Attempting to echo the urgency with which our Lord must certainly have addressed his disciples will help the hearer know how critically important the text is for our life and times.

²⁷And the slaves of the householder came and said to him,
'Master, did you not sow good seed in your field?
Where, then, did these weeds come from?'
²⁸He answered, 'An enemy has done this.'
The slaves said to him, 'Then do you want us to go and gather them?'
²⁹But he replied,
'No; for in gathering the weeds you would uproot the wheat along with them.
³⁰Let both of them grow together until the harvest;
and at harvest time I will tell the reapers,
Collect the weeds first and bind them in bundles to be burned,
but gather the wheat into my barn.'"

³⁶Then he left the crowds and went into the house.
And his disciples approached him, saying,
"Explain to us the parable of the weeds of the field."
³⁷He answered,
"The one who sows the good seed is the Son of Man;
³⁸the field is the world,
and the good seed are the children of the kingdom;
the weeds are the children of the evil one,
³⁹and the enemy who sowed them is the devil;
the harvest is the end of the age, and the reapers are angels.
⁴⁰Just as the weeds are collected and burned up with fire,
so will it be at the end of the age.

⁴¹"The Son of Man will send his angels,
and they will collect out of his kingdom all causes of sin and all evildoers,
⁴²and they will throw them into the furnace of fire,
where there will be weeping and gnashing of teeth.
⁴³Then the righteous will shine like the sun in the kingdom of their Father.
Let anyone with ears listen!"

The gospel of the Lord.

FIRST READING: 1 Kings 3:5-12

A reading from First Kings.

[5]At Gibeon the LORD appeared to Solomon in a dream by night;
and God said, "Ask what I should give you."
[6]And Solomon said,
"You have shown great and steadfast love to your servant my father David,
because he walked before you in faithfulness, in righteousness,
and in uprightness of heart toward you;
and you have kept for him this great and steadfast love,
and have given him a son to sit on his throne today.
[7]And now, O LORD my God,
you have made your servant king in place of my father David,
although I am only a little child;
I do not know how to go out or come in.
[8]And your servant is in the midst of the people whom you have chosen,
a great people, so numerous they cannot be numbered or counted.
[9]Give your servant therefore an understanding mind to govern your people,
able to discern between good and evil;
for who can govern this your great people?"

[10]It pleased the Lord that Solomon had asked this.
[11]God said to him,
"Because you have asked this,
and have not asked for yourself long life or riches,
or for the life of your enemies,
but have asked for yourself understanding to discern what is right,
[12]I now do according to your word.
Indeed I give you a wise and discerning mind;
no one like you has been before you
and no one like you shall arise after you."

The word of the Lord.   *or*   Word of God, word of life.

PSALMODY: Psalm 119:129-136

FIRST READING   *Gibeon = GIB-ee-un*
There are two voices to be heard: the voice of the servant of God, the new king, and the voice of God. One is the voice of a supplicant; the other of divine declaration. Help the assembly to hear the difference. Bring to the reading the sense of urgency that Solomon surely felt in this one-on-one with the Almighty.

SECOND READING: Romans 8:26-39

A reading from Romans.

^{26}The Spirit helps us in our weakness;
for we do not know how to pray as we ought,
but that very Spirit intercedes with sighs too deep for words.
^{27}And God, who searches the heart, knows what is the mind of the Spirit,
because the Spirit intercedes for the saints according to the will of God.

^{28}We know that all things work together for good for those who love God,
who are called according to his purpose.
^{29}For those whom he foreknew he also predestined
to be conformed to the image of his Son,
in order that he might be the firstborn within a large family.
^{30}And those whom he predestined he also called;
and those whom he called he also justified;
and those whom he justified he also glorified.

^{31}What then are we to say about these things?
If God is for us, who is against us?
^{32}He who did not withhold his own Son,
but gave him up for all of us,
will he not with him also give us everything else?
^{33}Who will bring any charge against God's elect?
It is God who justifies. ^{34}Who is to condemn?
It is Christ Jesus, who died, yes, who was raised,
who is at the right hand of God,
who indeed intercedes for us.
^{35}Who will separate us from the love of Christ?
Will hardship, or distress, or persecution,
or famine, or nakedness, or peril, or sword? ^{36}As it is written,
"For your sake we are being killed all day long;
we are accounted as sheep to be slaughtered."

^{37}No, in all these things we are more than conquerors
through him who loved us.
^{38}For I am convinced that neither death, nor life,
nor angels, nor rulers, nor things present, nor things to come, nor powers,
^{39}nor height, nor depth, nor anything else in all creation,
will be able to separate us from the love of God in Christ Jesus our Lord.

The word of the Lord.   *or*   Word of God, word of life.

SECOND READING
Resist strongly the temptation to read quickly, because the reading is a long one. It is also a complex reading, and both reader and hearer will need adequate time to hear and assimilate its meaning. Bring to the reading an intensity equal to that of the Spirit who "intercedes with sighs too deep for words." Be especially attentive to verses 28–30, which describe the love of the Father for the Son and for all whom he has called into relationship with him.

GOSPEL: Matthew 13:31-33, 44-52

The holy gospel according to Matthew.

³¹ ⌜Jesus⌝ put before ⌜the crowds⌝ another parable:
"The kingdom of heaven is like a mustard seed
that someone took and sowed in his field;
³²it is the smallest of all the seeds,
but when it has grown it is the greatest of shrubs and becomes a tree,
so that the birds of the air come and make nests in its branches."

³³He told them another parable:
"The kingdom of heaven is like yeast
that a woman took and mixed in with three measures of flour
until all of it was leavened."

⁴⁴"The kingdom of heaven is like treasure hidden in a field,
which someone found and hid;
then in his joy he goes and sells all that he has and buys that field.

⁴⁵"Again, the kingdom of heaven is like a merchant in search of fine pearls;
⁴⁶on finding one pearl of great value,
he went and sold all that he had and bought it.

⁴⁷"Again, the kingdom of heaven is like a net that was thrown into the sea
and caught fish of every kind;
⁴⁸when it was full, they drew it ashore,
sat down, and put the good into baskets but threw out the bad.
⁴⁹So it will be at the end of the age.
The angels will come out and separate the evil from the righteous
⁵⁰and throw them into the furnace of fire,
where there will be weeping and gnashing of teeth.

⁵¹"Have you understood all this?"
They answered, "Yes."
⁵²And he said to them,
"Therefore every scribe who has been trained for the kingdom of heaven
is like the master of a household
who brings out of his treasure what is new and what is old."

The gospel of the Lord.

GOSPEL
There are five pithy descriptions of the kingdom of heaven here. Allow a little room for each. A pause of some substance between them will allow the picture to develop and the point to be made. And having "understood all this," wrestle with verse 52 well in advance of Sunday and discover a delivery that will underscore its meaning.

SUNDAY, JULY 31–AUGUST 6
TIME AFTER PENTECOST — LECTIONARY 18

FIRST READING: Isaiah 55:1-5

A reading from Isaiah.

¹Ho, everyone who thirsts, come to the waters;
and you that have no money, come, buy and eat!
Come, buy wine and milk without money and without price.
²Why do you spend your money for that which is not bread,
and your labor for that which does not satisfy?
Listen carefully to me, and eat what is good,
and delight yourselves in rich food.

³Incline your ear, and come to me;
listen, so that you may live.
I will make with you an everlasting covenant,
my steadfast, sure love for David.
⁴See, I made him a witness to the peoples,
a leader and commander for the peoples.
⁵See, you shall call nations that you do not know,
and nations that do not know you shall run to you,
because of the LORD your God, the Holy One of Israel,
for he has glorified you.

The word of the Lord.   *or*   Word of God, word of life.

PSALMODY: Psalm 145:8-9, 14-21

SECOND READING: Romans 9:1-5

A reading from Romans.

¹I am speaking the truth in Christ—I am not lying;
my conscience confirms it by the Holy Spirit—
²I have great sorrow and unceasing anguish in my heart.

FIRST READING   *Isaiah = eye-ZAY-uh*

This reading provides a challenge in its first word, Ho. It clearly seems to be an imperative to "Listen up!" And it requires that kind of a spirited attack if it is to sound anything but flat and silly. This passage reaffirms God's commitment to the people of Israel, the very covenant God struck with David. These are words of promise. The reader will help the assembly to understand them by making them sound promising.

SECOND READING

The author's "great sorrow and unceasing anguish" set the tone for this reading. We hear Paul's agony that the Israelites have not embraced the righteousness that is rightfully theirs through faith in Christ Jesus. The reader would do well to read the remainder of the ninth chapter of Romans, to which this paragraph is the

³For I could wish that I myself were accursed
and cut off from Christ for the sake of my own people,
my kindred according to the flesh.
⁴They are Israelites, and to them belong the adoption, the glory,
the covenants, the giving of the law, the worship, and the promises;
⁵to them belong the patriarchs,
and from them, according to the flesh, comes the Messiah, who is over all,
God blessed forever. Amen.

The word of the Lord.   *or*   Word of God, word of life.

GOSPEL: Matthew 14:13-21

The holy gospel according to Matthew.

¹³Now when Jesus heard ⌜about the beheading of John the Baptist,⌝
he withdrew from there in a boat to a deserted place by himself.
But when the crowds heard it, they followed him on foot from the towns.
¹⁴When he went ashore, he saw a great crowd;
and he had compassion for them and cured their sick.

¹⁵When it was evening, the disciples came to him and said,
"This is a deserted place, and the hour is now late;
send the crowds away so that they may go into the villages
and buy food for themselves."
¹⁶Jesus said to them,
"They need not go away; you give them something to eat."
¹⁷They replied, "We have nothing here but five loaves and two fish."
¹⁸And he said, "Bring them here to me."
¹⁹Then he ordered the crowds to sit down on the grass.
Taking the five loaves and the two fish,
he looked up to heaven, and blessed and broke the loaves,
and gave them to the disciples, and the disciples gave them to the crowds.
²⁰And all ate and were filled;
and they took up what was left over of the broken pieces, twelve baskets full.
²¹And those who ate were about five thousand men,
besides women and children.

The gospel of the Lord.

---

introduction. Clearly the author's anguish is real when he says, "I could wish that I myself were accursed and cut off from Christ for the sake of my own people, my kindred according to the flesh." Help the assembly sense Paul's pain.

GOSPEL
Even when sorrowful and weary, Jesus has compassion for the great crowd and heals and feeds them. Establish that weariness and deep grief in the first sentence. It can carry the whole reading. Infuse the dialogue with the disciples with that same sense. It will provide the miracle with a slightly unexpected sound that may capture the ear of the hearers. Verse 21 demands a tone of wonder.

FIRST READING: 1 Kings 19:9-18

A reading from First Kings.

⁹At ⌐Horeb, the mount of God,⌐
⌐Elijah⌐ came to a cave, and spent the night there.
Then the word of the LORD came to him, saying,
"What are you doing here, Elijah?"
¹⁰He answered, "I have been very zealous for the LORD, the God of hosts;
for the Israelites have forsaken your covenant, thrown down your altars,
and killed your prophets with the sword.
I alone am left, and they are seeking my life, to take it away."
¹¹He said, "Go out and stand on the mountain before the LORD,
for the LORD is about to pass by."

Now there was a great wind, so strong that it was splitting mountains
and breaking rocks in pieces before the LORD,
but the LORD was not in the wind;
and after the wind an earthquake,
but the LORD was not in the earthquake;
¹²and after the earthquake a fire,
but the LORD was not in the fire;
and after the fire a sound of sheer silence.
¹³When Elijah heard it, he wrapped his face in his mantle
and went out and stood at the entrance of the cave.

Then there came a voice to him that said,
"What are you doing here, Elijah?"
¹⁴He answered,
"I have been very zealous for the LORD, the God of hosts;
for the Israelites have forsaken your covenant, thrown down your altars,
and killed your prophets with the sword.
I alone am left, and they are seeking my life, to take it away."
¹⁵Then the LORD said to him,
"Go, return on your way to the wilderness of Damascus;
when you arrive, you shall anoint Hazael as king over Aram.
¹⁶Also you shall anoint Jehu son of Nimshi as king over Israel;

FIRST READING   *Horeb = HOR-ub   Hazael = HAY-zuh-el   Aram = AR-um   Jehu = JEE-hoo   Nimshi =*
NIM-shee   Shaphat = SHAY-fat   Abel-meholah = AY-bul-muh-HOH-luh   Baal = BAY-ul
There are several names and places whose pronunciation require careful attention. The secret to
successfully reading these names aloud is simple: practice, repeatedly! Read the entire text over and over
again until the pronunciations come with ease. Elijah's discouragement is met by God's overwhelming
presence in the silence after the storm. God's definitive instructions to the prophet signal both God's power
and continuing presence among God's people. A long pause following verse 12 will help the assembly hear
the silence. Elijah's voice is surely a weary voice. God's voice is confident and authoritative.

and you shall anoint Elisha son of Shaphat of Abel-meholah
as prophet in your place.
¹⁷Whoever escapes from the sword of Hazael, Jehu shall kill;
and whoever escapes from the sword of Jehu, Elisha shall kill.
¹⁸Yet I will leave seven thousand in Israel,
all the knees that have not bowed to Baal,
and every mouth that has not kissed him."

The word of the Lord.   *or*   Word of God, word of life.

PSALMODY: Psalm 85:8-13

SECOND READING: Romans 10:5-15

A reading from Romans.

⁵Moses writes concerning the righteousness that comes from the law,
that "the person who does these things will live by them."
⁶But the righteousness that comes from faith says,
"Do not say in your heart, 'Who will ascend into heaven?'"
(that is, to bring Christ down)
⁷"or 'Who will descend into the abyss?'"
(that is, to bring Christ up from the dead).

⁸But what does it say?
   "The word is near you,
      on your lips and in your heart"
(that is, the word of faith that we proclaim);
⁹because if you confess with your lips that Jesus is Lord
and believe in your heart that God raised him from the dead,
you will be saved.
¹⁰For one believes with the heart and so is justified,
and one confesses with the mouth and so is saved.
¹¹The scripture says, "No one who believes in him will be put to shame."
¹²For there is no distinction between Jew and Greek;
the same Lord is Lord of all and is generous to all who call on him.
¹³For, "Everyone who calls on the name of the Lord shall be saved."

¹⁴But how are they to call on one in whom they have not believed?
And how are they to believe in one of whom they have never heard?
And how are they to hear without someone to proclaim him? ▸

SECOND READING
On the surface the text looks confusing. Paul is working with Moses' words in Deuteronomy 30:11-14
and is saying that if one desires to achieve righteousness by the law, one needs to live by the law. But the
righteousness that comes by faith is far easier to acquire since the word has come near to us in the person
of Jesus. Finally, the author salutes those who bring the name of Jesus to our hearing. (And that, dear reader,
is you!) The reading calls for a joyful and confident tone.

[15]And how are they to proclaim him unless they are sent?
As it is written,
"How beautiful are the feet of those who bring good news!"

The word of the Lord.　　　or　　　Word of God, word of life.

GOSPEL: Matthew 14:22-33

The holy gospel according to Matthew.

[22] ⌈Jesus⌉ made the disciples get into the boat
and go on ahead to the other side ⌈of the Sea of Galilee,⌉
while he dismissed the crowds.
[23]And after he had dismissed the crowds,
he went up the mountain by himself to pray.
When evening came, he was there alone,
[24]but by this time the boat, battered by the waves,
was far from the land, for the wind was against them.

[25]And early in the morning he came walking toward them on the sea.
[26]But when the disciples saw him walking on the sea,
they were terrified, saying, "It is a ghost!"
And they cried out in fear.
[27]But immediately Jesus spoke to them and said,
"Take heart, it is I; do not be afraid."

[28]Peter answered him,
"Lord, if it is you, command me to come to you on the water."
[29]He said, "Come."
So Peter got out of the boat, started walking on the water,
and came toward Jesus.
[30]But when he noticed the strong wind, he became frightened,
and beginning to sink, he cried out,
"Lord, save me!"
[31]Jesus immediately reached out his hand and caught him, saying to him,
"You of little faith, why did you doubt?"
[32]When they got into the boat, the wind ceased.
[33]And those in the boat worshiped him, saying,
"Truly you are the Son of God."

The gospel of the Lord.

GOSPEL
Take time in preparing the reading to visualize the action—all the action—in detail. Attempt to recapture
that vision in the voicing of the text. Take plenty of time. Allow the assembly sufficient time to see the gospel
as well.

Sunday, August 14–20
Time after Pentecost — Lectionary 20

FIRST READING: Isaiah 56:1, 6-8

A reading from Isaiah.

¹Thus says the LORD:
　　Maintain justice, and do what is right,
for soon my salvation will come,
　　and my deliverance be revealed.

⁶And the foreigners who join themselves to the LORD,
　　to minister to him, to love the name of the LORD,
　　and to be his servants,
all who keep the sabbath, and do not profane it,
　　and hold fast my covenant—
⁷these I will bring to my holy mountain,
　　and make them joyful in my house of prayer;
their burnt offerings and their sacrifices will be accepted on my altar;
　　for my house shall be called a house of prayer for all peoples.
⁸Thus says the Lord GOD,
　　who gathers the outcasts of Israel,
I will gather others to them
　　besides those already gathered.

The word of the Lord.　　　　*or*　　　　Word of God, word of life.

PSALMODY: Psalm 67

FIRST READING　　*Isaiah = eye-ZAY-uh*
The reading calls for the sound of the authoritative yet inviting voice of God. It illustrates the wideness of God's mercy and God's desire to gather "the outcasts of Israel" and others. The sound we are striving for is a combination of firmness and warmth.

SECOND READING: Romans 11:1-2a, 29-32

A reading from Romans.

⌐Paul writes:¬
¹I ask, then, has God rejected his people?
By no means! I myself am an Israelite,
a descendant of Abraham, a member of the tribe of Benjamin.
²God has not rejected his people whom he foreknew.

²⁹For the gifts and the calling of God are irrevocable.
³⁰Just as you were once disobedient to God
but have now received mercy because of their disobedience,
³¹so they have now been disobedient in order that,
by the mercy shown to you, they too may now receive mercy.
³²For God has imprisoned all in disobedience so that he may be merciful to all.

The word of the Lord.   *or*   Word of God, word of life.

GOSPEL: Matthew 15:[10-20] 21-28

The holy gospel according to Matthew.

[¹⁰ ⌐Jesus¬ called the crowd to him and said to them,
"Listen and understand:
¹¹it is not what goes into the mouth that defiles a person,
but it is what comes out of the mouth that defiles."
¹²Then the disciples approached and said to him,
"Do you know that the Pharisees took offense
when they heard what you said?"
¹³He answered,
"Every plant that my heavenly Father has not planted will be uprooted.
¹⁴Let them alone; they are blind guides of the blind.
And if one blind person guides another, both will fall into a pit."
¹⁵But Peter said to him, "Explain this parable to us."
¹⁶Then he said, "Are you also still without understanding?
¹⁷Do you not see that whatever goes into the mouth enters the stomach,
and goes out into the sewer?
¹⁸But what comes out of the mouth proceeds from the heart,
and this is what defiles.

SECOND READING

This brief text is packed with some heavy theological thinking. The apostle's point is that God has not forsaken the Jews (God's promises are "irrevocable"), but has used their disobedience to open God's promises to the Gentiles even as God will use Gentile disobedience (and God's mercy to the Gentiles) to illustrate God's mercy to the Jews. To read this one well the lector must have this little argument set clearly in mind before reading it for others.

¹⁹For out of the heart come evil intentions, murder, adultery,
fornication, theft, false witness, slander.
²⁰These are what defile a person,
but to eat with unwashed hands does not defile."]

²¹Jesus left that place and went away to the district of Tyre and Sidon.
²²Just then a Canaanite woman from that region came out
and started shouting,
"Have mercy on me, Lord, Son of David;
my daughter is tormented by a demon."
²³But he did not answer her at all.
And his disciples came and urged him, saying,
"Send her away, for she keeps shouting after us."
²⁴He answered, "I was sent only to the lost sheep of the house of Israel."
²⁵But she came and knelt before him, saying,
"Lord, help me."
²⁶He answered,
"It is not fair to take the children's food and throw it to the dogs."
²⁷She said, "Yes, Lord,
yet even the dogs eat the crumbs that fall from their masters' table."
²⁸Then Jesus answered her,
"Woman, great is your faith! Let it be done for you as you wish."
And her daughter was healed instantly.

The gospel of the Lord.

GOSPEL   *Sidon = SY-dun   Canaanite = KAY-nuh-nyt*
In either its longer or abbreviated form, the gospel's principal challenge is to make the dialogue believable. It requires some decisions about the various tones our Lord may have taken in reply to the various questions and assertions thrown his way. In preparation for the reading, wrestle with the variety of emotions Jesus may have felt and the different tacks he may have taken vocally in order to be clearly heard. This is no small challenge.

FIRST READING: Isaiah 51:1-6

A reading from Isaiah.

¹Listen to me, you that pursue righteousness,
    you that seek the LORD.
Look to the rock from which you were hewn,
    and to the quarry from which you were dug.
²Look to Abraham your father
    and to Sarah who bore you;
for he was but one when I called him,
    but I blessed him and made him many.
³For the LORD will comfort Zion;
    he will comfort all her waste places,
and will make her wilderness like Eden,
    her desert like the garden of the LORD;
joy and gladness will be found in her,
    thanksgiving and the voice of song.

⁴Listen to me, my people,
    and give heed to me, my nation;
for a teaching will go out from me,
    and my justice for a light to the peoples.
⁵I will bring near my deliverance swiftly,
    my salvation has gone out and my arms will rule the peoples;
the coastlands wait for me,
    and for my arm they hope.

⁶Lift up your eyes to the heavens,
    and look at the earth beneath;
for the heavens will vanish like smoke,
    the earth will wear out like a garment,
    and those who live on it will die like gnats;
but my salvation will be forever,
    and my deliverance will never be ended.

The word of the Lord.   *or*   Word of God, word of life.

FIRST READING   *Isaiah = eye-ZAY-uh*
Look, listen, and learn! These three words summarize the hopeful prophecy of promise for God's people. Listen up, says Almighty God, and learn of my power and my love. The reading calls for extra energy and enthusiasm. Appreciate and help the assembly to see the marvelous images the words create: "Look to the rock from which you were hewn." "[Abraham] was but one when I called him." "The earth will wear out like a garment, and those who live on it will die like gnats." "[The LORD] will make her wilderness like Eden." "My salvation will be forever, and my deliverance will never be ended."

PSALMODY: Psalm 138

SECOND READING: Romans 12:1-8

A reading from Romans.

¹I appeal to you therefore, brothers and sisters, by the mercies of God,
to present your bodies as a living sacrifice,
holy and acceptable to God,
which is your spiritual worship.
²Do not be conformed to this world,
but be transformed by the renewing of your minds,
so that you may discern what is the will of God—
what is good and acceptable and perfect.

³For by the grace given to me I say to everyone among you
not to think of yourself more highly than you ought to think,
but to think with sober judgment,
each according to the measure of faith that God has assigned.
⁴For as in one body we have many members,
and not all the members have the same function,
⁵so we, who are many, are one body in Christ,
and individually we are members one of another.
⁶We have gifts that differ according to the grace given to us:
prophecy, in proportion to faith; ⁷ministry, in ministering;
the teacher, in teaching; ⁸the exhorter, in exhortation;
the giver, in generosity; the leader, in diligence;
the compassionate, in cheerfulness.

The word of the Lord.   *or*   Word of God, word of life.

SECOND READING   *prophecy = PROF-uh-see*
Interestingly, each sentence in this text stands alone nicely. One might have the best chance of helping the assembly hear the reading by reading each sentence (verses 1, 2, 3, 4–5, and 6–8) as though it were unrelated to the one before. Do not hurry—there is a lot to learn here. Also note that in verse 6 the word "prophecy" is a noun.

GOSPEL: Matthew 16:13-20

The holy gospel according to Matthew.

¹³Now when Jesus came into the district of Caesarea Philippi,
he asked his disciples, "Who do people say that the Son of Man is?"
¹⁴And they said,
"Some say John the Baptist, but others Elijah,
and still others Jeremiah or one of the prophets."
¹⁵He said to them, "But who do you say that I am?"
¹⁶Simon Peter answered,
"You are the Messiah, the Son of the living God."

¹⁷And Jesus answered him,
"Blessed are you, Simon son of Jonah!
For flesh and blood has not revealed this to you, but my Father in heaven.
¹⁸And I tell you, you are Peter, and on this rock I will build my church,
and the gates of Hades will not prevail against it.
¹⁹I will give you the keys of the kingdom of heaven,
and whatever you bind on earth will be bound in heaven,
and whatever you loose on earth will be loosed in heaven."
²⁰Then he sternly ordered the disciples not to tell anyone
that he was the Messiah.

The gospel of the Lord.

GOSPEL   *Caesarea Philippi = sez-uh-REE-uh fih-LIP-eye   Jeremiah = jehr-uh-MY-uh   Hades = HAY-deez*
In verse 14, solid pauses at the commas and after Jeremiah will allow the assembly to imagine input from various disciples. A significant pause following verse 19 will set off Christ's celebration of the Petrine confession and his initiation of the Office of the Keys. An excellent reader will see the scene before reading it, and in the sound of the reader's voice the assembly will see it as well.

Sunday, August 28–September 3
Time after Pentecost — Lectionary 22

FIRST READING: Jeremiah 15:15-21

A reading from Jeremiah.

[15]O LORD, you know;
  remember me and visit me,
  and bring down retribution for me on my persecutors.
In your forbearance do not take me away;
  know that on your account I suffer insult.
[16]Your words were found, and I ate them,
  and your words became to me a joy and the delight of my heart;
for I am called by your name,
  O LORD, God of hosts.
[17]I did not sit in the company of merrymakers,
  nor did I rejoice;
under the weight of your hand I sat alone,
  for you had filled me with indignation.
[18]Why is my pain unceasing,
  my wound incurable, refusing to be healed?
Truly, you are to me like a deceitful brook,
  like waters that fail.

[19]Therefore thus says the LORD:
If you turn back, I will take you back,
  and you shall stand before me.
If you utter what is precious, and not what is worthless,
  you shall serve as my mouth.
It is they who will turn to you,
  not you who will turn to them.
[20]And I will make you to this people
  a fortified wall of bronze;
they will fight against you,
  but they shall not prevail over you,
for I am with you
  to save you and deliver you, says the LORD. ▸

FIRST READING *Jeremiah = jehr-uh-MY-uh*
Embrace the lament of the prophet. The word pictures are wonderful—consider them carefully. "Your words were found, and I ate them" (made them a part of my very being!). "Under the weight of your hand I sat alone" (indignation at the failure of the people to listen separates the prophet from the community). "You are to me like a deceitful brook" (drying up when I need water the most). Give the hearer time to capture and consider the images as well. Verses 19–21 is the promising voice of God.

²¹I will deliver you out of the hand of the wicked,
 and redeem you from the grasp of the ruthless.

The word of the Lord.   *or*   Word of God, word of life.

PSALMODY: Psalm 26:1-8

SECOND READING: Romans 12:9-21

A reading from Romans.

⁹Let love be genuine;
hate what is evil, hold fast to what is good;
¹⁰love one another with mutual affection;
outdo one another in showing honor.
¹¹Do not lag in zeal, be ardent in spirit, serve the Lord.
¹²Rejoice in hope, be patient in suffering, persevere in prayer.
¹³Contribute to the needs of the saints;
extend hospitality to strangers.

¹⁴Bless those who persecute you; bless and do not curse them.
¹⁵Rejoice with those who rejoice, weep with those who weep.
¹⁶Live in harmony with one another;
do not be haughty, but associate with the lowly;
do not claim to be wiser than you are.
¹⁷Do not repay anyone evil for evil,
but take thought for what is noble in the sight of all.
¹⁸If it is possible, so far as it depends on you,
live peaceably with all.

¹⁹Beloved, never avenge yourselves,
but leave room for the wrath of God;
for it is written,
"Vengeance is mine, I will repay, says the Lord."
²⁰No, "if your enemies are hungry, feed them;
if they are thirsty, give them something to drink;
for by doing this you will heap burning coals on their heads."
²¹Do not be overcome by evil, but overcome evil with good.

The word of the Lord.   *or*   Word of God, word of life.

SECOND READING
These are simple, central imperatives for the Christian life. This is loving instruction on how to live lovingly. Do not succumb to the temptation to read quickly. Savor and celebrate the sense of the community life that adhering to such instruction would produce. Help the hearer to understand the importance of every phrase.

GOSPEL: Matthew 16:21-28

The holy gospel according to Matthew.

²¹From that time on
⌐after Peter confessed that Jesus was the Messiah,⌐
Jesus began to show his disciples that he must go to Jerusalem
and undergo great suffering
at the hands of the elders and chief priests and scribes,
and be killed, and on the third day be raised.
²²And Peter took him aside and began to rebuke him, saying,
"God forbid it, Lord! This must never happen to you."
²³But he turned and said to Peter,
"Get behind me, Satan!
You are a stumbling block to me;
for you are setting your mind not on divine things but on human things."

²⁴Then Jesus told his disciples,
"If any want to become my followers,
let them deny themselves and take up their cross and follow me.
²⁵For those who want to save their life will lose it,
and those who lose their life for my sake will find it.
²⁶For what will it profit them if they gain the whole world but forfeit their life?
Or what will they give in return for their life?

²⁷"For the Son of Man is to come with his angels in the glory of his Father,
and then he will repay everyone for what has been done.
²⁸Truly I tell you,
there are some standing here who will not taste death
before they see the Son of Man coming in his kingdom."

The gospel of the Lord.

GOSPEL
A poorly prepared reader may stumble toward the end of verse 21, which is one long sentence. Avoid that trap through preparation: read the pericope several times in the week before, aloud as well as silently.

Sunday, September 4–10

Time after Pentecost — Lectionary 23

FIRST READING: Ezekiel 33:7-11

A reading from Ezekiel.

⁷So you, mortal, I have made a sentinel for the house of Israel;
whenever you hear a word from my mouth,
you shall give them warning from me.
⁸If I say to the wicked, "O wicked ones, you shall surely die,"
and you do not speak to warn the wicked to turn from their ways,
the wicked shall die in their iniquity,
but their blood I will require at your hand.
⁹But if you warn the wicked to turn from their ways,
and they do not turn from their ways,
the wicked shall die in their iniquity, but you will have saved your life.

¹⁰Now you, mortal, say to the house of Israel,
Thus you have said:
"Our transgressions and our sins weigh upon us,
and we waste away because of them; how then can we live?"
¹¹Say to them, As I live, says the Lord GOD,
I have no pleasure in the death of the wicked,
but that the wicked turn from their ways and live;
turn back, turn back from your evil ways;
for why will you die, O house of Israel?

The word of the Lord.   *or*   Word of God, word of life.

PSALMODY: Psalm 119:33-40

SECOND READING: Romans 13:8-14

A reading from Romans.

⁸Owe no one anything, except to love one another;
for the one who loves another has fulfilled the law.
⁹The commandments, "You shall not commit adultery;
You shall not murder; You shall not steal; You shall not covet";

FIRST READING   *Ezekiel = eh-ZEEK-ee-el*
God is speaking to his prophet, Ezekiel—the Immortal to the mortal. The prophet is the early warning device for the people (the "sentinel for the house of Israel"). His charge is to declare both the judgment of God and the grace of God to God's people, so that they might be moved to repentance. Verse 10 is a bit tricky. Introduced by the words, "Thus you have said," God prepares the prophet to address the despair that the contrite may feel ("we waste away because of [our sins]"). The prophet's reply, the announcement of the grace of God, is the substance of verse 11. Take care to help the people distinguish between God's address to the prophet and the prophet's relaying God's word to the people.

and any other commandment, are summed up in this word,
"Love your neighbor as yourself."
[10]Love does no wrong to a neighbor;
therefore, love is the fulfilling of the law.

[11]Besides this, you know what time it is,
how it is now the moment for you to wake from sleep.
For salvation is nearer to us now than when we became believers;
[12]the night is far gone, the day is near.
Let us then lay aside the works of darkness and put on the armor of light;
[13]let us live honorably as in the day, not in reveling and drunkenness,
not in debauchery and licentiousness,
not in quarreling and jealousy.
[14]Instead, put on the Lord Jesus Christ,
and make no provision for the flesh, to gratify its desires.

The word of the Lord.   *or*   Word of God, word of life.

GOSPEL: Matthew 18:15-20

The holy gospel according to Matthew.

⌈Jesus said to the disciples:⌉
[15]"If another member of the church sins against you,
go and point out the fault when the two of you are alone.
If the member listens to you, you have regained that one.
[16]But if you are not listened to, take one or two others along with you,
so that every word may be confirmed by the evidence of two or three witnesses.
[17]If the member refuses to listen to them, tell it to the church;
and if the offender refuses to listen even to the church,
let such a one be to you as a Gentile and a tax collector.

[18]"Truly I tell you, whatever you bind on earth will be bound in heaven,
and whatever you loose on earth will be loosed in heaven.
[19]Again, truly I tell you,
if two of you agree on earth about anything you ask,
it will be done for you by my Father in heaven.

[20]"For where two or three are gathered in my name, I am there among them."

The gospel of the Lord.

SECOND READING   *licentiousness = ly-SEN-chus-ness*
This reading is a straightforward reminder that if one genuinely loves the neighbor, one will do no wrong toward the neighbor. That reminder is followed by an appeal to "put on the armor of light" . . . "put on the Lord Jesus Christ." This is an encouraging word designed to wake up and motivate the complacent. Give it that kind of energy!

GOSPEL
Our Lord's ardent instruction to the Twelve relates to lovingly holding the community together, rather than establishing a minimal standard for excommunication. It requires a reconciling tone on the part of the gospel reader. Verse 18 might be more effectively connected to verses 15–17, while verse 19 might be helpfully attached to verse 20.

FIRST READING: Genesis 50:15-21

A reading from Genesis.

¹⁵Realizing that their father was dead, Joseph's brothers said,
"What if Joseph still bears a grudge against us
and pays us back in full for all the wrong that we did to him?"
¹⁶So they approached Joseph, saying,
"Your father gave this instruction before he died,
¹⁷'Say to Joseph: I beg you,
forgive the crime of your brothers and the wrong they did in harming you.'
Now therefore please forgive the crime
of the servants of the God of your father."
Joseph wept when they spoke to him.
¹⁸Then his brothers also wept, fell down before him, and said,
"We are here as your slaves."

¹⁹But Joseph said to them, "Do not be afraid!
Am I in the place of God?
²⁰Even though you intended to do harm to me,
God intended it for good, in order to preserve a numerous people,
as he is doing today.
²¹So have no fear; I myself will provide for you and your little ones."
In this way he reassured them, speaking kindly to them.

The word of the Lord.   *or*   Word of God, word of life.

PSALMODY: Psalm 103:[1-7] 8-13

FIRST READING

The mercy of God is evident in Joseph's forgiveness of his brothers. They had sold him into slavery (and would have left him for dead in the wilderness!), but God had spared and blessed Joseph beyond imagining. At the death of their father, the brothers fear retribution. The point of the text is to be found in Joseph's rhetorical question, "Am I in the place of God?" In fact, Joseph does show his brothers mercy and pity not unlike that of God's. The reading sounds compassionate.

SECOND READING: Romans 14:1-12

A reading from Romans.

¹Welcome those who are weak in faith,
but not for the purpose of quarreling over opinions.
²Some believe in eating anything, while the weak eat only vegetables.
³Those who eat must not despise those who abstain,
and those who abstain must not pass judgment on those who eat;
for God has welcomed them.
⁴Who are you to pass judgment on servants of another?
It is before their own lord that they stand or fall.
And they will be upheld, for the Lord is able to make them stand.

⁵Some judge one day to be better than another,
while others judge all days to be alike.
Let all be fully convinced in their own minds.
⁶Those who observe the day, observe it in honor of the Lord.
Also those who eat, eat in honor of the Lord,
since they give thanks to God;
while those who abstain, abstain in honor of the Lord
and give thanks to God.

⁷We do not live to ourselves, and we do not die to ourselves.
⁸If we live, we live to the Lord,
and if we die, we die to the Lord;
so then, whether we live or whether we die, we are the Lord's.
⁹For to this end Christ died and lived again,
so that he might be Lord of both the dead and the living.

¹⁰Why do you pass judgment on your brother or sister?
Or you, why do you despise your brother or sister?
For we will all stand before the judgment seat of God.
¹¹For it is written,
    "As I live, says the Lord, every knee shall bow to me,
        and every tongue shall give praise to God."
¹²So then, each of us will be accountable to God.

The word of the Lord.   *or*   Word of God, word of life.

SECOND READING
A simple point is being made. The author urges the hearer not to pass judgment on the servants of God ("servants of another"). That which the faithful choose to do or to abstain from doing is a choice made to honor God. We are urged to honor the choices of those whose decisions may differ from our own. It is an important message for the church, then and now. Bring to the reading a sense of urgency and the hearer in our day will be helped.

GOSPEL: Matthew 18:21-35

The holy gospel according to Matthew.

²¹Peter came and said to ⌈Jesus,⌉
"Lord, if another member of the church sins against me,
how often should I forgive? As many as seven times?"
²²Jesus said to him,
"Not seven times, but, I tell you, seventy-seven times.

²³"For this reason the kingdom of heaven may be compared to a king
who wished to settle accounts with his slaves.
²⁴When he began the reckoning,
one who owed him ten thousand talents was brought to him;
²⁵and, as he could not pay, his lord ordered him to be sold,
together with his wife and children and all his possessions,
and payment to be made.
²⁶So the slave fell on his knees before him, saying,
'Have patience with me, and I will pay you everything.'
²⁷And out of pity for him, the lord of that slave released him
and forgave him the debt.

²⁸"But that same slave, as he went out,
came upon one of his fellow slaves who owed him a hundred denarii;
and seizing him by the throat, he said, 'Pay what you owe.'
²⁹Then his fellow slave fell down and pleaded with him,
'Have patience with me, and I will pay you.'
³⁰But he refused;
then he went and threw him into prison until he would pay the debt.
³¹When his fellow slaves saw what had happened, they were greatly distressed,
and they went and reported to their lord all that had taken place.
³²Then his lord summoned him and said to him,
'You wicked slave!
I forgave you all that debt because you pleaded with me.
³³Should you not have had mercy on your fellow slave, as I had mercy on you?'
³⁴And in anger his lord handed him over to be tortured
until he would pay his entire debt.

³⁵"So my heavenly Father will also do to every one of you,
if you do not forgive your brother or sister from your heart."

The gospel of the Lord.

GOSPEL *denarii = den-AR-ee-eye*
This action-packed story is preceded by Peter's genuine exploration of magnanimity in forgiveness and Jesus' startling reply. Allow it to stand alone—and to introduce the parable. Pick up the pace for the parabolic illustration. Vary the pace of the story at its unexpected turning points: verse 27 (the slave's release); verse 30a (the forgiven one's unwillingness to forgive); and verse 35 ("So my heavenly Father will . . ."). Bring a great deal of energy to the telling of the story.

FIRST READING: Jonah 3:10—4:11

A reading from Jonah.

¹⁰When God saw what ⌐the people of Nineveh⌐ did,
how they turned from their evil ways,
God changed his mind about the calamity
that he had said he would bring upon them;
and he did not do it.

⁴:¹But this was very displeasing to Jonah, and he became angry.
²He prayed to the LORD and said,
"O LORD! Is not this what I said while I was still in my own country?
That is why I fled to Tarshish at the beginning;
for I knew that you are a gracious God and merciful,
slow to anger, and abounding in steadfast love,
and ready to relent from punishing.
³And now, O LORD, please take my life from me,
for it is better for me to die than to live."
⁴And the LORD said, "Is it right for you to be angry?"
⁵Then Jonah went out of the city and sat down east of the city,
and made a booth for himself there.
He sat under it in the shade, waiting to see what would become of the city.

⁶The LORD God appointed a bush, and made it come up over Jonah,
to give shade over his head, to save him from his discomfort;
so Jonah was very happy about the bush.
⁷But when dawn came up the next day,
God appointed a worm that attacked the bush, so that it withered.
⁸When the sun rose, God prepared a sultry east wind,
and the sun beat down on the head of Jonah so that he was faint
and asked that he might die.
He said, "It is better for me to die than to live."

⁹But God said to Jonah,
"Is it right for you to be angry about the bush?"
And he said, "Yes, angry enough to die." ▸

FIRST READING   *Nineveh = NIN-uh-vuh   Tarshish = TAR-shish*
This is a biting and marvelously ironic dialogue between God and the prophet Jonah. Jonah didn't want to be God's messenger in the first place. (God finally had to transport him in the belly of a great fish.) Now Jonah is angry because the people listened to him, repented, and are being spared by God. God's point here, demonstrated in the bush that appears and disappears, is that God's compassion considerably exceeds human compassion. Jonah's whining is melodramatic in the extreme. An energetic reading that gives us a taste of that will help the hearer get the point.

[10]Then the LORD said,
"You are concerned about the bush, for which you did not labor
and which you did not grow;
it came into being in a night and perished in a night.
[11]And should I not be concerned about Nineveh, that great city,
in which there are more than a hundred and twenty thousand persons
who do not know their right hand from their left, and also many animals?"

The word of the Lord.   *or*   Word of God, word of life.

PSALMODY: Psalm 145:1-8

SECOND READING: Philippians 1:21-30

A reading from Philippians.

[21]For to me, living is Christ and dying is gain.
[22]If I am to live in the flesh, that means fruitful labor for me;
and I do not know which I prefer.
[23]I am hard pressed between the two:
my desire is to depart and be with Christ, for that is far better;
[24]but to remain in the flesh is more necessary for you.
[25]Since I am convinced of this, I know that I will remain
and continue with all of you for your progress and joy in faith,
[26]so that I may share abundantly in your boasting in Christ Jesus
when I come to you again.

[27]Only, live your life in a manner worthy of the gospel of Christ,
so that, whether I come and see you or am absent and hear about you,
I will know that you are standing firm in one spirit,
striving side by side with one mind for the faith of the gospel,
[28]and are in no way intimidated by your opponents.
For them this is evidence of their destruction, but of your salvation.
And this is God's doing.
[29]For he has graciously granted you the privilege
not only of believing in Christ,
but of suffering for him as well—
[30]since you are having the same struggle that you saw I had
and now hear that I still have.

The word of the Lord.   *or*   Word of God, word of life.

SECOND READING   *Philippians = fih-LIP-ee-unz*
The author encourages hearers to live the Christian life and helps them come to grips with suffering. Living provides the occasion to witness to the faith in Christ Jesus; dying brings us directly into the presence of Christ. Both are attractive to the author. Both life and death (and even suffering!) are gifts of God for the faithful. That should be reflected in the tone of the reading.

GOSPEL: Matthew 20:1-16

The holy gospel according to Matthew.

⌐Jesus said to the disciples:⌐
[1]"The kingdom of heaven is like a landowner
who went out early in the morning to hire laborers for his vineyard.
[2]After agreeing with the laborers for the usual daily wage,
he sent them into his vineyard.
[3]When he went out about nine o'clock,
he saw others standing idle in the marketplace; [4]and he said to them,
'You also go into the vineyard, and I will pay you whatever is right.'
So they went.

[5]"When he went out again about noon and about three o'clock,
he did the same.
[6]And about five o'clock he went out and found others standing around;
and he said to them,
'Why are you standing here idle all day?'
[7]They said to him, 'Because no one has hired us.'
He said to them, 'You also go into the vineyard.'

[8]"When evening came, the owner of the vineyard said to his manager,
'Call the laborers and give them their pay,
beginning with the last and then going to the first.'
[9]When those hired about five o'clock came,
each of them received the usual daily wage.
[10]Now when the first came, they thought they would receive more;
but each of them also received the usual daily wage.
[11]And when they received it,
they grumbled against the landowner, [12]saying,
'These last worked only one hour, and you have made them equal to us
who have borne the burden of the day and the scorching heat.'
[13]But he replied to one of them,
'Friend, I am doing you no wrong;
did you not agree with me for the usual daily wage?
[14]Take what belongs to you and go;
I choose to give to this last the same as I give to you.
[15]Am I not allowed to do what I choose with what belongs to me?
Or are you envious because I am generous?'

[16]"So the last will be first, and the first will be last."

The gospel of the Lord.

GOSPEL
Beware the familiarity with the gospel that can lead to complacent proclamation. Strive to present a fresh telling of the story—as if for the first time. Do not rush the repetition of "he went out." Instead, allow each instance to underscore the persistence of the landowner (that is, God's pursuit of humankind).

SUNDAY, SEPTEMBER 25–OCTOBER 1
TIME AFTER PENTECOST — LECTIONARY 26

FIRST READING: Ezekiel 18:1-4, 25-32

A reading from Ezekiel.

¹The word of the LORD came to me:
²What do you mean by repeating this proverb concerning the land of Israel,
"The parents have eaten sour grapes,
and the children's teeth are set on edge"?
³As I live, says the Lord GOD,
this proverb shall no more be used by you in Israel.
⁴Know that all lives are mine;
the life of the parent as well as the life of the child is mine:
it is only the person who sins that shall die.

²⁵Yet you say, "The way of the Lord is unfair."
Hear now, O house of Israel: Is my way unfair?
Is it not your ways that are unfair?
²⁶When the righteous turn away from their righteousness
and commit iniquity,
they shall die for it;
for the iniquity that they have committed they shall die.
²⁷Again,
when the wicked turn away from the wickedness they have committed
and do what is lawful and right,
they shall save their life.
²⁸Because they considered
and turned away from all the transgressions that they had committed,
they shall surely live; they shall not die.
²⁹Yet the house of Israel says, "The way of the Lord is unfair."
O house of Israel, are my ways unfair?
Is it not your ways that are unfair?

³⁰Therefore I will judge you, O house of Israel,
all of you according to your ways, says the Lord GOD.
Repent and turn from all your transgressions;
otherwise iniquity will be your ruin.

FIRST READING   *Ezekiel = eh-ZEE-kee-el*
The people of Ezekiel's day were complaining that God unfairly punishes children for the sins of their forebears. In this text God aims to help the prophet set the record straight. The bottom line is that each person is accountable for his or her actions; that God desires the death of no one; and that people should "turn, then, and live." This text demands a particularly deliberate reading. Read slowly and with a sense of divine authority and compassion.

³¹Cast away from you
all the transgressions that you have committed against me,
and get yourselves a new heart and a new spirit!
Why will you die, O house of Israel?
³²For I have no pleasure in the death of anyone, says the Lord GOD.
Turn, then, and live.

The word of the Lord.   *or*   Word of God, word of life.

PSALMODY: Psalm 25:1-9

SECOND READING: Philippians 2:1-13

A reading from Philippians.

¹If then there is any encouragement in Christ,
any consolation from love, any sharing in the Spirit,
any compassion and sympathy,
²make my joy complete:
be of the same mind, having the same love,
being in full accord and of one mind.
³Do nothing from selfish ambition or conceit,
but in humility regard others as better than yourselves.
⁴Let each of you look not to your own interests,
but to the interests of others.

⁵Let the same mind be in you that was in Christ Jesus,
   ⁶who, though he was in the form of God,
      did not regard equality with God as something to be exploited,
   ⁷but emptied himself, taking the form of a slave,
      being born in human likeness.
And being found in human form, ⁸he humbled himself
      and became obedient to the point of death—
      even death on a cross.

⁹Therefore God also highly exalted him
      and gave him the name that is above every name,
   ¹⁰so that at the name of Jesus every knee should bend,
      in heaven and on earth and under the earth, ▸

SECOND READING   *Philippians = fih-LIP-ee-unz*
This is Paul's heartfelt pastoral encouragement for the people. "Be of the same mind"—let Christ's thoughts, Christ's attitude, be your own. The central portion of the text is an ancient poem or hymn in praise of the Lord Jesus. It is extraordinarily beautiful. Take adequate time! Help the hearer feel Paul's genuine care and concern for those to whom he was writing. Care about the people in the pew, and help them to hear your concern.

¹¹and every tongue should confess that Jesus Christ is Lord,
to the glory of God the Father.

¹²Therefore, my beloved, just as you have always obeyed me,
not only in my presence, but much more now in my absence,
work out your own salvation with fear and trembling;
¹³for it is God who is at work in you,
enabling you both to will and to work for his good pleasure.

The word of the Lord.   *or*   Word of God, word of life.

GOSPEL: Matthew 21:23-32

The holy gospel according to Matthew.

²³When ⌐Jesus⌐ entered the temple,
the chief priests and the elders of the people
came to him as he was teaching, and said,
"By what authority are you doing these things,
and who gave you this authority?"
²⁴Jesus said to them, "I will also ask you one question;
if you tell me the answer,
then I will also tell you by what authority I do these things.
²⁵Did the baptism of John come from heaven, or was it of human origin?"
And they argued with one another,
"If we say, 'From heaven,' he will say to us,
'Why then did you not believe him?'
²⁶But if we say, 'Of human origin,' we are afraid of the crowd;
for all regard John as a prophet."
²⁷So they answered Jesus, "We do not know."
And he said to them,
"Neither will I tell you by what authority I am doing these things.

²⁸"What do you think? A man had two sons;
he went to the first and said,
'Son, go and work in the vineyard today.'
²⁹He answered, 'I will not'; but later he changed his mind and went.
³⁰The father went to the second and said the same;
and he answered, 'I go, sir'; but he did not go.
³¹Which of the two did the will of his father?"
They said, "The first."
Jesus said to them, "Truly I tell you,
the tax collectors and the prostitutes are going into the kingdom of God
ahead of you.
³²For John came to you in the way of righteousness
and you did not believe him,
but the tax collectors and the prostitutes believed him;
and even after you saw it,
you did not change your minds and believe him."

The gospel of the Lord.

GOSPEL
This highly animated account (including Jesus' sly reply to the challenge of the elders; their huddled conclave; and the parable of the bad boys) cuts to the quick in verse 31. Work every angle. A lively reading will help the assembly hear that our Lord is deadly serious.

FIRST READING: Isaiah 5:1-7

A reading from Isaiah.

¹Let me sing for my beloved
   my love-song concerning his vineyard:
My beloved had a vineyard on a very fertile hill.
    ²He dug it and cleared it of stones,
and planted it with choice vines;
   he built a watchtower in the midst of it,
and hewed out a wine vat in it;
   he expected it to yield grapes, but it yielded wild grapes.

³And now, inhabitants of Jerusalem and people of Judah,
   judge between me and my vineyard.
⁴What more was there to do for my vineyard that I have not done in it?
   When I expected it to yield grapes, why did it yield wild grapes?

⁵And now I will tell you what I will do to my vineyard.
   I will remove its hedge, and it shall be devoured;
I will break down its wall, and it shall be trampled down.
    ⁶I will make it a waste;
it shall not be pruned or hoed,
   and it shall be overgrown with briers and thorns;
I will also command the clouds that they rain no rain upon it.

⁷For the vineyard of the LORD of hosts is the house of Israel,
   and the people of Judah are his pleasant planting;
he expected justice, but saw bloodshed;
   righteousness, but heard a cry!

The word of the Lord.   *or*   Word of God, word of life.

PSALMODY: Psalm 80:7-15

FIRST READING   *Isaiah = eye-ZAY-uh*
The prophet crafts an important parable here that details God's anger and resolve toward a people who have failed to live up to the covenant relationship they enjoy with God. It sounds at first like a love song (with the planting of a vineyard as the extended metaphor), but suddenly turns sour as it details the failings of Israel and Judah. A vivid reading will help the hearer consider what kind of yield might be perceived from God's contemporary planting, the church.

SECOND READING: Philippians 3:4b-14

A reading from Philippians.

⌐Paul writes:⌐
[4b]If anyone else has reason to be confident in the flesh, I have more:
[5]circumcised on the eighth day,
a member of the people of Israel, of the tribe of Benjamin,
a Hebrew born of Hebrews;
as to the law, a Pharisee;
[6]as to zeal, a persecutor of the church;
as to righteousness under the law, blameless.

[7]Yet whatever gains I had,
these I have come to regard as loss because of Christ.
[8]More than that, I regard everything as loss
because of the surpassing value of knowing Christ Jesus my Lord.
For his sake I have suffered the loss of all things,
and I regard them as rubbish,
in order that I may gain Christ [9]and be found in him,
not having a righteousness of my own that comes from the law,
but one that comes through faith in Christ,
the righteousness from God based on faith.

[10]I want to know Christ and the power of his resurrection
and the sharing of his sufferings by becoming like him in his death,
[11]if somehow I may attain the resurrection from the dead.
[12]Not that I have already obtained this or have already reached the goal
but I press on to make it my own,
because Christ Jesus has made me his own.
[13]Beloved, I do not consider that I have made it my own;
but this one thing I do:
forgetting what lies behind and straining forward to what lies ahead,
[14]I press on toward the goal
for the prize of the heavenly call of God in Christ Jesus.

The word of the Lord.   *or*   Word of God, word of life.

SECOND READING   *Philippians = fih-LIP-ee-unz*
This well known text from the mind and heart of Paul first details his bragging rights as a member of the chosen people, even a learned and zealous member. He goes on to say that these things pale in significance to the "value of knowing Christ Jesus" and "having a righteousness . . . that comes through faith." The reading demands a vigorous reading born of commitment and hope.

GOSPEL: Matthew 21:33-46

The holy gospel according to Matthew.

⌐Jesus said to the people:⌐
[33]"Listen to another parable.
There was a landowner who planted a vineyard,
put a fence around it, dug a wine press in it, and built a watchtower.
Then he leased it to tenants and went to another country.
[34]When the harvest time had come,
he sent his slaves to the tenants to collect his produce.
[35]But the tenants seized his slaves and beat one,
killed another, and stoned another.
[36]Again he sent other slaves, more than the first;
and they treated them in the same way.
[37]Finally he sent his son to them, saying,
'They will respect my son.'
[38]But when the tenants saw the son, they said to themselves,
'This is the heir; come, let us kill him and get his inheritance.'
[39]So they seized him, threw him out of the vineyard, and killed him.

[40]"Now when the owner of the vineyard comes,
what will he do to those tenants?"
[41]They said to him,
"He will put those wretches to a miserable death,
and lease the vineyard to other tenants
who will give him the produce at the harvest time."

[42]Jesus said to them, "Have you never read in the scriptures:
    'The stone that the builders rejected has become the cornerstone;
    this was the Lord's doing, and it is amazing in our eyes'?
[43]Therefore I tell you,
the kingdom of God will be taken away from you
and given to a people that produces the fruits of the kingdom.
[44]The one who falls on this stone will be broken to pieces;
and it will crush anyone on whom it falls."

[45]When the chief priests and the Pharisees heard his parables,
they realized that he was speaking about them.
[46]They wanted to arrest him,
but they feared the crowds, because they regarded him as a prophet.

The gospel of the Lord.

GOSPEL
With a deceptively innocent parable, Jesus leads everyone with ears to the damning indictment of verse 43.
Help the assembly hear from the beginning that the Lord knows exactly how the story ends.

SUNDAY, OCTOBER 9–15

TIME AFTER PENTECOST — LECTIONARY 28

FIRST READING: Isaiah 25:1-9

A reading from Isaiah.

¹O LORD, you are my God;
    I will exalt you, I will praise your name;
for you have done wonderful things,
    plans formed of old, faithful and sure.
²For you have made the city a heap,
    the fortified city a ruin;
the palace of aliens is a city no more,
    it will never be rebuilt.
³Therefore strong peoples will glorify you;
    cities of ruthless nations will fear you.
⁴For you have been a refuge to the poor,
    a refuge to the needy in their distress,
    a shelter from the rainstorm and a shade from the heat.
When the blast of the ruthless was like a winter rainstorm,
    ⁵the noise of aliens like heat in a dry place,
you subdued the heat with the shade of clouds;
    the song of the ruthless was stilled.

⁶On this mountain the LORD of hosts will make for all peoples
    a feast of rich food, a feast of well-aged wines,
    of rich food filled with marrow, of well-aged wines strained clear.
⁷And he will destroy on this mountain
    the shroud that is cast over all peoples,
    the sheet that is spread over all nations;
    he will swallow up death forever.
⁸Then the Lord GOD will wipe away the tears from all faces,
    and the disgrace of his people he will take away from all the earth,
    for the LORD has spoken.
⁹It will be said on that day,
    Lo, this is our God; we have waited for him, so that he might save us.
    This is the LORD for whom we have waited;
    let us be glad and rejoice in his salvation.

The word of the Lord.   *or*   Word of God, word of life.

FIRST READING   *Isaiah = eye-ZAY-uh*
This is a song of thanksgiving and demands that kind of joyful note. There are multiple word pictures here that require time to sink in. Particularly complex is the image of the feast in verse 6, in which each succeeding phrase amplifies the one before. Finally there is a declaration of the power of God over death (which is frequently read at funeral liturgies). "Rejoice in his salvation" is a good motto with which the reader might approach this text.

PSALMODY: Psalm 23

SECOND READING: Philippians 4:1-9

A reading from Philippians.

[1]My brothers and sisters,
whom I love and long for, my joy and crown,
stand firm in the Lord in this way, my beloved.

[2]I urge Euodia and I urge Syntyche to be of the same mind in the Lord.
[3]Yes, and I ask you also, my loyal companion,
help these women,
for they have struggled beside me in the work of the gospel,
together with Clement and the rest of my co-workers,
whose names are in the book of life.

[4]Rejoice in the Lord always; again I will say, Rejoice.
[5]Let your gentleness be known to everyone.
The Lord is near.
[6]Do not worry about anything,
but in everything by prayer and supplication with thanksgiving
let your requests be made known to God.
[7]And the peace of God, which surpasses all understanding,
will guard your hearts and your minds in Christ Jesus.

[8]Finally, beloved, whatever is true, whatever is honorable,
whatever is just, whatever is pure,
whatever is pleasing, whatever is commendable,
if there is any excellence and if there is anything worthy of praise,
think about these things.
[9]Keep on doing the things that you have learned and received
and heard and seen in me,
and the God of peace will be with you.

The word of the Lord.   *or*   Word of God, word of life.

SECOND READING   *Philippians = fih-LIP-ee-unz   Euodia = you-OH-dee-uh   Syntyche = SIN-tih-kih*
Wonderful words of encouragement are found here. Those words are prefaced by three verses that set the
letter in its historical context and help the reader make the reading sound like a letter. Encourage the hearer,
even as you, the reader, were encouraged by these words as you have considered them.

GOSPEL: Matthew 22:1-14

The holy gospel according to Matthew.

[1]Once more Jesus spoke to them in parables, saying:
[2]"The kingdom of heaven may be compared to a king
who gave a wedding banquet for his son.
[3]He sent his slaves to call those who had been invited to the wedding banquet,
but they would not come.
[4]Again he sent other slaves, saying,
'Tell those who have been invited:
Look, I have prepared my dinner,
my oxen and my fat calves have been slaughtered,
and everything is ready;
come to the wedding banquet.'
[5]But they made light of it and went away,
one to his farm, another to his business,
[6]while the rest seized his slaves, mistreated them, and killed them.
[7]The king was enraged.
He sent his troops, destroyed those murderers, and burned their city.

[8]"Then he said to his slaves,
'The wedding is ready, but those invited were not worthy.
[9]Go therefore into the main streets,
and invite everyone you find to the wedding banquet.'
[10]Those slaves went out into the streets and gathered all whom they found,
both good and bad; so the wedding hall was filled with guests.

[11]"But when the king came in to see the guests,
he noticed a man there who was not wearing a wedding robe,
[12]and he said to him,
'Friend, how did you get in here without a wedding robe?'
And he was speechless.
[13]Then the king said to the attendants,
'Bind him hand and foot, and throw him into the outer darkness,
where there will be weeping and gnashing of teeth.'

[14]"For many are called, but few are chosen."

The gospel of the Lord.

GOSPEL
Appropriate preparation for the proclamation of this gospel requires that the reader again be startled by the arrogance of the first invited, by the king's declaration to "invite everyone," and by his rage toward the man not wearing a wedding robe. Anything less will result in an unexceptional reading.

SUNDAY, OCTOBER 16–22
TIME AFTER PENTECOST — LECTIONARY 29

FIRST READING: Isaiah 45:1-7

A reading from Isaiah.

¹Thus says the LORD to his anointed, to Cyrus,
   whose right hand I have grasped
to subdue nations before him
   and strip kings of their robes,
to open doors before him—
   and the gates shall not be closed:
²I will go before you and level the mountains,
I will break in pieces the doors of bronze
   and cut through the bars of iron,
³I will give you the treasures of darkness
   and riches hidden in secret places,
so that you may know that it is I, the LORD,
   the God of Israel, who call you by your name.
⁴For the sake of my servant Jacob, and Israel my chosen,
I call you by your name,
   I surname you, though you do not know me.
⁵I am the LORD, and there is no other;
   besides me there is no god.
   I arm you, though you do not know me,
⁶so that they may know, from the rising of the sun
   and from the west,
that there is no one besides me;
   I am the LORD, and there is no other.
⁷I form light and create darkness,
   I make weal and create woe;
   I the LORD do all these things.

The word of the Lord.   *or*   Word of God, word of life.

PSALMODY: Psalm 96:1-9 [10-13]

FIRST READING   *Isaiah = eye-ZAY-uh   Cyrus = SY-rus*
This is a fascinating text and somewhat complex. The prophet puts this text in the mouth of God; thus the reader must assume God's voice for this reading. God announces that the benevolent despot, Cyrus, a non-Jew, will be God's anointed one and will serve God's purposes, though Cyrus does not know the God of Israel. This is a divine declaration of God's ability to get things done and of God's singular lordship over all things.

SECOND READING: 1 Thessalonians 1:1-10

A reading from First Thessalonians.

[1]Paul, Silvanus, and Timothy,
To the church of the Thessalonians
in God the Father and the Lord Jesus Christ:
Grace to you and peace.

[2]We always give thanks to God for all of you and mention you in our prayers,
constantly [3]remembering before our God and Father
your work of faith and labor of love and steadfastness of hope
in our Lord Jesus Christ.
[4]For we know, brothers and sisters beloved by God, that he has chosen you,
[5]because our message of the gospel came to you not in word only,
but also in power and in the Holy Spirit and with full conviction;
just as you know what kind of persons we proved to be among you for your sake.
[6]And you became imitators of us and of the Lord,
for in spite of persecution
you received the word with joy inspired by the Holy Spirit,
[7]so that you became an example to all the believers
in Macedonia and in Achaia.

[8]For the word of the Lord has sounded forth from you
not only in Macedonia and Achaia,
but in every place your faith in God has become known,
so that we have no need to speak about it.
[9]For the people of those regions report about us
what kind of welcome we had among you,
and how you turned to God from idols, to serve a living and true God,
[10]and to wait for his Son from heaven, whom he raised from the dead—
Jesus, who rescues us from the wrath that is coming.

The word of the Lord.   *or*   Word of God, word of life.

SECOND READING   *Thessalonians = thess-uh-LOHN-ee-unz   Silvanus = sil-VAY-nus   Macedonia = mass-uh-DOHN-ee-uh   Achaia = uh-KAY-uh*
This is the beginning of a letter. An understood "From" precedes the names of the authors, Paul, Silvanus, and Timothy. The sentence structure in this text strikes the contemporary ear as convoluted. In preparing, the reader will do well to be certain where each sentence will end. Only then will the message be clear to reader and hearer alike.

GOSPEL: Matthew 22:15-22

The holy gospel according to Matthew.

¹⁵The Pharisees went and plotted to entrap ⌐Jesus⌐ in what he said.
¹⁶So they sent their disciples to him, along with the Herodians, saying,
"Teacher, we know that you are sincere,
and teach the way of God in accordance with truth,
and show deference to no one;
for you do not regard people with partiality.
¹⁷Tell us, then, what you think.
Is it lawful to pay taxes to the emperor, or not?"
¹⁸But Jesus, aware of their malice, said,
"Why are you putting me to the test, you hypocrites?
¹⁹Show me the coin used for the tax."
And they brought him a denarius.
²⁰Then he said to them, "Whose head is this, and whose title?"
²¹They answered, "The emperor's."

Then he said to them,
"Give therefore to the emperor the things that are the emperor's,
and to God the things that are God's."
²²When they heard this, they were amazed;
and they left him and went away.

The gospel of the Lord.

GOSPEL   *Herodians = heh-ROH-dee-unz   denarius = deh-NAR-ee-us*
The tone of verses 15–17 is utterly deceitful! Our Lord's response is the picture of patience. Allow the assembly to enjoy the contrast.

✝ Sunday, October 23–29
Time after Pentecost — Lectionary 30

FIRST READING: Leviticus 19:1-2, 15-18

A reading from Leviticus.

¹The LORD spoke to Moses, saying:
²Speak to all the congregation of the people of Israel and say to them:
You shall be holy, for I the LORD your God am holy.

¹⁵You shall not render an unjust judgment;
you shall not be partial to the poor or defer to the great:
with justice you shall judge your neighbor.
¹⁶You shall not go around as a slanderer among your people,
and you shall not profit by the blood of your neighbor: I am the LORD.
¹⁷You shall not hate in your heart anyone of your kin;
you shall reprove your neighbor, or you will incur guilt yourself.
¹⁸You shall not take vengeance or bear a grudge against any of your people,
but you shall love your neighbor as yourself: I am the LORD.

The word of the Lord.   *or*   Word of God, word of life.

PSALMODY: Psalm 1

SECOND READING: 1 Thessalonians 2:1-8

A reading from First Thessalonians.

¹You yourselves know, brothers and sisters,
that our coming to you was not in vain,
²but though we had already suffered
and been shamefully mistreated at Philippi, as you know,
we had courage in our God to declare to you the gospel of God
in spite of great opposition.
³For our appeal does not spring from deceit or impure motives or trickery,
⁴but just as we have been approved by God
to be entrusted with the message of the gospel,
even so we speak, not to please mortals,
but to please God who tests our hearts. ▸

FIRST READING   *Leviticus = leh-VIT-ih-cus*
This text is a simple summary of some of God's expectations. The reading requires a voice whose authority backstops every stated expectation. In verse 2: "for I the LORD your God am holy." In verses 16 and 18: "I am the LORD." Allow each expectation to sink in. Read at a most deliberate pace. We can appreciate and celebrate God's expectations only to the degree that we can sort them out.

SECOND READING   *Thessalonians = thess-uh-LOHN-ee-unz   Philippi = fih-LIP-eye*
See how the apostle loves the Thessalonians! This reading is filled with tender concern. Preparation is essential, because the sentences are long and convoluted. The hearer will be helped to the degree that the reader can let the love shine in the reading of the text. The reading warrants some passion. Make it heartfelt.

⁵As you know and as God is our witness,
we never came with words of flattery or with a pretext for greed;
⁶nor did we seek praise from mortals, whether from you or from others,
⁷though we might have made demands as apostles of Christ.
But we were gentle among you,
like a nurse tenderly caring for her own children.
⁸So deeply do we care for you that we are determined to share with you
not only the gospel of God but also our own selves,
because you have become very dear to us.

The word of the Lord.   *or*   Word of God, word of life.

GOSPEL: Matthew 22:34-46

The holy gospel according to Matthew.

³⁴When the Pharisees heard that ⌈Jesus⌉ had silenced the Sadducees,
they gathered together,
³⁵and one of them, a lawyer, asked him a question to test him.
³⁶"Teacher, which commandment in the law is the greatest?"
³⁷He said to him,
" 'You shall love the Lord your God with all your heart,
and with all your soul, and with all your mind.'
³⁸This is the greatest and first commandment.
³⁹And a second is like it:
'You shall love your neighbor as yourself.'
⁴⁰On these two commandments hang all the law and the prophets."

⁴¹Now while the Pharisees were gathered together,
Jesus asked them this question:
⁴²"What do you think of the Messiah? Whose son is he?"
They said to him, "The son of David."
⁴³He said to them,
"How is it then that David by the Spirit calls him Lord, saying,
   ⁴⁴'The Lord said to my Lord,
      "Sit at my right hand, until I put your enemies under your feet" '?
⁴⁵If David thus calls him Lord, how can he be his son?"
⁴⁶No one was able to give him an answer,
nor from that day did anyone dare to ask him any more questions.

The gospel of the Lord.

GOSPEL   *Sadducees = SAD-yuh-seez*
The early verses beg for a "testing" tone. Jesus' patient reply ought to provide sharp contrast. A carefully considered reading might employ a playful voice (accompanied by a small smile) as our Lord asks a follow-up question and quotes Psalm 110. It is a side of the Savior the assembly does not often get to hear.

Sunday, October 30–November 5

Time after Pentecost — Lectionary 31

FIRST READING: Micah 3:5-12

A reading from Micah.

⁵Thus says the LORD concerning the prophets who lead my people astray,
who cry "Peace" when they have something to eat,
but declare war against those who put nothing into their mouths.
⁶Therefore it shall be night to you, without vision,
    and darkness to you, without revelation.
The sun shall go down upon the prophets,
    and the day shall be black over them;
⁷the seers shall be disgraced,
    and the diviners put to shame;
they shall all cover their lips, for there is no answer from God.
⁸But as for me, I am filled with power, with the spirit of the LORD,
    and with justice and might,
to declare to Jacob his transgression and to Israel his sin.

⁹Hear this, you rulers of the house of Jacob
    and chiefs of the house of Israel,
who abhor justice and pervert all equity,
¹⁰who build Zion with blood and Jerusalem with wrong!
¹¹Its rulers give judgment for a bribe,
    its priests teach for a price,
    its prophets give oracles for money;
yet they lean upon the LORD and say,
    "Surely the LORD is with us!
    No harm shall come upon us."
¹²Therefore because of you Zion shall be plowed as a field;
Jerusalem shall become a heap of ruins,
    and the mountain of the house a wooded height.

The word of the Lord.   *or*   Word of God, word of life.

PSALMODY: Psalm 43

FIRST READING

An acidic condemnation of other contemporary prophets (verses 5–7) precedes Micah's withering word of judgment. Though both halves of the reading are condemning, try to let the sound of contempt in the early going contrast with the righteous indignation in the later verses.

SECOND READING: 1 Thessalonians 2:9-13

A reading from First Thessalonians.

[9]You remember our labor and toil, brothers and sisters;
we worked night and day,
so that we might not burden any of you
while we proclaimed to you the gospel of God.
[10]You are witnesses, and God also,
how pure, upright, and blameless our conduct was toward you believers.
[11]As you know, we dealt with each one of you like a father with his children,
[12]urging and encouraging you and pleading that you lead a life worthy of God,
who calls you into his own kingdom and glory.

[13]We also constantly give thanks to God for this,
that when you received the word of God that you heard from us,
you accepted it not as a human word but as what it really is,
God's word, which is also at work in you believers.

The word of the Lord.   *or*   Word of God, word of life.

SECOND READING   *Thessalonians = thess-uh-LOHN-ee-unz*
The reading is very brief. A sense of urgency from the very beginning is required to give this reading the sense of importance it deserves.

GOSPEL: Matthew 23:1-12

The holy gospel according to Matthew.

[1]Jesus said to the crowds and to his disciples,
[2]"The scribes and the Pharisees sit on Moses' seat;
[3]therefore, do whatever they teach you and follow it;
but do not do as they do, for they do not practice what they teach.
[4]They tie up heavy burdens, hard to bear,
and lay them on the shoulders of others;
but they themselves are unwilling to lift a finger to move them.
[5]They do all their deeds to be seen by others;
for they make their phylacteries broad and their fringes long.
[6]They love to have the place of honor at banquets
and the best seats in the synagogues,
[7]and to be greeted with respect in the marketplaces,
and to have people call them rabbi.
[8]But you are not to be called rabbi,
for you have one teacher, and you are all students.
[9]And call no one your father on earth,
for you have one Father—the one in heaven.
[10]Nor are you to be called instructors,
for you have one instructor, the Messiah.

[11]"The greatest among you will be your servant.
[12]All who exalt themselves will be humbled,
and all who humble themselves will be exalted."

The gospel of the Lord.

GOSPEL   *phylacteries = fih-LAK-ter-eez*
A scathing critique of the scribes and the Pharisees (verses 1–7) might be profitably separated from the concluding verses by a pause following verse 7 and a gentler, instructive tone for verses 8–12.

SUNDAY, NOVEMBER 6–12

TIME AFTER PENTECOST — LECTIONARY 32

FIRST READING: Amos 5:18-24

Alternate Reading: Wisdom 6:12-16 (p. 504)

A reading from Amos.

¹⁸Alas for you who desire the day of the LORD!
    Why do you want the day of the LORD?
It is darkness, not light; ¹⁹as if someone fled from a lion,
    and was met by a bear; or went into the house
        and rested a hand against the wall, and was bitten by a snake.
²⁰Is not the day of the LORD darkness, not light,
    and gloom with no brightness in it?

²¹I hate, I despise your festivals,
    and I take no delight in your solemn assemblies.
²²Even though you offer me your burnt offerings and grain offerings,
    I will not accept them;
and the offerings of well-being of your fatted animals I will not look upon.
²³Take away from me the noise of your songs;
    I will not listen to the melody of your harps.
²⁴But let justice roll down like waters,
    and righteousness like an ever-flowing stream.

The word of the Lord.   *or*   Word of God, word of life.

PSALMODY: Psalm 70 or Wisdom 6:17-20

SECOND READING: 1 Thessalonians 4:13-18

A reading from First Thessalonians.

¹³We do not want you to be uninformed, brothers and sisters,
about those who have died,
so that you may not grieve as others do who have no hope.
¹⁴For since we believe that Jesus died and rose again,
even so, through Jesus, God will bring with him those who have died.
¹⁵For this we declare to you by the word of the Lord,
that we who are alive, who are left until the coming of the Lord,

---

FIRST READING
Verses 18-23 demand the sound of righteous cynicism. Their intensity will be amplified by an extremely deliberate delivery. The prophet, speaking for the Almighty, pronounces a stinging indictment of the peoples' festivals, assemblies, offerings, and songs. Verse 24 may profit from a dramatic shift in tone. Precede it with a solid pause, and give it the authority of a divine command.

SECOND READING   *Thessalonians = thess-uh-LOHN-ee-unz*
Sentence by sentence, this marvelous word of hope builds in intensity, wonder, and joy. The reader will want to begin with an intensity on which she or he can build. Allow the emotion to peak at the end of verse 17. Pause . . . then in verse 18 provide the hearers with their homework assignment.

will by no means precede those who have died.
[16]For the Lord himself, with a cry of command,
with the archangel's call and with the sound of God's trumpet,
will descend from heaven, and the dead in Christ will rise first.
[17]Then we who are alive, who are left,
will be caught up in the clouds together with them to meet the Lord in the air;
and so we will be with the Lord forever.

[18]Therefore encourage one another with these words.

The word of the Lord.   *or*   Word of God, word of life.

GOSPEL: Matthew 25:1-13

The holy gospel according to Matthew.

⌐Jesus said to the disciples:⌐
[1]"Then the kingdom of heaven will be like this.
Ten bridesmaids took their lamps and went to meet the bridegroom.
[2]Five of them were foolish, and five were wise.
[3]When the foolish took their lamps, they took no oil with them;
[4]but the wise took flasks of oil with their lamps.
[5]As the bridegroom was delayed, all of them became drowsy and slept.

[6]"But at midnight there was a shout,
'Look! Here is the bridegroom! Come out to meet him.'
[7]Then all those bridesmaids got up and trimmed their lamps.
[8]The foolish said to the wise,
'Give us some of your oil, for our lamps are going out.'
[9]But the wise replied,
'No! there will not be enough for you and for us;
you had better go to the dealers and buy some for yourselves.'
[10]And while they went to buy it, the bridegroom came,
and those who were ready went with him into the wedding banquet;
and the door was shut.
[11]Later the other bridesmaids came also, saying,
'Lord, lord, open to us.'
[12]But he replied, 'Truly I tell you, I do not know you.'

[13]"Keep awake therefore, for you know neither the day nor the hour."

The gospel of the Lord.

GOSPEL
The parable of the bridesmaids takes shape by twists and turns. Enjoy the telling of it. Help the assembly sense the developing tension. Allow verse 12 to sound like a slamming door. Follow it with a pause of substance and deliver the warning of verse 13 with appropriate gravity.

SUNDAY, NOVEMBER 13–19

TIME AFTER PENTECOST — LECTIONARY 33

FIRST READING: Zephaniah 1:7, 12-18

A reading from Zephaniah.

⁷Be silent before the Lord GOD!
　For the day of the LORD is at hand;
the LORD has prepared a sacrifice,
　he has consecrated his guests.

¹²At that time I will search Jerusalem with lamps,
　and I will punish the people who rest complacently on their dregs,
　those who say in their hearts,
"The LORD will not do good, nor will he do harm."
¹³Their wealth shall be plundered, and their houses laid waste.
Though they build houses, they shall not inhabit them;
though they plant vineyards, they shall not drink wine from them.

¹⁴The great day of the LORD is near, near and hastening fast;
the sound of the day of the LORD is bitter,
　the warrior cries aloud there.
¹⁵That day will be a day of wrath,
　a day of distress and anguish,
a day of ruin and devastation,
　a day of darkness and gloom,
a day of clouds and thick darkness,
　¹⁶a day of trumpet blast and battle cry
against the fortified cities and against the lofty battlements.

¹⁷I will bring such distress upon people
　that they shall walk like the blind;
　because they have sinned against the LORD,
their blood shall be poured out like dust, and their flesh like dung.
¹⁸Neither their silver nor their gold
　will be able to save them on the day of the LORD's wrath;
in the fire of his passion the whole earth shall be consumed;
for a full, a terrible end he will make of all the inhabitants of the earth.

The word of the Lord.　　　　*or*　　　　Word of God, word of life.

FIRST READING　　*Zephaniah = zef-uh-NY-uh*
This frightening text sets its own tone: "The sound of the day of the LORD is bitter" (verse 14b). Anything less, anything other, will sound noticeably incongruent. The well-prepared reading will begin with a bang and leave the assembly shaken and reflective!

PSALMODY: Psalm 90:1-8 [9-11] 12

SECOND READING: 1 Thessalonians 5:1-11

A reading from First Thessalonians.

¹Now concerning the times and the seasons, brothers and sisters,
you do not need to have anything written to you.
²For you yourselves know very well
that the day of the Lord will come like a thief in the night.
³When they say, "There is peace and security,"
then sudden destruction will come upon them,
as labor pains come upon a pregnant woman,
and there will be no escape!

⁴But you, beloved, are not in darkness,
for that day to surprise you like a thief;
⁵for you are all children of light and children of the day;
we are not of the night or of darkness.
⁶So then let us not fall asleep as others do,
but let us keep awake and be sober;
⁷for those who sleep sleep at night,
and those who are drunk get drunk at night.
⁸But since we belong to the day, let us be sober,
and put on the breastplate of faith and love,
and for a helmet the hope of salvation.
⁹For God has destined us not for wrath
but for obtaining salvation through our Lord Jesus Christ,
¹⁰who died for us,
so that whether we are awake or asleep we may live with him.
¹¹Therefore encourage one another and build up each other,
as indeed you are doing.

The word of the Lord.   *or*   Word of God, word of life.

SECOND READING   *Thessalonians = thess-uh-LOHN-ee-uns*
The epistle's author is as clear as day. The tone of the second reading, particularly from verse 4 on,
will contrast sharply with the first. For "the children of light and children of the day" these are words of
encouragement and consolation. For them the day of reckoning holds no fear.

GOSPEL: Matthew 25:14-30

The holy gospel according to Matthew.

⌐Jesus said to the disciples:⌐
[14]"For it is as if a man, going on a journey,
summoned his slaves and entrusted his property to them;
[15]to one he gave five talents, to another two, to another one,
to each according to his ability.
Then he went away.

[16]"The one who had received the five talents went off at once
and traded with them, and made five more talents.
[17]In the same way, the one who had the two talents made two more talents.
[18]But the one who had received the one talent went off
and dug a hole in the ground and hid his master's money.

[19]"After a long time the master of those slaves came
and settled accounts with them.
[20]Then the one who had received the five talents came forward,
bringing five more talents, saying,
'Master, you handed over to me five talents;
see, I have made five more talents.'
[21]His master said to him,
'Well done, good and trustworthy slave;
you have been trustworthy in a few things,
I will put you in charge of many things;
enter into the joy of your master.'
[22]And the one with the two talents also came forward, saying,
'Master, you handed over to me two talents;
see, I have made two more talents.'
[23]His master said to him,
'Well done, good and trustworthy slave;
you have been trustworthy in a few things,
I will put you in charge of many things;
enter into the joy of your master.'

GOSPEL
Great storytellers are highly invested, right from the beginning, in the tales they tell. This gospel requires that kind of psychic energy and emotional commitment from the outset. Help the hearer see each slave and share his accomplishment—or failure and condemnation.

²⁴"Then the one who had received the one talent also came forward, saying, 'Master, I knew that you were a harsh man, reaping where you did not sow, and gathering where you did not scatter seed; ²⁵so I was afraid, and I went and hid your talent in the ground. Here you have what is yours.' ²⁶But his master replied, 'You wicked and lazy slave! You knew, did you, that I reap where I did not sow, and gather where I did not scatter? ²⁷Then you ought to have invested my money with the bankers, and on my return I would have received what was my own with interest. ²⁸So take the talent from him, and give it to the one with the ten talents.

²⁹" 'For to all those who have, more will be given, and they will have an abundance; but from those who have nothing, even what they have will be taken away. ³⁰As for this worthless slave, throw him into the outer darkness, where there will be weeping and gnashing of teeth.' "

The gospel of the Lord.

CHRIST THE KING

SUNDAY, NOVEMBER 20–26
LAST SUNDAY AFTER PENTECOST — LECTIONARY 34

FIRST READING: Ezekiel 34:11-16, 20-24

A reading from Ezekiel.

[11]Thus says the Lord GOD:
I myself will search for my sheep, and will seek them out.
[12]As shepherds seek out their flocks
when they are among their scattered sheep,
so I will seek out my sheep.
I will rescue them from all the places to which they have been scattered
on a day of clouds and thick darkness.
[13]I will bring them out from the peoples and gather them from the countries,
and will bring them into their own land;
and I will feed them on the mountains of Israel,
by the watercourses, and in all the inhabited parts of the land.
[14]I will feed them with good pasture,
and the mountain heights of Israel shall be their pasture;
there they shall lie down in good grazing land,
and they shall feed on rich pasture on the mountains of Israel.
[15]I myself will be the shepherd of my sheep,
and I will make them lie down, says the Lord GOD.
[16]I will seek the lost, and I will bring back the strayed,
and I will bind up the injured, and I will strengthen the weak,
but the fat and the strong I will destroy.
I will feed them with justice.

[20]Therefore, thus says the Lord GOD to them:
I myself will judge between the fat sheep and the lean sheep.
[21]Because you pushed with flank and shoulder,
and butted at all the weak animals with your horns
until you scattered them far and wide,
[22]I will save my flock, and they shall no longer be ravaged;
and I will judge between sheep and sheep.

[23]I will set up over them one shepherd, my servant David,
and he shall feed them:

FIRST READING   *Ezekiel = eh-ZEEK-ee-el*
Read twice as loud and half as fast as you are initially inclined. This helpful rule of thumb for readers in the assembly is particularly applicable here. These are divine declarations, and the Lord GOD is seldom characterized as soft-spoken. Declare God's commitment and intention. Solid pauses after each "thus says the Lord GOD" and before the concluding "I, the LORD, have spoken" will help.

he shall feed them and be their shepherd.
²⁴And I, the LORD, will be their God,
and my servant David shall be prince among them;
I, the LORD, have spoken.

The word of the Lord.   *or*   Word of God, word of life.

PSALMODY: Psalm 95:1-7a

SECOND READING: Ephesians 1:15-23

A reading from Ephesians.

¹⁵I have heard of your faith in the Lord Jesus
and your love toward all the saints,
and for this reason ¹⁶I do not cease to give thanks for you
as I remember you in my prayers.
¹⁷I pray that the God of our Lord Jesus Christ, the Father of glory,
may give you a spirit of wisdom and revelation as you come to know him,
¹⁸so that, with the eyes of your heart enlightened,
you may know what is the hope to which he has called you,
what are the riches of his glorious inheritance among the saints,
¹⁹and what is the immeasurable greatness of his power for us who believe,
according to the working of his great power.

²⁰God put this power to work in Christ
when he raised him from the dead
and seated him at his right hand in the heavenly places,
²¹far above all rule and authority and power and dominion,
and above every name that is named,
not only in this age but also in the age to come.
²²And he has put all things under his feet
and has made him the head over all things for the church,
²³which is his body, the fullness of him who fills all in all.

The word of the Lord.   *or*   Word of God, word of life.

SECOND READING   *Ephesians = eh-FEE-zhunz*
This reading moves from a blessing upon the Christians in Ephesus to a marvelous description of Christ the King. Don't rush it. Some of the sentences are long and a bit complicated. The reader will want to map them out in rehearsal, then give a reading that makes it clear from the start where each sentence is going. Give the hearer time to absorb the power of God at work in Christ.

GOSPEL: Matthew 25:31-46

The holy gospel according to Matthew.

⌜Jesus said to the disciples:⌝
[31]"When the Son of Man comes in his glory, and all the angels with him,
then he will sit on the throne of his glory.
[32]All the nations will be gathered before him,
and he will separate people one from another
as a shepherd separates the sheep from the goats,
[33]and he will put the sheep at his right hand and the goats at the left.

[34]"Then the king will say to those at his right hand,
'Come, you that are blessed by my Father,
inherit the kingdom prepared for you from the foundation of the world;
[35]for I was hungry and you gave me food,
I was thirsty and you gave me something to drink,
I was a stranger and you welcomed me,
[36]I was naked and you gave me clothing,
I was sick and you took care of me,
I was in prison and you visited me.'
[37]Then the righteous will answer him,
'Lord, when was it that we saw you hungry and gave you food,
or thirsty and gave you something to drink?
[38]And when was it that we saw you a stranger and welcomed you,
or naked and gave you clothing?
[39]And when was it that we saw you sick or in prison and visited you?'
[40]And the king will answer them,
'Truly I tell you,
just as you did it to one of the least of these who are members of my family,
you did it to me.'

[41]"Then he will say to those at his left hand,
'You that are accursed,
depart from me into the eternal fire prepared for the devil and his angels;
[42]for I was hungry and you gave me no food,
I was thirsty and you gave me nothing to drink,
[43]I was a stranger and you did not welcome me,
naked and you did not give me clothing,
sick and in prison and you did not visit me.'

GOSPEL
The text anticipates the coming of the Son of Man in glory and Christ the King's "last word." It is a sobering scene. Strive for a judicial tone mingled, at the end, with not a little sadness.

⁴⁴Then they also will answer,
'Lord, when was it that we saw you hungry or thirsty
or a stranger or naked or sick or in prison,
and did not take care of you?'
⁴⁵Then he will answer them,
'Truly I tell you,
just as you did not do it to one of the least of these,
you did not do it to me.'
⁴⁶And these will go away into eternal punishment,
but the righteous into eternal life."

The gospel of the Lord.

Time after Pentecost
SEMICONTINUOUS SERIES

An alternative series with complementary First Readings and Psalms begins on page 215.

The Holy Trinity
First Sunday after Pentecost

FIRST READING: Genesis 1:1—2:4a

A reading from Genesis.

[1]In the beginning when God created the heavens and the earth,
[2]the earth was a formless void
and darkness covered the face of the deep,
while a wind from God swept over the face of the waters.
[3]Then God said,
"Let there be light"; and there was light.
[4]And God saw that the light was good;
and God separated the light from the darkness.
[5]God called the light Day,
and the darkness he called Night.
And there was evening and there was morning, the first day.

[6]And God said,
"Let there be a dome in the midst of the waters,
and let it separate the waters from the waters."
[7]So God made the dome and separated the waters that were under the dome
from the waters that were above the dome.
And it was so.
[8]God called the dome Sky.
And there was evening and there was morning, the second day.

[9]And God said,
"Let the waters under the sky be gathered together into one place,
and let the dry land appear."
And it was so.
[10]God called the dry land Earth,
and the waters that were gathered together he called Seas.
And God saw that it was good.
[11]Then God said,
"Let the earth put forth vegetation:
plants yielding seed,
and fruit trees of every kind on earth that bear fruit with the seed in it."
And it was so. ▸

FIRST READING
Length and familiarity both pose dangers for the reader of this pericope. Take steps to address these dangers. (1) Steep yourself in the text. Rediscover it by re-reading it with some frequency in preparation for Sunday. (2) Notice that the repetition in the reading develops a cadence or rhythm that helps to carry the story along. (3) Finally, remember the day. This Sunday, The Holy Trinity, is, as it were, God's "Name Day." Today we celebrate the majesty and the mystery of God. Help us imagine the Father, the Son, and the Holy Spirit engaged in the wild and wonderful task of creation. An expansive act of creation demands an expansive reading!

¹²The earth brought forth vegetation:
plants yielding seed of every kind,
and trees of every kind bearing fruit with the seed in it.
And God saw that it was good.
¹³And there was evening and there was morning, the third day.

¹⁴And God said,
"Let there be lights in the dome of the sky
to separate the day from the night;
and let them be for signs and for seasons and for days and years,
¹⁵and let them be lights in the dome of the sky to give light upon the earth."
And it was so.
¹⁶God made the two great lights—
the greater light to rule the day
and the lesser light to rule the night—and the stars.
¹⁷God set them in the dome of the sky to give light upon the earth,
¹⁸to rule over the day and over the night,
and to separate the light from the darkness.
And God saw that it was good.
¹⁹And there was evening and there was morning, the fourth day.

²⁰And God said,
"Let the waters bring forth swarms of living creatures,
and let birds fly above the earth across the dome of the sky."
²¹So God created the great sea monsters
and every living creature that moves, of every kind,
with which the waters swarm,
and every winged bird of every kind.
And God saw that it was good.
²²God blessed them, saying,
"Be fruitful and multiply and fill the waters in the seas,
and let birds multiply on the earth."
²³And there was evening and there was morning, the fifth day.

²⁴And God said,
"Let the earth bring forth living creatures of every kind:
cattle and creeping things and wild animals of the earth of every kind."
And it was so.
²⁵God made the wild animals of the earth of every kind,
and the cattle of every kind,
and everything that creeps upon the ground of every kind.
And God saw that it was good.

²⁶Then God said,
"Let us make humankind in our image,
according to our likeness;
and let them have dominion over the fish of the sea,
and over the birds of the air,
and over the cattle, and over all the wild animals of the earth,
and over every creeping thing that creeps upon the earth."
²⁷So God created humankind in his image,
in the image of God he created them;
male and female he created them.
²⁸God blessed them, and God said to them,
"Be fruitful and multiply, and fill the earth and subdue it;
and have dominion over the fish of the sea
and over the birds of the air
and over every living thing that moves upon the earth."
²⁹God said,
"See, I have given you every plant yielding seed
that is upon the face of all the earth,
and every tree with seed in its fruit;
you shall have them for food.
³⁰And to every beast of the earth, and to every bird of the air,
and to everything that creeps on the earth,
everything that has the breath of life,
I have given every green plant for food."
And it was so.
³¹God saw everything that he had made,
and indeed, it was very good.
And there was evening and there was morning, the sixth day.

²:¹Thus the heavens and the earth were finished,
and all their multitude.
²And on the seventh day God finished the work that he had done,
and he rested on the seventh day from all the work that he had done.
³So God blessed the seventh day and hallowed it,
because on it God rested from all the work that he had done in creation.

⁴These are the generations of the heavens and the earth
when they were created.

The word of the Lord.   *or*   Word of God, word of life.

PSALMODY: Psalm 8

SECOND READING: 2 Corinthians 13:11-13

A reading from Second Corinthians.

⌐Paul writes:⌐
¹¹Finally, brothers and sisters, farewell.
Put things in order, listen to my appeal,
agree with one another, live in peace;
and the God of love and peace will be with you.
¹²Greet one another with a holy kiss.
All the saints greet you.

¹³The grace of the Lord Jesus Christ, the love of God,
and the communion of the Holy Spirit be with all of you.

The word of the Lord.   *or*   Word of God, word of life.

GOSPEL: Matthew 28:16-20

The holy gospel according to Matthew.

¹⁶Now the eleven disciples went to Galilee,
to the mountain to which Jesus had directed them.
¹⁷When they saw him, they worshiped him; but some doubted.

¹⁸And Jesus came and said to them,
"All authority in heaven and on earth has been given to me.
¹⁹Go therefore and make disciples of all nations,
baptizing them in the name of the Father and of the Son
and of the Holy Spirit,
²⁰and teaching them to obey everything that I have commanded you.
And remember, I am with you always, to the end of the age."

The gospel of the Lord.

SECOND READING
This text is included because it is one of the early references to the Holy Trinity. Verse 13 is widely known as the Apostolic Greeting. It is the final lines of a letter to the church at Corinth. Watch the periods and commas, providing the pauses for which they call. Allow each sentence—each phrase—to stand alone as the final thoughts in a letter often do. Take your time.

GOSPEL
This is one of the Jesus' sayings that many in the assembly will know by heart. Combine authority and affection in a reading that sounds as though it comes from Jesus' heart.

FIRST READING: Isaiah 49:8-16a

A reading from Isaiah.

⁸Thus says the LORD:
In a time of favor I have answered you,
    on a day of salvation I have helped you;
I have kept you and given you as a covenant to the people,
to establish the land,
    to apportion the desolate heritages;
⁹saying to the prisoners, "Come out,"
    to those who are in darkness, "Show yourselves."
They shall feed along the ways,
    on all the bare heights shall be their pasture;
¹⁰they shall not hunger or thirst,
    neither scorching wind nor sun shall strike them down,
for he who has pity on them will lead them,
    and by springs of water will guide them.
¹¹And I will turn all my mountains into a road,
    and my highways shall be raised up.
¹²Lo, these shall come from far away,
    and lo, these from the north and from the west,
    and these from the land of Syene.

¹³Sing for joy, O heavens, and exult, O earth;
    break forth, O mountains, into singing!
For the LORD has comforted his people,
    and will have compassion on his suffering ones.

¹⁴But Zion said, "The LORD has forsaken me,
    my LORD has forgotten me."
¹⁵Can a woman forget her nursing child,
    or show no compassion for the child of her womb?
Even these may forget,
    yet I will not forget you.
¹⁶See, I have inscribed you on the palms of my hands.

The word of the Lord.   *or*   Word of God, word of life.

FIRST READING   *Isaiah = eye-ZAY-uh   Syene = sy-EE-nih*
The early verses of the text which celebrate the role and the action of "the servant" demand that the reader invest some time in a consideration of the whole 49th chapter if the reader's understanding is to develop into an intelligent reading. The three sentences of verses 15–16 are among the most poignant in scripture. Savor each one.

PSALMODY: Psalm 131

SECOND READING: 1 Corinthians 4:1-5

A reading from First Corinthians.

¹Think of us in this way,
as servants of Christ and stewards of God's mysteries.
²Moreover, it is required of stewards that they be found trustworthy.
³But with me it is a very small thing that I should be judged by you
or by any human court.
I do not even judge myself.
⁴I am not aware of anything against myself,
but I am not thereby acquitted.
It is the Lord who judges me.
⁵Therefore do not pronounce judgment before the time,
before the Lord comes,
who will bring to light the things now hidden in darkness
and will disclose the purposes of the heart.
Then each one will receive commendation from God.

The word of the Lord.   *or*   Word of God, word of life.

SECOND READING
Is there just a hint of arrogance in verse 4: "I am not aware of anything against myself"? Or is it apostolic confidence? A blending of the two tones may be the key to helping the assembly hear a very human Paul.

GOSPEL: Matthew 6:24-34

The holy gospel according to Matthew.

⌐Jesus said to the disciples:⌐
²⁴"No one can serve two masters;
for a slave will either hate the one and love the other,
or be devoted to the one and despise the other.
You cannot serve God and wealth.

²⁵"Therefore I tell you,
do not worry about your life,
what you will eat or what you will drink,
or about your body, what you will wear.
Is not life more than food, and the body more than clothing?
²⁶Look at the birds of the air;
they neither sow nor reap nor gather into barns,
and yet your heavenly Father feeds them.
Are you not of more value than they?
²⁷And can any of you by worrying
add a single hour to your span of life?
²⁸And why do you worry about clothing?
Consider the lilies of the field, how they grow;
they neither toil nor spin,
²⁹yet I tell you, even Solomon in all his glory
was not clothed like one of these.
³⁰But if God so clothes the grass of the field,
which is alive today and tomorrow is thrown into the oven,
will he not much more clothe you—you of little faith?

³¹"Therefore do not worry, saying,
'What will we eat?' or 'What will we drink?' or 'What will we wear?'
³²For it is the Gentiles who strive for all these things;
and indeed your heavenly Father knows that you need all these things.
³³But strive first for the kingdom of God and his righteousness,
and all these things will be given to you as well.

³⁴"So do not worry about tomorrow,
for tomorrow will bring worries of its own.
Today's trouble is enough for today."

The gospel of the Lord.

GOSPEL
Appropriately spaced pauses will allow the assembly to hear our Lord "think up" one phrase, one illustration after another in an attempt to teach his followers something about contentment. Do not merely read the text. Bring it to life.

SUNDAY, MAY 29–JUNE 4 *(if after Holy Trinity)*
TIME AFTER PENTECOST — LECTIONARY 9

FIRST READING: Genesis 6:9-22; 7:24; 8:14-19

A reading from Genesis:

⁹These are the descendants of Noah.
Noah was a righteous man, blameless in his generation;
Noah walked with God.
¹⁰And Noah had three sons, Shem, Ham, and Japheth.

¹¹Now the earth was corrupt in God's sight,
and the earth was filled with violence.
¹²And God saw that the earth was corrupt;
for all flesh had corrupted its ways upon the earth.
¹³And God said to Noah,
"I have determined to make an end of all flesh,
for the earth is filled with violence because of them;
now I am going to destroy them along with the earth.
¹⁴Make yourself an ark of cypress wood;
make rooms in the ark, and cover it inside and out with pitch.
¹⁵This is how you are to make it:
the length of the ark three hundred cubits, its width fifty cubits,
and its height thirty cubits.
¹⁶Make a roof for the ark, and finish it to a cubit above;
and put the door of the ark in its side;
make it with lower, second, and third decks.

¹⁷"For my part, I am going to bring a flood of waters on the earth,
to destroy from under heaven all flesh in which is the breath of life;
everything that is on the earth shall die.
¹⁸But I will establish my covenant with you;
and you shall come into the ark,
you, your sons, your wife, and your sons' wives with you.
¹⁹And of every living thing, of all flesh,
you shall bring two of every kind into the ark, to keep them alive with you;
they shall be male and female.
²⁰Of the birds according to their kinds,
and of the animals according to their kinds,

FIRST READING   *Japheth = JAY-fith*
Verses 9 and 10 provide a kind of on-ramp for the story. Take them slowly. Begin to accelerate at verse 11, as the story begins to unfold. Invest some time in finding a voice for God that brings some love to the many directions and instructions. Verses 6:22, 7:24, and 8:14 should each be set apart by a pause of substance to help the assembly sense the passage of time.

of every creeping thing of the ground according to its kind,
two of every kind shall come in to you, to keep them alive.
[21]Also take with you every kind of food that is eaten, and store it up;
and it shall serve as food for you and for them."
[22]Noah did this; he did all that God commanded him.

[7:24]And the waters swelled on the earth for one hundred fifty days.

[8:14]In the second month, on the twenty-seventh day of the month,
the earth was dry.
[15]Then God said to Noah,
[16]"Go out of the ark, you and your wife,
and your sons and your sons' wives with you.
[17]Bring out with you every living thing that is with you of all flesh—
birds and animals and every creeping thing that creeps on the earth—
so that they may abound on the earth,
and be fruitful and multiply on the earth."
[18]So Noah went out with his sons and his wife and his sons' wives.
[19]And every animal, every creeping thing, and every bird,
everything that moves on the earth, went out of the ark by families.

The word of the Lord.   *or*   Word of God, word of life.

PSALMODY: Psalm 46

SECOND READING: Romans 1:16-17; 3:22b-28 [29-31]

A reading from Romans.

[16]I am not ashamed of the gospel;
it is the power of God for salvation to everyone who has faith,
to the Jew first and also to the Greek.
[17]For in it the righteousness of God is revealed through faith for faith;
as it is written,
"The one who is righteous will live by faith."

[3:22b]For there is no distinction,
[23]since all have sinned and fall short of the glory of God;
[24]they are now justified by his grace as a gift,
through the redemption that is in Christ Jesus,
[25]whom God put forward as a sacrifice of atonement by his blood,
effective through faith.
He did this to show his righteousness,
because in his divine forbearance
he had passed over the sins previously committed;
[26]it was to prove at the present time that he himself is righteous
and that he justifies the one who has faith in Jesus.
[27]Then what becomes of boasting? It is excluded.
By what law? By that of works?
No, but by the law of faith.
[28]For we hold that a person is justified by faith
apart from works prescribed by the law.

[[29]Or is God the God of Jews only?
Is he not the God of Gentiles also?
Yes, of Gentiles also, [30]since God is one;
and he will justify the circumcised on the ground of faith
and the uncircumcised through that same faith.
[31]Do we then overthrow the law by this faith?
By no means! On the contrary, we uphold the law.]

The word of the Lord.   *or*   Word of God, word of life.

SECOND READING
Practice this one, repeatedly. This cutting jumps from the first chapter of the letter to the third in an effort to summarize its contents. Readings from Romans will occupy our attention all summer long. In simplest terms, the author says Gentiles and Jews alike are justified by faith in Jesus and that, having been justified, they desire to uphold the law. Punctuation is crucial to this reading as well. Slow down. Help the hearer follow the argument.

GOSPEL: Matthew 7:21-29

The holy gospel according to Matthew.

⌐Jesus said to the disciples:⌐
²¹"Not everyone who says to me, 'Lord, Lord,'
will enter the kingdom of heaven,
but only the one who does the will of my Father in heaven.
²²On that day many will say to me,
'Lord, Lord, did we not prophesy in your name,
and cast out demons in your name,
and do many deeds of power in your name?'
²³Then I will declare to them,
'I never knew you; go away from me, you evildoers.'

²⁴"Everyone then who hears these words of mine and acts on them
will be like a wise man who built his house on rock.
²⁵The rain fell, the floods came, and the winds blew and beat on that house,
but it did not fall, because it had been founded on rock.
²⁶And everyone who hears these words of mine and does not act on them
will be like a foolish man who built his house on sand.
²⁷The rain fell, and the floods came,
and the winds blew and beat against that house, and it fell—
and great was its fall!"

²⁸Now when Jesus had finished saying these things,
the crowds were astounded at his teaching,
²⁹for he taught them as one having authority, and not as their scribes.

The gospel of the Lord.

GOSPEL
This simple bit of instruction urges the hearer to be attentive to the words of Jesus and to act on them. Help the assembly hear the dialogue in verses 21–23. Modest astonishment or disbelief in the voice of the pious plea might contrast well to the understated voice of Jesus: "I never knew you." Allow a kind of warmth to enfold the warning in verses 24 to 27. A healthy pause between verses 27 and 28 will ready the hearer for the powerful observation contained in the final verses.

FIRST READING: Genesis 12:1-9

A reading from Genesis:

[1]The LORD said to Abram,
"Go from your country and your kindred and your father's house
to the land that I will show you.
[2]I will make of you a great nation, and I will bless you,
and make your name great, so that you will be a blessing.
[3]I will bless those who bless you,
and the one who curses you I will curse;
and in you all the families of the earth shall be blessed."

[4]So Abram went, as the LORD had told him; and Lot went with him.
Abram was seventy-five years old when he departed from Haran.
[5]Abram took his wife Sarai and his brother's son Lot,
and all the possessions that they had gathered,
and the persons whom they had acquired in Haran;
and they set forth to go to the land of Canaan.
When they had come to the land of Canaan,
[6]Abram passed through the land to the place at Shechem, to the oak of Moreh.
At that time the Canaanites were in the land.

[7]Then the LORD appeared to Abram, and said,
"To your offspring I will give this land."
So he built there an altar to the LORD, who had appeared to him.
[8]From there he moved on to the hill country on the east of Bethel,
and pitched his tent, with Bethel on the west and Ai on the east;
and there he built an altar to the LORD and invoked the name of the LORD.
[9]And Abram journeyed on by stages toward the Negeb.

The word of the Lord.   *or*   Word of God, word of life.

PSALMODY: Psalm 33:1-12

FIRST READING   *Abram = AY-brum   Haran = HAR-un   Canaan = KAY-nun   Shechem = SHEK-em
Moreh = MOR-eh   Ai = eye   Negeb = NEG-eb*
Solid pauses at the paragraph breaks will help to establish the passage of time. Investing time in practicing unfamiliar names (there are several here) is essential. The story has little chance of developing if the assembly senses the reader is struggling to pronounce names and addresses for the first time.

SECOND READING: Romans 4:13-25

A reading from Romans.

[13]The promise that he would inherit the world
did not come to Abraham or to his descendants through the law
but through the righteousness of faith.
[14]If it is the adherents of the law who are to be the heirs,
faith is null and the promise is void.
[15]For the law brings wrath;
but where there is no law, neither is there violation.

[16]For this reason it depends on faith,
in order that the promise may rest on grace
and be guaranteed to all his descendants,
not only to the adherents of the law
but also to those who share the faith of Abraham
(for he is the father of all of us,
[17]as it is written, "I have made you the father of many nations")—
in the presence of the God in whom he believed,
who gives life to the dead
and calls into existence the things that do not exist.

[18]Hoping against hope,
he believed that he would become "the father of many nations,"
according to what was said, "So numerous shall your descendants be."
[19]He did not weaken in faith when he considered his own body,
which was already as good as dead (for he was about a hundred years old),
or when he considered the barrenness of Sarah's womb.
[20]No distrust made him waver concerning the promise of God,
but he grew strong in his faith as he gave glory to God,
[21]being fully convinced that God was able to do what he had promised.
[22]Therefore his faith "was reckoned to him as righteousness."
[23]Now the words, "it was reckoned to him,"
were written not for his sake alone, [24]but for ours also.
It will be reckoned to us who believe in him
who raised Jesus our Lord from the dead,
[25]who was handed over to death for our trespasses
and was raised for our justification.

The word of the Lord.   *or*   Word of God, word of life.

SECOND READING
This is a determined, logical explication of the truth that our inheritance of God's promises rests on faith, not on our adherence to the law. The reading demands the voice of conviction. Long complex sentences require the reader to pay careful attention to commas and periods as well as to the logical sequence of thought often interrupted by parenthetical expressions. It is not an easy reading. Take some time to let the text soak into the reader's soul during the week of preparation.

GOSPEL: Matthew 9:9-13, 18-26

The holy gospel according to Matthew.

⁹As Jesus was walking along,
he saw a man called Matthew sitting at the tax booth;
and he said to him, "Follow me."
And he got up and followed him.

¹⁰And as he sat at dinner in the house,
many tax collectors and sinners came
and were sitting with him and his disciples.
¹¹When the Pharisees saw this, they said to his disciples,
"Why does your teacher eat with tax collectors and sinners?"
¹²But when he heard this, he said,
"Those who are well have no need of a physician,
but those who are sick.
¹³Go and learn what this means, 'I desire mercy, not sacrifice.'
For I have come to call not the righteous but sinners."

¹⁸While he was saying these things to them,
suddenly a leader of the synagogue came in and knelt before him, saying,
"My daughter has just died;
but come and lay your hand on her, and she will live."
¹⁹And Jesus got up and followed him, with his disciples.
²⁰Then suddenly a woman
who had been suffering from hemorrhages for twelve years
came up behind him and touched the fringe of his cloak,
²¹for she said to herself,
"If I only touch his cloak, I will be made well."
²²Jesus turned, and seeing her he said,
"Take heart, daughter; your faith has made you well."
And instantly the woman was made well.

²³When Jesus came to the leader's house
and saw the flute players and the crowd making a commotion,
²⁴he said, "Go away; for the girl is not dead but sleeping."
And they laughed at him.
²⁵But when the crowd had been put outside,
he went in and took her by the hand, and the girl got up.
²⁶And the report of this spread throughout that district.

The gospel of the Lord.

GOSPEL *synagogue = SIN-uh-gog hemorrhages = HEM-or-uh-juhz*
The challenge in this reading is that it tells four different stories and the third is interrupted by the fourth. A pause of significance between each of the paragraphs will be essential. A parenthetical pause coupled with an increased sense of urgency—to help the assembly hear the insertion of the story of the bleeding woman as an interruption—should precede verse 20. A final pause before verse 26 will help give that concluding verse the sense that the report of all this "spread throughout that district."

FIRST READING: Genesis 18:1-15 [21:1-7]

A reading from Genesis:

¹The LORD appeared to Abraham by the oaks of Mamre,
as he sat at the entrance of his tent in the heat of the day.
²He looked up and saw three men standing near him.
When he saw them, he ran from the tent entrance to meet them,
and bowed down to the ground.
³He said, "My lord, if I find favor with you, do not pass by your servant.
⁴Let a little water be brought, and wash your feet,
and rest yourselves under the tree.
⁵Let me bring a little bread, that you may refresh yourselves,
and after that you may pass on—since you have come to your servant."
So they said, "Do as you have said."

⁶And Abraham hastened into the tent to Sarah, and said,
"Make ready quickly three measures of choice flour,
knead it, and make cakes."
⁷Abraham ran to the herd, and took a calf, tender and good,
and gave it to the servant, who hastened to prepare it.
⁸Then he took curds and milk and the calf that he had prepared,
and set it before them;
and he stood by them under the tree while they ate.

⁹They said to him, "Where is your wife Sarah?"
And he said, "There, in the tent."
¹⁰Then one said,
"I will surely return to you in due season,
and your wife Sarah shall have a son."
And Sarah was listening at the tent entrance behind him.

¹¹Now Abraham and Sarah were old, advanced in age;
it had ceased to be with Sarah after the manner of women.
¹²So Sarah laughed to herself, saying,
"After I have grown old, and my husband is old, shall I have pleasure?" ▸

FIRST READING   *Mamre = MAM-rih*
One can simply read this story or one can breath life into it. Giving it birth, however, will take some significant time and some hard labor. Dig into the details. Experiment with the sound of Sarah's laughter. (It may well sound different in the middle of the story than at the story's ending.) Bring a frightened edge to Sarah's denial, and work at finding the definitive tone for the Lord's reply, "Oh yes, you did laugh."

¹³The LORD said to Abraham,
"Why did Sarah laugh, and say,
'Shall I indeed bear a child, now that I am old?'
¹⁴Is anything too wonderful for the LORD?
At the set time I will return to you, in due season,
and Sarah shall have a son."
¹⁵But Sarah denied, saying, "I did not laugh"; for she was afraid.
He said, "Oh yes, you did laugh."

[²¹˸¹The LORD dealt with Sarah as he had said,
and the LORD did for Sarah as he had promised.
²Sarah conceived and bore Abraham a son in his old age,
at the time of which God had spoken to him.
³Abraham gave the name Isaac to his son whom Sarah bore him.
⁴And Abraham circumcised his son Isaac when he was eight days old,
as God had commanded him.
⁵Abraham was a hundred years old when his son Isaac was born to him.
⁶Now Sarah said,
"God has brought laughter for me;
everyone who hears will laugh with me."
⁷And she said,
"Who would ever have said to Abraham that Sarah would nurse children?
Yet I have borne him a son in his old age."]

The word of the Lord.   *or*   Word of God, word of life.

PSALMODY: Psalm 116:1-2, 12-19

SECOND READING: Romans 5:1-8

A reading from Romans.

[1]Since we are justified by faith,
we have peace with God through our Lord Jesus Christ,
[2]through whom we have obtained access to this grace in which we stand;
and we boast in our hope of sharing the glory of God.
[3]And not only that, but we also boast in our sufferings,
knowing that suffering produces endurance,
[4]and endurance produces character,
and character produces hope,
[5]and hope does not disappoint us,
because God's love has been poured into our hearts
through the Holy Spirit that has been given to us.

[6]For while we were still weak,
at the right time Christ died for the ungodly.
[7]Indeed, rarely will anyone die for a righteous person—
though perhaps for a good person someone might actually dare to die.
[8]But God proves his love for us
in that while we still were sinners Christ died for us.

The word of the Lord.   *or*   Word of God, word of life.

SECOND READING
The author illustrates that it is Christ Jesus who has established the relationship between God and humankind "while we still were sinners." Verses 3-5 are one sentence and require careful attention to the commas, so that the sentence builds to a climax at the end of verse 5 and not with the words "and hope does not disappoint us." These are two powerful little readings that will be more powerful still if the reader will dedicate some quiet time during the week in which to meditate on the truth they proclaim.

GOSPEL: Matthew 9:35—10:8 [9-23]

The holy gospel according to Matthew.

³⁵Jesus went about all the cities and villages,
teaching in their synagogues,
and proclaiming the good news of the kingdom,
and curing every disease and every sickness.
³⁶When he saw the crowds, he had compassion for them,
because they were harassed and helpless, like sheep without a shepherd.
³⁷Then he said to his disciples,
"The harvest is plentiful, but the laborers are few;
³⁸therefore ask the Lord of the harvest to send out laborers into his harvest."
^{10:1}Then Jesus summoned his twelve disciples
and gave them authority over unclean spirits,
to cast them out, and to cure every disease and every sickness.

²These are the names of the twelve apostles:
first, Simon, also known as Peter, and his brother Andrew;
James son of Zebedee, and his brother John;
³Philip and Bartholomew; Thomas and Matthew the tax collector;
James son of Alphaeus, and Thaddaeus;
⁴Simon the Cananaean, and Judas Iscariot, the one who betrayed him.

⁵These twelve Jesus sent out with the following instructions:
"Go nowhere among the Gentiles, and enter no town of the Samaritans,
⁶but go rather to the lost sheep of the house of Israel.
⁷As you go, proclaim the good news,
'The kingdom of heaven has come near.'
⁸Cure the sick, raise the dead, cleanse the lepers, cast out demons.
You received without payment; give without payment.
[⁹Take no gold, or silver, or copper in your belts,
¹⁰no bag for your journey, or two tunics, or sandals, or a staff;
for laborers deserve their food.
¹¹Whatever town or village you enter, find out who in it is worthy,
and stay there until you leave.
¹²As you enter the house, greet it.
¹³If the house is worthy, let your peace come upon it;
but if it is not worthy, let your peace return to you.
¹⁴If anyone will not welcome you or listen to your words,
shake off the dust from your feet as you leave that house or town.

GOSPEL   *synagogues = SIN uh-gogz   Zebedee = ZEB-uh-dee   Alphaeus = al-FEE-us   Thaddaeus = THAD-ee-us   Cananaean = kay-nuh-NEE-un   Iscariot = is-CAR-ee-ut   Samaritans = suh-MAIR-it-uns   Gomorrah = guh-MOR-uh*
The temptation is to abbreviate the gospel by reading the shorter option. Resist it if you are able. The baptized will be helped in their daily proclamation of the gospel by these blunt warnings and terse instructions. Avoid with equal conviction the temptation to rush the reading because it is lengthy. Allow each imperative and every warning adequate opportunity to sink into the consciousness of the hearer.

15Truly I tell you,
it will be more tolerable for the land of Sodom and Gomorrah
on the day of judgment than for that town.

16"See, I am sending you out like sheep into the midst of wolves;
so be wise as serpents and innocent as doves.
17Beware of them, for they will hand you over to councils
and flog you in their synagogues;
18and you will be dragged before governors and kings because of me,
as a testimony to them and the Gentiles.
19When they hand you over,
do not worry about how you are to speak or what you are to say;
for what you are to say will be given to you at that time;
20for it is not you who speak,
but the Spirit of your Father speaking through you.

21"Brother will betray brother to death, and a father his child,
and children will rise against parents and have them put to death;
22and you will be hated by all because of my name.
But the one who endures to the end will be saved.
23When they persecute you in one town, flee to the next;
for truly I tell you,
you will not have gone through all the towns of Israel
before the Son of Man comes."]

The gospel of the Lord.

FIRST READING: Genesis 21:8-21

A reading from Genesis:

⁸The child ⌜Isaac⌝ grew, and was weaned;
and Abraham made a great feast on the day that Isaac was weaned.
⁹But Sarah saw the son of Hagar the Egyptian,
whom she had borne to Abraham,
playing with her son Isaac.
¹⁰So she said to Abraham,
"Cast out this slave woman with her son;
for the son of this slave woman shall not inherit along with my son Isaac."
¹¹The matter was very distressing to Abraham on account of his son.
¹²But God said to Abraham,
"Do not be distressed because of the boy and because of your slave woman;
whatever Sarah says to you, do as she tells you,
for it is through Isaac that offspring shall be named for you.
¹³As for the son of the slave woman, I will make a nation of him also,
because he is your offspring."

¹⁴So Abraham rose early in the morning, and took bread and a skin of water,
and gave it to Hagar, putting it on her shoulder, along with the child,
and sent her away.
And she departed, and wandered about in the wilderness of Beer-sheba.

¹⁵When the water in the skin was gone,
she cast the child under one of the bushes.
¹⁶Then she went and sat down opposite him a good way off,
about the distance of a bowshot;
for she said, "Do not let me look on the death of the child."
And as she sat opposite him, she lifted up her voice and wept.
¹⁷And God heard the voice of the boy;
and the angel of God called to Hagar from heaven, and said to her,
"What troubles you, Hagar?
Do not be afraid; for God has heard the voice of the boy where he is.
¹⁸Come, lift up the boy and hold him fast with your hand,
for I will make a great nation of him."

FIRST READING *Hagar = HAY-gar Beer-sheba = beer-SHE-buh Paran = PAR-un*
This story is highly dramatic and begs the reader to find the sound of recrimination for Sarah's voice; the sound of "scared to death" for Hagar; and the sound of blessed assurance for the angel of the Lord.

¹⁹Then God opened her eyes and she saw a well of water.
She went, and filled the skin with water, and gave the boy a drink.

²⁰God was with the boy, and he grew up;
he lived in the wilderness, and became an expert with the bow.
²¹He lived in the wilderness of Paran;
and his mother got a wife for him from the land of Egypt.

The word of the Lord.   *or*   Word of God, word of life.

PSALMODY: Psalm 86:1-10, 16-17

SECOND READING: Romans 6:1b-11

A reading from Romans.

¹ᵇShould we continue in sin in order that grace may abound?
²By no means! How can we who died to sin go on living in it?
³Do you not know that all of us who have been baptized into Christ Jesus
were baptized into his death?
⁴Therefore we have been buried with him by baptism into death,
so that, just as Christ was raised from the dead by the glory of the Father,
so we too might walk in newness of life.

⁵For if we have been united with him in a death like his,
we will certainly be united with him in a resurrection like his.
⁶We know that our old self was crucified with him
so that the body of sin might be destroyed,
and we might no longer be enslaved to sin.
⁷For whoever has died is freed from sin.
⁸But if we have died with Christ,
we believe that we will also live with him.
⁹We know that Christ, being raised from the dead, will never die again;
death no longer has dominion over him.
¹⁰The death he died, he died to sin, once for all;
but the life he lives, he lives to God.
¹¹So you also must consider yourselves dead to sin
and alive to God in Christ Jesus.

The word of the Lord.   *or*   Word of God, word of life.

SECOND READING

Previously the writer has expounded on the marvel of grace. In this text the writer urges us to "die to sin" and explains how "dying with Christ" in baptism ought to signal an end to our enslavement to sin. This is another very familiar section of scripture. Do not take it for granted! Reading and re-reading it this week will lead the reader to greater understanding and deeper appreciation of its beauty. Invest it with the energy such holy truth deserves.

GOSPEL: Matthew 10:24-39

The holy gospel according to Matthew.

⌜Jesus said to the twelve:⌝
²⁴"A disciple is not above the teacher, nor a slave above the master;
²⁵it is enough for the disciple to be like the teacher,
and the slave like the master.
If they have called the master of the house Beelzebul,
how much more will they malign those of his household!

²⁶"So have no fear of them;
for nothing is covered up that will not be uncovered,
and nothing secret that will not become known.
²⁷What I say to you in the dark, tell in the light;
and what you hear whispered, proclaim from the housetops.
²⁸Do not fear those who kill the body but cannot kill the soul;
rather fear him who can destroy both soul and body in hell.
²⁹Are not two sparrows sold for a penny?
Yet not one of them will fall to the ground apart from your Father.
³⁰And even the hairs of your head are all counted.
³¹So do not be afraid; you are of more value than many sparrows.

³²"Everyone therefore who acknowledges me before others,
I also will acknowledge before my Father in heaven;
³³but whoever denies me before others,
I also will deny before my Father in heaven.
³⁴Do not think that I have come to bring peace to the earth;
I have not come to bring peace, but a sword.
³⁵For I have come to set a man against his father,
and a daughter against her mother,
and a daughter-in-law against her mother-in-law;
³⁶and one's foes will be members of one's own household.
³⁷Whoever loves father or mother more than me is not worthy of me;
and whoever loves son or daughter more than me is not worthy of me;
³⁸and whoever does not take up the cross and follow me is not worthy of me.
³⁹Those who find their life will lose it,
and those who lose their life for my sake will find it."

The gospel of the Lord.

GOSPEL   *Beelzebul = bee-EL-zuh-bul*
These verses are loaded. The assembly will need time to appropriate them. A reading that brings the earnest intensity of a committed teacher will capture the spirit of the text. A reading that directs extra attention to the periods will help the hearer capture the meanings of the text. Deciding well in advance which sentences are naturally grouped with other sentences and which ought to stand alone.

FIRST READING: Genesis 22:1-14

A reading from Genesis:

¹God tested Abraham.
He said to him, "Abraham!"
And he said, "Here I am."
²He said,
"Take your son, your only son Isaac, whom you love,
and go to the land of Moriah, and offer him there as a burnt offering
on one of the mountains that I shall show you."

³So Abraham rose early in the morning, saddled his donkey,
and took two of his young men with him, and his son Isaac;
he cut the wood for the burnt offering,
and set out and went to the place in the distance that God had shown him.
⁴On the third day Abraham looked up and saw the place far away.
⁵Then Abraham said to his young men,
"Stay here with the donkey;
the boy and I will go over there;
we will worship, and then we will come back to you."

⁶Abraham took the wood of the burnt offering and laid it on his son Isaac,
and he himself carried the fire and the knife.
So the two of them walked on together.
⁷Isaac said to his father Abraham, "Father!"
And he said, "Here I am, my son."
He said, "The fire and the wood are here,
but where is the lamb for a burnt offering?"
⁸Abraham said,
"God himself will provide the lamb for a burnt offering, my son."
So the two of them walked on together.

⁹When they came to the place that God had shown him,
Abraham built an altar there and laid the wood in order.
He bound his son Isaac, and laid him on the altar, on top of the wood.
¹⁰Then Abraham reached out his hand and took the knife to kill his son. ▸

FIRST READING   *Moriah = moh-RY-uh*
Handle this horrific story with care. Allow verse 1 to stand as the headline for the account. A measured
reading in volume and pace will help allow the natural tension to develop. Provide the voice of Abraham
adequate uncertainty even when (or especially when) his statements appear certain. The agony of a man
caught between two great loves will emerge.

¹¹But the angel of the LORD called to him from heaven, and said,
"Abraham, Abraham!"
And he said, "Here I am."
¹² ⌜The angel⌝ said,
"Do not lay your hand on the boy or do anything to him;
for now I know that you fear God,
since you have not withheld your son, your only son, from me."
¹³And Abraham looked up and saw a ram, caught in a thicket by its horns.
Abraham went and took the ram
and offered it up as a burnt offering instead of his son.
¹⁴So Abraham called that place "The LORD will provide";
as it is said to this day,
"On the mount of the LORD it shall be provided."

The word of the Lord.   *or*   Word of God, word of life.

PSALMODY: Psalm 13

SECOND READING: Romans 6:12-23

A reading from Romans.

¹²Do not let sin exercise dominion in your mortal bodies,
to make you obey their passions.
¹³No longer present your members to sin as instruments of wickedness,
but present yourselves to God
as those who have been brought from death to life,
and present your members to God as instruments of righteousness.
¹⁴For sin will have no dominion over you,
since you are not under law but under grace.

¹⁵What then? Should we sin because we are not under law but under grace?
By no means!
¹⁶Do you not know that if you present yourselves to anyone as obedient slaves,
you are slaves of the one whom you obey,
either of sin, which leads to death,
or of obedience, which leads to righteousness?

SECOND READING
This is a tough one! The writer contrasts being a slave to sin to being a slave to righteousness. It's a neat concept, but it will require some careful reading and re-reading to be certain the lector follows the argument and can help the hearer follow it. Again, pay careful attention to the punctuation. It will provide the hearer with the time needed to grasp the author's argument.

¹⁷But thanks be to God that you, having once been slaves of sin,
have become obedient from the heart
to the form of teaching to which you were entrusted,
¹⁸and that you, having been set free from sin,
have become slaves of righteousness.
¹⁹I am speaking in human terms because of your natural limitations.
For just as you once presented your members as slaves to impurity
and to greater and greater iniquity,
so now present your members as slaves to righteousness for sanctification.

²⁰When you were slaves of sin,
you were free in regard to righteousness.
²¹So what advantage did you then get
from the things of which you now are ashamed?
The end of those things is death.
²²But now that you have been freed from sin and enslaved to God,
the advantage you get is sanctification.
The end is eternal life.
²³For the wages of sin is death,
but the free gift of God is eternal life in Christ Jesus our Lord.

The word of the Lord.   *or*   Word of God, word of life.

GOSPEL: Matthew 10:40-42

The holy gospel according to Matthew.

⌐Jesus said to the twelve:⌐
⁴⁰"Whoever welcomes you welcomes me,
and whoever welcomes me welcomes the one who sent me.
⁴¹Whoever welcomes a prophet in the name of a prophet
will receive a prophet's reward;
and whoever welcomes a righteous person in the name of a righteous person
will receive the reward of the righteous;
⁴²and whoever gives even a cup of cold water to one of these little ones
in the name of a disciple—
truly I tell you, none of these will lose their reward."

The gospel of the Lord.

GOSPEL
Everyone knows the Great Commission recorded at the end of Matthew's gospel. One might productively think of this little text as "Cold Water Commissioning." Jesus emphasizes the connection the disciples have with him and, in turn, with the Father. The reward, for even so small a gesture as a cup of cold water for a child, is certain. Stress the warm assurance in the last line.

FIRST READING: Genesis 24:34-38, 42-49, 58-67

A reading from Genesis:

⌐Laban, Rebekah's brother, received a visitor who said,⌐
³⁴"I am Abraham's servant.
³⁵The LORD has greatly blessed my master, and he has become wealthy;
he has given him flocks and herds, silver and gold,
male and female slaves, camels and donkeys.
³⁶And Sarah my master's wife bore a son to my master when she was old;
and he has given him all that he has.
³⁷My master made me swear, saying,
'You shall not take a wife for my son from the daughters of the Canaanites,
in whose land I live;
³⁸but you shall go to my father's house, to my kindred,
and get a wife for my son.'

⁴²"I came today to the spring, and said,
'O LORD, the God of my master Abraham,
if now you will only make successful the way I am going!
⁴³I am standing here by the spring of water;
let the young woman who comes out to draw,
to whom I shall say, "Please give me a little water from your jar to drink,"
⁴⁴and who will say to me, "Drink, and I will draw for your camels also"—
let her be the woman whom the Lord has appointed for my master's son.'

⁴⁵"Before I had finished speaking in my heart,
there was Rebekah coming out with her water jar on her shoulder;
and she went down to the spring, and drew.
I said to her, 'Please let me drink.'
⁴⁶She quickly let down her jar from her shoulder, and said,
'Drink, and I will also water your camels.'
So I drank, and she also watered the camels.
⁴⁷Then I asked her, 'Whose daughter are you?'
She said, 'The daughter of Bethuel, Nahor's son, whom Milcah bore to him.'
So I put the ring on her nose, and the bracelets on her arms.

FIRST READING   *Laban = LAY-bun   Canaanites = KAY-nuh-nytz   Bethuel = bih-THOO-el   Nahor = NAY-hor   Beer-lahai-roi = beer-luh-HI-roy   Negeb = NEG-eb*
Invest adequate time in mastering the unfamiliar pronunciations of the proper names in the story or the reading will surely come to a bad ending before it begins. Then invest all the joy and wonder one can muster in this happy story of God's provision of a spouse and comfort for Isaac.

⁴⁸Then I bowed my head and worshiped the LORD,
and blessed the LORD, the God of my master Abraham,
who had led me by the right way
to obtain the daughter of my master's kinsman for his son.
⁴⁹Now then, if you will deal loyally and truly with my master, tell me;
and if not, tell me, so that I may turn either to the right hand or to the left."

⁵⁸And they called Rebekah, and said to her, "Will you go with this man?"
She said, "I will."
⁵⁹So they sent away their sister Rebekah and her nurse
along with Abraham's servant and his men.
⁶⁰And they blessed Rebekah and said to her,
"May you, our sister, become thousands of myriads;
may your offspring gain possession of the gates of their foes."
⁶¹Then Rebekah and her maids rose up, mounted the camels,
and followed the man;
thus the servant took Rebekah, and went his way.

⁶²Now Isaac had come from Beer-lahai-roi, and was settled in the Negeb.
⁶³Isaac went out in the evening to walk in the field;
and looking up, he saw camels coming.
⁶⁴And Rebekah looked up,
and when she saw Isaac, she slipped quickly from the camel,
⁶⁵and said to the servant,
"Who is the man over there, walking in the field to meet us?"
The servant said, "It is my master."
So she took her veil and covered herself.
⁶⁶And the servant told Isaac all the things that he had done.

⁶⁷Then Isaac brought her into his mother Sarah's tent.
He took Rebekah, and she became his wife; and he loved her.
So Isaac was comforted after his mother's death.

The word of the Lord.   *or*   Word of God, word of life.

PSALMODY: Psalm 45:10-17 or Song of Solomon 2:8-13

SECOND READING: Romans 7:15-25a

A reading from Romans.

¹⁵I do not understand my own actions.
For I do not do what I want,
but I do the very thing I hate.
¹⁶Now if I do what I do not want, I agree that the law is good.
¹⁷But in fact it is no longer I that do it,
but sin that dwells within me.
¹⁸For I know that nothing good dwells within me, that is, in my flesh.
I can will what is right, but I cannot do it.
¹⁹For I do not do the good I want,
but the evil I do not want is what I do.
²⁰Now if I do what I do not want, it is no longer I that do it,
but sin that dwells within me.
²¹So I find it to be a law that when I want to do what is good,
evil lies close at hand.
²²For I delight in the law of God in my inmost self,
²³but I see in my members another law at war with the law of my mind,
making me captive to the law of sin that dwells in my members.

²⁴Wretched man that I am!
Who will rescue me from this body of death?
²⁵ᵃThanks be to God through Jesus Christ our Lord!

The word of the Lord.   *or*   Word of God, word of life.

SECOND READING

Take note! This is a difficult little text. Approach it with care. Read it slowly and with careful attention to every word. St. Paul's point is that God's law directs us toward right behavior but that we tend not to do the good that we want to do but rather the evil we hate. It is this reality that leads the writer and the hearer to the conclusion that our state is "wretched." A substantial pause before verse 24 is essential to establish the central question asked in the second half of that verse: "Who will rescue me from this body of death?" Another pause of substance might helpfully precede verse 25, which requires a voice firm with conviction born of deep faith: "Thanks be to God through Jesus Christ our Lord!" It is Jesus, and only Jesus, who can and does rescue us.

GOSPEL: Matthew 11:16-19, 25-30

The holy gospel according to Matthew.

⌈Jesus spoke to the crowd saying:⌉
¹⁶"To what will I compare this generation?
It is like children sitting in the marketplaces and calling to one another,
¹⁷'We played the flute for you, and you did not dance;
we wailed, and you did not mourn.'
¹⁸For John came neither eating nor drinking,
and they say, 'He has a demon';
¹⁹the Son of Man came eating and drinking, and they say,
'Look, a glutton and a drunkard, a friend of tax collectors and sinners!'
Yet wisdom is vindicated by her deeds."

²⁵At that time Jesus said,
"I thank you, Father, Lord of heaven and earth,
because you have hidden these things from the wise and the intelligent
and have revealed them to infants;
²⁶yes, Father, for such was your gracious will.
²⁷All things have been handed over to me by my Father;
and no one knows the Son except the Father,
and no one knows the Father except the Son
and anyone to whom the Son chooses to reveal him.

²⁸"Come to me, all you that are weary and are carrying heavy burdens,
and I will give you rest.
²⁹Take my yoke upon you, and learn from me;
for I am gentle and humble in heart,
and you will find rest for your souls.
³⁰For my yoke is easy, and my burden is light."

The gospel of the Lord.

GOSPEL
There are three very different sayings included in the gospel. Allow the hearer to sense their separateness. Pause, at length, between each. Each has its own sound. All are instructive and require the voice of the teacher. The first might have an edge to it. The second has a sense of confident gratitude. The third, perhaps, the sound of gentle invitation.

FIRST READING: Genesis 25:19-34

A reading from Genesis:

[19]These are the descendants of Isaac, Abraham's son:
Abraham was the father of Isaac,
[20]and Isaac was forty years old when he married Rebekah,
daughter of Bethuel the Aramean of Paddan-aram,
sister of Laban the Aramean.

[21]Isaac prayed to the LORD for his wife, because she was barren;
and the LORD granted his prayer, and his wife Rebekah conceived.
[22]The children struggled together within her; and she said,
"If it is to be this way, why do I live?"
So she went to inquire of the LORD.
[23]And the LORD said to her,

"Two nations are in your womb,
and two peoples born of you shall be divided;
the one shall be stronger than the other,
the elder shall serve the younger."

[24]When her time to give birth was at hand, there were twins in her womb.
[25]The first came out red, all his body like a hairy mantle;
so they named him Esau.
[26]Afterward his brother came out, with his hand gripping Esau's heel;
so he was named Jacob.
Isaac was sixty years old when she bore them.

[27]When the boys grew up, Esau was a skillful hunter, a man of the field,
while Jacob was a quiet man, living in tents.
[28]Isaac loved Esau, because he was fond of game;
but Rebekah loved Jacob.

FIRST READING   *Bethuel = bih-THOO-el Aramean = air-uh-MEE-un Paddan-aram = pad-un-AR-um*
Laban = LAY-bun
Nothing will so quickly sidetrack the attention of the assembly as will stumbling over the pronunciation of
"Bethuel the Aramean of Paddan-aram." Work on it. Then work at providing the written word all the pain,
agony, and mystery this odd little story demands.

[29]Once when Jacob was cooking a stew, Esau came in from the field, and he was famished.
[30]Esau said to Jacob,
"Let me eat some of that red stuff, for I am famished!"
(Therefore he was called Edom.)
[31]Jacob said, "First sell me your birthright."
[32]Esau said, "I am about to die; of what use is a birthright to me?"
[33]Jacob said, "Swear to me first."
So he swore to him, and sold his birthright to Jacob.
[34]Then Jacob gave Esau bread and lentil stew, and he ate and drank, and rose and went his way.
Thus Esau despised his birthright.

The word of the Lord.   *or*   Word of God, word of life.

PSALMODY: Psalm 119:105-112

SECOND READING: Romans 8:1-11

A reading from Romans.

[1]There is therefore now no condemnation for those who are in Christ Jesus.
[2]For the law of the Spirit of life in Christ Jesus
has set you free from the law of sin and of death.
[3]For God has done what the law, weakened by the flesh, could not do:
by sending his own Son in the likeness of sinful flesh,
and to deal with sin, he condemned sin in the flesh,
[4]so that the just requirement of the law might be fulfilled in us,
who walk not according to the flesh but according to the Spirit.
[5]For those who live according to the flesh
set their minds on the things of the flesh,
but those who live according to the Spirit
set their minds on the things of the Spirit.
[6]To set the mind on the flesh is death,
but to set the mind on the Spirit is life and peace.
[7]For this reason the mind that is set on the flesh is hostile to God;
it does not submit to God's law—indeed it cannot,
[8]and those who are in the flesh cannot please God.

[9]But you are not in the flesh; you are in the Spirit,
since the Spirit of God dwells in you.
Anyone who does not have the Spirit of Christ does not belong to him.
[10]But if Christ is in you, though the body is dead because of sin,
the Spirit is life because of righteousness.
[11]If the Spirit of him who raised Jesus from the dead dwells in you,
he who raised Christ from the dead will give life to your mortal bodies also
through his Spirit that dwells in you.

The word of the Lord.   *or*   Word of God, word of life.

SECOND READING
The stark contrast between "flesh" and "Spirit" runs through the whole of the reading. It is complex and not a little repetitive. Take one sentence, one clause, one thought at a time. Carefully observe the commas, semicolons, colons, and periods. Then read with confidence—this is good news! "If the Spirit of him who raised Jesus from the dead dwells in you" (and it does!), "he who raised Christ from the dead will give life to your mortal bodies also through his Spirit that dwells in you."

GOSPEL: Matthew 13:1-9, 18-23

The holy gospel according to Matthew.

¹That same day Jesus went out of the house and sat beside the sea.
²Such great crowds gathered around him
that he got into a boat and sat there,
while the whole crowd stood on the beach.
³And he told them many things in parables, saying:
"Listen! A sower went out to sow.
⁴And as he sowed, some seeds fell on the path,
and the birds came and ate them up.
⁵Other seeds fell on rocky ground, where they did not have much soil,
and they sprang up quickly, since they had no depth of soil.
⁶But when the sun rose, they were scorched;
and since they had no root, they withered away.
⁷Other seeds fell among thorns, and the thorns grew up and choked them.
⁸Other seeds fell on good soil and brought forth grain,
some a hundredfold, some sixty, some thirty.
⁹Let anyone with ears listen!"

¹⁸"Hear then the parable of the sower.
¹⁹When anyone hears the word of the kingdom and does not understand it,
the evil one comes and snatches away what is sown in the heart;
this is what was sown on the path.
²⁰As for what was sown on rocky ground,
this is the one who hears the word and immediately receives it with joy;
²¹yet such a person has no root, but endures only for a while,
and when trouble or persecution arises on account of the word,
that person immediately falls away.
²²As for what was sown among thorns,
this is the one who hears the word,
but the cares of the world and the lure of wealth choke the word,
and it yields nothing.
²³But as for what was sown on good soil,
this is the one who hears the word and understands it,
who indeed bears fruit and yields,
in one case a hundredfold, in another sixty, and in another thirty."

The gospel of the Lord.

GOSPEL

An animated telling of the parable to the crowd (verses 1–9), followed by a good healthy pause and a more instructive tone for its interpretation to the disciples (verses 18–23), will help hold the hearers' attention. Taking extra time in preparation to linger over the phrasing of familiar texts such as this leads not only to deeper understanding but new ways of voicing well-known words. Above all, avoid the temptation to hurry through a rich and instructive text we know so well.

FIRST READING: Genesis 28:10-19a

A reading from Genesis:

¹⁰Jacob left Beer-sheba and went toward Haran.
¹¹He came to a certain place and stayed there for the night,
because the sun had set.
Taking one of the stones of the place,
he put it under his head and lay down in that place.
¹²And he dreamed that there was a ladder set up on the earth,
the top of it reaching to heaven;
and the angels of God were ascending and descending on it.
¹³And the LORD stood beside him and said,
"I am the LORD, the God of Abraham your father and the God of Isaac;
the land on which you lie I will give to you and to your offspring;
¹⁴and your offspring shall be like the dust of the earth,
and you shall spread abroad to the west and to the east
and to the north and to the south;
and all the families of the earth shall be blessed in you and in your offspring.
¹⁵Know that I am with you and will keep you wherever you go,
and will bring you back to this land;
for I will not leave you until I have done what I have promised you."

¹⁶Then Jacob woke from his sleep and said,
"Surely the Lord is in this place—and I did not know it!"
¹⁷And he was afraid, and said,
"How awesome is this place!
This is none other than the house of God, and this is the gate of heaven."

¹⁸So Jacob rose early in the morning,
and he took the stone that he had put under his head
and set it up for a pillar and poured oil on the top of it.
¹⁹He called that place Bethel.

The word of the Lord.   *or*   Word of God, word of life.

FIRST READING   *Beer-sheba = beer-SHE-buh   Haran = HAR-un*
The telling of this wonderful story will be enriched if the reader invests some time in exploring what a dream sounds like. Bring to these verses the shimmering shape of a vision not quite completely formed. Provide a contrasting real-life sound to the verses following Jacob's waking.

PSALMODY: Psalm 139:1-12, 23-24

SECOND READING: Romans 8:12-25

A reading from Romans.

[12]So then, brothers and sisters, we are debtors, not to the flesh,
to live according to the flesh—
[13]for if you live according to the flesh, you will die;
but if by the Spirit you put to death the deeds of the body, you will live.
[14]For all who are led by the Spirit of God are children of God.

[15]For you did not receive a spirit of slavery to fall back into fear,
but you have received a spirit of adoption.
When we cry, "Abba! Father!"
[16]it is that very Spirit bearing witness with our spirit
that we are children of God,
[17]and if children, then heirs,
heirs of God and joint heirs with Christ—
if, in fact, we suffer with him so that we may also be glorified with him.

[18]I consider that the sufferings of this present time
are not worth comparing with the glory about to be revealed to us.
[19]For the creation waits with eager longing
for the revealing of the children of God;
[20]for the creation was subjected to futility,
not of its own will but by the will of the one who subjected it,
in hope [21]that the creation itself will be set free from its bondage to decay
and will obtain the freedom of the glory of the children of God.
[22]We know that the whole creation has been groaning in labor pains until now;
[23]and not only the creation, but we ourselves,
who have the first fruits of the Spirit,
groan inwardly while we wait for adoption, the redemption of our bodies.

[24]For in hope we were saved.
Now hope that is seen is not hope.
For who hopes for what is seen?
[25]But if we hope for what we do not see, we wait for it with patience.

The word of the Lord.   *or*   Word of God, word of life.

SECOND READING

The reader will want to spend extra time with this text. To begin, one might read it devotionally several times through. Sit quietly with the text in hand and allow the words to be addressed to you. As children of God, we must be prepared to suffer with Christ, until that time when we share in his glory. The certainty (and the patience) with which we wait for the revelation of the rule of God is a gift to us from the Spirit of God. A sense of confidence and certainty will help carry the meaning of the text to the assembly.

GOSPEL: Matthew 13:24-30, 36-43

The holy gospel according to Matthew.

²⁴ ⌐Jesus⌐ put before ⌐the crowds⌐ another parable:
"The kingdom of heaven may be compared to someone who sowed good
seed in his field;
²⁵but while everybody was asleep,
an enemy came and sowed weeds among the wheat, and then went away.
²⁶So when the plants came up and bore grain,
then the weeds appeared as well.
²⁷And the slaves of the householder came and said to him,
'Master, did you not sow good seed in your field?
Where, then, did these weeds come from?'
²⁸He answered, 'An enemy has done this.'
The slaves said to him, 'Then do you want us to go and gather them?'
²⁹But he replied,
'No; for in gathering the weeds you would uproot the wheat along with them.
³⁰Let both of them grow together until the harvest;
and at harvest time I will tell the reapers,
Collect the weeds first and bind them in bundles to be burned,
but gather the wheat into my barn.'"

³⁶Then he left the crowds and went into the house.
And his disciples approached him, saying,
"Explain to us the parable of the weeds of the field."
³⁷He answered, "The one who sows the good seed is the Son of Man;
³⁸the field is the world,
and the good seed are the children of the kingdom;
the weeds are the children of the evil one,
³⁹and the enemy who sowed them is the devil;
the harvest is the end of the age, and the reapers are angels.
⁴⁰Just as the weeds are collected and burned up with fire,
so will it be at the end of the age.

⁴¹"The Son of Man will send his angels,
and they will collect out of his kingdom all causes of sin and all evildoers,
⁴²and they will throw them into the furnace of fire,
where there will be weeping and gnashing of teeth.
⁴³Then the righteous will shine like the sun in the kingdom of their Father.
Let anyone with ears listen!"

The gospel of the Lord.

GOSPEL

A more animated telling of the parable (verses 24–30) can constructively contrast with a patient explanation of it (verses 36–43). Attempting to echo the urgency with which our Lord must certainly have addressed his disciples will help the hearer know how critically important the text is for our life and times.

FIRST READING: Genesis 29:15-28

A reading from Genesis:

[15]Laban said to Jacob,
"Because you are my kinsman, should you therefore serve me for nothing?
Tell me, what shall your wages be?"
[16]Now Laban had two daughters;
the name of the elder was Leah, and the name of the younger was Rachel.
[17]Leah's eyes were lovely, and Rachel was graceful and beautiful.
[18]Jacob loved Rachel; so he said,
"I will serve you seven years for your younger daughter Rachel."
[19]Laban said,
"It is better that I give her to you
than that I should give her to any other man; stay with me."
[20]So Jacob served seven years for Rachel,
and they seemed to him but a few days because of the love he had for her.

[21]Then Jacob said to Laban,
"Give me my wife that I may go in to her, for my time is completed."
[22]So Laban gathered together all the people of the place, and made a feast.
[23]But in the evening he took his daughter Leah and brought her to Jacob;
and he went in to her.
[24](Laban gave his maid Zilpah to his daughter Leah to be her maid.)
[25]When morning came, it was Leah!
And Jacob said to Laban, "What is this you have done to me?
Did I not serve with you for Rachel? Why then have you deceived me?"
[26]Laban said,
"This is not done in our country—giving the younger before the firstborn.
[27]Complete the week of this one, and we will give you the other also
in return for serving me another seven years."
[28]Jacob did so, and completed her week;
then Laban gave him his daughter Rachel as a wife.

The word of the Lord.   *or*   Word of God, word of life.

PSALMODY: Psalm 105:1-11, 45b or Psalm 128

FIRST READING   *Laban = LAY-bun   Zilpah = ZIL-puh*
Provide Laban's voice with a lack of sincerity in verses 15–20 and again in verses 26–27. (He knows exactly
what he's doing!) Verse 23 demands the sound of treachery. Do not underplay Jacob's righteous outrage.
Separate verse 28 from the rest of the text. It is a somewhat tempered happy ending.

SECOND READING: Romans 8:26-39

A reading from Romans.

26The Spirit helps us in our weakness;
for we do not know how to pray as we ought,
but that very Spirit intercedes with sighs too deep for words.
27And God, who searches the heart, knows what is the mind of the Spirit,
because the Spirit intercedes for the saints according to the will of God.

28We know that all things work together for good for those who love God,
who are called according to his purpose.
29For those whom he foreknew he also predestined
to be conformed to the image of his Son,
in order that he might be the firstborn within a large family.
30And those whom he predestined he also called;
and those whom he called he also justified;
and those whom he justified he also glorified.

31What then are we to say about these things?
If God is for us, who is against us?
32He who did not withhold his own Son,
but gave him up for all of us,
will he not with him also give us everything else?
33Who will bring any charge against God's elect?
It is God who justifies. 34Who is to condemn?
It is Christ Jesus, who died, yes, who was raised,
who is at the right hand of God,
who indeed intercedes for us.
35Who will separate us from the love of Christ?
Will hardship, or distress, or persecution,
or famine, or nakedness, or peril, or sword? 36As it is written,
"For your sake we are being killed all day long;
we are accounted as sheep to be slaughtered."

37No, in all these things we are more than conquerors
through him who loved us.
38For I am convinced that neither death, nor life,
nor angels, nor rulers, nor things present, nor things to come, nor powers,
39nor height, nor depth, nor anything else in all creation,
will be able to separate us from the love of God in Christ Jesus our Lord.

The word of the Lord.   *or*   Word of God, word of life.

SECOND READING
Resist strongly the temptation to read quickly because the reading is a long one. It is also a complex reading, and both reader and hearer will need adequate time to hear and assimilate its meaning. Bring to the reading an intensity equal to that of the Spirit who "intercedes with sighs too deep for words." Be especially attentive to verses 28–30, which describe the love of the Father for the Son and for all whom he has called into relationship with him.

GOSPEL: Matthew 13:31-33, 44-52

The holy gospel according to Matthew.

[31] ⌐Jesus⌐ put before ⌐the crowds⌐ another parable:
"The kingdom of heaven is like a mustard seed
that someone took and sowed in his field;
[32]it is the smallest of all the seeds,
but when it has grown it is the greatest of shrubs and becomes a tree,
so that the birds of the air come and make nests in its branches."

[33]He told them another parable:
"The kingdom of heaven is like yeast
that a woman took and mixed in with three measures of flour
until all of it was leavened."

[44]"The kingdom of heaven is like treasure hidden in a field,
which someone found and hid;
then in his joy he goes and sells all that he has and buys that field.

[45]"Again, the kingdom of heaven is like a merchant in search of fine pearls;
[46]on finding one pearl of great value,
he went and sold all that he had and bought it.

[47]"Again, the kingdom of heaven is like a net that was thrown into the sea
and caught fish of every kind;
[48]when it was full, they drew it ashore,
sat down, and put the good into baskets but threw out the bad.
[49]So it will be at the end of the age.
The angels will come out and separate the evil from the righteous
[50]and throw them into the furnace of fire,
where there will be weeping and gnashing of teeth.

[51]"Have you understood all this?"
They answered, "Yes."
[52]And he said to them,
"Therefore every scribe who has been trained for the kingdom of heaven
is like the master of a household
who brings out of his treasure what is new and what is old."

The gospel of the Lord.

GOSPEL
There are five pithy descriptions of the kingdom of heaven here. Allow a little room for each. A pause of some substance between them will allow the picture to develop and the point to be made. And having "understood all this," wrestle with verse 52 well in advance of Sunday and discover a delivery that will underscore its meaning.

SUNDAY, JULY 31–AUGUST 6
TIME AFTER PENTECOST — LECTIONARY 18

FIRST READING: Genesis 32:22-31

A reading from Genesis:

22 ⌜At night Jacob⌝ got up and took his two wives, his two maids,
and his eleven children, and crossed the ford of the Jabbok.
23He took them and sent them across the stream,
and likewise everything that he had.
24Jacob was left alone;
and a man wrestled with him until daybreak.

25When the man saw that he did not prevail against Jacob,
he struck him on the hip socket;
and Jacob's hip was put out of joint as he wrestled with him.
26Then he said, "Let me go, for the day is breaking."
But Jacob said, "I will not let you go, unless you bless me."
27So he said to him, "What is your name?"
And he said, "Jacob."
28Then the man said,
"You shall no longer be called Jacob, but Israel,
for you have striven with God and with humans, and have prevailed."
29Then Jacob asked him, "Please tell me your name."
But he said, "Why is it that you ask my name?"
And there he blessed him.

30So Jacob called the place Peniel, saying,
"For I have seen God face to face, and yet my life is preserved."
31The sun rose upon him as he passed Penuel, limping because of his hip.

The word of the Lord.   *or*   Word of God, word of life.

PSALMODY: Psalm 17:1-7, 15

FIRST READING   *Jabbok = JAB-uk   Peniel = puh-NY-ul   Penuel = puh-NOO-ul*
Jacob is running for his life, and verses 22–23 need to sound like it from the outset. Verse 24 needs to stand alone and be enveloped in a mysterious tone. Allow Jacob and the other combatant to "wrestle" the words out of the mouth of the opponent. Savor the mystery of verse 30 and delightful little detail at the end of verse 31, but watch for the difference between "Peniel" and "Penuel."

SECOND READING: Romans 9:1-5

A reading from Romans.

¹I am speaking the truth in Christ—I am not lying;
my conscience confirms it by the Holy Spirit—
²I have great sorrow and unceasing anguish in my heart.
³For I could wish that I myself were accursed
and cut off from Christ for the sake of my own people,
my kindred according to the flesh.
⁴They are Israelites, and to them belong the adoption, the glory,
the covenants, the giving of the law, the worship, and the promises;
⁵to them belong the patriarchs,
and from them, according to the flesh, comes the Messiah, who is over all,
God blessed forever. Amen.

The word of the Lord.   *or*   Word of God, word of life.

SECOND READING

The author's "great sorrow and unceasing anguish" set the tone for this reading. We hear Paul's agony that the Israelites have not embraced the righteousness that is rightfully theirs through faith in Christ Jesus. The reader would do well to read the remainder of the ninth chapter of Romans, to which this paragraph is the introduction. Clearly the author's anguish is real when he says, "I could wish that I myself were accursed and cut off from Christ for the sake of my own people, my kindred according to the flesh." Help the assembly sense Paul's pain.

GOSPEL: Matthew 14:13-21

The holy gospel according to Matthew.

[13]Now when Jesus heard ⌜about the beheading of John the Baptist,⌝
he withdrew from there in a boat to a deserted place by himself.
But when the crowds heard it, they followed him on foot from the towns.
[14]When he went ashore, he saw a great crowd;
and he had compassion for them and cured their sick.

[15]When it was evening, the disciples came to him and said,
"This is a deserted place, and the hour is now late;
send the crowds away so that they may go into the villages
and buy food for themselves."
[16]Jesus said to them,
"They need not go away; you give them something to eat."
[17]They replied, "We have nothing here but five loaves and two fish."
[18]And he said, "Bring them here to me."
[19]Then he ordered the crowds to sit down on the grass.
Taking the five loaves and the two fish,
he looked up to heaven, and blessed and broke the loaves,
and gave them to the disciples, and the disciples gave them to the crowds.
[20]And all ate and were filled;
and they took up what was left over of the broken pieces, twelve baskets full.
[21]And those who ate were about five thousand men,
besides women and children.

The gospel of the Lord.

GOSPEL

Even when sorrowful and weary, Jesus has compassion for the great crowd and heals and feeds them. Establish that weariness and deep grief in the first sentence. It can carry the whole reading. Infuse the dialogue with the disciples with that same sense. It will provide the miracle with a slightly unexpected sound that may capture the ear of the hearers. Verse 21 demands a tone of wonder.

SUNDAY, AUGUST 7–13
TIME AFTER PENTECOST — LECTIONARY 19

FIRST READING: Genesis 37:1-4, 12-28

A reading from Genesis:

¹Jacob settled in the land where his father had lived as an alien,
the land of Canaan.
²This is the story of the family of Jacob.

Joseph, being seventeen years old,
was shepherding the flock with his brothers;
he was a helper to the sons of Bilhah and Zilpah, his father's wives;
and Joseph brought a bad report of them to their father.
³Now Israel loved Joseph more than any other of his children,
because he was the son of his old age;
and he had made him a long robe with sleeves.
⁴But when his brothers saw that their father loved him more than all his
brothers, they hated him, and could not speak peaceably to him.

¹²Now his brothers went to pasture their father's flock near Shechem.
¹³And Israel said to Joseph,
"Are not your brothers pasturing the flock at Shechem?
Come, I will send you to them."
He answered, "Here I am."
¹⁴So he said to him,
"Go now, see if it is well with your brothers and with the flock;
and bring word back to me."
So he sent him from the valley of Hebron.

He came to Shechem, ¹⁵and a man found him wandering in the fields;
the man asked him, "What are you seeking?"
¹⁶"I am seeking my brothers," he said;
"tell me, please, where they are pasturing the flock."
¹⁷The man said,
"They have gone away, for I heard them say, 'Let us go to Dothan.'"
So Joseph went after his brothers, and found them at Dothan.
¹⁸They saw him from a distance,
and before he came near to them, they conspired to kill him. ▸

FIRST READING   *Canaan = KAY-nun   Bilhah = BILL-hah   Zilpah = ZILL-puh   Shechem = SHEK-um
Hebron = HE-brun   Dothan = DOH-thun   Ishmaelites = ISH-muh-lytz   Gilead = GIL-ee-ad   Midianite =
MID-ee-uh-nyt*
If the reading of this story does not fester with sounds of jealousy, conspiracy and contempt it will be a lost
opportunity. Find the story's points of climax and build to them. Tell the story—do not merely read it.

¹⁹They said to one another,
"Here comes this dreamer.
²⁰Come now, let us kill him and throw him into one of the pits;
then we shall say that a wild animal has devoured him,
and we shall see what will become of his dreams."
²¹But when Reuben heard it, he delivered him out of their hands, saying,
"Let us not take his life."
²²Reuben said to them,
"Shed no blood; throw him into this pit here in the wilderness,
but lay no hand on him"—
that he might rescue him out of their hand and restore him to his father.

²³So when Joseph came to his brothers,
they stripped him of his robe, the long robe with sleeves that he wore;
²⁴and they took him and threw him into a pit.
The pit was empty; there was no water in it.
²⁵Then they sat down to eat;
and looking up they saw a caravan of Ishmaelites coming from Gilead,
with their camels carrying gum, balm, and resin,
on their way to carry it down to Egypt.
²⁶Then Judah said to his brothers,
"What profit is it if we kill our brother and conceal his blood?
²⁷Come, let us sell him to the Ishmaelites,
and not lay our hands on him, for he is our brother, our own flesh."
And his brothers agreed.
²⁸When some Midianite traders passed by, they drew Joseph up,
lifting him out of the pit,
and sold him to the Ishmaelites for twenty pieces of silver.
And they took Joseph to Egypt.

The word of the Lord.   *or*   Word of God, word of life.

PSALMODY: Psalm 105:1-6, 16-22, 45b

SECOND READING: Romans 10:5-15

A reading from Romans.

[5]Moses writes concerning the righteousness that comes from the law,
that "the person who does these things will live by them."
[6]But the righteousness that comes from faith says,
"Do not say in your heart, 'Who will ascend into heaven?'"
(that is, to bring Christ down)
[7]"or 'Who will descend into the abyss?'"
(that is, to bring Christ up from the dead).

[8]But what does it say?
"The word is near you,
on your lips and in your heart"
(that is, the word of faith that we proclaim);
[9]because if you confess with your lips that Jesus is Lord
and believe in your heart that God raised him from the dead,
you will be saved.
[10]For one believes with the heart and so is justified,
and one confesses with the mouth and so is saved.
[11]The scripture says, "No one who believes in him will be put to shame."
[12]For there is no distinction between Jew and Greek;
the same Lord is Lord of all and is generous to all who call on him.
[13]For, "Everyone who calls on the name of the Lord shall be saved."

[14]But how are they to call on one in whom they have not believed?
And how are they to believe in one of whom they have never heard?
And how are they to hear without someone to proclaim him?
[15]And how are they to proclaim him unless they are sent?
As it is written,
"How beautiful are the feet of those who bring good news!"

The word of the Lord.   *or*   Word of God, word of life.

SECOND READING
On the surface the text looks confusing. Paul is working with Moses' words in Deuteronomy 30:11-14 and is saying that if one desires to achieve righteousness by the law, one needs to live by the law. But the righteousness that comes by faith is far easier to acquire since the word has come near to us in the person of Jesus. Finally, the author salutes those who bring the name of Jesus to our hearing. (And that, dear reader, is you!) The reading calls for a joyful and confident tone.

GOSPEL: Matthew 14:22-33

The holy gospel according to Matthew.

²² ⌈Jesus⌉ made the disciples get into the boat
and go on ahead to the other side ⌈of the Sea of Galilee,⌉
while he dismissed the crowds.
²³And after he had dismissed the crowds,
he went up the mountain by himself to pray.
When evening came, he was there alone,
²⁴but by this time the boat, battered by the waves,
was far from the land, for the wind was against them.

²⁵And early in the morning he came walking toward them on the sea.
²⁶But when the disciples saw him walking on the sea,
they were terrified, saying, "It is a ghost!"
And they cried out in fear.
²⁷But immediately Jesus spoke to them and said,
"Take heart, it is I; do not be afraid."

²⁸Peter answered him,
"Lord, if it is you, command me to come to you on the water."
²⁹He said, "Come."
So Peter got out of the boat, started walking on the water,
and came toward Jesus.
³⁰But when he noticed the strong wind, he became frightened,
and beginning to sink, he cried out,
"Lord, save me!"
³¹Jesus immediately reached out his hand and caught him, saying to him,
"You of little faith, why did you doubt?"
³²When they got into the boat, the wind ceased.
³³And those in the boat worshiped him, saying,
"Truly you are the Son of God."

The gospel of the Lord.

GOSPEL

Take time in preparing the reading to visualize the action—all the action—in detail. Attempt to recapture that vision in the voicing of the text. Take plenty of time. Allow the assembly sufficient time to see the gospel as well.

FIRST READING: Genesis 45:1-15

A reading from Genesis:

⌈After Judah offered himself in place of his brother Benjamin,⌉
¹Joseph could no longer control himself before all those who stood by him,
and he cried out, "Send everyone away from me."
So no one stayed with him when Joseph made himself known to his brothers.
²And he wept so loudly that the Egyptians heard it,
and the household of Pharaoh heard it.

³Joseph said to his brothers,
"I am Joseph. Is my father still alive?"
But his brothers could not answer him, so dismayed were they at his presence.

⁴Then Joseph said to his brothers, "Come closer to me."
And they came closer.
He said, "I am your brother, Joseph, whom you sold into Egypt.
⁵And now do not be distressed, or angry with yourselves,
because you sold me here;
for God sent me before you to preserve life.
⁶For the famine has been in the land these two years;
and there are five more years
in which there will be neither plowing nor harvest.
⁷God sent me before you to preserve for you a remnant on earth,
and to keep alive for you many survivors.
⁸So it was not you who sent me here, but God;
he has made me a father to Pharaoh,
and lord of all his house and ruler over all the land of Egypt.
⁹Hurry and go up to my father and say to him,
'Thus says your son Joseph,
God has made me lord of all Egypt; come down to me, do not delay.
¹⁰You shall settle in the land of Goshen,
and you shall be near me, you and your children and your children's children,
as well as your flocks, your herds, and all that you have. ▸

FIRST READING   *Pharaoh = FAIR-oh   Goshen = GOH-shun*
The character of Joseph is larger than life. A "little" reading will not do. The story begins and ends in tears—weeping of such proportion that "the household of Pharaoh heard it." Convincingly bringing that kind of emotion to a public reading demands significant rehearsal. Honor the scripture. Work at it.

¹¹I will provide for you there—
since there are five more years of famine to come—
so that you and your household, and all that you have,
will not come to poverty.'
¹²And now your eyes and the eyes of my brother Benjamin see
that it is my own mouth that speaks to you.
¹³You must tell my father how greatly I am honored in Egypt,
and all that you have seen.
Hurry and bring my father down here."
¹⁴Then he fell upon his brother Benjamin's neck and wept,
while Benjamin wept upon his neck.
¹⁵And he kissed all his brothers and wept upon them;
and after that his brothers talked with him.

The word of the Lord.   *or*   Word of God, word of life.

PSALMODY: Psalm 133

SECOND READING: Romans 11:1-2a, 29-32

A reading from Romans.

⌐Paul writes:¬
¹I ask, then, has God rejected his people?
By no means! I myself am an Israelite,
a descendant of Abraham, a member of the tribe of Benjamin.
²God has not rejected his people whom he foreknew.
²⁹For the gifts and the calling of God are irrevocable.

³⁰Just as you were once disobedient to God
but have now received mercy because of their disobedience,
³¹so they have now been disobedient in order that,
by the mercy shown to you, they too may now receive mercy.
³²For God has imprisoned all in disobedience so that he may be merciful to all.

The word of the Lord.   *or*   Word of God, word of life.

SECOND READING
This brief text is packed with some heavy theological thinking. The apostle's point is that God has not forsaken the Jews (God's promises are "irrevocable"), but has used their disobedience to open God's promises to the Gentiles even as God will use Gentile disobedience (and God's mercy to the Gentiles) to illustrate God's mercy to the Jews. To read this one well the lector must have this little argument set clearly in mind before reading it for others.

GOSPEL: Matthew 15:[10-20] 21-28

The holy gospel according to Matthew.

[¹⁰ ⌐Jesus⌐ called the crowd to him and said to them,
"Listen and understand:
¹¹it is not what goes into the mouth that defiles a person,
but it is what comes out of the mouth that defiles."
¹²Then the disciples approached and said to him,
"Do you know that the Pharisees took offense
when they heard what you said?"
¹³He answered,
"Every plant that my heavenly Father has not planted will be uprooted.
¹⁴Let them alone; they are blind guides of the blind.
And if one blind person guides another, both will fall into a pit."
¹⁵But Peter said to him, "Explain this parable to us."
¹⁶Then he said, "Are you also still without understanding?
¹⁷Do you not see that whatever goes into the mouth enters the stomach,
and goes out into the sewer?
¹⁸But what comes out of the mouth proceeds from the heart,
and this is what defiles.
¹⁹For out of the heart come evil intentions, murder, adultery,
fornication, theft, false witness, slander.
²⁰These are what defile a person,
but to eat with unwashed hands does not defile."]

²¹Jesus left that place and went away to the district of Tyre and Sidon.
²²Just then a Canaanite woman from that region came out and started shouting,
"Have mercy on me, Lord, Son of David;
my daughter is tormented by a demon."
²³But he did not answer her at all.
And his disciples came and urged him, saying,
"Send her away, for she keeps shouting after us."
²⁴He answered, "I was sent only to the lost sheep of the house of Israel."
²⁵But she came and knelt before him, saying, "Lord, help me."
²⁶He answered,
"It is not fair to take the children's food and throw it to the dogs."
²⁷She said, "Yes, Lord,
yet even the dogs eat the crumbs that fall from their masters' table."
²⁸Then Jesus answered her,
"Woman, great is your faith! Let it be done for you as you wish."
And her daughter was healed instantly.

The gospel of the Lord.

GOSPEL   *Sidon = SY-dun   Canaanite = KAY-nuh-nyt*
In either its longer or abbreviated form, the gospel's principal challenge is to make the dialogue believable. It requires some decisions about the various tones our Lord may have taken in reply to the various questions and assertions thrown his way. In preparation for the reading, wrestle with the variety of emotions Jesus may have felt and the different tacks he may have taken vocally in order to be clearly heard. This is no small challenge.

FIRST READING: Exodus 1:8—2:10

A reading from Exodus:

[8]Now a new king arose over Egypt, who did not know Joseph.
[9]He said to his people,
"Look, the Israelite people are more numerous and more powerful than we.
[10]Come, let us deal shrewdly with them,
or they will increase and, in the event of war,
join our enemies and fight against us and escape from the land."
[11]Therefore they set taskmasters over them to oppress them with forced labor.
They built supply cities, Pithom and Rameses, for Pharaoh.
[12]But the more they were oppressed, the more they multiplied and spread,
so that the Egyptians came to dread the Israelites.
[13]The Egyptians became ruthless in imposing tasks on the Israelites,
[14]and made their lives bitter with hard service in mortar and brick
and in every kind of field labor.
They were ruthless in all the tasks that they imposed on them.

[15]The king of Egypt said to the Hebrew midwives,
one of whom was named Shiphrah and the other Puah,
[16]"When you act as midwives to the Hebrew women,
and see them on the birthstool, if it is a boy, kill him;
but if it is a girl, she shall live."
[17]But the midwives feared God;
they did not do as the king of Egypt commanded them,
but they let the boys live.
[18]So the king of Egypt summoned the midwives and said to them,
"Why have you done this, and allowed the boys to live?"
[19]The midwives said to Pharaoh,
"Because the Hebrew women are not like the Egyptian women;
for they are vigorous and give birth before the midwife comes to them."

[20]So God dealt well with the midwives;
and the people multiplied and became very strong.
[21]And because the midwives feared God, he gave them families.

FIRST READING   *Pithom = PY-thum   Rameses = RAM-uh-seez   Pharaoh = FAIR-oh   Shiphrah = SHIF-ruh   Puah = POO-uh   Levi = LEE-vy   bitumen = buh-TYOO-mun*
The long stories in the semicontinuous series are dramatic in nature and sometimes cover a significant period of time. This is one of those. Reader and assembly alike will benefit from the reader's having plotted out the progress of the story long before beginning to read it aloud. Allow each episode its own space. Vary them in pace and tone. Bring the stories to life.

²²Then Pharaoh commanded all his people,
"Every boy that is born to the Hebrews you shall throw into the Nile,
but you shall let every girl live."
²:¹Now a man from the house of Levi went and married a Levite woman.
²The woman conceived and bore a son;
and when she saw that he was a fine baby, she hid him three months.
³When she could hide him no longer she got a papyrus basket for him,
and plastered it with bitumen and pitch;
she put the child in it and placed it among the reeds on the bank of the river.
⁴His sister stood at a distance, to see what would happen to him.

⁵The daughter of Pharaoh came down to bathe at the river,
while her attendants walked beside the river.
She saw the basket among the reeds and sent her maid to bring it.
⁶When she opened it, she saw the child.
He was crying, and she took pity on him,
"This must be one of the Hebrews' children," she said.
⁷Then his sister said to Pharaoh's daughter,
"Shall I go and get you a nurse from the Hebrew women
to nurse the child for you?"
⁸Pharaoh's daughter said to her, "Yes."
So the girl went and called the child's mother.
⁹Pharaoh's daughter said to her,
"Take this child and nurse it for me, and I will give you your wages."
So the woman took the child and nursed it.

¹⁰When the child grew up, she brought him to Pharaoh's daughter,
and she took him as her son.
She named him Moses,
"because," she said, "I drew him out of the water."

The word of the Lord.   *or*   Word of God, word of life.

PSALMODY: Psalm 124

SECOND READING: Romans 12:1-8

A reading from Romans.

¹I appeal to you therefore, brothers and sisters, by the mercies of God,
to present your bodies as a living sacrifice, holy and acceptable to God,
which is your spiritual worship.
²Do not be conformed to this world,
but be transformed by the renewing of your minds,
so that you may discern what is the will of God—
what is good and acceptable and perfect.

³For by the grace given to me I say to everyone among you
not to think of yourself more highly than you ought to think,
but to think with sober judgment,
each according to the measure of faith that God has assigned.
⁴For as in one body we have many members,
and not all the members have the same function,
⁵so we, who are many, are one body in Christ,
and individually we are members one of another.
⁶We have gifts that differ according to the grace given to us:
prophecy, in proportion to faith; ⁷ministry, in ministering;
the teacher, in teaching; ⁸the exhorter, in exhortation;
the giver, in generosity; the leader, in diligence;
the compassionate, in cheerfulness.

The word of the Lord.   *or*   Word of God, word of life.

SECOND READING   *prophecy = PROF-uh-see*
Interestingly, each sentence in this text stands alone nicely. One might have the best chance of helping the assembly hear the reading by reading each sentence (verses 1, 2, 3, 4–5, and 6–8) as though it were unrelated to the one before. Do not hurry—there is a lot to learn here. Also note that in verse 6 the word "prophecy" is a noun.

GOSPEL: Matthew 16:13-20

The holy gospel according to Matthew.

¹³Now when Jesus came into the district of Caesarea Philippi,
he asked his disciples, "Who do people say that the Son of Man is?"
¹⁴And they said,
"Some say John the Baptist, but others Elijah,
and still others Jeremiah or one of the prophets."
¹⁵He said to them, "But who do you say that I am?"
¹⁶Simon Peter answered,
"You are the Messiah, the Son of the living God."

¹⁷And Jesus answered him,
"Blessed are you, Simon son of Jonah!
For flesh and blood has not revealed this to you, but my Father in heaven.
¹⁸And I tell you, you are Peter, and on this rock I will build my church,
and the gates of Hades will not prevail against it.
¹⁹I will give you the keys of the kingdom of heaven,
and whatever you bind on earth will be bound in heaven,
and whatever you loose on earth will be loosed in heaven."
²⁰Then he sternly ordered the disciples not to tell anyone
that he was the Messiah.

The gospel of the Lord.

GOSPEL   *Caesarea Philippi = sez-uh-REE-uh fih-LIP-eye   Jeremiah = jehr-uh-MY-uh   Hades = HAY-deez*
In verse 14, solid pauses at the commas and after Jeremiah will allow the assembly to hear the voices
of various disciples. A significant pause following Verse 19 will set off Christ's celebration of the Petrine
confession and his initiation of the Office of the Keys. An excellent reader will see the scene before reading it,
and in the sound of the reader's voice the assembly will see it as well.

FIRST READING: Exodus 3:1-15

A reading from Exodus:

¹Moses was keeping the flock of his father-in-law Jethro,
the priest of Midian;
he led his flock beyond the wilderness, and came to Horeb,
the mountain of God.
²There the angel of the LORD appeared to him in a flame of fire out of a bush;
he looked, and the bush was blazing, yet it was not consumed.
³Then Moses said,
"I must turn aside and look at this great sight,
and see why the bush is not burned up."
⁴When the LORD saw that he had turned aside to see,
God called to him out of the bush, "Moses, Moses!"
And he said, "Here I am."
⁵Then he said,
"Come no closer! Remove the sandals from your feet,
for the place on which you are standing is holy ground."
⁶He said further,
"I am the God of your father, the God of Abraham,
the God of Isaac, and the God of Jacob."
And Moses hid his face, for he was afraid to look at God.

⁷Then the LORD said,
"I have observed the misery of my people who are in Egypt;
I have heard their cry on account of their taskmasters.
Indeed, I know their sufferings,
⁸and I have come down to deliver them from the Egyptians,
and to bring them up out of that land to a good and broad land,
a land flowing with milk and honey,
to the country of the Canaanites, the Hittites, the Amorites,
the Perizzites, the Hivites, and the Jebusites.
⁹The cry of the Israelites has now come to me;
I have also seen how the Egyptians oppress them.
¹⁰So come, I will send you to Pharaoh
to bring my people, the Israelites, out of Egypt."

FIRST READING   *Midian = MID-ee-un   Horeb = HOR-ub   Canaanites = KAY-nuh-nytz   Amorites = AM-oh-rytz   Perizzites = PEH-rih-zytz   Hivites = HIH-vytz   Jebusites = JEB-you-sytz   Pharaoh = FAIR-oh*
The reading announces and celebrates the name of God "for all generations." This is no small thing. Bringing the story to life is no small matter either. While the merit of memorizing readings remains a matter of debate, the closer this text is to the reader's immediate recollection, the more likely it will come to life in the hearing of the assembly. Then, of course, there is the matter of the Hittites, the Amorites, the Perizzites, the Hivites, and the Jebusites.

[11]But Moses said to God,
"Who am I that I should go to Pharaoh, and bring the Israelites out of Egypt?"
[12]He said, "I will be with you;
and this shall be the sign for you that it is I who sent you:
when you have brought the people out of Egypt,
you shall worship God on this mountain."

[13]But Moses said to God,
"If I come to the Israelites and say to them,
'The God of your ancestors has sent me to you,'
and they ask me, 'What is his name?' what shall I say to them?"
[14]God said to Moses,
"I AM WHO I AM."
He said further,
"Thus you shall say to the Israelites, 'I AM has sent me to you.'"
[15]God also said to Moses,
"Thus you shall say to the Israelites,
'The LORD, the God of your ancestors,
the God of Abraham, the God of Isaac, and the God of Jacob,
has sent me to you':

  "This is my name forever,
  and this my title for all generations."

The word of the Lord.   *or*   Word of God, word of life.

PSALMODY: Psalm 105:1-6, 23-26, 45b

SECOND READING: Romans 12:9-21

A reading from Romans.

[9]Let love be genuine;
hate what is evil, hold fast to what is good;
[10]love one another with mutual affection;
outdo one another in showing honor.
[11]Do not lag in zeal, be ardent in spirit, serve the Lord.
[12]Rejoice in hope, be patient in suffering, persevere in prayer.
[13]Contribute to the needs of the saints;
extend hospitality to strangers.

[14]Bless those who persecute you; bless and do not curse them.
[15]Rejoice with those who rejoice, weep with those who weep.
[16]Live in harmony with one another;
do not be haughty, but associate with the lowly;
do not claim to be wiser than you are.
[17]Do not repay anyone evil for evil,
but take thought for what is noble in the sight of all.
[18]If it is possible, so far as it depends on you,
live peaceably with all.

[19]Beloved, never avenge yourselves,
but leave room for the wrath of God;
for it is written,
"Vengeance is mine, I will repay, says the Lord."
[20]No, "if your enemies are hungry, feed them;
if they are thirsty, give them something to drink;
for by doing this you will heap burning coals on their heads."
[21]Do not be overcome by evil, but overcome evil with good.

The word of the Lord.   *or*   Word of God, word of life.

SECOND READING

These are simple, central imperatives for the Christian life. This is loving instruction on how to live lovingly. Do not succumb to the temptation to read quickly. Savor and celebrate the sense of the community life that adhering to such instruction would produce. Help the hearer to understand the importance of every phrase.

GOSPEL: Matthew 16:21–28

The holy gospel according to Matthew.

²¹From that time on
⌐after Peter confessed that Jesus was the Messiah,⌐
Jesus began to show his disciples that he must go to Jerusalem
and undergo great suffering
at the hands of the elders and chief priests and scribes,
and be killed, and on the third day be raised.
²²And Peter took him aside and began to rebuke him, saying,
"God forbid it, Lord! This must never happen to you."
²³But he turned and said to Peter,
"Get behind me, Satan!
You are a stumbling block to me;
for you are setting your mind not on divine things but on human things."

²⁴Then Jesus told his disciples,
"If any want to become my followers,
let them deny themselves and take up their cross and follow me.
²⁵For those who want to save their life will lose it,
and those who lose their life for my sake will find it.
²⁶For what will it profit them if they gain the whole world
but forfeit their life?
Or what will they give in return for their life?

²⁷"For the Son of Man is to come with his angels in the glory of his Father,
and then he will repay everyone for what has been done.
²⁸Truly I tell you,
there are some standing here who will not taste death
before they see the Son of Man coming in his kingdom."

The gospel of the Lord.

GOSPEL
A poorly prepared reader may stumble toward the end of verse 21, which is one long sentence. Avoid that trap through preparation: read the pericope several times in the week before, aloud as well as silently.

FIRST READING: Exodus 12:1-14

A reading from Exodus:

¹The LORD said to Moses and Aaron in the land of Egypt:
²This month shall mark for you the beginning of months;
it shall be the first month of the year for you.
³Tell the whole congregation of Israel
that on the tenth of this month they are to take a lamb for each family,
a lamb for each household.
⁴If a household is too small for a whole lamb,
it shall join its closest neighbor in obtaining one;
the lamb shall be divided in proportion to the number of people who eat of it.

⁵Your lamb shall be without blemish, a year-old male;
you may take it from the sheep or from the goats.
⁶You shall keep it until the fourteenth day of this month;
then the whole assembled congregation of Israel shall slaughter it at twilight.
⁷They shall take some of the blood and put it on the two doorposts
and the lintel of the houses in which they eat it.
⁸They shall eat the lamb that same night;
they shall eat it roasted over the fire
with unleavened bread and bitter herbs.
⁹Do not eat any of it raw or boiled in water,
but roasted over the fire, with its head, legs, and inner organs.
¹⁰You shall let none of it remain until the morning;
anything that remains until the morning you shall burn.

¹¹This is how you shall eat it:
your loins girded, your sandals on your feet, and your staff in your hand;
and you shall eat it hurriedly.
It is the passover of the LORD.
¹²For I will pass through the land of Egypt that night,
and I will strike down every firstborn in the land of Egypt,
both human beings and animals;
on all the gods of Egypt I will execute judgments:
I am the LORD.

FIRST READING
This is God's instructional introduction of the Seder for Moses and Aaron and all the people. In preparation, look carefully at the division of the lines of texts. Not every line ought to end with a pause. It is of particular importance that the sentences hang together—especially those detailing the preparation of the lamb in verses 5–10, which is, after all, a recipe. Three simple statements stand out, and a good reading will help the hearer focus on them: Verse 11b: "It is the passover of the LORD." Verse 12b: "I am the LORD." Verse 14a: "This day shall be a day of remembrance for you." Kick those up a notch!

¹³The blood shall be a sign for you on the houses where you live:
when I see the blood, I will pass over you,
and no plague shall destroy you when I strike the land of Egypt.

¹⁴This day shall be a day of remembrance for you.
You shall celebrate it as a festival to the LORD;
throughout your generations you shall observe it as a perpetual ordinance.

The word of the Lord.   *or*   Word of God, word of life.

PSALMODY: Psalm 149

SECOND READING: Romans 13:8-14

A reading from Romans.

⁸Owe no one anything, except to love one another;
for the one who loves another has fulfilled the law.
⁹The commandments, "You shall not commit adultery;
You shall not murder; You shall not steal; You shall not covet";
and any other commandment, are summed up in this word,
"Love your neighbor as yourself."
¹⁰Love does no wrong to a neighbor;
therefore, love is the fulfilling of the law.

¹¹Besides this, you know what time it is,
how it is now the moment for you to wake from sleep.
For salvation is nearer to us now than when we became believers;
¹²the night is far gone, the day is near.
Let us then lay aside the works of darkness and put on the armor of light;
¹³let us live honorably as in the day, not in reveling and drunkenness,
not in debauchery and licentiousness,
not in quarreling and jealousy.
¹⁴Instead, put on the Lord Jesus Christ,
and make no provision for the flesh, to gratify its desires.

The word of the Lord.   *or*   Word of God, word of life.

SECOND READING   *licentiousness = ly-SEN-chus-ness*
This reading is a straightforward reminder that if one genuinely loves the neighbor, one will do no wrong toward the neighbor. That reminder is followed by an appeal to "put on the armor of light" . . . "put on the Lord Jesus Christ." This is an encouraging word designed to wake up and motivate the complacent. Give it that kind of energy!

GOSPEL: Matthew 18:15-20

The holy gospel according to Matthew.

⌐Jesus said to the disciples:¬
[15]"If another member of the church sins against you,
go and point out the fault when the two of you are alone.
If the member listens to you, you have regained that one.
[16]But if you are not listened to, take one or two others along with you,
so that every word may be confirmed by the evidence of two or three witnesses.
[17]If the member refuses to listen to them, tell it to the church;
and if the offender refuses to listen even to the church,
let such a one be to you as a Gentile and a tax collector.

[18]"Truly I tell you, whatever you bind on earth will be bound in heaven,
and whatever you loose on earth will be loosed in heaven.
[19]Again, truly I tell you,
if two of you agree on earth about anything you ask,
it will be done for you by my Father in heaven.

[20]"For where two or three are gathered in my name, I am there among them."

The gospel of the Lord.

GOSPEL

Our Lord's ardent instruction to the Twelve relates to lovingly holding the community together, rather than establishing a minimal standard for excommunication. It requires a reconciling tone on the part of the gospel reader. Verse 18 might be more effectively connected to verses 15–17, while verse 19 might be helpfully attached to verse 20.

FIRST READING: Exodus 14:19-31

A reading from Exodus:

¹⁹The angel of God who was going before the Israelite army moved
and went behind them;
and the pillar of cloud moved from in front of them
and took its place behind them.
²⁰It came between the army of Egypt and the army of Israel.
And so the cloud was there with the darkness,
and it lit up the night;
one did not come near the other all night.

²¹Then Moses stretched out his hand over the sea.
The LORD drove the sea back by a strong east wind all night,
and turned the sea into dry land;
and the waters were divided.
²²The Israelites went into the sea on dry ground,
the waters forming a wall for them on their right and on their left.
²³The Egyptians pursued, and went into the sea after them,
all of Pharaoh's horses, chariots, and chariot drivers.
²⁴At the morning watch the LORD in the pillar of fire and cloud
looked down upon the Egyptian army,
and threw the Egyptian army into panic.
²⁵He clogged their chariot wheels so that they turned with difficulty.
The Egyptians said,
"Let us flee from the Israelites,
for the LORD is fighting for them against Egypt."

²⁶Then the LORD said to Moses,
"Stretch out your hand over the sea,
so that the water may come back upon the Egyptians,
upon their chariots and chariot drivers."
²⁷So Moses stretched out his hand over the sea,
and at dawn the sea returned to its normal depth.
As the Egyptians fled before it,
the LORD tossed the Egyptians into the sea. ▸

FIRST READING   *Pharaoh = FAIR-oh*
This is high drama. It lends itself to an expansive and energetic reading. Two cautionary notes: (1) Verse 20b is an oddly-constructed sentence. The reader will want to be certain in advance the meaning or image to convey. (2) A solid pause before verse 30 will establish the final sentences as a concluding summary of the implications of the narrative.

²⁸The waters returned and covered the chariots and the chariot drivers,
the entire army of Pharaoh that had followed them into the sea;
not one of them remained.
²⁹But the Israelites walked on dry ground through the sea,
the waters forming a wall for them on their right and on their left.

³⁰Thus the LORD saved Israel that day from the Egyptians;
and Israel saw the Egyptians dead on the seashore.
³¹Israel saw the great work that the LORD did against the Egyptians.
So the people feared the LORD
and believed in the LORD and in his servant Moses.

The word of the Lord.   *or*   Word of God, word of life.

PSALMODY: Psalm 114 or Exodus 15:1b-11, 20-21

SECOND READING: Romans 14:1-12

A reading from Romans.

[1]Welcome those who are weak in faith,
but not for the purpose of quarreling over opinions.
[2]Some believe in eating anything, while the weak eat only vegetables.
[3]Those who eat must not despise those who abstain,
and those who abstain must not pass judgment on those who eat;
for God has welcomed them.
[4]Who are you to pass judgment on servants of another?
It is before their own lord that they stand or fall.
And they will be upheld, for the Lord is able to make them stand.

[5]Some judge one day to be better than another,
while others judge all days to be alike.
Let all be fully convinced in their own minds.
[6]Those who observe the day, observe it in honor of the Lord.
Also those who eat, eat in honor of the Lord,
since they give thanks to God;
while those who abstain, abstain in honor of the Lord
and give thanks to God.

[7]We do not live to ourselves, and we do not die to ourselves.
[8]If we live, we live to the Lord,
and if we die, we die to the Lord;
so then, whether we live or whether we die, we are the Lord's.
[9]For to this end Christ died and lived again,
so that he might be Lord of both the dead and the living.

[10]Why do you pass judgment on your brother or sister?
Or you, why do you despise your brother or sister?
For we will all stand before the judgment seat of God.
[11]For it is written,
"As I live, says the Lord, every knee shall bow to me,
and every tongue shall give praise to God."
[12]So then, each of us will be accountable to God.

The word of the Lord. *or* Word of God, word of life.

SECOND READING
A simple point is being made. The author urges the hearer not to pass judgment on the servants of God ("servants of another"). That which the faithful choose to do or to abstain from doing is a choice made to honor God. We are urged to honor the choices of those whose decisions may differ from our own. It is an important message for the church, then and now. Bring to the reading a sense of urgency and the hearer in our day will be helped.

GOSPEL: Matthew 18:21-35

The holy gospel according to Matthew.

²¹Peter came and said to ⌐Jesus,⌐
"Lord, if another member of the church sins against me,
how often should I forgive? As many as seven times?"
²²Jesus said to him,
"Not seven times, but, I tell you, seventy-seven times.

²³"For this reason the kingdom of heaven may be compared to a king
who wished to settle accounts with his slaves.
²⁴When he began the reckoning,
one who owed him ten thousand talents was brought to him;
²⁵and, as he could not pay, his lord ordered him to be sold,
together with his wife and children and all his possessions,
and payment to be made.
²⁶So the slave fell on his knees before him, saying,
'Have patience with me, and I will pay you everything.'
²⁷And out of pity for him, the lord of that slave released him
and forgave him the debt.

²⁸"But that same slave, as he went out,
came upon one of his fellow slaves who owed him a hundred denarii;
and seizing him by the throat, he said, 'Pay what you owe.'
²⁹Then his fellow slave fell down and pleaded with him,
'Have patience with me, and I will pay you.'
³⁰But he refused;
then he went and threw him into prison until he would pay the debt.
³¹When his fellow slaves saw what had happened, they were greatly distressed,
and they went and reported to their lord all that had taken place.
³²Then his lord summoned him and said to him,
'You wicked slave!
I forgave you all that debt because you pleaded with me.
³³Should you not have had mercy on your fellow slave, as I had mercy on you?'
³⁴And in anger his lord handed him over to be tortured
until he would pay his entire debt.

³⁵"So my heavenly Father will also do to every one of you,
if you do not forgive your brother or sister from your heart."

The gospel of the Lord.

GOSPEL   *denarii = den-AR-ee-eye*
This action-packed story is preceded by Peter's genuine exploration of magnanimity in forgiveness and Jesus' startling reply. Allow it to stand alone—and to introduce the parable. Pick up the pace for the parabolic illustration. Vary the pace of the story at its unexpected turning points: verse 27 (the slave's release); verse 30a (the forgiven one's unwillingness to forgive); and verse 35 ("So my heavenly Father will . . ."). Bring a great deal of energy to the telling of the story.

Sunday, September 18–24

TIME AFTER PENTECOST — LECTIONARY 25

FIRST READING: Exodus 16:2-15

A reading from Exodus:

²The whole congregation of the Israelites complained
against Moses and Aaron in the wilderness.
³The Israelites said to them,
"If only we had died by the hand of the LORD in the land of Egypt,
when we sat by the fleshpots and ate our fill of bread;
for you have brought us out into this wilderness
to kill this whole assembly with hunger."

⁴Then the LORD said to Moses,
"I am going to rain bread from heaven for you,
and each day the people shall go out and gather enough for that day.
In that way I will test them,
whether they will follow my instruction or not.
⁵On the sixth day, when they prepare what they bring in,
it will be twice as much as they gather on other days."

⁶So Moses and Aaron said to all the Israelites,
"In the evening you shall know that it was the LORD
who brought you out of the land of Egypt,
⁷and in the morning you shall see the glory of the LORD,
because he has heard your complaining against the LORD.
For what are we, that you complain against us?"
⁸And Moses said,
"When the LORD gives you meat to eat in the evening
and your fill of bread in the morning,
because the LORD has heard the complaining that you utter against him—
what are we?
Your complaining is not against us but against the LORD."

⁹Then Moses said to Aaron,
"Say to the whole congregation of the Israelites,
'Draw near to the LORD, for he has heard your complaining.'" ▸

FIRST READING

If the reader fails to enter wholeheartedly into the scene as it is described in the text, the reading will be less than it ought to be. Hear the "whole congregation" complaining! Imagine God's choosing to say to Moses, "I am going to rain bread." See the "glory of the LORD" in the cloud! Then work at helping the assembly similarly to hear, imagine, and see.

TIME AFTER PENTECOST — SEMICONTINUOUS SERIES   369

¹⁰And as Aaron spoke to the whole congregation of the Israelites,
they looked toward the wilderness,
and the glory of the LORD appeared in the cloud.
¹¹The LORD spoke to Moses and said,
¹²"I have heard the complaining of the Israelites;
say to them, 'At twilight you shall eat meat,
and in the morning you shall have your fill of bread;
then you shall know that I am the LORD your God.'"

¹³In the evening quails came up and covered the camp;
and in the morning there was a layer of dew around the camp.
¹⁴When the layer of dew lifted,
there on the surface of the wilderness was a fine flaky substance,
as fine as frost on the ground.
¹⁵When the Israelites saw it, they said to one another,
"What is it?" For they did not know what it was.
Moses said to them,
"It is the bread that the LORD has given you to eat."

The word of the Lord.   *or*   Word of God, word of life.

PSALMODY: Psalm 105:1-6, 37-45

SECOND READING: Philippians 1:21-30

A reading from Philippians.

²¹For to me, living is Christ and dying is gain.
²²If I am to live in the flesh, that means fruitful labor for me;
and I do not know which I prefer.
²³I am hard pressed between the two:
my desire is to depart and be with Christ, for that is far better;
²⁴but to remain in the flesh is more necessary for you.
²⁵Since I am convinced of this, I know that I will remain
and continue with all of you for your progress and joy in faith,
²⁶so that I may share abundantly in your boasting in Christ Jesus
when I come to you again.

²⁷Only, live your life in a manner worthy of the gospel of Christ,
so that, whether I come and see you or am absent and hear about you,
I will know that you are standing firm in one spirit,
striving side by side with one mind for the faith of the gospel,
²⁸and are in no way intimidated by your opponents.
For them this is evidence of their destruction, but of your salvation.
And this is God's doing.
²⁹For he has graciously granted you the privilege
not only of believing in Christ,
but of suffering for him as well—
³⁰since you are having the same struggle that you saw I had
and now hear that I still have.

The word of the Lord.   *or*   Word of God, word of life.

SECOND READING   *Philippians = fih-LIP-ee-unz*
The author encourages hearers to live the Christian life and helps them come to grips with suffering. Living provides the occasion to witness to the faith in Christ Jesus; dying brings us directly into the presence of Christ. Both are attractive to the author. Both life and death (and even suffering!) are gifts of God for the faithful. That should be reflected in the tone of the reading.

GOSPEL: Matthew 20:1-16

The holy gospel according to Matthew.

⌐Jesus said to the disciples:⌐
[1]"The kingdom of heaven is like a landowner
who went out early in the morning to hire laborers for his vineyard.
[2]After agreeing with the laborers for the usual daily wage,
he sent them into his vineyard.
[3]When he went out about nine o'clock,
he saw others standing idle in the marketplace; [4]and he said to them,
'You also go into the vineyard, and I will pay you whatever is right.'
So they went.

[5]"When he went out again about noon and about three o'clock,
he did the same.
[6]And about five o'clock he went out and found others standing around;
and he said to them,
'Why are you standing here idle all day?'
[7]They said to him, 'Because no one has hired us.'
He said to them, 'You also go into the vineyard.'

[8]"When evening came, the owner of the vineyard said to his manager,
'Call the laborers and give them their pay,
beginning with the last and then going to the first.'
[9]When those hired about five o'clock came,
each of them received the usual daily wage.
[10]Now when the first came, they thought they would receive more;
but each of them also received the usual daily wage.
[11]And when they received it,
they grumbled against the landowner, [12]saying,
'These last worked only one hour, and you have made them equal to us
who have borne the burden of the day and the scorching heat.'
[13]But he replied to one of them,
'Friend, I am doing you no wrong;
did you not agree with me for the usual daily wage?
[14]Take what belongs to you and go;
I choose to give to this last the same as I give to you.
[15]Am I not allowed to do what I choose with what belongs to me?
Or are you envious because I am generous?'

[16]"So the last will be first, and the first will be last."

The gospel of the Lord.

GOSPEL
Beware the familiarity with the gospel that can lead to complacent proclamation. Strive to present a fresh telling of the story—as if for the first time. Do not rush the repetition of "he went out." Instead, allow each instance to underscore the persistence of the landowner (that is, God's pursuit of humankind).

SUNDAY, SEPTEMBER 25–OCTOBER 1
TIME AFTER PENTECOST — LECTIONARY 26

FIRST READING: Exodus 17:1-7

A reading from Exodus:

¹From the wilderness of Sin
the whole congregation of the Israelites journeyed by stages,
as the LORD commanded.
They camped at Rephidim, but there was no water for the people to drink.
²The people quarreled with Moses, and said, "Give us water to drink."
Moses said to them,
"Why do you quarrel with me? Why do you test the LORD?"
³But the people thirsted there for water;
and the people complained against Moses and said,
"Why did you bring us out of Egypt,
to kill us and our children and livestock with thirst?"

⁴So Moses cried out to the LORD,
"What shall I do with this people? They are almost ready to stone me."
⁵The LORD said to Moses,
"Go on ahead of the people, and take some of the elders of Israel with you;
take in your hand the staff with which you struck the Nile, and go.
⁶I will be standing there in front of you on the rock at Horeb.
Strike the rock, and water will come out of it,
so that the people may drink."
Moses did so, in the sight of the elders of Israel.
⁷He called the place Massah and Meribah,
because the Israelites quarreled and tested the LORD, saying,
"Is the LORD among us or not?"

The word of the Lord.   *or*   Word of God, word of life.

PSALMODY: Psalm 78:1-4, 12-16

FIRST READING   *Rephidim = REF-uh-dim   Horeb = HOR-ub   Massah = MASS-ah   Meribah = MEH-rih-bah*
Sense the thirst. Feel the anger and fear. Season the dialogue with them. Contrast those emotions with the LORD's patient instruction to Moses. Allow verse 6c ("Moses did so . . .") to stand alone. Do not "throw away" verse 7, but do not make more of it than an archeological footnote.

SECOND READING: Philippians 2:1-13

A reading from Philippians.

¹If then there is any encouragement in Christ,
any consolation from love, any sharing in the Spirit,
any compassion and sympathy,
²make my joy complete:
be of the same mind, having the same love,
being in full accord and of one mind.
³Do nothing from selfish ambition or conceit,
but in humility regard others as better than yourselves.
⁴Let each of you look not to your own interests,
but to the interests of others.

⁵Let the same mind be in you that was in Christ Jesus,
⁶who, though he was in the form of God,
did not regard equality with God as something to be exploited,
⁷but emptied himself, taking the form of a slave,
being born in human likeness.
And being found in human form, ⁸he humbled himself
and became obedient to the point of death—
even death on a cross.

⁹Therefore God also highly exalted him
and gave him the name that is above every name,
¹⁰so that at the name of Jesus every knee should bend,
in heaven and on earth and under the earth,
¹¹and every tongue should confess that Jesus Christ is Lord,
to the glory of God the Father.

¹²Therefore, my beloved, just as you have always obeyed me,
not only in my presence, but much more now in my absence,
work out your own salvation with fear and trembling;
¹³for it is God who is at work in you,
enabling you both to will and to work for his good pleasure.

The word of the Lord.   *or*   Word of God, word of life.

SECOND READING   *Philippians = fih-LIP-ee-unz*
This is Paul's heartfelt pastoral encouragement for the people. "Be of the same mind"—let Christ's thoughts, Christ's attitude, be your own. The central portion of the text is an ancient poem or hymn in praise of the Lord Jesus. It is extraordinarily beautiful. Take adequate time! Help the hearer feel Paul's genuine care and concern for those to whom he was writing. Care about the people in the pew, and help them to hear your concern.

GOSPEL: Matthew 21:23-32

The holy gospel according to Matthew.

23When ⌈Jesus⌉ entered the temple,
the chief priests and the elders of the people
came to him as he was teaching, and said,
"By what authority are you doing these things,
and who gave you this authority?"
24Jesus said to them, "I will also ask you one question;
if you tell me the answer,
then I will also tell you by what authority I do these things.
25Did the baptism of John come from heaven, or was it of human origin?"
And they argued with one another,
"If we say, 'From heaven,' he will say to us,
'Why then did you not believe him?'
26But if we say, 'Of human origin,' we are afraid of the crowd;
for all regard John as a prophet."
27So they answered Jesus, "We do not know."
And he said to them,
"Neither will I tell you by what authority I am doing these things.

28"What do you think? A man had two sons;
he went to the first and said,
'Son, go and work in the vineyard today.'
29He answered, 'I will not'; but later he changed his mind and went.
30The father went to the second and said the same;
and he answered, 'I go, sir'; but he did not go.
31Which of the two did the will of his father?"
They said, "The first."
Jesus said to them, "Truly I tell you,
the tax collectors and the prostitutes are going into the kingdom of God
ahead of you.
32For John came to you in the way of righteousness
and you did not believe him,
but the tax collectors and the prostitutes believed him;
and even after you saw it,
you did not change your minds and believe him."

The gospel of the Lord.

GOSPEL
This highly animated account (including Jesus' sly reply to the challenge of the elders; their huddled conclave; and the parable of the bad boys) cuts to the quick in verse 31. Work every angle. A lively reading will help the assembly hear that our Lord is deadly serious.

Sunday, October 2–8

FIRST READING: Exodus 20:1-4, 7-9, 12-20

A reading from Exodus:

¹God spoke all these words:

²I am the Lord your God, who brought you out of the land of Egypt,
out of the house of slavery;
³you shall have no other gods before me.
⁴You shall not make for yourself an idol,
whether in the form of anything that is in heaven above,
or that is on the earth beneath,
or that is in the water under the earth.

⁷You shall not make wrongful use of the name of the Lord your God,
for the Lord will not acquit anyone who misuses his name.

⁸Remember the sabbath day, and keep it holy.
⁹Six days you shall labor and do all your work.

¹²Honor your father and your mother,
so that your days may be long in the land that the Lord your God is giving you.
¹³You shall not murder.
¹⁴You shall not commit adultery.
¹⁵You shall not steal.
¹⁶You shall not bear false witness against your neighbor.
¹⁷You shall not covet your neighbor's house;
you shall not covet your neighbor's wife,
or male or female slave, or ox, or donkey,
or anything that belongs to your neighbor.

¹⁸When all the people witnessed the thunder and lightning,
the sound of the trumpet, and the mountain smoking,

FIRST READING

Help the assembly sense the scene long before it is described so vividly in verse 18. God is speaking against a backdrop of "thunder and lightning, the sound of the trumpet, and the mountain smoking." Give each sentence from the beginning through the end of the ten commandments a separate life. Deliver each with authority, and allow it to hang in the air—in the consciousness of the hearer—for a while before proceeding to the next.

they were afraid and trembled and stood at a distance,
¹⁹and said to Moses,
"You speak to us, and we will listen;
but do not let God speak to us, or we will die."
²⁰Moses said to the people,
"Do not be afraid; for God has come only to test you
and to put the fear of him upon you so that you do not sin."

The word of the Lord.   *or*   Word of God, word of life.

PSALMODY: Psalm 19

SECOND READING: Philippians 3:4b-14

A reading from Philippians.

⌈Paul writes:⌉
⁴ᵇIf anyone else has reason to be confident in the flesh, I have more:
⁵circumcised on the eighth day,
a member of the people of Israel, of the tribe of Benjamin,
a Hebrew born of Hebrews; as to the law, a Pharisee;
⁶as to zeal, a persecutor of the church;
as to righteousness under the law, blameless.

⁷Yet whatever gains I had,
these I have come to regard as loss because of Christ.
⁸More than that, I regard everything as loss
because of the surpassing value of knowing Christ Jesus my Lord.
For his sake I have suffered the loss of all things,
and I regard them as rubbish,
in order that I may gain Christ ⁹and be found in him,
not having a righteousness of my own that comes from the law,
but one that comes through faith in Christ,
the righteousness from God based on faith.

¹⁰I want to know Christ and the power of his resurrection
and the sharing of his sufferings by becoming like him in his death,
¹¹if somehow I may attain the resurrection from the dead. ▸

SECOND READING   *Philippians = fih-LIP-ee-unz*
This well known little text from the mind and heart of Paul first details his bragging rights as a member of the chosen people, even a learned and zealous member. He goes on to say that these things pale in significance to the "value of knowing Christ Jesus" and "having a righteousness . . . that comes through faith." The reading demands a vigorous reading born of commitment and hope.

[12]Not that I have already obtained this or have already reached the goal
but I press on to make it my own,
because Christ Jesus has made me his own.
[13]Beloved, I do not consider that I have made it my own;
but this one thing I do:
forgetting what lies behind and straining forward to what lies ahead,
[14]I press on toward the goal
for the prize of the heavenly call of God in Christ Jesus.

The word of the Lord. *or* Word of God, word of life.

GOSPEL: Matthew 21:33-46

The holy gospel according to Matthew.

⌜Jesus said to the people:⌝
³³"Listen to another parable.
There was a landowner who planted a vineyard,
put a fence around it, dug a wine press in it, and built a watchtower.
Then he leased it to tenants and went to another country.
³⁴When the harvest time had come,
he sent his slaves to the tenants to collect his produce.
³⁵But the tenants seized his slaves and beat one,
killed another, and stoned another.
³⁶Again he sent other slaves, more than the first;
and they treated them in the same way.
³⁷Finally he sent his son to them, saying,
'They will respect my son.'
³⁸But when the tenants saw the son, they said to themselves,
'This is the heir; come, let us kill him and get his inheritance.'
³⁹So they seized him, threw him out of the vineyard, and killed him.

⁴⁰"Now when the owner of the vineyard comes,
what will he do to those tenants?"
⁴¹They said to him,
"He will put those wretches to a miserable death,
and lease the vineyard to other tenants
who will give him the produce at the harvest time."

⁴²Jesus said to them, "Have you never read in the scriptures:
'The stone that the builders rejected has become the cornerstone;
this was the Lord's doing, and it is amazing in our eyes'?
⁴³Therefore I tell you,
the kingdom of God will be taken away from you
and given to a people that produces the fruits of the kingdom.
⁴⁴The one who falls on this stone will be broken to pieces;
and it will crush anyone on whom it falls."

⁴⁵When the chief priests and the Pharisees heard his parables,
they realized that he was speaking about them.
⁴⁶They wanted to arrest him,
but they feared the crowds, because they regarded him as a prophet.

The gospel of the Lord.

GOSPEL
With a deceptively innocent parable, Jesus leads everyone with ears to the damning indictment of verse 43.
Help the assembly hear from the beginning that the Lord knows exactly how the story ends.

SUNDAY, OCTOBER 9–15
TIME AFTER PENTECOST — LECTIONARY 28

FIRST READING: Exodus 32:1-14

A reading from Exodus:

[1]When the people saw that Moses delayed to come down from the mountain,
the people gathered around Aaron, and said to him,
"Come, make gods for us, who shall go before us;
as for this Moses, the man who brought us up out of the land of Egypt,
we do not know what has become of him."
[2]Aaron said to them,
"Take off the gold rings that are on the ears of your wives, your sons,
and your daughters, and bring them to me."
[3]So all the people took off the gold rings from their ears,
and brought them to Aaron.
[4]He took the gold from them, formed it in a mold, and cast an image of a calf;
and they said, "These are your gods, O Israel,
who brought you up out of the land of Egypt!"
[5]When Aaron saw this, he built an altar before it;
and Aaron made proclamation and said,
"Tomorrow shall be a festival to the LORD."
[6]They rose early the next day,
and offered burnt offerings and brought sacrifices of well-being;
and the people sat down to eat and drink, and rose up to revel.

[7]The LORD said to Moses,
"Go down at once!
Your people, whom you brought up out of the land of Egypt,
have acted perversely;
[8]they have been quick to turn aside from the way that I commanded them;
they have cast for themselves an image of a calf,
and have worshiped it and sacrificed to it, and said,
'These are your gods, O Israel,
who brought you up out of the land of Egypt!'"
[9]The LORD said to Moses,
"I have seen this people, how stiff-necked they are.

FIRST READING

This reading is a gold mine for the reader ready to work at it. The raw emotion and rage described in the text itself present the vocal challenge. Take note: "The people . . . rose up to revel." God says, "Let me alone, so that my wrath may burn hot against them." Moses "implored the LORD." An excellent reading demands a dramatic pause before verse 14 and will bring the sound of utter astonishment to the statement "And the LORD changed his mind. . . ."

[10]Now let me alone,
so that my wrath may burn hot against them and I may consume them;
and of you I will make a great nation."
[11]But Moses implored the LORD his God, and said,
"O LORD, why does your wrath burn hot against your people,
whom you brought out of the land of Egypt with great power
and with a mighty hand?
[12]Why should the Egyptians say,
'It was with evil intent that he brought them out
to kill them in the mountains,
and to consume them from the face of the earth'?
Turn from your fierce wrath;
change your mind and do not bring disaster on your people.
[13]Remember Abraham, Isaac, and Israel, your servants,
how you swore to them by your own self, saying to them,
'I will multiply your descendants like the stars of heaven,
and all this land that I have promised I will give to your descendants,
and they shall inherit it forever.'"
[14]And the LORD changed his mind
about the disaster that he planned to bring on his people.

The word of the Lord. *or* Word of God, word of life.

PSALMODY: Psalm 106:1-6, 19-23

SECOND READING: Philippians 4:1-9

A reading from Philippians.

¹My brothers and sisters,
whom I love and long for, my joy and crown,
stand firm in the Lord in this way, my beloved.

²I urge Euodia and I urge Syntyche to be of the same mind in the Lord.
³Yes, and I ask you also, my loyal companion,
help these women,
for they have struggled beside me in the work of the gospel,
together with Clement and the rest of my co-workers,
whose names are in the book of life.

⁴Rejoice in the Lord always; again I will say, Rejoice.
⁵Let your gentleness be known to everyone.
The Lord is near.
⁶Do not worry about anything,
but in everything by prayer and supplication with thanksgiving
let your requests be made known to God.
⁷And the peace of God, which surpasses all understanding,
will guard your hearts and your minds in Christ Jesus.

⁸Finally, beloved, whatever is true, whatever is honorable,
whatever is just, whatever is pure,
whatever is pleasing, whatever is commendable,
if there is any excellence and if there is anything worthy of praise,
think about these things.
⁹Keep on doing the things that you have learned and received
and heard and seen in me,
and the God of peace will be with you.

The word of the Lord.   *or*   Word of God, word of life.

SECOND READING   *Philippians = fih-LIP-ee-unz   Euodia = you-OH-dee-uh   Syntyche = SIN-tih-kih*
Wonderful words of encouragement are found here. Those words are prefaced by three verses that set the
letter in its historical context and help the reader make the reading sound like a letter. Encourage the hearer,
even as you, the reader, were encouraged by these words as you have considered them.

GOSPEL: Matthew 22:1-14

The holy gospel according to Matthew.

[1]Once more Jesus spoke to them in parables, saying:
[2]"The kingdom of heaven may be compared to a king
who gave a wedding banquet for his son.
[3]He sent his slaves to call those who had been invited to the wedding banquet,
but they would not come.
[4]Again he sent other slaves, saying,
'Tell those who have been invited:
Look, I have prepared my dinner,
my oxen and my fat calves have been slaughtered,
and everything is ready;
come to the wedding banquet.'
[5]But they made light of it and went away,
one to his farm, another to his business,
[6]while the rest seized his slaves, mistreated them, and killed them.
[7]The king was enraged.
He sent his troops, destroyed those murderers, and burned their city.

[8]"Then he said to his slaves,
'The wedding is ready, but those invited were not worthy.
[9]Go therefore into the main streets,
and invite everyone you find to the wedding banquet.'
[10]Those slaves went out into the streets and gathered all whom they found,
both good and bad; so the wedding hall was filled with guests.

[11]"But when the king came in to see the guests,
he noticed a man there who was not wearing a wedding robe,
[12]and he said to him,
'Friend, how did you get in here without a wedding robe?'
And he was speechless.
[13]Then the king said to the attendants,
'Bind him hand and foot, and throw him into the outer darkness,
where there will be weeping and gnashing of teeth.'

[14]"For many are called, but few are chosen."

The gospel of the Lord.

GOSPEL
Appropriate preparation for the proclamation of this gospel requires that the reader again be startled by the arrogance of the first invited, by the king's declaration to "invite everyone," and by his rage toward the man not wearing a wedding robe. Anything less will result in an unexceptional reading.

FIRST READING: Exodus 33:12-23

A reading from Exodus:

¹²Moses said to the LORD,
"See, you have said to me, 'Bring up this people';
but you have not let me know whom you will send with me.
Yet you have said,
'I know you by name, and you have also found favor in my sight.'
¹³Now if I have found favor in your sight, show me your ways,
so that I may know you and find favor in your sight.
Consider too that this nation is your people."
¹⁴He said, "My presence will go with you, and I will give you rest."
¹⁵And he said to him,
"If your presence will not go, do not carry us up from here.
¹⁶For how shall it be known that I have found favor in your sight,
I and your people, unless you go with us?
In this way, we shall be distinct, I and your people,
from every people on the face of the earth."

¹⁷The LORD said to Moses,
"I will do the very thing that you have asked;
for you have found favor in my sight, and I know you by name."
¹⁸Moses said, "Show me your glory, I pray."
¹⁹And he said, "I will make all my goodness pass before you,
and will proclaim before you the name, 'The LORD';
and I will be gracious to whom I will be gracious,
and will show mercy on whom I will show mercy.
²⁰But," he said, "you cannot see my face;
for no one shall see me and live."

²¹And the LORD continued,
"See, there is a place by me where you shall stand on the rock;
²²and while my glory passes by I will put you in a cleft of the rock,
and I will cover you with my hand until I have passed by;
²³then I will take away my hand, and you shall see my back;
but my face shall not be seen."

The word of the Lord.   *or*   Word of God, word of life.

FIRST READING
We are privileged to overhear an earnest and intimate conversation. Moses' request, "Show me your glory, I pray," calls for a tentative reading that will be complemented by the LORD's gentle and gracious acquiescence.

PSALMODY: Psalm 99

SECOND READING: 1 Thessalonians 1:1-10

A reading from First Thessalonians.

¹Paul, Silvanus, and Timothy,
To the church of the Thessalonians
in God the Father and the Lord Jesus Christ:
Grace to you and peace.

²We always give thanks to God for all of you and mention you in our prayers,
constantly ³remembering before our God and Father
your work of faith and labor of love and steadfastness of hope
in our Lord Jesus Christ.
⁴For we know, brothers and sisters beloved by God, that he has chosen you,
⁵because our message of the gospel came to you not in word only,
but also in power and in the Holy Spirit and with full conviction;
just as you know what kind of persons we proved to be among you for your sake.
⁶And you became imitators of us and of the Lord,
for in spite of persecution
you received the word with joy inspired by the Holy Spirit,
⁷so that you became an example to all the believers in Macedonia and in Achaia.

⁸For the word of the Lord has sounded forth from you
not only in Macedonia and Achaia,
but in every place your faith in God has become known,
so that we have no need to speak about it.
⁹For the people of those regions report about us
what kind of welcome we had among you,
and how you turned to God from idols, to serve a living and true God,
¹⁰and to wait for his Son from heaven, whom he raised from the dead—
Jesus, who rescues us from the wrath that is coming.

The word of the Lord.   *or*   Word of God, word of life.

SECOND READING   *Thessalonians = thess-uh-LOHN-ee-unz   Silvanus = sil-VAY-nus   Macedonia = mass-uh-DOHN-ee-uh   Achaia = uh-KAY-uh*
This is the beginning of a letter. An understood "From" precedes the names of the authors, Paul, Silvanus, and Timothy. The sentence structure in this text strikes the contemporary ear as convoluted. In preparing, the reader will do well to be certain where each sentence will end. Only then will the message be clear to reader and hearer alike.

GOSPEL: Matthew 22:15-22

The holy gospel according to Matthew.

[15]The Pharisees went and plotted to entrap ⌐Jesus⌐ in what he said.
[16]So they sent their disciples to him, along with the Herodians, saying,
"Teacher, we know that you are sincere,
and teach the way of God in accordance with truth,
and show deference to no one; for you do not regard people with partiality.
[17]Tell us, then, what you think.
Is it lawful to pay taxes to the emperor, or not?"
[18]But Jesus, aware of their malice, said,
"Why are you putting me to the test, you hypocrites?
[19]Show me the coin used for the tax."
And they brought him a denarius.
[20]Then he said to them, "Whose head is this, and whose title?"
[21]They answered, "The emperor's."

Then he said to them,
"Give therefore to the emperor the things that are the emperor's,
and to God the things that are God's."
[22]When they heard this, they were amazed;
and they left him and went away.

The gospel of the Lord.

GOSPEL   *Herodians = heh-ROH-dee-unz   denarius = deh-NAR-ee-us*
The tone of verses 15–17 is utterly deceitful! Our Lord's response is the picture of patience. Allow the
assembly to enjoy the contrast.

FIRST READING: Deuteronomy 34:1-12

A reading from Deuteronomy:

¹Moses went up from the plains of Moab to Mount Nebo,
to the top of Pisgah, which is opposite Jericho,
and the LORD showed him the whole land:
Gilead as far as Dan, ²all Naphtali, the land of Ephraim and Manasseh,
all the land of Judah as far as the Western Sea,
³the Negeb, and the Plain—that is, the valley of Jericho,
the city of palm trees—as far as Zoar.
⁴The LORD said to him,
"This is the land of which I swore to Abraham, to Isaac, and to Jacob, saying,
'I will give it to your descendants';
I have let you see it with your eyes, but you shall not cross over there."

⁵Then Moses, the servant of the LORD,
died there in the land of Moab, at the LORD's command.
⁶He was buried in a valley in the land of Moab, opposite Beth-peor,
but no one knows his burial place to this day.
⁷Moses was one hundred twenty years old when he died;
his sight was unimpaired and his vigor had not abated.
⁸The Israelites wept for Moses in the plains of Moab thirty days;
then the period of mourning for Moses was ended.

⁹Joshua son of Nun was full of the spirit of wisdom,
because Moses had laid his hands on him;
and the Israelites obeyed him, doing as the LORD had commanded Moses.

¹⁰Never since has there arisen a prophet in Israel like Moses,
whom the LORD knew face to face.
¹¹He was unequaled for all the signs and wonders
that the LORD sent him to perform in the land of Egypt,
against Pharaoh and all his servants and his entire land,
¹²and for all the mighty deeds and all the terrifying displays of power
that Moses performed in the sight of all Israel.

The word of the Lord.   *or*   Word of God, word of life.

FIREST READING *Deuteronomy = dew-ter-ON-uh-mee   Moab = MOH-ub   Nebo = NEE-boh   Pisgah = PIZ-guh   Gilead = GILL-ee-ad   Naphtali = NAF-tuh-lye   Ephraim = EEF-rih-um   Manasseh = muh-NAS-uh   Negeb = NEG-ub   Zoar = ZOH-ur   Beth-peor = beth-PEE-or   Pharaoh = FAIR-oh*
Until Naphtali, Ephraim, and Manasseh flow as trippingly from the reader's lips as Cleveland, St. Louis, and Des Moines, the reading is not yet ready. This tribute to the LORD's servant, Moses, demands, in sequence, the solemnity of an obituary and the ringing praise of a eulogy.

PSALMODY: Psalm 90:1-6, 13-17

SECOND READING: 1 Thessalonians 2:1-8

A reading from First Thessalonians.

¹You yourselves know, brothers and sisters,
that our coming to you was not in vain,
²but though we had already suffered
and been shamefully mistreated at Philippi, as you know,
we had courage in our God to declare to you the gospel of God
in spite of great opposition.
³For our appeal does not spring from deceit or impure motives or trickery,
⁴but just as we have been approved by God
to be entrusted with the message of the gospel,
even so we speak, not to please mortals,
but to please God who tests our hearts.

⁵As you know and as God is our witness,
we never came with words of flattery or with a pretext for greed;
⁶nor did we seek praise from mortals, whether from you or from others,
⁷though we might have made demands as apostles of Christ.
But we were gentle among you,
like a nurse tenderly caring for her own children.
⁸So deeply do we care for you that we are determined to share with you
not only the gospel of God but also our own selves,
because you have become very dear to us.

The word of the Lord.   *or*   Word of God, word of life.

SECOND READING   *Thessalonians = thess-uh-LOHN-ee-unz   Philippi = fih-LIP-eye*
See how the apostle loves the Thessalonians! This reading is filled with tender concern. Preparation is essential, because the sentences are long and convoluted. The hearer will be helped to the degree that the reader can let the love shine in the reading of the text. The reading warrants some passion. Make it heartfelt.

GOSPEL: Matthew 22:34-46

The holy gospel according to Matthew.

³⁴When the Pharisees heard that ⌈Jesus⌉ had silenced the Sadducees,
they gathered together,
³⁵and one of them, a lawyer, asked him a question to test him.
³⁶"Teacher, which commandment in the law is the greatest?"
³⁷He said to him,
" 'You shall love the Lord your God with all your heart,
and with all your soul, and with all your mind.'
³⁸This is the greatest and first commandment.
³⁹And a second is like it:
'You shall love your neighbor as yourself.'
⁴⁰On these two commandments hang all the law and the prophets."

⁴¹Now while the Pharisees were gathered together,
Jesus asked them this question:
⁴²"What do you think of the Messiah? Whose son is he?"
They said to him, "The son of David."
⁴³He said to them,
"How is it then that David by the Spirit calls him Lord, saying,
⁴⁴"The Lord said to my Lord,
"Sit at my right hand, until I put your enemies under your feet" '?
⁴⁵If David thus calls him Lord, how can he be his son?"
⁴⁶No one was able to give him an answer,
nor from that day did anyone dare to ask him any more questions.

The gospel of the Lord.

GOSPEL   *Sadducees = SAD-yuh-seez*
The early verses beg for a "testing" tone. Jesus' patient reply ought to provide sharp contrast. A carefully considered reading might employ a playful voice (accompanied by a small smile) as our Lord asks a follow-up question and quotes Psalm 110. It is a side of the Savior the assembly does not often get to hear.

☩ SUNDAY, OCTOBER 30–NOVEMBER 5

TIME AFTER PENTECOST — LECTIONARY 31

FIRST READING: Joshua 3:7-17

A reading from Joshua:

⁷The LORD said to Joshua,
"This day I will begin to exalt you in the sight of all Israel,
so that they may know that I will be with you as I was with Moses.
⁸You are the one who shall command the priests
who bear the ark of the covenant,
'When you come to the edge of the waters of the Jordan,
you shall stand still in the Jordan.'"

⁹Joshua then said to the Israelites,
"Draw near and hear the words of the LORD your God."
¹⁰Joshua said,
"By this you shall know that among you is the living God
who without fail
will drive out from before you the Canaanites, Hittites, Hivites,
Perizzites, Girgashites, Amorites, and Jebusites:
¹¹the ark of the covenant of the Lord of all the earth
is going to pass before you into the Jordan.
¹²So now select twelve men from the tribes of Israel,
one from each tribe.
¹³When the soles of the feet of the priests who bear the ark of the LORD,
the Lord of all the earth, rest in the waters of the Jordan,
the waters of the Jordan flowing from above shall be cut off;
they shall stand in a single heap."

¹⁴When the people set out from their tents to cross over the Jordan,
the priests bearing the ark of the covenant were in front of the people.
¹⁵Now the Jordan overflows all its banks throughout the time of harvest.
So when those who bore the ark had come to the Jordan,
and the feet of the priests bearing the ark were dipped in the edge of the water,
¹⁶the waters flowing from above stood still,
rising up in a single heap far off at Adam, the city that is beside Zarethan,
while those flowing toward the sea of the Arabah, the Dead Sea,
were wholly cut off.

FIRST READING   *Canaanites = KAY-nuh-nytz   Hivites = HIH-vytz   Perizzites = PEAR-ih-zytz*
Girgashites = GUR-guh-shytz   Amorites = AM-uh-rytz   Jebusites = JEB-you-sytz   Zarethan = ZAIR-uh-than   Arabah = AIR-uh-buh
The wonder and joy of the entry into the land of promise will be diminished if the reader stumbles over names such as Girgashites and Zarethan. There is no substitute for reading the texts aloud—repeatedly—before the day of the assembly. Likewise, there is no reward quite like that of a reading the lector knows has captured the attention and imagination of the hearer.

Then the people crossed over opposite Jericho.

¹⁷While all Israel were crossing over on dry ground,
the priests who bore the ark of the covenant of the LORD
stood on dry ground in the middle of the Jordan,
until the entire nation finished crossing over the Jordan.

The word of the Lord.   *or*   Word of God, word of life.

PSALMODY: Psalm 107:1-7, 33-37

SECOND READING: 1 Thessalonians 2:9-13

A reading from First Thessalonians.

⁹You remember our labor and toil, brothers and sisters;
we worked night and day,
so that we might not burden any of you
while we proclaimed to you the gospel of God.
¹⁰You are witnesses, and God also,
how pure, upright, and blameless our conduct was toward you believers.
¹¹As you know, we dealt with each one of you like a father with his children,
¹²urging and encouraging you and pleading that you lead a life worthy of God,
who calls you into his own kingdom and glory.

¹³We also constantly give thanks to God for this,
that when you received the word of God that you heard from us,
you accepted it not as a human word but as what it really is,
God's word, which is also at work in you believers.

The word of the Lord.   *or*   Word of God, word of life.

SECOND READING   *Thessalonians = thess-uh-LOHN-ee-unz*
The reading is very brief. A sense of urgency from the very beginning is required to give this reading the
sense of importance it deserves.

GOSPEL: Matthew 23:1-12

The holy gospel according to Matthew.

¹Jesus said to the crowds and to his disciples,
²"The scribes and the Pharisees sit on Moses' seat;
³therefore, do whatever they teach you and follow it;
but do not do as they do, for they do not practice what they teach.
⁴They tie up heavy burdens, hard to bear,
and lay them on the shoulders of others;
but they themselves are unwilling to lift a finger to move them.
⁵They do all their deeds to be seen by others;
for they make their phylacteries broad and their fringes long.
⁶They love to have the place of honor at banquets
and the best seats in the synagogues,
⁷and to be greeted with respect in the marketplaces,
and to have people call them rabbi.
⁸But you are not to be called rabbi,
for you have one teacher, and you are all students.
⁹And call no one your father on earth,
for you have one Father—the one in heaven.
¹⁰Nor are you to be called instructors,
for you have one instructor, the Messiah.

¹¹"The greatest among you will be your servant.
¹²All who exalt themselves will be humbled,
and all who humble themselves will be exalted."

The gospel of the Lord.

GOSPEL   *phylacteries = fih-LAK-ter-eez*
A scathing critique of the scribes and the Pharisees (verses 1–7) might be profitably separated from the concluding verses by a pause following verse 7 and a gentler, instructive tone for verses 8–12.

Sunday, November 6–12
TIME AFTER PENTECOST — LECTIONARY 32

FIRST READING: Joshua 24:1-3a, 14-25

A reading from Joshua:

¹Joshua gathered all the tribes of Israel to Shechem,
and summoned the elders, the heads, the judges, and the officers of Israel;
and they presented themselves before God.
²And Joshua said to all the people,
"Thus says the LORD, the God of Israel:
Long ago your ancestors—Terah and his sons Abraham and Nahor—
lived beyond the Euphrates and served other gods.
³ªThen I took your father Abraham from beyond the River
and led him through all the land of Canaan and made his offspring many.

¹⁴"Now therefore revere the LORD,
and serve him in sincerity and in faithfulness;
put away the gods that your ancestors served beyond the River and in Egypt,
and serve the LORD.
¹⁵Now if you are unwilling to serve the LORD,
choose this day whom you will serve,
whether the gods your ancestors served in the region beyond the River
or the gods of the Amorites in whose land you are living;
but as for me and my household, we will serve the LORD."

¹⁶Then the people answered,
"Far be it from us that we should forsake the LORD to serve other gods;
¹⁷for it is the LORD our God
who brought us and our ancestors up from the land of Egypt,
out of the house of slavery, and who did those great signs in our sight.
He protected us along all the way that we went,
and among all the peoples through whom we passed;
¹⁸and the LORD drove out before us all the peoples,
the Amorites who lived in the land.
Therefore we also will serve the LORD, for he is our God." ▶

FIRST READING   *Shechem = SHEK-um   Terah = TEH-ruh   Nahor = NAY-hor   Euphrates = you-FRAY-teez   Amorites = AM-uh-rytz*
Joshua's famous "Choose this day whom you will serve" speech is but one of the treasures to be unearthed here. The dramatic dialogue between leader and people from verse 16 forward is nothing less than stirring. Take plenty of time. Allow the conviction on both sides to swell as the reading progresses. Warning: an unrehearsed reading will derail, nine times out of ten, at verse 19. It will be misread unless the reader knows what is coming in verse 20.

¹⁹But Joshua said to the people,
"You cannot serve the LORD, for he is a holy God.
He is a jealous God;
he will not forgive your transgressions or your sins.
²⁰If you forsake the LORD and serve foreign gods,
then he will turn and do you harm, and consume you,
after having done you good."
²¹And the people said to Joshua,
"No, we will serve the LORD!"
²²Then Joshua said to the people,
"You are witnesses against yourselves
that you have chosen the LORD, to serve him."
And they said, "We are witnesses."
²³He said, "Then put away the foreign gods that are among you,
and incline your hearts to the LORD, the God of Israel."
²⁴The people said to Joshua,
"The LORD our God we will serve, and him we will obey."
²⁵So Joshua made a covenant with the people that day,
and made statutes and ordinances for them at Shechem.

The word of the Lord.   *or*   Word of God, word of life.

PSALMODY: Psalm 78:1-7

SECOND READING: 1 Thessalonians 4:13-18

A reading from First Thessalonians.

¹³We do not want you to be uninformed, brothers and sisters,
about those who have died,
so that you may not grieve as others do who have no hope.
¹⁴For since we believe that Jesus died and rose again,
even so, through Jesus, God will bring with him those who have died.
¹⁵For this we declare to you by the word of the Lord,
that we who are alive, who are left until the coming of the Lord,
will by no means precede those who have died.
¹⁶For the Lord himself, with a cry of command,
with the archangel's call and with the sound of God's trumpet,
will descend from heaven, and the dead in Christ will rise first.

SECOND READING   *Thessalonians = thess-uh-LOHN-ee-unz*
Sentence by sentence, this marvelous word of hope builds in intensity, wonder, and joy. The reader will want
to begin with an intensity on which she or he can build. Allow the emotion to peak at the end of verse 17.
Pause . . . then in verse 18 provide the hearers with their homework assignment.

¹⁷Then we who are alive, who are left,
will be caught up in the clouds together with them to meet the Lord in the air;
and so we will be with the Lord forever.

¹⁸Therefore encourage one another with these words.

The word of the Lord.   *or*   Word of God, word of life.

GOSPEL: Matthew 25:1-13

The holy gospel according to Matthew.

⌐Jesus said to the disciples:¬
¹"Then the kingdom of heaven will be like this.
Ten bridesmaids took their lamps and went to meet the bridegroom.
²Five of them were foolish, and five were wise.
³When the foolish took their lamps, they took no oil with them;
⁴but the wise took flasks of oil with their lamps.
⁵As the bridegroom was delayed, all of them became drowsy and slept.

⁶"But at midnight there was a shout,
'Look! Here is the bridegroom! Come out to meet him.'
⁷Then all those bridesmaids got up and trimmed their lamps.
⁸The foolish said to the wise,
'Give us some of your oil, for our lamps are going out.'
⁹But the wise replied,
'No! there will not be enough for you and for us;
you had better go to the dealers and buy some for yourselves.'
¹⁰And while they went to buy it, the bridegroom came,
and those who were ready went with him into the wedding banquet;
and the door was shut.
¹¹Later the other bridesmaids came also, saying,
'Lord, lord, open to us.'
¹²But he replied, 'Truly I tell you, I do not know you.'

¹³"Keep awake therefore, for you know neither the day nor the hour."

The gospel of the Lord.

GOSPEL
The parable of the bridesmaids takes shape by twists and turns. Enjoy the telling of it. Help the assembly sense the developing tension. Allow verse 12 to sound like a slamming door. Follow it with a pause of substance and deliver the warning of verse 13 with appropriate gravity.

FIRST READING: Judges 4:1-7

A reading from Judges:

¹The Israelites again did what was evil in the sight of the LORD,
after Ehud died.
²So the LORD sold them into the hand of King Jabin of Canaan,
who reigned in Hazor;
the commander of his army was Sisera, who lived in Harosheth-ha-goiim.
³Then the Israelites cried out to the LORD for help;
for he had nine hundred chariots of iron,
and had oppressed the Israelites cruelly twenty years.

⁴At that time Deborah, a prophetess, wife of Lappidoth, was judging Israel.
⁵She used to sit under the palm of Deborah
between Ramah and Bethel in the hill country of Ephraim;
and the Israelites came up to her for judgment.
⁶She sent and summoned Barak son of Abinoam from Kedesh in Naphtali,
and said to him,
"The LORD, the God of Israel, commands you,
'Go, take position at Mount Tabor,
bringing ten thousand from the tribe of Naphtali and the tribe of Zebulun.
⁷I will draw out Sisera, the general of Jabin's army,
to meet you by the Wadi Kishon with his chariots and his troops;
and I will give him into your hand.'"

The word of the Lord.   *or*   Word of God, word of life.

PSALMODY: Psalm 123

FIRST READING   *Ehud = EE-hud   Jabin = JAY-bin   Hazor = HAY-zor   Sisera = SIS-uh-ruh   Harosheth-ha-goiim = huh-RO-sheth-huh-GOY-im   Lappidoth = LAP-uh-doth   Ramah = RAY-muh   Ephraim = EEF-ruh-im   Barak = BAR-uk   Abinoam = uh-BIH-no-um   Kedesh = KEE-desh   Naphtali = NAF-tuh-lye   Tabor = TAY-bor   Zebulun = ZEB-you-lun   Wadi Kishon = WAH-dee KY-shun*
Deborah was courageous; so must the reader be—armed with courage that comes from preparation! Practice, over and over.

SECOND READING: 1 Thessalonians 5:1-11

A reading from First Thessalonians.

[1]Now concerning the times and the seasons, brothers and sisters,
you do not need to have anything written to you.
[2]For you yourselves know very well
that the day of the Lord will come like a thief in the night.
[3]When they say, "There is peace and security,"
then sudden destruction will come upon them,
as labor pains come upon a pregnant woman,
and there will be no escape!

[4]But you, beloved, are not in darkness,
for that day to surprise you like a thief;
[5]for you are all children of light and children of the day;
we are not of the night or of darkness.
[6]So then let us not fall asleep as others do,
but let us keep awake and be sober;
[7]for those who sleep sleep at night,
and those who are drunk get drunk at night.
[8]But since we belong to the day, let us be sober,
and put on the breastplate of faith and love,
and for a helmet the hope of salvation.
[9]For God has destined us not for wrath
but for obtaining salvation through our Lord Jesus Christ,
[10]who died for us,
so that whether we are awake or asleep we may live with him.
[11]Therefore encourage one another and build up each other,
as indeed you are doing.

The word of the Lord.   *or*   Word of God, word of life.

SECOND READING   *Thessalonians = thess-uh-LOHN-ee-uns*
The epistle's author is as clear as day. The tone of the second reading, particularly from verse 4 on, will contrast sharply with the First. For "the children of light and children of the day" these are words of encouragement and consolation. For them the day of reckoning holds no fear.

GOSPEL: Matthew 25:14-30

The holy gospel according to Matthew.

⌈Jesus said to the disciples:⌉
[14]"For it is as if a man, going on a journey,
summoned his slaves and entrusted his property to them;
[15]to one he gave five talents, to another two, to another one,
to each according to his ability.
Then he went away.

[16]"The one who had received the five talents went off at once
and traded with them, and made five more talents.
[17]In the same way, the one who had the two talents made two more talents.
[18]But the one who had received the one talent went off
and dug a hole in the ground and hid his master's money.

[19]"After a long time the master of those slaves came
and settled accounts with them.
[20]Then the one who had received the five talents came forward,
bringing five more talents, saying,
'Master, you handed over to me five talents;
see, I have made five more talents.'
[21]His master said to him,
'Well done, good and trustworthy slave;
you have been trustworthy in a few things,
I will put you in charge of many things;
enter into the joy of your master.'
[22]And the one with the two talents also came forward, saying,
'Master, you handed over to me two talents;
see, I have made two more talents.'
[23]His master said to him,
'Well done, good and trustworthy slave;
you have been trustworthy in a few things,
I will put you in charge of many things;
enter into the joy of your master.'

GOSPEL

Great storytellers are highly invested, right from the beginning, in the tales they tell. This gospel requires that kind of psychic energy and emotional commitment from the outset. Help the hearer see each slave and share his accomplishment—or failure and condemnation.

[24]"Then the one who had received the one talent also came forward, saying, 'Master, I knew that you were a harsh man, reaping where you did not sow, and gathering where you did not scatter seed; [25]so I was afraid, and I went and hid your talent in the ground. Here you have what is yours.' [26]But his master replied, 'You wicked and lazy slave! You knew, did you, that I reap where I did not sow, and gather where I did not scatter? [27]Then you ought to have invested my money with the bankers, and on my return I would have received what was my own with interest. [28]So take the talent from him, and give it to the one with the ten talents.

[29]" 'For to all those who have, more will be given, and they will have an abundance; but from those who have nothing, even what they have will be taken away. [30]As for this worthless slave, throw him into the outer darkness, where there will be weeping and gnashing of teeth.' "

The gospel of the Lord.

CHRIST THE KING
SUNDAY, NOVEMBER 20–26
LAST SUNDAY AFTER PENTECOST — LECTIONARY 34

FIRST READING: Ezekiel 34:11-16, 20-24

A reading from Ezekiel:

¹¹Thus says the Lord GOD:
I myself will search for my sheep, and will seek them out.
¹²As shepherds seek out their flocks
when they are among their scattered sheep,
so I will seek out my sheep.
I will rescue them from all the places to which they have been scattered
on a day of clouds and thick darkness.
¹³I will bring them out from the peoples and gather them from the countries,
and will bring them into their own land;
and I will feed them on the mountains of Israel,
by the watercourses, and in all the inhabited parts of the land.
¹⁴I will feed them with good pasture,
and the mountain heights of Israel shall be their pasture;
there they shall lie down in good grazing land,
and they shall feed on rich pasture on the mountains of Israel.
¹⁵I myself will be the shepherd of my sheep,
and I will make them lie down, says the Lord GOD.
¹⁶I will seek the lost, and I will bring back the strayed,
and I will bind up the injured, and I will strengthen the weak,
but the fat and the strong I will destroy.
I will feed them with justice.

²⁰Therefore, thus says the Lord GOD to them:
I myself will judge between the fat sheep and the lean sheep.
²¹Because you pushed with flank and shoulder,
and butted at all the weak animals with your horns
until you scattered them far and wide,
²²I will save my flock, and they shall no longer be ravaged;
and I will judge between sheep and sheep.

FIRST READING   *Ezekiel = eh-ZEEK-ee-el*
Read twice as loud and half as fast as you are initially inclined. This helpful rule of thumb for readers in the assembly is particularly applicable here. These are divine declarations, and the Lord GOD is seldom characterized as soft spoken. Declare God's commitment and intention. Solid pauses after each "thus says the Lord GOD" and before the concluding "I, the LORD, have spoken" will help.

²³I will set up over them one shepherd, my servant David,
and he shall feed them:
he shall feed them and be their shepherd.
²⁴And I, the LORD, will be their God,
and my servant David shall be prince among them;
I, the LORD, have spoken.

The word of the Lord.   *or*   Word of God, word of life.

PSALMODY: Psalm 100

SECOND READING: Ephesians 1:15-23

A reading from Ephesians.

¹⁵I have heard of your faith in the Lord Jesus
and your love toward all the saints,
and for this reason ¹⁶I do not cease to give thanks for you
as I remember you in my prayers.
¹⁷I pray that the God of our Lord Jesus Christ, the Father of glory,
may give you a spirit of wisdom and revelation as you come to know him,
¹⁸so that, with the eyes of your heart enlightened,
you may know what is the hope to which he has called you,
what are the riches of his glorious inheritance among the saints,
¹⁹and what is the immeasurable greatness of his power for us who believe,
according to the working of his great power.

²⁰God put this power to work in Christ
when he raised him from the dead
and seated him at his right hand in the heavenly places,
²¹far above all rule and authority and power and dominion,
and above every name that is named,
not only in this age but also in the age to come.
²²And he has put all things under his feet
and has made him the head over all things for the church,
²³which is his body, the fullness of him who fills all in all.

The word of the Lord.   *or*   Word of God, word of life.

SECOND READING   *Ephesians = eh-FEE-zhunz*
This reading moves from a blessing upon the Christians in Ephesus to a marvelous description of Christ the King. Don't rush it. Some of the sentences are long and a bit complicated. The reader will want to map them out in rehearsal, then give a reading that makes it clear from the start where each sentence is going. Give the hearer time to absorb the power of God at work in Christ.

GOSPEL: Matthew 25:31-46

The holy gospel according to Matthew.

⌐Jesus said to the disciples:¬
[31]"When the Son of Man comes in his glory, and all the angels with him,
then he will sit on the throne of his glory.
[32]All the nations will be gathered before him,
and he will separate people one from another
as a shepherd separates the sheep from the goats,
[33]and he will put the sheep at his right hand and the goats at the left.

[34]"Then the king will say to those at his right hand,
'Come, you that are blessed by my Father,
inherit the kingdom prepared for you from the foundation of the world;
[35]for I was hungry and you gave me food,
I was thirsty and you gave me something to drink,
I was a stranger and you welcomed me,
[36]I was naked and you gave me clothing,
I was sick and you took care of me,
I was in prison and you visited me.'
[37]Then the righteous will answer him,
'Lord, when was it that we saw you hungry and gave you food,
or thirsty and gave you something to drink?
[38]And when was it that we saw you a stranger and welcomed you,
or naked and gave you clothing?
[39]And when was it that we saw you sick or in prison and visited you?'
[40]And the king will answer them,
'Truly I tell you,
just as you did it to one of the least of these who are members of my family,
you did it to me.'

[41]"Then he will say to those at his left hand,
'You that are accursed,
depart from me into the eternal fire prepared for the devil and his angels;
[42]for I was hungry and you gave me no food,
I was thirsty and you gave me nothing to drink,
[43]I was a stranger and you did not welcome me,
naked and you did not give me clothing,
sick and in prison and you did not visit me.'

GOSPEL
The text anticipates the coming of the Son of Man in glory and Christ the King's "last word." It is a sobering scene. Strive for a judicial tone mingled, at the end, with not a little sadness.

[44]Then they also will answer,
'Lord, when was it that we saw you hungry or thirsty
or a stranger or naked or sick or in prison,
and did not take care of you?'
[45]Then he will answer them,
'Truly I tell you,
just as you did not do it to one of the least of these,
you did not do it to me.'
[46]And these will go away into eternal punishment,
but the righteous into eternal life."

The gospel of the Lord.

Lesser Festivals
AND OCCASIONS

✠ Andrew, Apostle

NOVEMBER 30

FIRST READING: Ezekiel 3:16-21

A reading from Ezekiel.

[16]At the end of seven days, the word of the LORD came to me:
[17]Mortal, I have made you a sentinel for the house of Israel;
whenever you hear a word from my mouth,
you shall give them warning from me.
[18]If I say to the wicked, "You shall surely die,"
and you give them no warning,
or speak to warn the wicked from their wicked way,
in order to save their life,
those wicked persons shall die for their iniquity;
but their blood I will require at your hand.
[19]But if you warn the wicked,
and they do not turn from their wickedness, or from their wicked way,
they shall die for their iniquity; but you will have saved your life.

[20]Again, if the righteous turn from their righteousness and commit iniquity,
and I lay a stumbling block before them, they shall die;
because you have not warned them, they shall die for their sin,
and their righteous deeds that they have done shall not be remembered;
but their blood I will require at your hand.
[21]If, however, you warn the righteous not to sin, and they do not sin,
they shall surely live, because they took warning;
and you will have saved your life.

The word of the Lord.   *or*   Word of God, word of life.

PSALMODY: Psalm 19:1-6

FIRST READING   *Ezekiel = eh-ZEEK-ee-el*
This dire warning needs to sound precisely that—dire. These are words designed to put the fear of God in the prophet and the people in the pew. While the reader will always want to explore words to be emphasized for impact and clarity, there is good reason to emphasize "your hand" and "your life" in verses 18 and 19; and, in the last line, "and you will have saved your life."

SECOND READING: Romans 10:10-18

A reading from Romans.

¹⁰One believes with the heart and so is justified,
and one confesses with the mouth and so is saved.
¹¹The scripture says,
"No one who believes in him will be put to shame."
¹²For there is no distinction between Jew and Greek;
the same Lord is Lord of all and is generous to all who call on him.
¹³For, "Everyone who calls on the name of the Lord shall be saved."

¹⁴But how are they to call on one in whom they have not believed?
And how are they to believe in one of whom they have never heard?
And how are they to hear without someone to proclaim him?
¹⁵And how are they to proclaim him unless they are sent?
As it is written,
"How beautiful are the feet of those who bring good news!"
¹⁶But not all have obeyed the good news; for Isaiah says,
"Lord, who has believed our message?"
¹⁷So faith comes from what is heard,
and what is heard comes through the word of Christ.
¹⁸But I ask, have they not heard? Indeed they have; for
    "Their voice has gone out to all the earth,
        and their words to the ends of the world."

The word of the Lord.   *or*   Word of God, word of life.

SECOND READING   *Isaiah = eye-ZAY-uh*
Reader, take note: the beautiful feet about which the lesson speaks are your own! Paul is agonizing here over those who have heard and not believed. The sequence of simple, pointed statements and questions ought to build to verse 18. There, "Indeed they have," ought to stand alone, separated from the reading by a good dramatic pause both before and after.

GOSPEL: John 1:35-42

The holy gospel according to John.

[35]The next day John again was standing with two of his disciples, [36]and as he watched Jesus walk by, he exclaimed,
"Look, here is the Lamb of God!"
[37]The two disciples heard him say this, and they followed Jesus.
[38]When Jesus turned and saw them following, he said to them,
"What are you looking for?"
They said to him,
"Rabbi" (which translated means Teacher),
"where are you staying?"
[39]He said to them, "Come and see."

They came and saw where he was staying,
and they remained with him that day.
It was about four o'clock in the afternoon.
[40]One of the two who heard John speak and followed him
was Andrew, Simon Peter's brother.
[41]He first found his brother Simon and said to him,
"We have found the Messiah" (which is translated Anointed).
[42]He brought Simon to Jesus, who looked at him and said,
"You are Simon son of John.
You are to be called Cephas" (which is translated Peter).

The gospel of the Lord.

GOSPEL   *Cephas = SEE-fus*
The call of Andrew is set in a gospel that includes (at least at first glace) several odd little remarks. "Rabbi, where are you staying?" "It was about four o'clock in the afternoon." "You are to be called Cephas." If the reading as a whole is to have meaning for the hearer, first the reader must settle on the meanings and intentions of every word and phrase.

For Thomas, Apostle (observed by some churches on Dec. 21), see page 457.

STEPHEN, DEACON AND MARTYR
DECEMBER 26

FIRST READING: 2 Chronicles 24:17-22

A reading from Second Chronicles.

[17]Now after the death of Jehoiada the officials of Judah came
and did obeisance to the king;
then the king listened to them.
[18]They abandoned the house of the LORD, the God of their ancestors,
and served the sacred poles and the idols.
And wrath came upon Judah and Jerusalem for this guilt of theirs.
[19]Yet he sent prophets among them to bring them back to the LORD;
they testified against them, but they would not listen.

[20]Then the spirit of God took possession of Zechariah
son of the priest Jehoiada;
he stood above the people and said to them,
"Thus says God:
Why do you transgress the commandments of the LORD,
so that you cannot prosper?
Because you have forsaken the LORD, he has also forsaken you."
[21]But they conspired against him,
and by command of the king
they stoned him to death in the court of the house of the LORD.
[22]King Joash did not remember the kindness that Jehoiada,
Zechariah's father, had shown him, but killed his son.
As he was dying, he said, "May the LORD see and avenge!"

The word of the Lord.   *or*   Word of God, word of life.

PSALMODY: Psalm 17:1-9, 15

FIRST READING   *Jehoiada = juh-HOY-uh-duh   Zechariah = zek-uh-RY-uh   Joash = JO-ash*
This dramatic and tragic account requires a bold, carefully paced reading. Fill the room with the sound of
the telling of it! Help the hearer sense the gravity of the events. This is a rough and tumble story. Help the
assembly feel the grit of it.

SECOND READING: Acts 6:8—7:2a, 51-60

A reading from Acts.

⁸Stephen, full of grace and power,
did great wonders and signs among the people.
⁹Then some of those who belonged to the synagogue of the Freedmen
(as it was called),
Cyrenians, Alexandrians, and others of those from Cilicia and Asia,
stood up and argued with Stephen.
¹⁰But they could not withstand
the wisdom and the Spirit with which he spoke.
¹¹Then they secretly instigated some men to say,
"We have heard him speak blasphemous words against Moses and God."

¹²They stirred up the people as well as the elders and the scribes;
then they suddenly confronted him, seized him,
and brought him before the council.
¹³They set up false witnesses who said,
"This man never stops saying things against this holy place and the law;
¹⁴for we have heard him say that this Jesus of Nazareth
will destroy this place and will change the customs that Moses handed on to us."
¹⁵And all who sat in the council looked intently at him,
and they saw that his face was like the face of an angel.
⁷:¹Then the high priest asked him,
"Are these things so?"
²ᵃAnd Stephen replied: "Brothers and fathers, listen to me.

⁵¹"You stiff-necked people, uncircumcised in heart and ears,
you are forever opposing the Holy Spirit, just as your ancestors used to do.
⁵²Which of the prophets did your ancestors not persecute?
They killed those who foretold the coming of the Righteous One,
and now you have become his betrayers and murderers.
⁵³You are the ones that received the law as ordained by angels,
and yet you have not kept it."

⁵⁴When they heard these things, they became enraged
and ground their teeth at Stephen.
⁵⁵But filled with the Holy Spirit,
he gazed into heaven and saw the glory of God
and Jesus standing at the right hand of God. ▸

SECOND READING   *Cyrenians = sy-REE-nee-unz   Cilicia = sil-LISH-yuh*
Few biblical stories match this one for dramatic action combined with exquisite turns of phrase. Take advantage of both. Vary the pace and volume of the reading as the action demands. Savor the well-turned phrase. Sometimes an increase in the intensity of the delivery of a sentence is more useful than increased volume. This may be true in verse 60.

⁵⁶"Look," he said,
"I see the heavens opened
and the Son of Man standing at the right hand of God!"

⁵⁷But they covered their ears,
and with a loud shout all rushed together against him.
⁵⁸Then they dragged him out of the city and began to stone him;
and the witnesses laid their coats at the feet of a young man named Saul.
⁵⁹While they were stoning Stephen, he prayed,
"Lord Jesus, receive my spirit."
⁶⁰Then he knelt down and cried out in a loud voice,
"Lord, do not hold this sin against them."
When he had said this, he died.

The word of the Lord.   *or*   Word of God, word of life.

GOSPEL: Matthew 23:34-39

The holy gospel according to Matthew.

⌜Jesus said:⌝
³⁴"Therefore I send you prophets, sages, and scribes,
some of whom you will kill and crucify,
and some you will flog in your synagogues and pursue from town to town,
³⁵so that upon you may come all the righteous blood shed on earth,
from the blood of righteous Abel to the blood of Zechariah son of Barachiah,
whom you murdered between the sanctuary and the altar.
³⁶Truly I tell you, all this will come upon this generation.

³⁷"Jerusalem, Jerusalem,
the city that kills the prophets and stones those who are sent to it!
How often have I desired to gather your children together
as a hen gathers her brood under her wings,
and you were not willing!
³⁸See, your house is left to you, desolate.
³⁹For I tell you, you will not see me again until you say,
'Blessed is the one who comes in the name of the Lord.' "

The gospel of the Lord.

GOSPEL   *Zechariah = zek-uh-RY-uh   Barachiah = bar-uh-KY-uh*
A depth of weariness and abiding sorrow, anchored in continual disappointment, might provide a helpful clue as to the sound of this gospel.

JOHN, APOSTLE AND EVANGELIST

FIRST READING: Genesis 1:1-5, 26-31

A reading from Genesis.

[1]In the beginning when God created the heavens and the earth,
[2]the earth was a formless void
and darkness covered the face of the deep,
while a wind from God swept over the face of the waters.
[3]Then God said, "Let there be light"; and there was light.
[4]And God saw that the light was good;
and God separated the light from the darkness.
[5]God called the light Day, and the darkness he called Night.
And there was evening and there was morning, the first day.

[26]Then God said,
"Let us make humankind in our image, according to our likeness;
and let them have dominion over the fish of the sea,
and over the birds of the air, and over the cattle,
and over all the wild animals of the earth,
and over every creeping thing that creeps upon the earth."

    [27]So God created humankind in his image,
        in the image of God he created them;
        male and female he created them.
[28]God blessed them, and God said to them,
"Be fruitful and multiply, and fill the earth and subdue it;
and have dominion over the fish of the sea
and over the birds of the air
and over every living thing that moves upon the earth."

[29]God said,
"See, I have given you every plant yielding seed
that is upon the face of all the earth,
and every tree with seed in its fruit;
you shall have them for food. ▸

FIRST READING

The three appointed readings serve as a kind of summary of the writing of John the Evangelist as outlined in the first verse of the second reading: "We declare to you what was from the beginning, what we have heard, what we have seen . . . concerning the word of life. . . . " Allow this creation account to ring out with the truth that "in the beginning was the Word" (John 1). "Power" is the operative word in sounding out this text.

³⁰And to every beast of the earth, and to every bird of the air,
and to everything that creeps on the earth,
everything that has the breath of life,
I have given every green plant for food."
And it was so.

³¹God saw everything that he had made,
and indeed, it was very good.
And there was evening and there was morning, the sixth day.

The word of the Lord.   *or*   Word of God, word of life.

PSALMODY: Psalm 116:12-19

SECOND READING: 1 John 1:1—2:2

A reading from First John.

¹We declare to you what was from the beginning,
what we have heard, what we have seen with our eyes,
what we have looked at and touched with our hands,
concerning the word of life—
²this life was revealed, and we have seen it and testify to it,
and declare to you the eternal life that was with the Father
and was revealed to us—
³we declare to you what we have seen and heard
so that you also may have fellowship with us;
and truly our fellowship is with the Father and with his Son Jesus Christ.
⁴We are writing these things so that our joy may be complete.

⁵This is the message we have heard from him and proclaim to you,
that God is light and in him there is no darkness at all.
⁶If we say that we have fellowship with him
while we are walking in darkness,
we lie and do not do what is true;
⁷but if we walk in the light as he himself is in the light,
we have fellowship with one another,
and the blood of Jesus his Son cleanses us from all sin.
⁸If we say that we have no sin, we deceive ourselves,
and the truth is not in us.

SECOND READING
The topic sentence is verse 2:1b: "We have an advocate with the Father, Jesus Christ the righteous." Invest all the tenderness and earnest truth-telling of an eyewitness to the love of God in Christ Jesus (which the evangelist was!) in building to that point.

⁹If we confess our sins,
he who is faithful and just will forgive us our sins
and cleanse us from all unrighteousness.
¹⁰If we say that we have not sinned, we make him a liar,
and his word is not in us.

²:¹My little children,
I am writing these things to you so that you may not sin.
But if anyone does sin, we have an advocate with the Father,
Jesus Christ the righteous;
²and he is the atoning sacrifice for our sins,
and not for ours only but also for the sins of the whole world.

The word of the Lord.   *or*   Word of God, word of life.

GOSPEL: John 21:20-25

The holy gospel according to John.

²⁰Peter turned and saw the disciple whom Jesus loved following them;
he was the one who had reclined next to Jesus at the supper and had said,
"Lord, who is it that is going to betray you?"
²¹When Peter saw him, he said to Jesus,
"Lord, what about him?"
²²Jesus said to him,
"If it is my will that he remain until I come, what is that to you?
Follow me!"
²³So the rumor spread in the community that this disciple would not die.
Yet Jesus did not say to him that he would not die, but,
"If it is my will that he remain until I come, what is that to you?"

²⁴This is the disciple who is testifying to these things
and has written them, and we know that his testimony is true.
²⁵But there are also many other things that Jesus did;
if every one of them were written down,
I suppose that the world itself could not contain
the books that would be written.

The gospel of the Lord.

GOSPEL
There is almost an air of embarrassment about this odd little story at the end of John's gospel, included today, perhaps, to give the assembly a sense of the person of the apostle and evangelist. It requires a conversational tone but one tinged with the intensity of one who is talking about matters of life and death. The final verse of the gospel brings us to the grandeur and power with which the appointed readings began.

The Holy Innocents, Martyrs

FIRST READING: Jeremiah 31:15-17

A reading from Jeremiah.

¹⁵Thus says the LORD:
A voice is heard in Ramah,
   lamentation and bitter weeping.
Rachel is weeping for her children;
    she refuses to be comforted for her children,
    because they are no more.
¹⁶Thus says the LORD:
Keep your voice from weeping,
   and your eyes from tears;
for there is a reward for your work,
says the LORD:
    they shall come back from the land of the enemy;
¹⁷there is hope for your future,
 says the LORD:
    your children shall come back to their own country.

The word of the Lord.   *or*   Word of God, word of life.

PSALMODY: Psalm 124

SECOND READING: 1 Peter 4:12-19

A reading from First Peter.

¹²Beloved, do not be surprised at the fiery ordeal
that is taking place among you to test you,
as though something strange were happening to you.
¹³But rejoice insofar as you are sharing Christ's sufferings,
so that you may also be glad and shout for joy when his glory is revealed.
¹⁴If you are reviled for the name of Christ, you are blessed,
because the spirit of glory, which is the Spirit of God, is resting on you.
¹⁵But let none of you suffer as a murderer, a thief,
a criminal, or even as a mischief maker.

FIRST READING   *Jeremiah = jehr-eh-MY-uh   Ramah = RAY-muh*
The tone in verse 15 is heart-rending lament. Separate verses 15 and 16 with a significant pause. Allow the pain to settle into the soul of the hearer. In contrast, the voice of the Lord in verses 16 and 17 should be quietly gentle and reassuring, acknowledging the grief of Rachel but not allowing it the last word.

SECOND READING
A sound of confident, authoritative teaching will capture the essence of the lesson. Do not hurry these profound truths. Consider the use of well placed pauses as means of controlling the pace by affording each new idea a moment to settle into the consciousness of the hearer: after verses 13, 14, 16, 17, and 18. Scripture is rarely read too slowly in the assembly. There is no hurry.

¹⁶Yet if any of you suffers as a Christian, do not consider it a disgrace,
but glorify God because you bear this name.
¹⁷For the time has come for judgment to begin with the household of God;
if it begins with us,
what will be the end for those who do not obey the gospel of God?
¹⁸And
    "If it is hard for the righteous to be saved,
    what will become of the ungodly and the sinners?"
¹⁹Therefore, let those suffering in accordance with God's will
entrust themselves to a faithful Creator, while continuing to do good.

The word of the Lord.　　　*or*　　　Word of God, word of life.

GOSPEL: Matthew 2:13-18

The holy gospel according to Matthew.

¹³Now after ⌈the wise men⌉ had left,
an angel of the Lord appeared to Joseph in a dream and said,
"Get up, take the child and his mother, and flee to Egypt,
and remain there until I tell you;
for Herod is about to search for the child, to destroy him."
¹⁴Then Joseph got up, took the child and his mother by night,
and went to Egypt,
¹⁵and remained there until the death of Herod.
This was to fulfill what had been spoken by the Lord through the prophet,
"Out of Egypt I have called my son."

¹⁶When Herod saw that he had been tricked by the wise men,
he was infuriated,
and he sent and killed all the children in and around Bethlehem
who were two years old or under,
according to the time that he had learned from the wise men.
¹⁷Then was fulfilled what had been spoken through the prophet Jeremiah:
    ¹⁸"A voice was heard in Ramah,
        wailing and loud lamentation,
    Rachel weeping for her children;
        she refused to be consoled, because they are no more."

The gospel of the Lord.

GOSPEL　　*Jeremiah = jehr-eh-MY-uh　Ramah = RAY-muh*
The gospel contains two distinct sounds. The story in verses 13–15a might move briskly and be set apart
from its interpretation in verse 15b by a pause. A voice of stunned disbelief might helpfully capture the
scope of the horror and grief in verses 17 and 18.

NAME OF JESUS

JANUARY 1

FIRST READING: Numbers 6:22-27

A reading from Numbers.

²²The LORD spoke to Moses, saying:
²³Speak to Aaron and his sons, saying,
Thus you shall bless the Israelites:
You shall say to them,
 ²⁴The LORD bless you and keep you;
 ²⁵the LORD make his face to shine upon you, and be gracious to you;
 ²⁶the LORD lift up his countenance upon you, and give you peace.

²⁷So they shall put my name on the Israelites, and I will bless them.

The word of the Lord.   *or*   Word of God, word of life.

PSALMODY: Psalm 8

SECOND READING: Galatians 4:4-7
OR PHILIPPIANS 2:5-11, following

A reading from Galatians.

⁴When the fullness of time had come,
God sent his Son, born of a woman, born under the law,
⁵in order to redeem those who were under the law,
so that we might receive adoption as children.
⁶And because you are children,
God has sent the Spirit of his Son into our hearts,
crying, "Abba! Father!"
⁷So you are no longer a slave but a child,
and if a child then also an heir, through God.

The word of the Lord.   *or*   Word of God, word of life.

FIRST READING   *Israelites = IZ-rul-eyts*
The assembly has heard these good words thousands of times, but help them sense Moses' hearing them for the first time. Do not hurry. Imagine each phrase of the benediction sinking into the head of the one who was supposed to repeat it to his brother.

SECOND READING (Galatians)   *Galatians = guh-LAY-shunz   Abba = AH-buh*
There is a tendency to rush tiny texts. Resist the temptation. Each sentence bears a profound truth. Allow the assembly to hear each one and to embrace it before sharing the next.

OR: Philippians 2:5-11

A reading from Philippians.

⁵Let the same mind be in you that was in Christ Jesus,
  ⁶who, though he was in the form of God,
     did not regard equality with God
     as something to be exploited,
  ⁷but emptied himself,
     taking the form of a slave,
     being born in human likeness.
  And being found in human form,
    ⁸he humbled himself
    and became obedient to the point of death—
    even death on a cross.
⁹Therefore God also highly exalted him
    and gave him the name that is above every name,
¹⁰so that at the name of Jesus
    every knee should bend,
in heaven and on earth and under the earth,
¹¹and every tongue should confess
    that Jesus Christ is Lord,
    to the glory of God the Father.

The word of the Lord.   *or*   Word of God, word of life.

SECOND READING (Philippians)   *Philippians = fih-LIP-ee-unz*
There is a natural flow to this text much like that of a poem or hymn (which is what it originally was). Listen for it in preparation. Repeat it in rehearsal. Recreate it in proclamation.

GOSPEL: Luke 2:15-21

The holy gospel according to Luke.

[15]When the angels had left them and gone into heaven,
the shepherds said to one another,
"Let us go now to Bethlehem
and see this thing that has taken place,
which the Lord has made known to us."
[16]So they went with haste and found Mary and Joseph,
and the child lying in the manger.
[17]When they saw this,
they made known what had been told them about this child;
[18]and all who heard it were amazed at what the shepherds told them.
[19]But Mary treasured all these words and pondered them in her heart.
[20]The shepherds returned,
glorifying and praising God for all they had heard and seen,
as it had been told them.

[21]After eight days had passed, it was time to circumcise the child;
and he was called Jesus,
the name given by the angel before he was conceived in the womb.

The gospel of the Lord.

GOSPEL
Work at recapturing the wonder of telling the story told on Christmas Eve. Then pause. (Eight days pass!)
Announce the name that "is above every name" with joy and wonder.

☩ CONFESSION OF PETER
JANUARY 18

FIRST READING: Acts 4:8-13

A reading from Acts.

⁸Peter, filled with the Holy Spirit, said to the authorities,
"Rulers of the people and elders,
⁹if we are questioned today
because of a good deed done to someone who was sick
and are asked how this man has been healed,
¹⁰let it be known to all of you, and to all the people of Israel,
that this man is standing before you in good health
by the name of Jesus Christ of Nazareth,
whom you crucified, whom God raised from the dead.
¹¹This Jesus is
  'the stone that was rejected by you, the builders;
  it has become the cornerstone.'
¹²There is salvation in no one else,
for there is no other name under heaven given among mortals
by which we must be saved."

¹³Now when they saw the boldness of Peter and John
and realized that they were uneducated and ordinary men,
they were amazed and recognized them as companions of Jesus.

The word of the Lord.   *or*   Word of God, word of life.

PSALMODY: Psalm 18:1-6, 16-19

FIRST READING
Verses 8–12 call for the sound of oration in the public square. Fill the room with the sound of bold and faithful witness to the "name of Jesus Christ of Nazareth." Pause dramatically before attempting to capture the amazement in the reaction of the authorities in verse 13.

SECOND READING: 1 Corinthians 10:1-5

A reading from First Corinthians.

[1]I do not want you to be unaware, brothers and sisters,
that our ancestors were all under the cloud,
and all passed through the sea,
[2]and all were baptized into Moses in the cloud and in the sea,
[3]and all ate the same spiritual food,
[4]and all drank the same spiritual drink.
For they drank from the spiritual rock that followed them,
and the rock was Christ.
[5]Nevertheless, God was not pleased with most of them,
and they were struck down in the wilderness.

The word of the Lord.   *or*   Word of God, word of life.

GOSPEL: Matthew 16:13-19

The holy gospel according to Matthew.

[13]Now when Jesus came into the district of Caesarea Philippi,
he asked his disciples, "Who do people say that the Son of Man is?"
[14]And they said,
"Some say John the Baptist, but others Elijah,
and still others Jeremiah or one of the prophets."
[15]He said to them, "But who do you say that I am?"
[16]Simon Peter answered,
"You are the Messiah, the Son of the living God."

[17]And Jesus answered him,
"Blessed are you, Simon son of Jonah!
For flesh and blood has not revealed this to you,
but my Father in heaven.
[18]And I tell you, you are Peter,
and on this rock I will build my church,
and the gates of Hades will not prevail against it.
[19]I will give you the keys of the kingdom of heaven,
and whatever you bind on earth will be bound in heaven,
and whatever you loose on earth will be loosed in heaven."

The gospel of the Lord.

SECOND READING
The first four verses of the reading describe—with conviction—the wandering of the children of Israel in the desert—with Christ! But it takes a stunningly sharp turn in verse 5 as it describes God's "nevertheless" displeasure. A breathless astonishment in the reading of that verse might be just right.

GOSPEL   *Caesarea Philippi = sez-uh-REE-uh fih-LIP-eye   Jeremiah = jehr-eh-MY-uh   Hades = HAY-deez*
Familiarity, perhaps more than any other factor, tempts readers to rush. Resist. Someone in the assembly is hearing the story for the first time. A careful, well-paced presentation (capturing the divine authority in Jesus' voice) will help someone else in the assembly hear the story as if for the first time.

CONVERSION OF PAUL

JANUARY 25

FIRST READING: Acts 9:1-22

A reading from Acts.

¹Saul, still breathing threats and murder against the disciples of the Lord,
went to the high priest
²and asked him for letters to the synagogues at Damascus,
so that if he found any who belonged to the Way, men or women,
he might bring them bound to Jerusalem.

³Now as he was going along and approaching Damascus,
suddenly a light from heaven flashed around him.
⁴He fell to the ground and heard a voice saying to him,
"Saul, Saul, why do you persecute me?"
⁵He asked, "Who are you, Lord?"
The reply came, "I am Jesus, whom you are persecuting.
⁶But get up and enter the city,
and you will be told what you are to do."
⁷The men who were traveling with him stood speechless
because they heard the voice but saw no one.
⁸Saul got up from the ground,
and though his eyes were open, he could see nothing;
so they led him by the hand and brought him into Damascus.
⁹For three days he was without sight, and neither ate nor drank.

¹⁰Now there was a disciple in Damascus named Ananias.
The Lord said to him in a vision, "Ananias."
He answered, "Here I am, Lord."
¹¹The Lord said to him,
"Get up and go to the street called Straight,
and at the house of Judas look for a man of Tarsus named Saul.
At this moment he is praying,
¹²and he has seen in a vision a man named Ananias come in
and lay his hands on him so that he might regain his sight."
¹³But Ananias answered,
"Lord, I have heard from many about this man,
how much evil he has done to your saints in Jerusalem; ▸

FIRST READING   *synagogues = SIN-uh-gogz   Ananias = an-uh-NY-us*
This is one of the great stories of scripture that never fails to capture the attention and the imagination. It is a long reading that contains subtle shifts of pace and tone from paragraph to paragraph. An excellent reading will require thoughtful preparation and repeated reading of the text aloud in the days before the assembly gathers.

¹⁴and here he has authority from the chief priests
to bind all who invoke your name."
¹⁵But the Lord said to him,
"Go, for he is an instrument whom I have chosen
to bring my name before Gentiles and kings and before the people of Israel;
¹⁶I myself will show him how much he must suffer for the sake of my name."

¹⁷So Ananias went and entered the house.
He laid his hands on Saul and said,
"Brother Saul, the Lord Jesus, who appeared to you on your way here,
has sent me so that you may regain your sight
and be filled with the Holy Spirit."
¹⁸And immediately something like scales fell from his eyes,
and his sight was restored.
Then he got up and was baptized,
¹⁹and after taking some food, he regained his strength.

For several days he was with the disciples in Damascus,
²⁰and immediately he began to proclaim Jesus in the synagogues, saying,
"He is the Son of God."
²¹All who heard him were amazed and said,
"Is not this the man who made havoc in Jerusalem
among those who invoked this name?
And has he not come here
for the purpose of bringing them bound before the chief priests?"
²²Saul became increasingly more powerful
and confounded the Jews who lived in Damascus
by proving that Jesus was the Messiah.

The word of the Lord.   *or*   Word of God, word of life.

PSALMODY: Psalm 67

SECOND READING: Galatians 1:11-24

A reading from Galatians.

⌐Paul writes:⌐
[11]I want you to know, brothers and sisters,
that the gospel that was proclaimed by me is not of human origin;
[12]for I did not receive it from a human source,
nor was I taught it,
but I received it through a revelation of Jesus Christ.

[13]You have heard, no doubt, of my earlier life in Judaism.
I was violently persecuting the church of God and was trying to destroy it.
[14]I advanced in Judaism beyond many among my people of the same age,
for I was far more zealous for the traditions of my ancestors.

[15]But when God, who had set me apart before I was born
and called me through his grace,
was pleased [16]to reveal his Son to me,
so that I might proclaim him among the Gentiles,
I did not confer with any human being,
[17]nor did I go up to Jerusalem to those who were already apostles before me,
but I went away at once into Arabia,
and afterwards I returned to Damascus.
[18]Then after three years I did go up to Jerusalem to visit Cephas
and stayed with him fifteen days;
[19]but I did not see any other apostle except James the Lord's brother.
[20]In what I am writing to you, before God, I do not lie!
[21]Then I went into the regions of Syria and Cilicia,
[22]and I was still unknown by sight to the churches of Judea that are in Christ;
[23]they only heard it said,
"The one who formerly was persecuting us
is now proclaiming the faith he once tried to destroy."
[24]And they glorified God because of me.

The word of the Lord.   *or*   Word of God, word of life.

SECOND READING   *Galatians = guh-LAY-shunz   Cephas = SEE-fus   Cilicia = sih-LISH-yuh*
In this unique context the assembly is allowed to hear Paul's take on the holy adventure recorded in Acts, just heard. Exploit the immediacy generated in the words, "You have heard, no doubt, of my earlier life . . . ." Invest enough time in preparation to allow the character of the apostle to come to life in his speaking.

GOSPEL: Luke 21:10-19

The holy gospel according to Luke.

[10] ⌐Jesus⌐ said to ⌐the disciples,⌐
"Nation will rise against nation, and kingdom against kingdom;
[11]there will be great earthquakes,
and in various places famines and plagues;
and there will be dreadful portents and great signs from heaven.

[12]"But before all this occurs, they will arrest you and persecute you;
they will hand you over to synagogues and prisons,
and you will be brought before kings and governors because of my name.
[13]This will give you an opportunity to testify.
[14]So make up your minds not to prepare your defense in advance;
[15]for I will give you words and a wisdom
that none of your opponents will be able to withstand or contradict.
[16]You will be betrayed even by parents and brothers,
by relatives and friends;
and they will put some of you to death.
[17]You will be hated by all because of my name.
[18]But not a hair of your head will perish.
[19]By your endurance you will gain your souls."

The gospel of the Lord.

GOSPEL   *synagogues = SIN-uh-gogz*
Our Lord's encouragement to endure might most effectively describe the impending struggles if presented in an understated voice of certain confidence rather than one of dramatic prediction.

PRESENTATION OF OUR LORD

FEBRUARY 2

FIRST READING: Malachi 3:1-4

A reading from Malachi:

¹See, I am sending my messenger to prepare the way before me,
and the Lord whom you seek will suddenly come to his temple.
The messenger of the covenant in whom you delight—
indeed, he is coming, says the LORD of hosts.
²But who can endure the day of his coming,
and who can stand when he appears?

For he is like a refiner's fire and like fullers' soap;
³he will sit as a refiner and purifier of silver,
and he will purify the descendants of Levi
and refine them like gold and silver,
until they present offerings to the LORD in righteousness.
⁴Then the offering of Judah and Jerusalem will be pleasing to the LORD
as in the days of old and as in former years.

The word of the Lord.   *or*   Word of God, word of life.

PSALMODY: Psalm 84 or Psalm 24:7-10

FIRST READING   *Malachi = MAL-uh-ky   Levi = LEE-vy*
If the hearer is to sense the delightfully ironic nature of the reading, the reader will want to invest some time in thinking through the text before bringing it to voice. Most people in the pew will understand the prophet speaking about Jesus and his sudden coming to the temple as an infant. In view of that, delight in the disconnect in verses 2 and 3 between a babe in arms and the powerful purifier.

SECOND READING: Hebrews 2:14-18

A reading from Hebrews.

¹⁴Since, therefore, the children share flesh and blood,
⌐Jesus⌐ himself likewise shared the same things,
so that through death he might destroy the one who has the power of death,
that is, the devil,
¹⁵and free those who all their lives were held in slavery by the fear of death.

¹⁶For it is clear that he did not come to help angels,
but the descendants of Abraham.
¹⁷Therefore he had to become like his brothers and sisters in every respect,
so that he might be a merciful and faithful high priest in the service of God,
to make a sacrifice of atonement for the sins of the people.
¹⁸Because he himself was tested by what he suffered,
he is able to help those who are being tested.

The word of the Lord.   *or*   Word of God, word of life.

GOSPEL: Luke 2:22-40

The holy gospel according to Luke.

²²When the time came for their purification according to the law of Moses,
⌐Mary and Joseph⌐ brought ⌐Jesus⌐ up to Jerusalem to present him to the Lord
²³(as it is written in the law of the Lord,
"Every firstborn male shall be designated as holy to the Lord"),
²⁴and they offered a sacrifice
according to what is stated in the law of the Lord,
"a pair of turtledoves or two young pigeons."

²⁵Now there was a man in Jerusalem whose name was Simeon;
this man was righteous and devout,
looking forward to the consolation of Israel,
and the Holy Spirit rested on him.
²⁶It had been revealed to him by the Holy Spirit
that he would not see death before he had seen the Lord's Messiah.
²⁷Guided by the Spirit, Simeon came into the temple;
and when the parents brought in the child Jesus,
to do for him what was customary under the law,

SECOND READING

Reading to the assembly goes beyond sentences and sounds. This brief description of the incarnation and atonement of humankind merits devotional consideration and a kind of prayerful inculcation of its truth into the psyche of the reader during the days preceding the assembly. Then the reading will proceed not only from the reader's lips but the reader's heart.

²⁸Simeon took him in his arms and praised God, saying,
>²⁹"Master, now you are dismissing your servant in peace,
>>according to your word;
>³⁰for my eyes have seen your salvation,
>>³¹which you have prepared in the presence of all peoples,
>³²a light for revelation to the Gentiles
>>and for glory to your people Israel."

³³And the child's father and mother were amazed
at what was being said about him.

³⁴Then Simeon blessed them and said to his mother Mary,
"This child is destined for the falling and the rising of many in Israel,
and to be a sign that will be opposed
³⁵so that the inner thoughts of many will be revealed—
and a sword will pierce your own soul too."

³⁶There was also a prophet,
Anna the daughter of Phanuel, of the tribe of Asher.
She was of a great age,
having lived with her husband seven years after her marriage,
³⁷then as a widow to the age of eighty-four.
She never left the temple
but worshiped there with fasting and prayer night and day.
³⁸At that moment she came, and began to praise God
and to speak about the child
to all who were looking for the redemption of Jerusalem.

³⁹When they had finished everything required by the law of the Lord,
they returned to Galilee, to their own town of Nazareth.
⁴⁰The child grew and became strong, filled with wisdom;
and the favor of God was upon him.

The gospel of the Lord.

GOSPEL   *Simeon = SIM-ee-un   Phanuel = FAN-oo-el*
The same kind of investment of energy and enthusiasm is essential both in reading the gospel and preaching a sermon. If you are doing both, approach the preparation for the reading of the story of the presentation of the child with the same prayerful intention focused on the preparation of the homily so that the assembly might "see God's salvation" in both.

For Matthias, Apostle (observed by some churches on Feb. 24), see page 442.

JOSEPH, GUARDIAN OF JESUS

FIRST READING: 2 Samuel 7:4, 8-16

A reading from Second Samuel.

⁴That same night the word of the LORD came to Nathan:
⁸Now therefore thus you shall say to my servant David:
Thus says the LORD of hosts:
I took you from the pasture, from following the sheep
to be prince over my people Israel;
⁹and I have been with you wherever you went,
and have cut off all your enemies from before you;
and I will make for you a great name,
like the name of the great ones of the earth.
¹⁰And I will appoint a place for my people Israel and will plant them,
so that they may live in their own place, and be disturbed no more;
and evildoers shall afflict them no more, as formerly,
¹¹from the time that I appointed judges over my people Israel;
and I will give you rest from all your enemies.

Moreover the LORD declares to you that the LORD will make you a house.
¹²When your days are fulfilled and you lie down with your ancestors,
I will raise up your offspring after you,
who shall come forth from your body,
and I will establish his kingdom.
¹³He shall build a house for my name,
and I will establish the throne of his kingdom forever.
¹⁴I will be a father to him, and he shall be a son to me.
When he commits iniquity, I will punish him with a rod such as mortals use,
with blows inflicted by human beings.
¹⁵But I will not take my steadfast love from him,
as I took it from Saul, whom I put away from before you.
¹⁶Your house and your kingdom shall be made sure forever before me;
your throne shall be established forever.

The word of the Lord.   *or*   Word of God, word of life.

FIRST READING

It would be easy for the recitation of what God had done to slip unnoticed into what is still promised in the future in the third part of verse 9. Giving the word "will" a little extra emphasis will prevent that. The last part of verse 11 begins the prophecy of the house of David, which culminated in Jesus' birth. If you lean on the word "I" at the start of verse 14, it will help the hearer understand why Joseph is called guardian of Jesus, not father.

PSALMODY: Psalm 89:1-29

SECOND READING: Romans 4:13-18

A reading from Romans.

¹³For the promise that he would inherit the world
did not come to Abraham or to his descendants through the law
but through the righteousness of faith.
¹⁴If it is the adherents of the law who are to be the heirs,
faith is null and the promise is void.
¹⁵For the law brings wrath;
but where there is no law, neither is there violation.

¹⁶For this reason it depends on faith,
in order that the promise may rest on grace
and be guaranteed to all his descendants,
not only to the adherents of the law
but also to those who share the faith of Abraham
(for he is the father of all of us,
¹⁷as it is written, "I have made you the father of many nations")—
in the presence of the God in whom he believed,
who gives life to the dead and calls into existence the things that do not exist.
¹⁸Hoping against hope,
he believed that he would become "the father of many nations,"
according to what was said,
"So numerous shall your descendants be."

The word of the Lord.   *or*   Word of God, word of life.

SECOND READING
The theme of fathers continues as we hear Abraham described using that term. Back in the first verse of this reading, though, emphasize the word "righteousness," since we will soon hear Joseph described as "a righteous man."

GOSPEL: Matthew 1:16, 18-21, 24a

The holy gospel according to Matthew.

[16]Jacob was the father of Joseph the husband of Mary,
of whom Jesus was born, who is called the Messiah.

[18]Now the birth of Jesus the Messiah took place in this way.
When his mother Mary had been engaged to Joseph,
but before they lived together,
she was found to be with child from the Holy Spirit.
[19]Her husband Joseph, being a righteous man
and unwilling to expose her to public disgrace,
planned to dismiss her quietly.
[20]But just when he had resolved to do this,
an angel of the Lord appeared to him in a dream and said,
"Joseph, son of David, do not be afraid to take Mary as your wife,
for the child conceived in her is from the Holy Spirit.
[21]She will bear a son, and you are to name him Jesus,
for he will save his people from their sins."

[24a]When Joseph awoke from sleep,
he did as the angel of the Lord commanded him.

The gospel of the Lord.

GOSPEL

The first sentence is the end of the genealogy. For the sake of comprehension, pause slightly between each of the four parts of the sentence. Take note of the human compassion in verse 19, followed by the divine revelation.

Annunciation of Our Lord

March 25

FIRST READING: Isaiah 7:10-14

A reading from Isaiah.

¹⁰The LORD spoke to Ahaz, saying,
¹¹Ask a sign of the LORD your God;
let it be deep as Sheol or high as heaven.
¹²But Ahaz said, I will not ask,
and I will not put the LORD to the test.
¹³Then Isaiah said:
"Hear then, O house of David!
Is it too little for you to weary mortals, that you weary my God also?
¹⁴Therefore the Lord himself will give you a sign.
Look, the young woman is with child and shall bear a son,
and shall name him Immanuel."

The word of the Lord.   *or*   Word of God, word of life.

PSALMODY: Psalm 45 or Psalm 40:5-10

FIRST READING   *Isaiah = eye-ZAY-uh*
Ahaz' refusal to seek a sign (when asked!) is likely an act of unfaith and needs to sound like it. The Lord will provide signs at God's own time. Regardless of the young woman Isaiah may have had in mind, the assembly will hear the prophet's words with reference to the virgin Mary. That was a sign of stunning importance and needs to sound like it.

SECOND READING: Hebrews 10:4-10

A reading from Hebrews.

⁴It is impossible for the blood of bulls and goats to take away sins.
⁵Consequently, when Christ came into the world, he said,
　　"Sacrifices and offerings you have not desired,
　　　but a body you have prepared for me;
　　⁶in burnt offerings and sin offerings
　　　you have taken no pleasure.
　　⁷Then I said, 'See, God, I have come to do your will, O God'
　　　(in the scroll of the book it is written of me)."
⁸When he said above,
"You have neither desired nor taken pleasure in sacrifices
and offerings and burnt offerings and sin offerings"
(these are offered according to the law),
⁹then he added, "See, I have come to do your will."
He abolishes the first in order to establish the second.
¹⁰And it is by God's will that we have been sanctified
through the offering of the body of Jesus Christ once for all.

The word of the Lord.　　　　*or*　　　　Word of God, word of life.

SECOND READING
The voice of a patient teacher might be sought here. Take adequate time to think this lesson through before attempting to vocalize it. The syntax is not simple but the point is. That point is clearly made in verse 10. Carefully lead the hearers to the author's conclusion.

GOSPEL: Luke 1:26-38

The holy gospel according to Luke.

²⁶In the sixth month the angel Gabriel was sent by God
to a town in Galilee called Nazareth,
²⁷to a virgin engaged to a man whose name was Joseph,
of the house of David.
The virgin's name was Mary.
²⁸And he came to her and said,
"Greetings, favored one! The Lord is with you."
²⁹But she was much perplexed by his words
and pondered what sort of greeting this might be.

³⁰The angel said to her,
"Do not be afraid, Mary, for you have found favor with God.
³¹And now, you will conceive in your womb and bear a son,
and you will name him Jesus.
³²He will be great, and will be called the Son of the Most High,
and the Lord God will give to him the throne of his ancestor David.
³³He will reign over the house of Jacob forever,
and of his kingdom there will be no end."
³⁴Mary said to the angel,
"How can this be, since I am a virgin?"
³⁵The angel said to her,
"The Holy Spirit will come upon you,
and the power of the Most High will overshadow you;
therefore the child to be born will be holy;
he will be called Son of God.
³⁶And now, your relative Elizabeth in her old age has also conceived a son;
and this is the sixth month for her who was said to be barren.
³⁷For nothing will be impossible with God."

³⁸Then Mary said, "Here am I, the servant of the Lord;
let it be with me according to your word."

Then the angel departed from her.

The gospel of the Lord.

GOSPEL
The verb in verse 29 is "perplexed," but what Mary felt might more likely have been fear. Helping the assembly hear the fear in Mary's pondering will take some doing. It will be worth the effort and may well inform the tone the reader selects in shaping Mary's resolve in verse 38. Tell the story as if the assembly did not already know its ending.

MARK, EVANGELIST

April 25

FIRST READING: Isaiah 52:7-10

A reading from Isaiah.

⁷How beautiful upon the mountains
    are the feet of the messenger who announces peace,
who brings good news,
    who announces salvation,
    who says to Zion, "Your God reigns."
⁸Listen! Your sentinels lift up their voices,
    together they sing for joy;
for in plain sight they see
    the return of the LORD to Zion.
⁹Break forth together into singing,
    you ruins of Jerusalem;
for the LORD has comforted his people,
    he has redeemed Jerusalem.
¹⁰The LORD has bared his holy arm
    before the eyes of all the nations;
and all the ends of the earth shall see
    the salvation of our God.

The word of the Lord.   *or*   Word of God, word of life.

PSALMODY: Psalm 57

SECOND READING: 2 Timothy 4:6-11, 18

A reading from Second Timothy.

⌈Paul writes:⌉
⁶As for me, I am already being poured out as a libation,
and the time of my departure has come.
⁷I have fought the good fight,
I have finished the race,
I have kept the faith.

FIRST READING   *Isaiah = eye-ZAY-uh*
Think Handel! Hear the joyous strains of his *Messiah*. This is music to the ears of the defeated and exiled.
Allow the magnificent images of each verse a clarion sounding in the hearing of the assembly!

SECOND READING   *Demas = DEE-mus*   *Thessalonica = thes-uh-loh-NY-kuh*   *Crescens = CRES-enz*
Galatia = guh-LAY-shuh   *Dalmatia = dal-MAY-shuh*
Paul is tired. He is discouraged. He is feeling very much alone. His glass is more than half empty and his
hope (though clearly stated) does not seek a booming voice. The break between verses 11 and 18 calls for
a significant pause. The hearers will relate well to a tentatively voiced conclusion of an exhausted apostle in
verse 18.

^{8}From now on there is reserved for me the crown of righteousness,
which the Lord, the righteous judge, will give me on that day,
and not only to me
but also to all who have longed for his appearing.

^{9}Do your best to come to me soon,
^{10}for Demas, in love with this present world,
has deserted me and gone to Thessalonica;
Crescens has gone to Galatia, Titus to Dalmatia.
^{11}Only Luke is with me.
Get Mark and bring him with you, for he is useful in my ministry.

^{18}The Lord will rescue me from every evil attack
and save me for his heavenly kingdom.
To him be the glory forever and ever. Amen.

The word of the Lord.   *or*   Word of God, word of life.

GOSPEL: Mark 1:1-15

The holy gospel according to Mark.

^{1}The beginning of the good news of Jesus Christ, the Son of God.
^{2}As it is written in the prophet Isaiah,
  "See, I am sending my messenger ahead of you,
    who will prepare your way;
    ^{3}the voice of one crying out in the wilderness:
      'Prepare the way of the Lord,
      make his paths straight,' "
^{4}John the baptizer appeared in the wilderness,
proclaiming a baptism of repentance for the forgiveness of sins.
^{5}And people from the whole Judean countryside
and all the people of Jerusalem were going out to him,
and were baptized by him in the river Jordan, confessing their sins.
^{6}Now John was clothed with camel's hair,
with a leather belt around his waist,
and he ate locusts and wild honey.
^{7}He proclaimed, "The one who is more powerful than I is coming after me;
I am not worthy to stoop down and untie the thong of his sandals.
^{8}I have baptized you with water;
but he will baptize you with the Holy Spirit." ▸

GOSPEL
This sweeping introduction to the Gospel of Mark covers a substantial time span. Plot the pauses carefully to help the hearer sense both the drama and the passage of time: after verse 1, verse 4, verse 8, verse 11, verse 12, verse 13. The people in the pew are in no hurry. They came specifically to hear the gospel.

⁹In those days Jesus came from Nazareth of Galilee
and was baptized by John in the Jordan.
¹⁰And just as he was coming up out of the water,
he saw the heavens torn apart and the Spirit descending like a dove on him.
¹¹And a voice came from heaven,
"You are my Son, the Beloved; with you I am well pleased."

¹²And the Spirit immediately drove him out into the wilderness.
¹³He was in the wilderness forty days, tempted by Satan;
and he was with the wild beasts; and the angels waited on him.

¹⁴Now after John was arrested, Jesus came to Galilee,
proclaiming the good news of God, ¹⁵and saying,
"The time is fulfilled, and the kingdom of God has come near;
repent, and believe in the good news."

The gospel of the Lord.

Philip and James, Apostles

May 1

FIRST READING: Isaiah 30:18-21

A reading from Isaiah.

> ¹⁸The LORD waits to be gracious to you;
>   therefore he will rise up to show mercy to you.
> For the LORD is a God of justice;
>   blessed are all those who wait for him.
>
> ¹⁹Truly, O people in Zion, inhabitants of Jerusalem,
> you shall weep no more.
> He will surely be gracious to you at the sound of your cry;
> when he hears it, he will answer you.
> ²⁰Though the Lord may give you the bread of adversity
> and the water of affliction,
> yet your Teacher will not hide himself any more,
> but your eyes shall see your Teacher.
> ²¹And when you turn to the right or when you turn to the left,
> your ears shall hear a word behind you, saying,
> "This is the way; walk in it."

The word of the Lord.   *or*   Word of God, word of life.

PSALMODY: Psalm 44:1-3, 20-26

FIRST READING   *Isaiah = eye-ZAY-uh*
These powerful words, much like a fine diamond, merit a splendid setting. Pause significantly following the announcement of the reading before launching into the prophet's words. Pause significantly as well as at the end of the reading before announcing that this is holy word. Bring every ounce of intensity at your disposal to these wonderful words.

SECOND READING: 2 Corinthians 4:1-6

A reading from Second Corinthians.

[1]Since it is by God's mercy that we are engaged in this ministry,
we do not lose heart.
[2]We have renounced the shameful things that one hides;
we refuse to practice cunning or to falsify God's word;
but by the open statement of the truth
we commend ourselves to the conscience of everyone in the sight of God.
[3]And even if our gospel is veiled,
it is veiled to those who are perishing.
[4]In their case the god of this world has blinded the minds of the unbelievers,
to keep them from seeing the light of the gospel of the glory of Christ,
who is the image of God.

[5]For we do not proclaim ourselves;
we proclaim Jesus Christ as Lord
and ourselves as your slaves for Jesus' sake.
[6]For it is the God who said, "Let light shine out of darkness,"
who has shone in our hearts
to give the light of the knowledge of the glory of God
in the face of Jesus Christ.

The word of the Lord.   *or*   Word of God, word of life.

SECOND READING
The tone of this lesson is very nearly conversational. A reading of quiet confidence will do it justice. Verse 6 is not a simple one. It will take some reading and rereading to ensure that the hearer (who only gets to hear it once) hears it well.

GOSPEL: John 14:8-14

The holy gospel according to John.

[8]Philip said to ⌜Jesus,⌝
"Lord, show us the Father, and we will be satisfied."
[9]Jesus said to him,
"Have I been with you all this time, Philip,
and you still do not know me?
Whoever has seen me has seen the Father.
How can you say, 'Show us the Father'?
[10]Do you not believe that I am in the Father and the Father is in me?
The words that I say to you I do not speak on my own;
but the Father who dwells in me does his works.
[11]Believe me that I am in the Father and the Father is in me;
but if you do not, then believe me because of the works themselves.

[12]"Very truly, I tell you,
the one who believes in me will also do the works that I do and,
in fact, will do greater works than these,
because I am going to the Father.
[13]I will do whatever you ask in my name,
so that the Father may be glorified in the Son.
[14]If in my name you ask me for anything, I will do it."

The gospel of the Lord.

GOSPEL
Our Lord had no script; what he said, he gave thought to first. That takes time. Help the assembly to hear a conversation. Help the assembly hear Jesus looking for the right words.

MATTHIAS, APOSTLE

May 14

FIRST READING: Isaiah 66:1-2

A reading from Isaiah.

¹Thus says the LORD:
Heaven is my throne
 and the earth is my footstool;
what is the house that you would build for me,
 and what is my resting place?
²All these things my hand has made,
 and so all these things are mine, says the LORD.
But this is the one to whom I will look,
 to the humble and contrite in spirit,
 who trembles at my word.

The word of the Lord.   *or*   Word of God, word of life.

PSALMODY: Psalm 56

SECOND READING: Acts 1:15-26

A reading from Acts.

¹⁵In those days Peter stood up among the believers
(together the crowd numbered about one hundred twenty persons)
and said,
¹⁶"Friends, the scripture had to be fulfilled,
which the Holy Spirit through David foretold concerning Judas,
who became a guide for those who arrested Jesus—
¹⁷for he was numbered among us and was allotted his share in this ministry."
¹⁸(Now this man acquired a field with the reward of his wickedness;
and falling headlong, he burst open in the middle
and all his bowels gushed out.
¹⁹This became known to all the residents of Jerusalem,
so that the field was called in their language Hakeldama,
that is, Field of Blood.)

FIRST READING   *Isaiah = eye-ZAY-uh*
Quiet authority is perhaps the most helpful sound for a reading that so succinctly details the credentials of the authentic apostle. A deliberate pace will help establish the sound of authority.

SECOND READING   *Hakeldama = huh-KEL-duh-muh   Barsabbas = bar-SAB-us   Matthias = muh-THY-us*
The reading will be helpfully divided between two voices—that of Peter as public speaker and that of the narrator who details the action as well as commenting on it in two parenthetical asides. Work at both feeling and giving expression to a rising tension as the faithful prayerfully attempt to discern the will of God by rolling the dice.

[20]"For it is written in the book of Psalms,
    'Let his homestead become desolate,
        and let there be no one to live in it';
and
    'Let another take his position of overseer.'

[21]"So one of the men who have accompanied us
during all the time that the Lord Jesus went in and out among us,
[22]beginning from the baptism of John
until the day when he was taken up from us—
one of these must become a witness with us to his resurrection."
[23]So they proposed two,
Joseph called Barsabbas, who was also known as Justus, and Matthias.
[24]Then they prayed and said,
"Lord, you know everyone's heart.
Show us which one of these two you have chosen
[25]to take the place in this ministry and apostleship
from which Judas turned aside to go to his own place."
[26]And they cast lots for them, and the lot fell on Matthias;
and he was added to the eleven apostles.

The word of the Lord.　　*or*　　Word of God, word of life.

GOSPEL: Luke 6:12-16

The holy gospel according to Luke.

[12]During those days ⌐Jesus⌐ went out to the mountain to pray;
and he spent the night in prayer to God.
[13]And when day came, he called his disciples and chose twelve of them,
whom he also named apostles:
[14]Simon, whom he named Peter, and his brother Andrew,
and James, and John, and Philip, and Bartholomew,
[15]and Matthew, and Thomas, and James son of Alphaeus,
and Simon, who was called the Zealot,
[16]and Judas son of James, and Judas Iscariot, who became a traitor.

The gospel of the Lord.

GOSPEL　　*Alphaeus = al-FEE-us　Iscariot = is-CAR-ee-ut*
This gospel is so much more than a list. It is a revelation. Reveal each name in turn.

FIRST READING: 1 Samuel 2:1-10

A reading from First Samuel.

¹Hannah prayed and said,

"My heart exults in the LORD;
  my strength is exalted in my God.
My mouth derides my enemies,
  because I rejoice in my victory.

²"There is no Holy One like the LORD,
  no one besides you;
  there is no Rock like our God.
³Talk no more so very proudly,
  let not arrogance come from your mouth;
for the LORD is a God of knowledge,
  and by him actions are weighed.
⁴The bows of the mighty are broken,
  but the feeble gird on strength.
⁵Those who were full have hired themselves out for bread,
  but those who were hungry are fat with spoil.
The barren has borne seven,
  but she who has many children is forlorn.
⁶The LORD kills and brings to life;
  he brings down to Sheol and raises up.
⁷The LORD makes poor and makes rich;
  he brings low, he also exalts.
⁸He raises up the poor from the dust;
  he lifts the needy from the ash heap,
to make them sit with princes
  and inherit a seat of honor.
For the pillars of the earth are the LORD'S,
  and on them he has set the world.

⁹"He will guard the feet of his faithful ones,
  but the wicked shall be cut off in darkness;

FIRST READING   *Sheol = sheh-OHL*
Poems are pictures painted with vowels and consonants. The reader will not only want to consciously slow down in the sharing of this poem with the assembly, but be particularly attentive to the consonants (b, p, t, d) whose distinct enunciation give the reading its color. Carefully clipped consonants that sound exaggerated to the speaker will be heard by the assembly not as exaggeration, but as clarity.

for not by might does one prevail.
¹⁰The LORD! His adversaries shall be shattered;
   the Most High will thunder in heaven.
The LORD will judge the ends of the earth;
   he will give strength to his king,
   and exalt the power of his anointed."

The word of the Lord.   *or*   Word of God, word of life.

PSALMODY: Psalm 113

SECOND READING: Romans 12:9-16b

A reading from Romans.

⁹Let love be genuine;
hate what is evil, hold fast to what is good;
¹⁰love one another with mutual affection;
outdo one another in showing honor.
¹¹Do not lag in zeal, be ardent in spirit, serve the Lord.
¹²Rejoice in hope, be patient in suffering, persevere in prayer.
¹³Contribute to the needs of the saints;
extend hospitality to strangers.

¹⁴Bless those who persecute you; bless and do not curse them.
¹⁵Rejoice with those who rejoice, weep with those who weep.
¹⁶ᵇLive in harmony with one another;
do not be haughty, but associate with the lowly.

The word of the Lord.   *or*   Word of God, word of life.

GOSPEL: Luke 1:39-57

The holy gospel according to Luke.

³⁹In those days Mary set out
and went with haste to a Judean town in the hill country,
⁴⁰where she entered the house of Zechariah and greeted Elizabeth.
⁴¹When Elizabeth heard Mary's greeting, the child leaped in her womb. ▸

SECOND READING
Holy admonition—and a lot of it! Allow each imperative its own space and its own power. Take plenty of time because the author has plenty to say. Here too (as in the first reading), attention to the consonants will pay dividends. "Do not lag in zeal, be ardent in suffering," and similar phrases will be lost if hurried or less than precisely enunciated.

GOSPEL   *Zechariah = zek-uh-RY-uh*
Mary's poem in the gospel both parallels and rivals Hannah's in First Samuel (first reading). The same principles apply. Additionally, the reader would be well advised to insert a solid pause between verses 55 and 56 as well as between verses 56 and 57.

And Elizabeth was filled with the Holy Spirit
[42]and exclaimed with a loud cry,
"Blessed are you among women, and blessed is the fruit of your womb.
[43]And why has this happened to me,
that the mother of my Lord comes to me?
[44]For as soon as I heard the sound of your greeting,
the child in my womb leaped for joy.
[45]And blessed is she who believed
that there would be a fulfillment of what was spoken to her by the Lord."

[46]And Mary said,
    "My soul magnifies the Lord,
        [47]and my spirit rejoices in God my Savior,
    [48]for he has looked with favor on the lowliness of his servant.
        Surely, from now on all generations will call me blessed;
    [49]for the Mighty One has done great things for me,
        and holy is his name.
    [50]His mercy is for those who fear him
        from generation to generation.
    [51]He has shown strength with his arm;
        he has scattered the proud in the thoughts of their hearts.
    [52]He has brought down the powerful from their thrones,
        and lifted up the lowly;
    [53]he has filled the hungry with good things,
        and sent the rich away empty.
    [54]He has helped his servant Israel,
        in remembrance of his mercy,
    [55]according to the promise he made to our ancestors,
        to Abraham and to his descendants forever."

[56]And Mary remained with her about three months
and then returned to her home.

[57]Now the time came for Elizabeth to give birth,
and she bore a son.

The gospel of the Lord.

Barnabas, Apostle

June 11

FIRST READING: Isaiah 42:5-12

A reading from Isaiah.

⁵Thus says God, the LORD,
    who created the heavens and stretched them out,
    who spread out the earth and what comes from it,
who gives breath to the people upon it
    and spirit to those who walk in it:
⁶I am the LORD, I have called you in righteousness,
    I have taken you by the hand and kept you;
I have given you as a covenant to the people,
    a light to the nations,
    ⁷to open the eyes that are blind,
to bring out the prisoners from the dungeon,
    from the prison those who sit in darkness.
⁸I am the LORD, that is my name;
    my glory I give to no other,
    nor my praise to idols.
⁹See, the former things have come to pass,
    and new things I now declare;
before they spring forth,
    I tell you of them.

¹⁰Sing to the LORD a new song,
    his praise from the end of the earth!
Let the sea roar and all that fills it,
    the coastlands and their inhabitants.
¹¹Let the desert and its towns lift up their voice,
    the villages that Kedar inhabits;
let the inhabitants of Sela sing for joy,
    let them shout from the tops of the mountains.
¹²Let them give glory to the LORD,
    and declare his praise in the coastlands.

The word of the Lord.   *or*   Word of God, word of life.

FIRST READING   *Isaiah = eye-ZAY-uh*
The reading calls out for increased volume as it declares both the LORD's name and the LORD's intention and invites God's people to sing and shout! An excellent reading will allow the volume to grow from the text itself. Volume overlaid on the reading for volume's sake will not serve the assembly well.

PSALMODY: Psalm 112

SECOND READING: Acts 11:19-30; 13:1-3

A reading from Acts.

[19]Now those who were scattered
because of the persecution that took place over Stephen
traveled as far as Phoenicia, Cyprus, and Antioch,
and they spoke the word to no one except Jews.
[20]But among them were some men of Cyprus and Cyrene who,
on coming to Antioch, spoke to the Hellenists also,
proclaiming the Lord Jesus.
[21]The hand of the Lord was with them,
and a great number became believers and turned to the Lord.
[22]News of this came to the ears of the church in Jerusalem,
and they sent Barnabas to Antioch.

[23]When he came and saw the grace of God, he rejoiced,
and he exhorted them all
to remain faithful to the Lord with steadfast devotion;
[24]for he was a good man, full of the Holy Spirit and of faith.
And a great many people were brought to the Lord.
[25]Then Barnabas went to Tarsus to look for Saul,
[26]and when he had found him, he brought him to Antioch.
So it was that for an entire year
they met with the church and taught a great many people,
and it was in Antioch that the disciples were first called "Christians."

[27]At that time prophets came down from Jerusalem to Antioch.
[28]One of them named Agabus stood up and predicted by the Spirit
that there would be a severe famine over all the world;
and this took place during the reign of Claudius.
[29]The disciples determined that according to their ability,
each would send relief to the believers living in Judea;
[30]this they did, sending it to the elders by Barnabas and Saul.

[13:1]Now in the church at Antioch there were prophets and teachers:
Barnabas, Simeon who was called Niger,
Lucius of Cyrene, Manaen a member of the court of Herod the ruler,
and Saul.

SECOND READING   *Phoenicia = fuh-NEESH-yuh   Cyrene = sy-REE-nuh   Agabus = AH-guh-bus*
Simeon = SIM-ee-un   Niger = NY-ger   Lucius = LOO-shus   Manaen = MAN-ih-en
This thick narrative detailing the Barnabas story presents a real challenge. It is the reader who brings extra energy to the reading—a genuine enthusiasm for introducing the assembly to St. Barnabas—who will hold the hearers' attention. Each of the four episodes will productively be introduced by a healthy pause.

²While they were worshiping the Lord and fasting,
the Holy Spirit said,
"Set apart for me Barnabas and Saul
for the work to which I have called them."
³Then after fasting and praying
they laid their hands on them and sent them off.

The word of the Lord.   *or*   Word of God, word of life.

GOSPEL: Matthew 10:7-16

The holy gospel according to Matthew.

⌐Jesus said to the twelve:⌐
⁷"As you go, proclaim the good news,
'The kingdom of heaven has come near.'
⁸Cure the sick, raise the dead, cleanse the lepers, cast out demons.
You received without payment; give without payment.
⁹Take no gold, or silver, or copper in your belts,
¹⁰no bag for your journey, or two tunics, or sandals, or a staff;
for laborers deserve their food.

¹¹"Whatever town or village you enter, find out who in it is worthy,
and stay there until you leave.
¹²As you enter the house, greet it.
¹³If the house is worthy, let your peace come upon it;
but if it is not worthy, let your peace return to you.
¹⁴If anyone will not welcome you or listen to your words,
shake off the dust from your feet as you leave that house or town.
¹⁵Truly I tell you,
it will be more tolerable for the land of Sodom and Gomorrah
on the day of judgment than for that town.

¹⁶"See, I am sending you out like sheep into the midst of wolves;
so be wise as serpents and innocent as doves."

The gospel of the Lord.

GOSPEL   *Gomorrah = guh-MOR-uh*
A rising sense of excitement at the outset of this apostolic mission might well build from verses 7 to 15. The instructions are somewhat disjointed and will sound more genuine if interspersed with appropriate pauses. Verse 16 will most effectively stand by itself and have the sound of the dire warning which it is.

JOHN THE BAPTIST

FIRST READING: Malachi 3:1-4

A reading from Malachi.

¹See, I am sending my messenger to prepare the way before me,
and the Lord whom you seek will suddenly come to his temple.
The messenger of the covenant in whom you delight—
indeed, he is coming, says the LORD of hosts.
²But who can endure the day of his coming,
and who can stand when he appears?

For he is like a refiner's fire and like fullers' soap;
³he will sit as a refiner and purifier of silver,
and he will purify the descendants of Levi
and refine them like gold and silver,
until they present offerings to the LORD in righteousness.
⁴Then the offering of Judah and Jerusalem will be pleasing to the LORD
as in the days of old and as in former years.

The word of the Lord.   *or*   Word of God, word of life.

PSALMODY: Psalm 141

SECOND READING: Acts 13:13-26

A reading from Acts:

¹³Paul and his companions set sail from Paphos
and came to Perga in Pamphylia.
John, however, left them and returned to Jerusalem;
¹⁴but they went on from Perga and came to Antioch in Pisidia.
And on the sabbath day they went into the synagogue and sat down.
¹⁵After the reading of the law and the prophets,
the officials of the synagogue sent them a message, saying,
"Brothers, if you have any word of exhortation for the people, give it."

FIRST READING   *Malachi = MAL-uh-ky   Levi = LEE-vy*
In Matthew 11:10, Jesus uses the first line of this text to identify John the Baptizer, whose birth is commemorated by the church today. The prophet's point is that the coming of the Messiah will be a day of defining and refining. It will force the children of God to "clean up their act." This text demands the sound of an important warning for all who hear it.

[16]So Paul stood up and with a gesture began to speak:
"You Israelites, and others who fear God, listen.
[17]The God of this people Israel chose our ancestors
and made the people great during their stay in the land of Egypt,
and with uplifted arm he led them out of it.
[18]For about forty years he put up with them in the wilderness.
[19]After he had destroyed seven nations in the land of Canaan,
he gave them their land as an inheritance
[20]for about four hundred fifty years.
After that he gave them judges until the time of the prophet Samuel.
[21]Then they asked for a king;
and God gave them Saul son of Kish, a man of the tribe of Benjamin,
who reigned for forty years.
[22]When he had removed him, he made David their king.
In his testimony about him he said,
'I have found David, son of Jesse, to be a man after my heart,
who will carry out all my wishes.'
[23]Of this man's posterity God has brought to Israel a Savior,
Jesus, as he promised;
[24]before his coming John had already proclaimed a baptism of repentance
to all the people of Israel.
[25]And as John was finishing his work, he said,
'What do you suppose that I am? I am not he.
No, but one is coming after me;
I am not worthy to untie the thong of the sandals on his feet.'

[26]"My brothers, you descendants of Abraham's family,
and others who fear God,
to us the message of this salvation has been sent."

The word of the Lord.   *or*   Word of God, word of life.

SECOND READING   *Paphos = PA-fus*   *Pamphylia = pam-FIL-yuh*   *Pisidia = pih-SID-yuh*
synagogue = SIN-uh-gog
Paul's quick summary of the history of God's relationship with God's people leads him to the conclusion that
through Jesus, whom John the Baptist proclaimed and extolled, "the message of salvation" has been sent
to humankind. The reading should build to that grand conclusion in verse 26. Bring lots of energy and joy to
this recital of the love of God for God's chosen.

GOSPEL: Luke 1:57-67 [68-80]

The holy gospel according to Luke.

⁵⁷Now the time came for Elizabeth to give birth, and she bore a son.
⁵⁸Her neighbors and relatives heard
that the Lord had shown his great mercy to her,
and they rejoiced with her.

⁵⁹On the eighth day they came to circumcise the child,
and they were going to name him Zechariah after his father.
⁶⁰But his mother said, "No; he is to be called John."
⁶¹They said to her, "None of your relatives has this name."
⁶²Then they began motioning to his father
to find out what name he wanted to give him.
⁶³He asked for a writing tablet and wrote,
"His name is John."
And all of them were amazed.
⁶⁴Immediately his mouth was opened and his tongue freed,
and he began to speak, praising God.
⁶⁵Fear came over all their neighbors,
and all these things were talked about
throughout the entire hill country of Judea.
⁶⁶All who heard them pondered them and said,
"What then will this child become?"
For, indeed, the hand of the Lord was with him.

⁶⁷Then his father Zechariah was filled with the Holy Spirit
and spoke this prophecy:
　　[⁶⁸"Blessed be the Lord God of Israel,
　　　　for he has looked favorably on his people and redeemed them.
　　⁶⁹He has raised up a mighty savior for us
　　　　in the house of his servant David,
　　⁷⁰as he spoke through the mouth of his holy prophets from of old,
　　　　⁷¹that we would be saved from our enemies
　　　　　　and from the hand of all who hate us.
　　⁷²Thus he has shown the mercy promised to our ancestors,
　　　　and has remembered his holy covenant,
　　⁷³the oath that he swore to our ancestor Abraham,
　　　　to grant us ⁷⁴that we, being rescued from the hands of our enemies,

---

GOSPEL　　*Zechariah = zek-uh-RY-uh*
Some advice: resist every inclination to save time and abbreviate the gospel. The story is dramatic. The
song is exquisite. Relish both. Read them with all the joy and wonder they deserve.

might serve him without fear, [75]in holiness and righteousness
    before him all our days.

[76]"And you, child, will be called the prophet of the Most High;
    for you will go before the Lord to prepare his ways,
[77]to give knowledge of salvation to his people
    by the forgiveness of their sins.
[78]By the tender mercy of our God,
    the dawn from on high will break upon us,
[79]to give light to those who sit in darkness and in the shadow of death,
    to guide our feet into the way of peace."

[80]The child grew and became strong in spirit,
and he was in the wilderness until the day he appeared publicly to Israel.]

The gospel of the Lord.

✠ PETER AND PAUL, APOSTLES

JUNE 29

FIRST READING: Acts 12:1-11

A reading from Acts.

¹About that time King Herod laid violent hands
upon some who belonged to the church.
²He had James, the brother of John, killed with the sword.
³After he saw that it pleased the Jews,
he proceeded to arrest Peter also.
(This was during the festival of Unleavened Bread.)
⁴When he had seized him, he put him in prison
and handed him over to four squads of soldiers to guard him,
intending to bring him out to the people after the Passover.
⁵While Peter was kept in prison,
the church prayed fervently to God for him.

⁶The very night before Herod was going to bring him out,
Peter, bound with two chains,
was sleeping between two soldiers,
while guards in front of the door
were keeping watch over the prison.
⁷Suddenly an angel of the Lord appeared
and a light shone in the cell.
He tapped Peter on the side and woke him, saying,
"Get up quickly." And the chains fell off his wrists.
⁸The angel said to him,
"Fasten your belt and put on your sandals."
He did so. Then he said to him,
"Wrap your cloak around you and follow me."
⁹Peter went out and followed him;
he did not realize that what was happening with the angel's help was real;
he thought he was seeing a vision.
¹⁰After they had passed the first and the second guard,
they came before the iron gate leading into the city.
It opened for them of its own accord,
and they went outside and walked along a lane,
when suddenly the angel left him.

FIRST READING
At least two themes are present in this reading. It establishes the sort of danger the apostles were in as they witnessed to the risen Christ, and it demonstrates that God's miraculous interventions were not limited to the time before Jesus. By adopting a good story-telling tone, the reader can draw the listeners into this tale, and especially the angel's urgent directions.

¹¹Then Peter came to himself and said,
"Now I am sure that the Lord has sent his angel
and rescued me from the hands of Herod
and from all that the Jewish people were expecting."

The word of the Lord.   *or*   Word of God, word of life.

PSALMODY: Psalm 87:1-3, 5-7

SECOND READING: 2 Timothy 4:6-8, 17-18

A reading from Second Timothy.

⁶As for me, I am already being poured out as a libation,
and the time of my departure has come.
⁷I have fought the good fight,
I have finished the race, I have kept the faith.
⁸From now on there is reserved for me the crown of righteousness,
which the Lord, the righteous judge, will give me on that day,
and not only to me but also to all who have longed for his appearing.

¹⁷But the Lord stood by me and gave me strength,
so that through me the message might be fully proclaimed
and all the Gentiles might hear it.
So I was rescued from the lion's mouth.
¹⁸The Lord will rescue me from every evil attack
and save me for his heavenly kingdom.
To him be the glory forever and ever. Amen.

The word of the Lord.   *or*   Word of God, word of life.

SECOND READING
This is meant to be heard as Paul's valedictory farewell address, but it could be applied to Peter or any of the apostles. A sound of serene confidence will convey our shared assurance of God's gracious protection and salvation.

GOSPEL: John 21:15-19

The holy gospel according to John.

[15]When they had finished breakfast,
Jesus said to Simon Peter,
"Simon son of John, do you love me more than these?"
He said to him, "Yes, Lord; you know that I love you."
Jesus said to him, "Feed my lambs."
[16]A second time he said to him,
"Simon son of John, do you love me?"
He said to him, "Yes, Lord; you know that I love you."
Jesus said to him, "Tend my sheep."
[17]He said to him the third time,
"Simon son of John, do you love me?"
Peter felt hurt because he said to him the third time, "Do you love me?"
And he said to him,
"Lord, you know everything; you know that I love you."
Jesus said to him, "Feed my sheep.
[18]Very truly, I tell you, when you were younger,
you used to fasten your own belt and to go wherever you wished.
But when you grow old, you will stretch out your hands,
and someone else will fasten a belt around you
and take you where you do not wish to go."
[19](He said this to indicate the kind of death by which he would glorify God.)
After this he said to him, "Follow me."

The gospel of the Lord.

GOSPEL

Jesus' questioning of Peter is generally seen as a threefold counterpart to Peter's threefold denial just days earlier. Imagine how the dialog might have taken place, and try to recreate that in your reading. Bring increased passion to each of Peter's successive confessions of faith. Stressing Jesus' words "do not wish" will allow resonance with the apostles' captivity and martyrdom. Then perhaps insert a slight pause before the reading's closing words, "Follow me."

Thomas, Apostle

July 3

FIRST READING: Judges 6:36-40

A reading from Judges.

³⁶Gideon said to God,
"In order to see whether you will deliver Israel by my hand, as you have said,
³⁷I am going to lay a fleece of wool on the threshing floor;
if there is dew on the fleece alone, and it is dry on all the ground,
then I shall know that you will deliver Israel by my hand, as you have said."
³⁸And it was so.
When he rose early next morning and squeezed the fleece,
he wrung enough dew from the fleece to fill a bowl with water.

³⁹Then Gideon said to God, "Do not let your anger burn against me,
let me speak one more time;
let me, please, make trial with the fleece just once more;
let it be dry only on the fleece, and on all the ground let there be dew."
⁴⁰And God did so that night.
It was dry on the fleece only, and on all the ground there was dew.

The word of the Lord.   *or*   Word of God, word of life.

PSALMODY: Psalm 136:1-4, 23-26

SECOND READING: Ephesians 4:11-16

A reading from Ephesians.

¹¹The gifts ⌈Christ⌉ gave were that some would be apostles,
some prophets, some evangelists, some pastors and teachers,
¹²to equip the saints for the work of ministry,
for building up the body of Christ,
¹³until all of us come to the unity of the faith
and of the knowledge of the Son of God,
to maturity, to the measure of the full stature of Christ. ▸

FIRST READING   *Gideon = GID-ee-un*
Gideon was, by all accounts, not the sharpest knife in the drawer when God called him. Using some care (and that apparent truth), one might hear and convey some humor in this reading as God's would-be servant struggles with self-doubt.

SECOND READING   *Ephesians = eh-FEE-zhunz*
Map each of these three complicated little sentences mentally for their meaning before attempting to discover their sound. An excellent reading will be preceded by considerable thought.

¹⁴We must no longer be children,
tossed to and fro and blown about by every wind of doctrine,
by people's trickery, by their craftiness in deceitful scheming.
¹⁵But speaking the truth in love,
we must grow up in every way into him who is the head, into Christ,
¹⁶from whom the whole body,
joined and knit together by every ligament with which it is equipped,
as each part is working properly,
promotes the body's growth in building itself up in love.

The word of the Lord.   *or*   Word of God, word of life.

GOSPEL: John 14:1-7

The holy gospel according to John.

⌐Jesus said to the disciples:⌐
¹"Do not let your hearts be troubled.
Believe in God, believe also in me.
²In my Father's house there are many dwelling places.
If it were not so, would I have told you that I go to prepare a place for you?
³And if I go and prepare a place for you,
I will come again and will take you to myself,
so that where I am, there you may be also.
⁴And you know the way to the place where I am going."

⁵Thomas said to him, "Lord, we do not know where you are going.
How can we know the way?"
⁶Jesus said to him, "I am the way, and the truth, and the life.
No one comes to the Father except through me.
⁷If you know me, you will know my Father also.
From now on you do know him and have seen him."

The gospel of the Lord.

GOSPEL
While every reading has more than one legitimate and helpful shape, the reader of this text might wish to consider rendering our Lord's reply—"I AM . . . the way . . . and the truth . . . and the life"—in concert with evangelist's emphasis on that name throughout the gospel.

Mary Magdalene, Apostle

July 22

FIRST READING: Ruth 1:6-18

Or Exodus 2:1-10, following

A reading from Ruth:

⁶⌐Naomi⌐ started to return with her daughters-in-law ⌐Orpah and Ruth⌐
from the country of Moab,
for she had heard in the country of Moab
that the LORD had considered his people
and given them food.
⁷So she set out from the place where she had been living,
she and her two daughters-in-law,
and they went on their way to go back to the land of Judah.
⁸But Naomi said to her two daughters-in-law,
"Go back each of you to your mother's house.
May the LORD deal kindly with you,
as you have dealt with the dead and with me.
⁹The LORD grant that you may find security,
each of you in the house of your husband."
Then she kissed them, and they wept aloud.

¹⁰They said to her, "No, we will return with you to your people."
¹¹But Naomi said,
"Turn back, my daughters, why will you go with me?
Do I still have sons in my womb that they may become your husbands?
¹²Turn back, my daughters, go your way,
for I am too old to have a husband.
Even if I thought there was hope for me,
even if I should have a husband tonight and bear sons,
¹³would you then wait until they were grown?
Would you then refrain from marrying?
No, my daughters, it has been far more bitter for me than for you,
because the hand of the LORD has turned against me."

¹⁴Then they wept aloud again.
Orpah kissed her mother-in-law, but Ruth clung to her. ▸

FIRST READING (Ruth)   *Moab = MO-ab*
The faithful tenacity of Ruth parallels that of Mary Magdalene whom the church commemorates and about whom the gospel will speak. It is a profound story of love and loyalty. Ruth's song of faithfulness ("Do not press me to leave you . . . ") is among some of the most beautiful of scripture. Pour yourself into this lesson. Give the reading all you've got!

¹⁵So she said,
"See, your sister-in-law has gone back to her people and to her gods;
return after your sister-in-law."
¹⁶But Ruth said,
"Do not press me to leave you
or to turn back from following you!
Where you go, I will go;
where you lodge, I will lodge;
your people shall be my people,
and your God my God.
¹⁷Where you die, I will die—
there will I be buried.
May the LORD do thus and so to me,
and more as well,
if even death parts me from you!"
¹⁸When Naomi saw that she was determined to go with her,
she said no more to her.

The word of the Lord.   *or*   Word of God, word of life.

OR: Exodus 2:1-10

A reading from Exodus.

¹Now a man from the house of Levi went and married a Levite woman.
²The woman conceived and bore a son;
and when she saw that he was a fine baby, she hid him three months.
³When she could hide him no longer she got a papyrus basket for him,
and plastered it with bitumen and pitch;
she put the child in it and placed it among the reeds on the bank of the river.
⁴His sister stood at a distance, to see what would happen to him.

⁵The daughter of Pharaoh came down to bathe at the river,
while her attendants walked beside the river.
She saw the basket among the reeds and sent her maid to bring it.
⁶When she opened it, she saw the child.
He was crying, and she took pity on him.
"This must be one of the Hebrews' children," she said.
⁷Then his sister said to Pharaoh's daughter,
"Shall I go and get you a nurse from the Hebrew women
to nurse the child for you?"

FIRST READING (Exodus)   *Levi = LEE-vy   Pharaoh = FAIR-oh*
It is the tenderness and attentiveness of the Pharaoh's daughter, Moses' sister, and Moses' mother that finds a parallel in Mary Magdalene's Easter morning pursuit of the Savior. Share the story softly and tenderly.

⁸Pharaoh's daughter said to her, "Yes."
So the girl went and called the child's mother.
⁹Pharaoh's daughter said to her,
"Take this child and nurse it for me, and I will give you your wages."
So the woman took the child and nursed it.

¹⁰When the child grew up, she brought him to Pharaoh's daughter,
and she took him as her son.
She named him Moses, "because," she said,
"I drew him out of the water."

The word of the Lord.   *or*   Word of God, word of life.

PSALMODY: Psalm 73:23-28

SECOND READING: Acts 13:26-33a

A reading from Acts.

²⁶"My brothers, you descendants of Abraham's family,
and others who fear God,
to us the message of this salvation has been sent.
²⁷Because the residents of Jerusalem and their leaders did not recognize him
or understand the words of the prophets that are read every sabbath,
they fulfilled those words by condemning him.
²⁸Even though they found no cause for a sentence of death,
they asked Pilate to have him killed.
²⁹When they had carried out everything that was written about him,
they took him down from the tree and laid him in a tomb.

³⁰"But God raised him from the dead;
³¹and for many days he appeared to those who came up with him
from Galilee to Jerusalem,
and they are now his witnesses to the people.
³²And we bring you the good news that what God promised to our ancestors
³³ᵃhe has fulfilled for us, their children, by raising Jesus."

The word of the Lord.   *or*   Word of God, word of life.

SECOND READING
This Acts text is something of a mini-sermon. Preach it, brother! Preach it, sister! Notice the "reader's job description" hidden in this reading: "We bring you the good news that what God promised to our ancestors he has fulfilled for us, their children, by raising Jesus."

GOSPEL: John 20:1-2, 11-18

The holy gospel according to John.

[1]Early on the first day of the week, while it was still dark,
Mary Magdalene came to the tomb
and saw that the stone had been removed from the tomb.
[2]So she ran and went to Simon Peter and the other disciple,
the one whom Jesus loved, and said to them,
"They have taken the Lord out of the tomb,
and we do not know where they have laid him."

[11]Mary stood weeping outside the tomb.
As she wept, she bent over to look into the tomb;
[12]and she saw two angels in white,
sitting where the body of Jesus had been lying,
one at the head and the other at the feet.
[13]They said to her, "Woman, why are you weeping?"
She said to them,
"They have taken away my Lord,
and I do not know where they have laid him."
[14]When she had said this, she turned around and saw Jesus standing there,
but she did not know that it was Jesus.
[15]Jesus said to her,
"Woman, why are you weeping? Whom are you looking for?"
Supposing him to be the gardener, she said to him,
"Sir, if you have carried him away, tell me where you have laid him,
and I will take him away."

[16]Jesus said to her, "Mary!"
She turned and said to him in Hebrew,
"Rabbouni!" (which means Teacher).
[17]Jesus said to her,
"Do not hold on to me, because I have not yet ascended to the Father.
But go to my brothers and say to them,
'I am ascending to my Father and your Father, to my God and your God.' "
[18]Mary Magdalene went and announced to the disciples,
"I have seen the Lord";
and she told them that he had said these things to her.

The gospel of the Lord.

GOSPEL
Verse 2b is very nearly repeated word for word in verse 13b. Verse 13a is repeated in verse 15a. The differences in the words' delivery need to be established by the context and the speaker. Take time to sit with the text in preparing the reading. Attempt to "hear it" before attempting to "voice it."

FIRST READING: 1 Kings 19:9-18

A reading from First Kings.

⁹At Horeb, the mount of God,
⌈Elijah⌉ came to a cave, and spent the night there.
Then the word of the LORD came to him, saying,
"What are you doing here, Elijah?"
¹⁰He answered, "I have been very zealous for the LORD, the God of hosts;
for the Israelites have forsaken your covenant, thrown down your altars,
and killed your prophets with the sword.
I alone am left, and they are seeking my life, to take it away."
¹¹He said, "Go out and stand on the mountain before the LORD,
for the LORD is about to pass by."

Now there was a great wind, so strong that it was splitting mountains
and breaking rocks in pieces before the LORD,
but the LORD was not in the wind;
and after the wind an earthquake,
but the LORD was not in the earthquake;
¹²and after the earthquake a fire,
but the LORD was not in the fire;
and after the fire a sound of sheer silence.
¹³When Elijah heard it, he wrapped his face in his mantle
and went out and stood at the entrance of the cave.

Then there came a voice to him that said,
"What are you doing here, Elijah?"
¹⁴He answered,
"I have been very zealous for the LORD, the God of hosts;
for the Israelites have forsaken your covenant, thrown down your altars,
and killed your prophets with the sword.
I alone am left, and they are seeking my life, to take it away."
¹⁵Then the LORD said to him,
"Go, return on your way to the wilderness of Damascus;
when you arrive, you shall anoint Hazael as king over Aram.
¹⁶Also you shall anoint Jehu son of Nimshi as king over Israel; ▸

FIRST READING   *Hazael = HAY-zih-el   Aram = AIR-um   Jehu = JEE-hoo   Nimshi = NIM-she*
Shaphat = SHAH-fut   Abel-meholah = aye-bul-muh-HO-luh
The authoritative voice of God contrasts in both episodes recorded here with the despair in the voice of the prophet. Consider a quieter, smaller voice for verse 11 than the directive voice of verses 15–18. Consider as well a great, dramatic pause following verse 12 to allow the "sound of sheer silence" to settle over the assembly.

and you shall anoint Elisha son of Shaphat of Abel-meholah
as prophet in your place.
¹⁷Whoever escapes from the sword of Hazael, Jehu shall kill;
and whoever escapes from the sword of Jehu, Elisha shall kill.
¹⁸Yet I will leave seven thousand in Israel,
all the knees that have not bowed to Baal,
and every mouth that has not kissed him."

The word of the Lord.   *or*   Word of God, word of life.

PSALMODY: Psalm 7:1-10

SECOND READING: Acts 11:27—12:3a

A reading from Acts.

²⁷At that time ⌐when Barnabas and Saul were in Antioch,⌐
prophets came down from Jerusalem to Antioch.
²⁸One of them named Agabus stood up and predicted by the Spirit
that there would be a severe famine over all the world;
and this took place during the reign of Claudius.
²⁹The disciples determined that according to their ability,
each would send relief to the believers living in Judea;
this they did, sending it to the elders by Barnabas and Saul.

¹²:¹About that time
King Herod laid violent hands upon some who belonged to the church.
²He had James, the brother of John, killed with the sword.
³ᵃAfter he saw that it pleased the Jews, he proceeded to arrest Peter also.

The word of the Lord.   *or*   Word of God, word of life.

SECOND READING   *Agabus = AH-guh-bus*
This reading is included because verse 12:2 records the martyrdom of St. James. Verses 27–29 set the time frame. Build to verse 12:2. Allow verse 12:3 to stand as a quietly understated but sorrowful afterthought.

GOSPEL: Mark 10:35-45

The holy gospel according to Mark.

[35]James and John, the sons of Zebedee,
came forward to ⌈Jesus⌉ and said to him,
 "Teacher, we want you to do for us whatever we ask of you."
[36]And he said to them, "What is it you want me to do for you?"
[37]And they said to him,
"Grant us to sit, one at your right hand and one at your left, in your glory."
[38]But Jesus said to them,
"You do not know what you are asking.
Are you able to drink the cup that I drink,
or be baptized with the baptism that I am baptized with?"
[39]They replied, "We are able."
Then Jesus said to them,
"The cup that I drink you will drink;
and with the baptism with which I am baptized, you will be baptized;
[40]but to sit at my right hand or at my left is not mine to grant,
but it is for those for whom it has been prepared."

[41]When the ten heard this, they began to be angry with James and John.
[42]So Jesus called them and said to them,
"You know that among the Gentiles
those whom they recognize as their rulers lord it over them,
and their great ones are tyrants over them.
[43]But it is not so among you;
but whoever wishes to become great among you must be your servant,
[44]and whoever wishes to be first among you must be slave of all.
[45]For the Son of Man came not to be served but to serve,
and to give his life a ransom for many."

The gospel of the Lord.

GOSPEL   *Zebedee = ZEB-eh-dee*
There is a certain irony that the gospel appointed for the commemoration of St. James contains a story that presents him in such an unflattering light. That might inform the tone of the reading. James's longing is one to which we are easily able to relate. Allow the voice of Jesus to love the misdirected apostle and all those who are within the sound of his voice.

FIRST READING: Isaiah 61:7-11

A reading from Isaiah.

⁷Because their shame was double,
  and dishonor was proclaimed as their lot,
therefore they shall possess a double portion;
  everlasting joy shall be theirs.

⁸For I the LORD love justice,
  I hate robbery and wrongdoing;
I will faithfully give them their recompense,
  and I will make an everlasting covenant with them.
⁹Their descendants shall be known among the nations,
  and their offspring among the peoples;
all who see them shall acknowledge
  that they are a people whom the LORD has blessed.
¹⁰I will greatly rejoice in the LORD,
  my whole being shall exult in my God;
for he has clothed me with the garments of salvation,
  he has covered me with the robe of righteousness,
as a bridegroom decks himself with a garland,
  and as a bride adorns herself with her jewels.
¹¹For as the earth brings forth its shoots,
  and as a garden causes what is sown in it to spring up,
so the Lord GOD will cause righteousness and praise
  to spring up before all the nations.

The word of the Lord.   *or*   Word of God, word of life.

PSALMODY: Psalm 34:1-9

FIRST READING   *Isaiah = eye-ZAY-uh*
Today, we hear God's promises to all those who suffer injustice as explicitly applicable to the virgin Mary. Verses 7–9 come from the promising voice of God. Verses 10–11 come from the voice of the one richly blessed. (Notice how verse 10 anticipates the Magnificat, the song of Mary that is recorded in the gospel.) The words of blessing should carry a tone of authority. The words of the one blessed ought to be characterized by great joy.

SECOND READING: Galatians 4:4-7

A reading from Galatians.

⁴When the fullness of time had come,
God sent his Son, born of a woman, born under the law,
⁵in order to redeem those who were under the law,
so that we might receive adoption as children.
⁶And because you are children,
God has sent the Spirit of his Son into our hearts,
crying, "Abba! Father!"
⁷So you are no longer a slave but a child,
and if a child then also an heir, through God.

The word of the Lord.   *or*   Word of God, word of life.

GOSPEL: Luke 1:46-55

The holy gospel according to Luke.

⁴⁶Mary said,
"My soul magnifies the Lord,
    ⁴⁷and my spirit rejoices in God my Savior,
⁴⁸for he has looked with favor on the lowliness of his servant.
    Surely, from now on all generations will call me blessed;
⁴⁹for the Mighty One has done great things for me,
    and holy is his name.
⁵⁰His mercy is for those who fear him
    from generation to generation.
⁵¹He has shown strength with his arm;
    he has scattered the proud in the thoughts of their hearts.
⁵²He has brought down the powerful from their thrones,
    and lifted up the lowly;
⁵³he has filled the hungry with good things,
    and sent the rich away empty.
⁵⁴He has helped his servant Israel,
    in remembrance of his mercy,
⁵⁵according to the promise he made to our ancestors,
    to Abraham and to his descendants forever."

The gospel of the Lord.

SECOND READING   *Galatians = guh-LAY-shuns   Abba = AH-buh*
"God sent his Son, born of a woman" (Mary, mother of our Lord!) to redeem us and adopt us as God's own. Because we have become God's children we may address Almighty God with a child's affectionate nickname ("Abba" = Daddy!). The final verse summarizes this wonderful reality and requires a voice of great conviction.

GOSPEL
Familiarity breeds . . . caution in the careful reader. Rediscover the wonder of the words of Mary's song. Use it devotionally in the days before the celebration. Help the hearer sense Mary's ecstatic reaction again—for the first time.

BARTHOLOMEW, APOSTLE

AUGUST 24

FIRST READING: Exodus 19:1-6

A reading from Exodus.

¹On the third new moon
after the Israelites had gone out of the land of Egypt,
on that very day, they came into the wilderness of Sinai.
²They had journeyed from Rephidim, entered the wilderness of Sinai,
and camped in the wilderness;
Israel camped there in front of the mountain.
³Then Moses went up to God;
the LORD called to him from the mountain, saying,
"Thus you shall say to the house of Jacob, and tell the Israelites:
⁴You have seen what I did to the Egyptians,
and how I bore you on eagles' wings and brought you to myself.
⁵Now therefore, if you obey my voice and keep my covenant,
you shall be my treasured possession out of all the peoples.
Indeed, the whole earth is mine,
⁶but you shall be for me a priestly kingdom and a holy nation.
These are the words that you shall speak to the Israelites."

The word of the Lord.   *or*   Word of God, word of life.

PSALMODY: Psalm 12

SECOND READING: 1 Corinthians 12:27-31a

A reading from First Corinthians.

²⁷Now you are the body of Christ and individually members of it.
²⁸And God has appointed in the church first apostles,
second prophets, third teachers;
then deeds of power, then gifts of healing,
forms of assistance, forms of leadership,
various kinds of tongues.

FIRST READING   *Israelites = IS-rul-eytz   Rephidim = REF-ih-dim   Sinai = SY-ny*
In six succinct verses, God's particular affection for Israel finds expression. This is a powerful statement of election and love. It calls for the sound of both power and affection.

SECOND READING
Lists can present problems for the reader, but they need not. Rather than "rattling them off," take adequate time to consider the variety of gifts and the order in which the author places them. Allow the rhetorical questions to hang in the air a while. Pause, perhaps, before urging the hearer to "strive."

²⁹Are all apostles? Are all prophets? Are all teachers?
Do all work miracles? Do all possess gifts of healing?
³⁰Do all speak in tongues? Do all interpret?
^{31a}But strive for the greater gifts.

The word of the Lord.   *or*   Word of God, word of life.

GOSPEL: John 1:43-51

The holy gospel according to John.

⁴³The next day Jesus decided to go to Galilee.
He found Philip and said to him, "Follow me."
⁴⁴Now Philip was from Bethsaida, the city of Andrew and Peter.
⁴⁵Philip found Nathanael and said to him,
"We have found him
about whom Moses in the law and also the prophets wrote,
Jesus son of Joseph from Nazareth."
⁴⁶Nathanael said to him, "Can anything good come out of Nazareth?"
Philip said to him, "Come and see."

⁴⁷When Jesus saw Nathanael coming toward him, he said of him,
"Here is truly an Israelite in whom there is no deceit!"
⁴⁸Nathanael asked him, "Where did you get to know me?"
Jesus answered, "I saw you under the fig tree before Philip called you."
⁴⁹Nathanael replied,
"Rabbi, you are the Son of God! You are the King of Israel!"
⁵⁰Jesus answered,
"Do you believe because I told you that I saw you under the fig tree?
You will see greater things than these."
⁵¹And he said to him,
"Very truly, I tell you, you will see heaven opened
and the angels of God ascending and descending upon the Son of Man."

The gospel of the Lord.

GOSPEL   *Bethsaida = beth-SAY-ih-duh*
Give the gospel enough room to develop, the story enough time to unfold. Allow verse 44 to stand by itself.
Pause between Nathanael's skepticism and Philip's invitation. Pause between verses 46 and 47. (Let them
catch up to Jesus!) There may well be an understated affection in Jesus' words in verse 50. He may even be
teasing Nathanael a bit there in contrast to the pure promise of verse 51.

HOLY CROSS DAY
SEPTEMBER 14

FIRST READING: Numbers 21:4b-9

A reading from Numbers.

⌜From Mount Hor the Israelites set out,⌝
⁴ᵇbut the people became impatient on the way.
⁵The people spoke against God and against Moses,
"Why have you brought us up out of Egypt to die in the wilderness?
For there is no food and no water, and we detest this miserable food."
⁶Then the LORD sent poisonous serpents among the people,
and they bit the people, so that many Israelites died.

⁷The people came to Moses and said,
"We have sinned by speaking against the LORD and against you;
pray to the LORD to take away the serpents from us."
So Moses prayed for the people.
⁸And the LORD said to Moses,
"Make a poisonous serpent, and set it on a pole;
and everyone who is bitten shall look at it and live."
⁹So Moses made a serpent of bronze, and put it upon a pole;
and whenever a serpent bit someone,
that person would look at the serpent of bronze and live.

The word of the Lord.   *or*   Word of God, word of life.

PSALMODY: Psalm 98:1-4 or Psalm 78:1-2, 34-38

SECOND READING: 1 Corinthians 1:18-24

A reading from First Corinthians.

¹⁸The message about the cross is foolishness to those who are perishing,
but to us who are being saved it is the power of God.
¹⁹For it is written,
    "I will destroy the wisdom of the wise,
        and the discernment of the discerning I will thwart."

FIRST READING
Haste will lay this text waste. Take some time. A significant amount of time elapses in these five and a half verses. Pick the pauses with care. Use them to good effect. Consider pauses between verses 4b and 5, 5 and 6, 6 and 7, 7a and 7b, 7b and 8, 8 and 9. It will not prove too much.

SECOND READING
This is an apostolic "one-two punch" if ever there was one. Let 'em have it. "Christ crucified!" It's the gospel truth.

²⁰Where is the one who is wise?
Where is the scribe?
Where is the debater of this age?
Has not God made foolish the wisdom of the world?

²¹For since, in the wisdom of God,
the world did not know God through wisdom,
God decided, through the foolishness of our proclamation,
to save those who believe.
²²For Jews demand signs and Greeks desire wisdom,
²³but we proclaim Christ crucified,
a stumbling block to Jews and foolishness to Gentiles,
²⁴but to those who are the called, both Jews and Greeks,
Christ the power of God and the wisdom of God.

The word of the Lord.　　　　*or*　　　　Word of God, word of life.

GOSPEL: John 3:13-17

The holy gospel according to John.

⌜Jesus said:⌝
¹³"No one has ascended into heaven
except the one who descended from heaven,
the Son of Man.
¹⁴And just as Moses lifted up the serpent in the wilderness,
so must the Son of Man be lifted up,
¹⁵that whoever believes in him may have eternal life.

¹⁶"For God so loved the world that he gave his only Son,
so that everyone who believes in him may not perish
but may have eternal life.
¹⁷Indeed, God did not send the Son into the world to condemn the world,
but in order that the world might be saved through him."

The gospel of the Lord.

GOSPEL
Take care not to "recite" verse 16. Take care not to "spotlight" it. Keep it in the context of our Lord's larger statement.

MATTHEW, APOSTLE AND EVANGELIST
SEPTEMBER 21

FIRST READING: Ezekiel 2:8—3:11

A reading from Ezekiel.

⁸You, mortal, hear what I say to you;
do not be rebellious like that rebellious house;
open your mouth and eat what I give you.
⁹I looked, and a hand was stretched out to me,
and a written scroll was in it.
¹⁰He spread it before me;
it had writing on the front and on the back,
and written on it were words of lamentation and mourning and woe.

^{3:1}He said to me, O mortal, eat what is offered to you;
eat this scroll, and go, speak to the house of Israel.
²So I opened my mouth, and he gave me the scroll to eat.
³He said to me, Mortal, eat this scroll that I give you
and fill your stomach with it.
Then I ate it; and in my mouth it was as sweet as honey.

⁴He said to me: Mortal, go to the house of Israel
and speak my very words to them.
⁵For you are not sent to a people of obscure speech and difficult language,
but to the house of Israel—
⁶not to many peoples of obscure speech and difficult language,
whose words you cannot understand.
Surely, if I sent you to them, they would listen to you.
⁷But the house of Israel will not listen to you,
for they are not willing to listen to me;
because all the house of Israel have a hard forehead and a stubborn heart.
⁸See, I have made your face hard against their faces,
and your forehead hard against their foreheads.
⁹Like the hardest stone, harder than flint, I have made your forehead;
do not fear them or be dismayed at their looks,
for they are a rebellious house.

FIRST READING   *Ezekiel = eh-ZEEK-ee-el*
The well-prepared reader will want to pull out all the stops for this reading. But preparation will take some time and some considerable rehearsal. It is God's voice and a frightening vision. The ominous tone of verses 2:8—3:3a should contrast dramatically to the prophet's discovery in verse 3b. The instructions in verses 4–11 can build in intensity and volume to "'Thus says the Lord GoD,' whether they hear or refuse to hear." A "big" reading that develops from the setting and meaning of the reading will move the assembly.

¹⁰He said to me: Mortal, all my words that I shall speak to you
receive in your heart and hear with your ears;
¹¹then go to the exiles, to your people, and speak to them.
Say to them, "Thus says the Lord GOD";
whether they hear or refuse to hear.

The word of the Lord.   *or*   Word of God, word of life.

PSALMODY: Psalm 119:33-40

SECOND READING: Ephesians 2:4-10

A reading from Ephesians.

⁴God, who is rich in mercy,
out of the great love with which he loved us
⁵even when we were dead through our trespasses,
made us alive together with Christ—
by grace you have been saved—
⁶and raised us up with him
and seated us with him in the heavenly places in Christ Jesus,
⁷so that in the ages to come
he might show the immeasurable riches of his grace
in kindness toward us in Christ Jesus.
⁸For by grace you have been saved through faith,
and this is not your own doing;
it is the gift of God—
⁹not the result of works, so that no one may boast.
¹⁰For we are what he has made us,
created in Christ Jesus for good works,
which God prepared beforehand to be our way of life.

The word of the Lord.   *or*   Word of God, word of life.

SECOND READING   *Ephesians = eh-FEE-zhunz*
The text is rich but the sentences are long and require careful navigation. There is no substitute for practice.
This means reading the text aloud, repeatedly, in preparation for the day of the assembly.

GOSPEL: Matthew 9:9-13

The holy gospel according to Matthew.

⁹As Jesus was walking along,
he saw a man called Matthew sitting at the tax booth;
and he said to him, "Follow me."
And he got up and followed him.

¹⁰And as he sat at dinner in the house,
many tax collectors and sinners came
and were sitting with him and his disciples.
¹¹When the Pharisees saw this, they said to his disciples,
"Why does your teacher eat with tax collectors and sinners?"
¹²But when he heard this, he said,
"Those who are well have no need of a physician,
but those who are sick.
¹³Go and learn what this means,
'I desire mercy, not sacrifice.'
For I have come to call not the righteous but sinners."

The gospel of the Lord.

GOSPEL
Jesus came "to call not the righteous but sinners." Blessed St. Matthew is an apostolic example of that truth.
Bring all the heartfelt intensity at your disposal to the words of Jesus. He meant it. Thanks be to God!

Michael and All Angels

FIRST READING: Daniel 10:10-14; 12:1-3

A reading from Daniel.

¹⁰A hand touched me and roused me to my hands and knees.
¹¹He said to me, "Daniel, greatly beloved,
pay attention to the words that I am going to speak to you.
Stand on your feet, for I have now been sent to you."
So while he was speaking this word to me, I stood up trembling.
¹²He said to me, "Do not fear, Daniel,
for from the first day that you set your mind to gain understanding
and to humble yourself before your God,
your words have been heard, and I have come because of your words.
¹³But the prince of the kingdom of Persia opposed me twenty-one days.
So Michael, one of the chief princes, came to help me,
and I left him there with the prince of the kingdom of Persia,
¹⁴and have come to help you understand what is to happen to your people
at the end of days.
For there is a further vision for those days.

¹²:¹"At that time Michael, the great prince,
the protector of your people, shall arise.
There shall be a time of anguish,
such as has never occurred since nations first came into existence.
But at that time your people shall be delivered,
everyone who is found written in the book.
²Many of those who sleep in the dust of the earth shall awake,
some to everlasting life, and some to shame and everlasting contempt.
³Those who are wise shall shine like the brightness of the sky,
and those who lead many to righteousness,
like the stars forever and ever."

The word of the Lord.   *or*   Word of God, word of life.

FIRST READING
Help the assembly sense Daniel's fear and trembling in verses 10 and 11 as he struggles to stand at the outset of his vision. The prophecy following contains expressions of hope and expressions of doom in equal measure. The voice of the vision must be the voice of authority.

PSALMODY: Psalm 103:1-5, 20-22

SECOND READING: Revelation 12:7-12

A reading from Revelation.

⁷War broke out in heaven;
Michael and his angels fought against the dragon.
The dragon and his angels fought back,
⁸but they were defeated,
and there was no longer any place for them in heaven.
⁹The great dragon was thrown down,
that ancient serpent, who is called the Devil and Satan,
the deceiver of the whole world—
he was thrown down to the earth,
and his angels were thrown down with him.

¹⁰Then I heard a loud voice in heaven, proclaiming,
   "Now have come the salvation and the power
      and the kingdom of our God
      and the authority of his Messiah,
   for the accuser of our comrades has been thrown down,
      who accuses them day and night before our God.
¹¹But they have conquered him by the blood of the Lamb
      and by the word of their testimony,
   for they did not cling to life even in the face of death.
¹²Rejoice then, you heavens
      and those who dwell in them!
   But woe to the earth and the sea,
      for the devil has come down to you
   with great wrath,
      because he knows that his time is short!"

The word of the Lord.   *or*   Word of God, word of life.

SECOND READING
The action here is on a cosmic level and sets the tone for the reading. It is the story of the advent of evil in the world. An expansive reading is called for—one that paints the picture with broad strokes.

GOSPEL: Luke 10:17-20

The holy gospel according to Luke.

¹⁷The seventy returned with joy, saying,
"Lord, in your name even the demons submit to us!"
¹⁸He said to them,
"I watched Satan fall from heaven like a flash of lightning.
¹⁹See, I have given you authority to tread on snakes and scorpions,
and over all the power of the enemy;
and nothing will hurt you.
²⁰Nevertheless, do not rejoice at this,
that the spirits submit to you,
but rejoice that your names are written in heaven."

The gospel of the Lord.

GOSPEL
Set in this context, the gospel clearly suggests that Jesus was a pre-existent eyewitness to the battle described in the second reading. That is something of an eye-opener for the disciples (and the assembly!) and explains in some part his authority over evil. But the real cause for rejoicing is found in the last line of the text. This is pure gospel. Allow the assembled baptized to know that Jesus is speaking about them.

Luke, Evangelist

October 18

FIRST READING: Isaiah 43:8-13

Or Isaiah 35:5-8, following

A reading from Isaiah.

⁸Bring forth the people who are blind, yet have eyes,
  who are deaf, yet have ears!
⁹Let all the nations gather together,
  and let the peoples assemble.
Who among them declared this,
  and foretold to us the former things?
Let them bring their witnesses to justify them,
  and let them hear and say, "It is true."
¹⁰You are my witnesses, says the LORD,
  and my servant whom I have chosen,
so that you may know and believe me
  and understand that I am he.
Before me no god was formed,
  nor shall there be any after me.
¹¹I, I am the LORD,
  and besides me there is no savior.
¹²I declared and saved and proclaimed,
  when there was no strange god among you;
  and you are my witnesses, says the LORD.
¹³I am God, and also henceforth I am He;
  there is no one who can deliver from my hand;
  I work and who can hinder it?

The word of the Lord.   *or*   Word of God, word of life.

OR: Isaiah 35:5-8

A reading from Isaiah.

⁵Then the eyes of the blind shall be opened,
  and the ears of the deaf unstopped;
⁶then the lame shall leap like a deer,

FIRST READING (Isaiah 43)   *Isaiah = eye-ZAY-uh*
Almighty God is taking on all comers in verses 8 and 9—defying any witness to testify against God's sovereignty. Those to whom these words are addressed are witnesses to God's singular divinity. Today we remember St. Luke as God's witness, but a powerful delivery of this text will remind the assembly that we, too, are witnesses to God's saving power. Consider the possibility of delivering the rhetorical question in verse 13b ("who can hinder it?") in a dramatically diminished volume as a means of allowing it to "hang in the air" at the reading's end.

and the tongue of the speechless sing for joy.
For waters shall break forth in the wilderness,
    and streams in the desert;
⁷the burning sand shall become a pool,
    and the thirsty ground springs of water;
the haunt of jackals shall become a swamp,
    the grass shall become reeds and rushes.

⁸A highway shall be there,
    and it shall be called the Holy Way;
the unclean shall not travel on it,
    but it shall be for God's people;
    no traveler, not even fools, shall go astray.

The word of the Lord.   *or*   Word of God, word of life.

PSALMODY: Psalm 124

SECOND READING: 2 Timothy 4:5-11

A reading from Second Timothy.

⁵As for you, always be sober, endure suffering,
do the work of an evangelist, carry out your ministry fully.

⁶As for me, I am already being poured out as a libation,
and the time of my departure has come.
⁷I have fought the good fight, I have finished the race, I have kept the faith.
⁸From now on there is reserved for me the crown of righteousness,
which the Lord, the righteous judge, will give me on that day,
and not only to me but also to all who have longed for his appearing.

⁹Do your best to come to me soon,
¹⁰for Demas, in love with this present world,
has deserted me and gone to Thessalonica;
Crescens has gone to Galatia, Titus to Dalmatia.
¹¹Only Luke is with me.
Get Mark and bring him with you, for he is useful in my ministry.

The word of the Lord.   *or*   Word of God, word of life.

FIRST READING (Isaiah 35)   *Isaiah = eye-ZAY-uh*
The words of verses 5 and 6 have a certain, special poignancy when read on the day of St. Luke, Evangelist (and, by tradition, physician). Here God promises relief and safe passage. It is a hopeful text rich with promise. Do not miss the sassy little twist ("not even fools") at the end of verse 8.

SECOND READING   *Demas = DEE-mus   Thessalonica = thes-uh-loh-NY-kuh   Crescens = CRES-enz
Galatia = guh-LAY-shuh   Dalmatia = dal-MAY-shuh*
In the context of today's commemoration this lesson salutes Luke's faithfulness and encourages every hearer to "do the work of an evangelist." An encouraging, confident, and upbeat sound might be just right.

GOSPEL: Luke 1:1-4; 24:44-53

The holy gospel according to Luke.

⌐Luke writes:⌐
¹Since many have undertaken to set down an orderly account
of the events that have been fulfilled among us,
²just as they were handed on to us
by those who from the beginning were eyewitnesses
and servants of the word,
³I too decided, after investigating everything carefully from the very first,
to write an orderly account for you, most excellent Theophilus,
⁴so that you may know the truth concerning the things
about which you have been instructed.

²⁴:⁴⁴Before he ascended, Jesus said to the disciples and their companions:
"These are my words that I spoke to you while I was still with you—
that everything written about me in the law of Moses,
the prophets, and the psalms must be fulfilled."
⁴⁵Then he opened their minds to understand the scriptures,
⁴⁶and he said to them, "Thus it is written,
that the Messiah is to suffer and to rise from the dead on the third day,
⁴⁷and that repentance and forgiveness of sins is to be proclaimed in his name
to all nations, beginning from Jerusalem.
⁴⁸You are witnesses of these things.
⁴⁹And see, I am sending upon you what my Father promised;
so stay here in the city
until you have been clothed with power from on high."

⁵⁰Then he led them out as far as Bethany,
and, lifting up his hands, he blessed them.
⁵¹While he was blessing them,
he withdrew from them and was carried up into heaven.
⁵²And they worshiped him, and returned to Jerusalem with great joy;
⁵³and they were continually in the temple blessing God.

The gospel of the Lord.

GOSPEL   *Theophilus = thee-OFF-il-us*
The welding of the beginning and the ending of Luke's gospel provides the assembly an opportunity to hear the evangelist's preamble, a summary of the messianic mission fulfilled, and our Lord's apostolic commissioning all at once. Attentive listeners will hear Isaiah's contention echoed in Jesus' words, "You are witnesses of these things." Maintain the encouraging, upbeat tone established in the second reading.

✝ # SIMON AND JUDE, APOSTLES
OCTOBER 28

FIRST READING: Jeremiah 26:[1-6] 7-16

A reading from Jeremiah.

[¹At the beginning of the reign of King Jehoiakim son of Josiah of Judah,
this word came from the LORD:
²Thus says the LORD:
Stand in the court of the LORD'S house,
and speak to all the cities of Judah
that come to worship in the house of the LORD;
speak to them all the words that I command you;
do not hold back a word.
³It may be that they will listen, all of them,
and will turn from their evil way,
that I may change my mind about the disaster
that I intend to bring on them because of their evil doings.
⁴You shall say to them:
Thus says the LORD: If you will not listen to me,
to walk in my law that I have set before you,
⁵and to heed the words of my servants the prophets
whom I send to you urgently—
though you have not heeded—
⁶then I will make this house like Shiloh,
and I will make this city a curse for all the nations of the earth.]

⁷The priests and the prophets and all the people
heard Jeremiah speaking these words in the house of the LORD.
⁸And when Jeremiah had finished speaking
all that the LORD had commanded him to speak to all the people,
then the priests and the prophets and all the people laid hold of him,
saying, "You shall die!
⁹Why have you prophesied in the name of the LORD, saying,
'This house shall be like Shiloh,
and this city shall be desolate, without inhabitant'?"
And all the people gathered around Jeremiah in the house of the LORD. ▶

FIRST READING   *Jeremiah = jehr-eh-MY-uh   Jehoiakim = jeh-HOY-uh-kim   Josiah = joh-SY-uh*
The word from the Lord, spoken by the prophet Jeremiah, is a blunt and threatening word. It is not well received by the priests and other "prophets-for-hire." Interestingly it is the "people in the pew" who recognize the word as genuine and call on the religious leaders to spare Jeremiah's life. It is a "big"—dramatic—story that demands a big reading. Bring it to life by bringing some real energy to the reading.

¹⁰When the officials of Judah heard these things,
they came up from the king's house to the house of the LORD
and took their seat in the entry of the New Gate of the house of the LORD.
¹¹Then the priests and the prophets said to the officials and to all the people,
"This man deserves the sentence of death
because he has prophesied against this city,
as you have heard with your own ears."

¹²Then Jeremiah spoke to all the officials and all the people, saying,
"It is the LORD who sent me to prophesy
against this house and this city all the words you have heard.
¹³Now therefore amend your ways and your doings,
and obey the voice of the LORD your God,
and the LORD will change his mind about the disaster
that he has pronounced against you.
¹⁴But as for me, here I am in your hands.
Do with me as seems good and right to you.
¹⁵Only know for certain that if you put me to death,
you will be bringing innocent blood upon yourselves
and upon this city and its inhabitants,
for in truth the LORD sent me to you to speak all these words in your ears."

¹⁶Then the officials and all the people said to the priests and the prophets,
"This man does not deserve the sentence of death,
for he has spoken to us in the name of the LORD our God."

The word of the Lord.   *or*   Word of God, word of life.

PSALMODY: Psalm 11

SECOND READING: 1 John 4:1-6

A reading from First John.

¹Beloved, do not believe every spirit,
but test the spirits to see whether they are from God;
for many false prophets have gone out into the world.
²By this you know the Spirit of God:
every spirit that confesses that Jesus Christ has come in the flesh is from God,
³and every spirit that does not confess Jesus is not from God.
And this is the spirit of the antichrist,

SECOND READING
These are instructions (the kind needed in the first reading) on how to discern between the word of the false prophet and the word of the genuine article. The counsel needs to sound firm but loving.

of which you have heard that it is coming;
and now it is already in the world.

⁴Little children, you are from God, and have conquered them;
for the one who is in you is greater than the one who is in the world.
⁵They are from the world;
therefore what they say is from the world, and the world listens to them.

⁶We are from God.
Whoever knows God listens to us,
and whoever is not from God does not listen to us.
From this we know the spirit of truth and the spirit of error.

The word of the Lord.   *or*   Word of God, word of life.

GOSPEL: John 14:21-27

The holy gospel according to John.

⌐Jesus said to the disciples:⌐
²¹"They who have my commandments and keep them
are those who love me;
and those who love me will be loved by my Father,
and I will love them and reveal myself to them."
²²Judas (not Iscariot) said to him,
"Lord, how is it that you will reveal yourself to us, and not to the world?"
²³Jesus answered him,
"Those who love me will keep my word, and my Father will love them,
and we will come to them and make our home with them.
²⁴Whoever does not love me does not keep my words;
and the word that you hear is not mine, but is from the Father who sent me.

²⁵"I have said these things to you while I am still with you.
²⁶But the Advocate, the Holy Spirit, whom the Father will send in my name,
will teach you everything,
and remind you of all that I have said to you.
²⁷Peace I leave with you; my peace I give to you.
I do not give to you as the world gives.
Do not let your hearts be troubled, and do not let them be afraid."

The gospel of the Lord.

GOSPEL   *Iscariot = is-CAR-ee-ut*
This little enigmatic lesson in verses 21–24 underscores the need for the instructive, promised Spirit of God.
One can almost see several quizzical faces among the twelve. Pauses between verses 24 and 25, verses 26
and 27, and between the second and third sentences of verse 27 will amplify the words' beauty and their
innate tenderness.

REFORMATION DAY
OCTOBER 31

FIRST READING: Jeremiah 31:31-34

A reading from Jeremiah.

³¹The days are surely coming, says the LORD,
when I will make a new covenant
with the house of Israel and the house of Judah.
³²It will not be like the covenant that I made with their ancestors
when I took them by the hand to bring them out of the land of Egypt—
a covenant that they broke, though I was their husband, says the LORD.

³³But this is the covenant that I will make with the house of Israel
after those days, says the LORD:
I will put my law within them,
and I will write it on their hearts;
and I will be their God, and they shall be my people.
³⁴No longer shall they teach one another,
or say to each other, "Know the LORD,"
for they shall all know me,
from the least of them to the greatest, says the LORD;
for I will forgive their iniquity, and remember their sin no more.

The word of the Lord.   *or*   Word of God, word of life.

PSALMODY: Psalm 46

FIRST READING   *Jeremiah = jehr-eh-MY-uh*
The voice is the voice of God. It requires the ring of authority, of power and might. A subtle change between the first paragraph and the second will also be helpful. In the first paragraph Almighty God recalls the unfaithfulness of God's people (some sadness? some anger?); in the second, God's overwhelming desire to forgive sets the tone of voice.

SECOND READING: Romans 3:19-28

A reading from Romans.

[19]Now we know that whatever the law says,
it speaks to those who are under the law,
so that every mouth may be silenced,
and the whole world may be held accountable to God.
[20]For "no human being will be justified in his sight"
by deeds prescribed by the law,
for through the law comes the knowledge of sin.

[21]But now, apart from law, the righteousness of God has been disclosed,
and is attested by the law and the prophets,
[22]the righteousness of God through faith in Jesus Christ for all who believe.
For there is no distinction,
[23]since all have sinned and fall short of the glory of God;
[24]they are now justified by his grace as a gift,
through the redemption that is in Christ Jesus,
[25]whom God put forward as a sacrifice of atonement by his blood,
effective through faith.
He did this to show his righteousness,
because in his divine forbearance
he had passed over the sins previously committed;
[26]it was to prove at the present time that he himself is righteous
and that he justifies the one who has faith in Jesus.

[27]Then what becomes of boasting?
It is excluded.
By what law? By that of works?
No, but by the law of faith.
[28]For we hold that a person is justified by faith
apart from works prescribed by the law.

The word of the Lord.   *or*   Word of God, word of life.

SECOND READING
The second reading amplifies the first reading. The Romans text makes several, simple, sequential points. (1) No one will be justified by doing the works prescribed in the law (2) because all people "fall short" in attempting to keep the law. (3) Now we are justified by God's grace, (4) which is a gift in the sacrifice of Christ Jesus received by faith. Verse 28 is both the topic sentence and the punch line of the lesson. Allow the whole reading to lead the assembly to its hopeful conclusion.

GOSPEL: John 8:31-36

The holy gospel according to John.

[31]Jesus said to the Jews who had believed in him,
"If you continue in my word, you are truly my disciples;
[32]and you will know the truth,
and the truth will make you free."
[33]They answered him,
"We are descendants of Abraham and have never been slaves to anyone.
What do you mean by saying, 'You will be made free'?"

[34]Jesus answered them,
"Very truly, I tell you, everyone who commits sin is a slave to sin.
[35]The slave does not have a permanent place in the household;
the son has a place there forever.

[36]"So if the Son makes you free, you will be free indeed."

The gospel of the Lord.

GOSPEL
Perhaps the assembly would profit from a sound of gentleness in the voice of Jesus, considering those to whom he is speaking: "the Jews who had believed in him." Verse 32 has become something of a battle cry in contemporary parlance. A softer, kinder delivery may help the assembly hear it more clearly.

ALL SAINTS DAY
NOVEMBER 1

FIRST READING: Revelation 7:9-17

A reading from Revelation.

⁹After this I looked,
and there was a great multitude that no one could count,
from every nation, from all tribes and peoples and languages,
standing before the throne and before the Lamb, robed in white,
with palm branches in their hands.
¹⁰They cried out in a loud voice, saying,
  "Salvation belongs to our God who is seated on the throne, and to the Lamb!"
¹¹And all the angels stood around the throne
and around the elders and the four living creatures,
and they fell on their faces before the throne and worshiped God,
¹²singing,
  "Amen! Blessing and glory and wisdom
   and thanksgiving and honor
   and power and might
   be to our God forever and ever! Amen."

¹³Then one of the elders addressed me, saying,
"Who are these, robed in white, and where have they come from?"
¹⁴I said to him, "Sir, you are the one that knows."
Then he said to me, "These are they who have come out of the great ordeal;
they have washed their robes and made them white in the blood of the Lamb.
¹⁵For this reason they are before the throne of God,
   and worship him day and night within his temple,
   and the one who is seated on the throne will shelter them.
¹⁶They will hunger no more, and thirst no more;
   the sun will not strike them,
   nor any scorching heat;
¹⁷for the Lamb at the center of the throne will be their shepherd,
   and he will guide them to springs of the water of life,
   and God will wipe away every tear from their eyes."

The word of the Lord.   *or*   Word of God, word of life.

FIRST READING
First and foremost this is a vision. Revelation! A sense of wonder is essential. See the scene! Fill in the details in your mind before you begin to read. Help the hearer see what you see. As with the first reading, this text declares that God sustains God's own and that they will take their place around the heavenly throne forever.

PSALMODY: Psalm 34:1-10, 22

SECOND READING: 1 John 3:1-3

A reading from First John.

[1]See what love the Father has given us,
that we should be called children of God;
and that is what we are.
The reason the world does not know us is that it did not know him.
[2]Beloved, we are God's children now;
what we will be has not yet been revealed.
What we do know is this:
when he is revealed, we will be like him, for we will see him as he is.
[3]And all who have this hope in him purify themselves,
just as he is pure.

The word of the Lord.   *or*   Word of God, word of life.

SECOND READING

The reading of this passage will be enhanced by attention to the tenses and cases: the simple but profound indicative of "that is what we are," and the contrast between present and future in verse 2. A note of serene confidence might well carry the entire reading.

GOSPEL: Matthew 5:1-12

The holy gospel according to Matthew.

When Jesus saw the crowds, he went up the mountain;
and after he sat down, his disciples came to him.
²Then he began to speak, and taught them, saying:
    ³"Blessed are the poor in spirit, for theirs is the kingdom of heaven.
    ⁴"Blessed are those who mourn, for they will be comforted.
    ⁵"Blessed are the meek, for they will inherit the earth.
    ⁶"Blessed are those who hunger and thirst for righteousness,
for they will be filled.
    ⁷"Blessed are the merciful, for they will receive mercy.
    ⁸"Blessed are the pure in heart, for they will see God.
    ⁹"Blessed are the peacemakers, for they will be called children of God.
    ¹⁰"Blessed are those who are persecuted for righteousness' sake,
for theirs is the kingdom of heaven.
    ¹¹"Blessed are you when people revile you and persecute you
and utter all kinds of evil against you falsely on my account
¹²Rejoice and be glad,
for your reward is great in heaven,
for in the same way they persecuted the prophets who were before you."

The gospel of the Lord.

GOSPEL
It may be possible to bring the assembly to the mountain of Matthew 5 by allowing each "Blessed are" to hang in the air a bit once it has been voiced. Give the hearer a sense of our Lord's "thinking up" the Beatitudes rather than "reading" them. A reading textured with thoughtful pauses may help the people in the pew to hear them as for the first time.

FIRST READING: Ecclesiastes 3:1-13

A reading from Ecclesiastes.

¹For everything there is a season, and a time for every matter under heaven:
　²a time to be born, and a time to die;
　a time to plant, and a time to pluck up what is planted;
　³a time to kill, and a time to heal;
　a time to break down, and a time to build up;
　⁴a time to weep, and a time to laugh;
　a time to mourn, and a time to dance;
　⁵a time to throw away stones, and a time to gather stones together;
　a time to embrace, and a time to refrain from embracing;
　⁶a time to seek, and a time to lose;
　a time to keep, and a time to throw away;
　⁷a time to tear, and a time to sew;
　a time to keep silence, and a time to speak;
　⁸a time to love, and a time to hate;
　a time for war, and a time for peace.

⁹What gain have the workers from their toil?
¹⁰I have seen the business that God has given to everyone to be busy with.
¹¹He has made everything suitable for its time;
moreover he has put a sense of past and future into their minds,
yet they cannot find out what God has done from the beginning to the end.
¹²I know that there is nothing better for them than to be happy
and enjoy themselves as long as they live;
¹³moreover, it is God's gift
that all should eat and drink and take pleasure in all their toil.

The word of the Lord.　　　*or*　　　Word of God, word of life.

PSALMODY: Psalm 8

FIRST READING　　*Ecclesiastes = eh-klee-zee-ASS-teez*
An excellent reading will result from the reader's conscious discovery of his or her own rhythm for these familiar contrasting seasons. This takes time. It requires reading and rereading the text. It demands a studied reconsideration of one of the most familiar cuttings from scripture. There is no shortcut. Make time.

SECOND READING: Revelation 21:1-6a

A reading from Revelation.

¹I saw a new heaven and a new earth;
for the first heaven and the first earth had passed away,
and the sea was no more.
²And I saw the holy city, the new Jerusalem,
coming down out of heaven from God,
prepared as a bride adorned for her husband.
³And I heard a loud voice from the throne saying,
 "See, the home of God is among mortals.
 He will dwell with them;
 they will be his peoples,
 and God himself will be with them;
 ⁴he will wipe every tear from their eyes.
 Death will be no more;
 mourning and crying and pain will be no more,
 for the first things have passed away."

⁵And the one who was seated on the throne said,
"See, I am making all things new."
Also he said,
"Write this, for these words are trustworthy and true."
⁶ᵃThen he said to me,
"It is done! I am the Alpha and the Omega, the beginning and the end."

The word of the Lord.   *or*   Word of God, word of life.

SECOND READING
The reader, by careful preparation, can begin to "see" John's vision and to "hear" the voice from the throne, and thus help the assembly capture the revelation as well. Dreams and visions are often larger than life. They call for expansive oral interpretation.

GOSPEL: Matthew 25:31-46

The holy gospel according to Matthew.

⌐Jesus said to the disciples:⌐
[31]"When the Son of Man comes in his glory, and all the angels with him,
then he will sit on the throne of his glory.
[32]All the nations will be gathered before him,
and he will separate people one from another
as a shepherd separates the sheep from the goats,
[33]and he will put the sheep at his right hand and the goats at the left.

[34]"Then the king will say to those at his right hand,
'Come, you that are blessed by my Father,
inherit the kingdom prepared for you from the foundation of the world;
[35]for I was hungry and you gave me food,
I was thirsty and you gave me something to drink,
I was a stranger and you welcomed me,
[36]I was naked and you gave me clothing,
I was sick and you took care of me,
I was in prison and you visited me.'
[37]Then the righteous will answer him,
'Lord, when was it that we saw you hungry and gave you food,
or thirsty and gave you something to drink?
[38]And when was it that we saw you a stranger and welcomed you,
or naked and gave you clothing?
[39]And when was it that we saw you sick or in prison and visited you?'
[40]And the king will answer them,
'Truly I tell you,
just as you did it to one of the least of these who are members of my family,
you did it to me.'

[41]"Then he will say to those at his left hand,
'You that are accursed,
depart from me into the eternal fire prepared for the devil and his angels;
[42]for I was hungry and you gave me no food,
I was thirsty and you gave me nothing to drink,
[43]I was a stranger and you did not welcome me,
naked and you did not give me clothing,
sick and in prison and you did not visit me.'

GOSPEL
The same challenges and opportunities face the gospel reader on this occasion as faced the lector for the first reading. Texts that are very familiar and texts that have repeating patterns require more preparation time if they are to be heard "new." This vision of the end time gives sharp definition to how humanity ought be engaged in the meantime. It bears repeating.

⁴⁴Then they also will answer,
'Lord, when was it that we saw you hungry or thirsty
or a stranger or naked or sick or in prison,
and did not take care of you?'
⁴⁵Then he will answer them,
'Truly I tell you,
just as you did not do it to one of the least of these,
you did not do it to me.'
⁴⁶And these will go away into eternal punishment,
but the righteous into eternal life."

The gospel of the Lord.

✝ DAY OF THANKSGIVING

FIRST READING: Deuteronomy 8:7-18

A reading from Deuteronomy.

[7]For the LORD your God is bringing you into a good land,
a land with flowing streams,
with springs and underground waters welling up in valleys and hills,
[8]a land of wheat and barley,
of vines and fig trees and pomegranates,
a land of olive trees and honey,
[9]a land where you may eat bread without scarcity,
where you will lack nothing,
a land whose stones are iron and from whose hills you may mine copper.
[10]You shall eat your fill
and bless the LORD your God for the good land that he has given you.

[11]Take care that you do not forget the LORD your God,
by failing to keep his commandments, his ordinances, and his statutes,
which I am commanding you today.
[12]When you have eaten your fill
and have built fine houses and live in them,
[13]and when your herds and flocks have multiplied,
and your silver and gold is multiplied,
and all that you have is multiplied,
[14]then do not exalt yourself, forgetting the LORD your God,
who brought you out of the land of Egypt, out of the house of slavery,
[15]who led you through the great and terrible wilderness,
an arid wasteland with poisonous snakes and scorpions.
He made water flow for you from flint rock,
[16]and fed you in the wilderness with manna that your ancestors did not know,
to humble you and to test you,
and in the end to do you good.
[17]Do not say to yourself,
"My power and the might of my own hand have gotten me this wealth."

FIRST READING   *Deuteronomy = dew-ter-ON-uh-mee   pomegranates = POM-uh-gran-utz*
This glorious reading begins by piling up images of plenty—let the wonder of that come through in your voice. Then, let the assembly hear the contrast as you move into the caution beginning at verse 11: "do not forget," "do not exalt yourself." The reading concludes back on a positive note.

[18]But remember the LORD your God,
for it is he who gives you power to get wealth,
so that he may confirm his covenant that he swore to your ancestors,
as he is doing today.

The word of the Lord.   *or*   Word of God, word of life.

PSALMODY: Psalm 65

SECOND READING: 2 Corinthians 9:6-15

A reading from Second Corinthians.

[6]The point is this:
the one who sows sparingly will also reap sparingly,
and the one who sows bountifully will also reap bountifully.
[7]Each of you must give as you have made up your mind,
not reluctantly or under compulsion,
for God loves a cheerful giver.
[8]And God is able to provide you with every blessing in abundance,
so that by always having enough of everything,
you may share abundantly in every good work.
[9]As it is written,
    "He scatters abroad, he gives to the poor;
    his righteousness endures forever."
[10]He who supplies seed to the sower and bread for food
will supply and multiply your seed for sowing
and increase the harvest of your righteousness.
[11]You will be enriched in every way for your great generosity,
which will produce thanksgiving to God through us;
[12]for the rendering of this ministry not only supplies the needs of the saints
but also overflows with many thanksgivings to God.
[13]Through the testing of this ministry
you glorify God by your obedience to the confession of the gospel of Christ
and by the generosity of your sharing with them and with all others,
[14]while they long for you and pray for you
because of the surpassing grace of God that he has given you.
[15]Thanks be to God for his indescribable gift!

The word of the Lord.   *or*   Word of God, word of life.

SECOND READING
The concepts in this teaching are not difficult, but will come across better to the listeners if the reader has them clearly understood beforehand. Be generous with your preparation, as you are inviting the hearers to be generous in their living.

GOSPEL: Luke 17:11-19

The holy gospel according to Luke.

[11]On the way to Jerusalem
Jesus was going through the region between Samaria and Galilee.
[12]As he entered a village, ten lepers approached him.
Keeping their distance, [13]they called out, saying,
"Jesus, Master, have mercy on us!"
[14]When he saw them, he said to them,
"Go and show yourselves to the priests."
And as they went, they were made clean.
[15]Then one of them, when he saw that he was healed, turned back,
praising God with a loud voice.
[16]He prostrated himself at Jesus' feet and thanked him.
And he was a Samaritan.
[17]Then Jesus asked, "Were not ten made clean?
But the other nine, where are they?
[18]Was none of them found to return and give praise to God
except this foreigner?"
[19]Then he said to him,
"Get up and go on your way;
your faith has made you well."

The gospel of the Lord.

GOSPEL

Two simple sentences in the gospel might productively stand out. Verse 14b, "And as they went, they were made clean," because it is the miracle. Verse 16b, "And he was a Samaritan," because it is miraculous. They need not be loudly read, but both would profit from parenthetical pauses.

Appendix

ALTERNATE READINGS
FROM THE APOCRYPHAL BOOKS

SECOND SUNDAY OF CHRISTMAS

FIRST READING: Sirach 24:1-12

A reading from Sirach.

¹Wisdom praises herself,
  and tells of her glory in the midst of her people.
²In the assembly of the Most High she opens her mouth,
  and in the presence of his hosts she tells of her glory:

³"I came forth from the mouth of the Most High,
  and covered the earth like a mist.
⁴I dwelt in the highest heavens,
  and my throne was in a pillar of cloud.
⁵Alone I compassed the vault of heaven
  and traversed the depths of the abyss.
⁶Over waves of the sea, over all the earth,
  and over every people and nation I have held sway.
⁷Among all these I sought a resting place;
  in whose territory should I abide?

⁸"Then the Creator of all things gave me a command,
  and my Creator chose the place for my tent.
He said, 'Make your dwelling in Jacob,
  and in Israel receive your inheritance.'
⁹Before the ages, in the beginning, he created me,
  and for all the ages I shall not cease to be.
¹⁰In the holy tent I ministered before him,
  and so I was established in Zion.

¹¹"Thus in the beloved city he gave me a resting place,
  and in Jerusalem was my domain.
¹²I took root in an honored people,
  in the portion of the Lord, his heritage."

The word of the Lord.   *or*   Word of God, word of life.

PSALMODY: Wisdom 10:15-21 or Psalm 147:12-20

Readings continue on page 30.

FIRST READING   *Sirach = SIHR-ahk*
Verses 1 and 2 announce what is to be heard. Pause thereafter. Then help the assembly hear the voice of Jesus. It is a delightfully revealing opportunity to peek behind the curtain of the gospel (John 1).

Sixth Sunday after Epiphany

SUNDAY, FEBRUARY 11-17   (if before Transfiguration)

LECTIONARY 6

FIRST READING: Sirach 15:15-20

A reading from Sirach.

¹⁵If you choose,
>   you can keep the commandments,
>   and to act faithfully is a matter of your own choice.
¹⁶He has placed before you fire and water;
>   stretch out your hand for whichever you choose.

¹⁷Before each person are life and death,
>   and whichever one chooses will be given.
¹⁸For great is the wisdom of the Lord;
>   he is mighty in power and sees everything;
¹⁹his eyes are on those who fear him,
>   and he knows every human action.
²⁰He has not commanded anyone to be wicked,
>   and he has not given anyone permission to sin.

The word of the Lord.   *or*   Word of God, word of life.

PSALMODY: Psalm 119:1-8

Readings continue on page 57.

FIRST READING   *Sirach = SIHR-ahk*
This concise alternative to Deuteronomy 30 is utterly straightforward. Give each sentence its due.

ALTERNATE READINGS FROM THE APOCRYPHAL BOOKS

RESURRECTION OF OUR LORD
VIGIL OF EASTER

SIXTH READING: Baruch 3:9-15, 32—4:4

A reading from Baruch.

⁹Hear the commandments of life, O Israel;
  give ear, and learn wisdom!
¹⁰Why is it, O Israel, why is it that you are in the land of your enemies,
  that you are growing old in a foreign country,
that you are defiled with the dead,
  ¹¹that you are counted among those in Hades?
¹²You have forsaken the fountain of wisdom.
¹³If you had walked in the way of God,
  you would be living in peace forever.
¹⁴Learn where there is wisdom,
  where there is strength,
  where there is understanding,
so that you may at the same time discern
  where there is length of days, and life,
  where there is light for the eyes, and peace.

¹⁵Who has found her place?
  And who has entered her storehouses?

³²But the one who knows all things knows her,
  he found her by his understanding.
The one who prepared the earth for all time
  filled it with four-footed creatures;
³³the one who sends forth the light, and it goes;
  he called it, and it obeyed him, trembling;
³⁴the stars shone in their watches, and were glad;
  he called them, and they said, "Here we are!"
  They shone with gladness for him who made them.
³⁵This is our God;
  no other can be compared to him.
³⁶He found the whole way to knowledge,
  and gave her to his servant Jacob
  and to Israel, whom he loved. ▸

SIXTH READING *Baruch = bah-ROOK   Hades = HAY-deez*
The words of the Apocrypha (including these) contain advantage and disadvantage in their unfamiliarity.
Because they are unfamiliar they will land with a certain freshness on the ears of the assembly. Because they
are unfamiliar their line of reasoning will take longer for the hearer to discern. Discover the various natural
pause points in the reading and take advantage of them. Allow the assembly adequate time to appropriate
the less familiar.

³⁷Afterward she appeared on earth
   and lived with humankind.
⁴:¹She is the book of the commandments of God,
   the law that endures forever.
All who hold her fast will live,
   and those who forsake her will die.
²Turn, O Jacob, and take her;
   walk toward the shining of her light.
³Do not give your glory to another,
   or your advantages to an alien people.
⁴Happy are we, O Israel,
   for we know what is pleasing to God.

The word of the Lord.   *or*   Word of God, word of life.

RESPONSE: Psalm 19

Readings continue on page 157.

SUNDAY, JULY 17–23

TIME AFTER PENTECOST — LECTIONARY 16

Complementary Series

FIRST READING: Wisdom 12:13, 16-19

A reading from the Wisdom of Solomon.

¹³For neither is there any god besides you, whose care is for all people,
to whom you should prove that you have not judged unjustly.

¹⁶For your strength is the source of righteousness,
and your sovereignty over all causes you to spare all.
¹⁷For you show your strength when people doubt the completeness
    of your power,
and you rebuke any insolence among those who know it.
¹⁸Although you are sovereign in strength, you judge with mildness,
and with great forbearance you govern us;
for you have power to act whenever you choose.

¹⁹Through such works you have taught your people
that the righteous must be kind,
and you have filled your children with good hope,
because you give repentance for sins.

The word of the Lord.   *or*   Word of God, word of life.

PSALMODY: Psalm 86:11-17

Readings continue on page 246.

FIRST READING
This brief reading is a tough one. Some help may be had in reading chapters 12—14, but not a great
deal. Those who desire to read this celebration of the providence of God well will need to invest some
time in wrestling a personal understanding out of each sentence before attempting to knit them together
meaningfully for the assembly.

SUNDAY, NOVEMBER 6–12
TIME AFTER PENTECOST — LECTIONARY 32
Complementary Series

FIRST READING: Wisdom 6:12-16

A reading from the Wisdom of Solomon.

¹²Wisdom is radiant and unfading,
   and she is easily discerned by those who love her,
   and is found by those who seek her.
¹³She hastens to make herself known to those who desire her.
¹⁴One who rises early to seek her will have no difficulty,
   for she will be found sitting at the gate.
¹⁵To fix one's thought on her is perfect understanding,
   and one who is vigilant on her account will soon be free from care,
¹⁶because she goes about seeking those worthy of her,
   and she graciously appears to them in their paths,
   and meets them in every thought.

The word of the Lord.   *or*   Word of God, word of life.

PSALMODY: Wisdom 6:17-20 or Psalm 70

Readings continue on page 292.

FIRST READING
Four exquisite sentences celebrate the gifts of wisdom and her readiness to be embraced. The sentences are not especially complex ones, but they will be unfamiliar to many in the assembly. An excellent reading will be preceded by a thorough personal understanding on the part of the reader.

Index

PROVERBS

ECCLESIASTES

SONG OF SOLOMON

ISAIAH